**Murdock Learning Resource
Center
George Fox College**
Newberg, Oregon 97132

DEMCO

Minorities at Risk

Minorities at Risk
A Global View of Ethnopolitical Conflicts

Ted Robert Gurr

with contributions by

Barbara Harff
Monty G. Marshall
James R. Scarritt

UNITED STATES
INSTITUTE OF PEACE PRESS

Washington, D.C.

United States Institute of Peace
1550 M Street, N.W.
Washington, D.C. 20005

First published 1993

Printed in the United States of America

The paper used in this publication meets the minimum requirements of American National Standard for Information Sciences—Permanence of Paper for Printed Library Materials, ANSI Z39.48-1984.

Library of Congress Cataloging-in-Publication Data
Gurr, Ted Robert, 1936–
    Minorities at risk / by Ted Robert Gurr; with contributions by Barbara Harff, Monty G. Marshall, James R. Scarritt.
        p.   cm.
    Includes bibliographical references and index.
    ISBN 1-878379-25-9 (alk. paper)—ISBN 1-878379-24-0 (pbk.: alk. paper)
    1. Ethnic relations—Case studies. 2. International relations—Case studies. 3. Conflict management—Case studies. 4. Minorities—Case studies. I. United States Institute of Peace. II. Title.
GN496.G87 1993
305.8—dc20   92-45737
                                                                         CIP

Contents

Maps

Foreword

Some twenty million refugees are currently fleeing from communal or ethnically based conflicts around the world. Ethnic conflict has devastated Yugoslavia and threatens the stability of many of the successor republics of the Soviet Union. There are protracted conflicts in the Middle East and Southeast Asia. Many countries in Western Europe are beset by antagonism toward immigrant groups of Third World origin. Indeed, conflicts between ethnic groups or with the states in which they reside are a serious and growing challenge to domestic and international security.

As this monumental study makes abundantly clear, ethnically based conflict is a pervasive worldwide phenomenon, one that often erupts into brutality and violence. This violence frequently crosses national borders and the conflict becomes entwined with larger regional or global issues. It is only natural, therefore, that the subject of ethnopolitical conflict has been a major interest of the United States Institute of Peace. Among other projects, we supported Ted Robert Gurr's pioneering research with a fellowship from the Jennings Randolph Program for International Peace and with a subsequent award from our Grant Program to help him complete this volume.

The resulting book, *Minorities at Risk,* is an ambitious and unprecedented effort to identify the multiple expressions of ethnic conflict in the contemporary world. Some of its statistically based findings have important policy implications. For example, deliberate discrimination by dominant groups is a much more important source of minorities' disadvantages and grievances than are the cultural differences that divide minorities from majorities. Moreover, economic inequalities are more resistant to change than are political inequalities. Other findings challenge accepted notions. For instance, rebellions by ethnonationalists have increased steadily in every decade since the 1950s, not just in recent years. The source of the most rapidly rising type of communal conflict is neither nationalism nor religious fundamentalism, but the demands of indigenous peoples for protection of their lands and rights.

But Professor Gurr does more than just compare the disadvantages and conflicts of ethnic groups. In a lengthy chapter on settling ethnopolitical conflicts, he demonstrates that few of them are completely intractable. His evidence confirms the view that open governments are more likely than authoritarian ones to accommodate the interests of minorities, yet he notes that some autocratic regimes have also made serious efforts to achieve equality among groups and have granted substantial concessions to regional minorities. Communal conflicts of all types, from every part of the world, have been restrained or transformed by political accommodations and reforms, including governmental arrangements such as autonomy, pluralism, and power sharing. That's good news for those of us in the conflict resolution field, but, as *Minorities at Risk* clearly shows, we have plenty of work left to do.

Samuel W. Lewis, President
United States Institute of Peace

Preface

The Bosnians, the Kurds and Shi'is of Iraq, and black South Africans are among the most visible of more than two hundred ethnic and religious minorities and subordinate majorities throughout the world who are contesting the terms of their in corporation into "the world order."[1] Politically active communal groups, most of them disadvantaged, in 1990 numbered some 900 million people, about one-sixth of the world's population. Since 1945 more than fifty of these peoples have fought protracted campaigns of protest, terrorism, and rebellion against the states that govern them. Ethnonationalists such as the Eritreans and the Québecois are on the verge of independence and ten others have secured some regional autonomy. Ethnoclasses such as African Americans in the United States and Muslims in Western Europe have won greater civil rights and are vigorously advocating cultural pluralism. Other groups, such as the indigenous Maya of Guatemala and Palestinian nationalists in the Middle East, have suffered badly from internal wars and repression but continue to support risky campaigns for greater political rights and autonomy.

This book is the first comprehensive report of the Minorities at Risk project, a global survey of 233 politically active communal groups. Chapter 1 defines, identifies, and categorizes the groups. Chapter 2 analyzes the traits that differentiate them from dominant groups, giving special attention to material and political inequalities and discrimination. Chapter 3 examines the connections between minorities' objective disadvantages and their grievances. Those grievances have driven upward trends in political protest and rebellion on behalf of communal interests in every world region and every type of group since 1945, as is demonstrated in chapter 4. The evidence is integrated in chapter 5 in a theoretical framework, which sketches an explanation of why disadvantaged minorities mobilize to assert their interests, and how development, democracy, and international circumstances shape their choices of protest or rebellion. Chapters 6 through 9 provide in-depth assessments of the status and prospects of communal minorities in the western democracies and Japan, the former Soviet bloc (by Monty G. Marshall, University of Iowa), North Africa and the Middle East (by Barbara Harff, U.S. Naval Academy), and Africa south of the Sahara (by James R. Scarritt, University of Colorado). Outcomes of ethnopolitical conflicts are evaluated in chapter 10, which contends that few of these conflicts are completely intractable and shows that many have been settled or restrained by political accommodations and reformist strategies. The concluding chapter summarizes the principal findings of the study.

Most of what scholars know about communal conflicts, and most policy guidance for responding to them, is based on substantive studies of one or several cases. The cumulative knowledge is extensive but before now there was no firm basis for generalizing a set of findings beyond the groups or region examined in each particular study.[2] This study differs in one fundamental way from virtually all previous work on communal conflict: it is based on the analysis of information and coded data for *all* the politically significant communal groups that meet the general criteria described in chapter 1. Thus there is a systematic, empirical core to the Minorities at Risk study that heretofore has been lacking from the literature on this topic.

The inherent limitation of broad comparative research is that it does not capture the details and nuances of each particular communal group's traits, grievances, and conflicts. The data we have coded on 233 groups are numerical abstractions of complex social situations, perceptions, and political actions. Yet we are closely familiar with many of the details and complexities of ethnopolitical status and actions, because the coding is based on our compilation and interpretations of voluminous scholarly and journalistic materials on each of the groups in the study. This substantive material is used selectively in chapters 1 through 5 to provide examples and interpretations of the general relationships observed in the coded data. Chapters 6 through 9 offer more fine-grained descriptions and analysis: each of these chapters identifies patterns of minority status and conflicts that are distinctive to countries in one world region, then uses comparative case studies to illustrate and amplify the generalizations. Chapter 10's analysis of the settlement of communal conflicts is based almost entirely on substantive comparisons of strategies and outcomes observed among the 233 groups.

In short, this book attempts an integrated substantive and empirical analysis of communal status and conflict since the end of World War II, with special attention to the decade of the 1980s. Area specialists may conclude that too little attention has been given in this project to some features of the groups and countries with which they are intimately familiar. In most cases the explanation is that hard choices had to be made about which details to include. The justification is that some simplification is necessary for the kind of general mapping reported here. Empirical social scientists may object that the indicators used for comparative analysis are "soft" or imprecise: they are derived by coding nonstandardized source materials and have not been fully tested for reliability and validity.[3] But there are no standard sources of statistical or substantive information on communal groups. Such groups have only recently and gradually been recognized as a major type of actor in domestic and international politics. Therefore it is better to have coded data on some of their most important social and political traits than to plead statistically self-righteous ignorance. We also concede fallibility. It is inevitable that some errors of fact and questionable judgments have intruded, and we invite specialists to criticize and correct our substantive observations and the group codings reported in the Appendix.

Acknowledgments

The author began what became the Minorities at Risk project in 1986 at the University of Colorado's Center for Comparative Politics. The encouragement and advice of my colleagues Barbara Harff and James R. Scarritt played a major role in shaping the project. An initial list of groups was derived from previous work on group discrimination and separatism[4] and cross-checked against reports of the Minority Rights Group (London) and Cultural Survival (Cambridge, Massachusetts). Extensive background files of materials on each group then were compiled, evaluated, and coded. Monty G. Marshall surveyed and coded Asian, Soviet, and East European groups, with contributions by Steven Kurth, and developed the Minorities data base.

Detailed studies of protracted Asian conflicts were prepared by
Scott McDonald and Shin-wha Lee at the University of Maryland, with contributions by Amy Hwang. Latin American
groups were analyzed by Michael Hartman, then a research as-
sistant at the United States Institute of Peace. Middle Eastern
minorities were coded by Monty G. Marshall and Deina Ali
AbdelKader, with contributions by Christina Perlioni, at the
University of Maryland. Most African groups were identified
and coded by a research group directed by Professor Scarritt at
the University of Colorado, Boulder, whose members were Martha L. Gibson, Keith Jaggers, Kook Shin Kim, Michael Obert,
and Joshua B. Rubongoya. The author coded groups in Western Europe, North America, the Horn of Africa, and South Africa, with assistance from James Atkins, Douglas Emory, Sean
Keller, Christopher Moore, and Goitom Telahun. The statistical
analyses reported in this book were carried out by Scott Mc-
Donald with the assistance of Shin-wha Lee. Sean Keller played
a key role in establishing the project's information management
system and prepared the graphics and maps reproduced in this
book.

The research was supported by the United States Institute of
Peace, which awarded the author a Jennings Randolph fellowship in 1988–89 and provided a subsequent grant for continued work on the project at the University of Maryland's Center
for International Development and Conflict Management. Support for the project also has been provided by the Academic
Support Program of the U.S. Department of Defense. This
book was written during a semester's leave awarded by the University of Maryland's General Research Board.

Special thanks are due to colleagues who have tried to save
us from the risks, unavoidable in a project on this scale, of fac-
tual error, oversight, and oversimplification. Working papers
for this book have benefited from the comments of Oystein
Gaasholt; John Harbeson; Barbara Harff; Martin O. Heisler;
Edy Kaufman; Herbert Kelman; David Little; Hugh Miall;
John M. Richardson, Jr.; Donald S. Rothchild; William Safran;
Stanley Samarasinghe; Peter Wallensteen; and several anony-
mous readers of a draft of the book manuscript. Our assistants
and graduate students have also read and commented on a
number of chapters.

This volume incorporates some evidence and interpretations
from three papers published elsewhere.[5] Three other published
papers extend or build upon some of the analyses reported
here.[6]

Minorities at Risk

1. Identifying Communal Groups

Communal groups antedated the emergence of the modern state system, they have endured in most countries despite policies of assimilation and integration, and they promise to persist and reemerge whenever and however international boundaries are redrawn. But most communal groups lack statelike political organization and many, such as the Chinese of Malaysia and the mixed Serb, Croat, and Bosnian Muslim towns of the western Serbian borderlands, are dispersed among other peoples. Communal groups thus are "fuzzy sets" of people, more persistent than most associational groups but not precisely bounded either politically or socially. In essence, communal groups are psychological communities: groups whose core members share a distinctive and enduring collective identity based on cultural traits and lifeways that matter to them and to others with whom they interact.[1]

People have many possible bases for communal identity: shared historical experiences or myths, religious beliefs, language, ethnicity, region of residence, and, in castelike systems, customary occupations. Communal groups—which also are referred to as ethnic groups, minorities, and peoples—usually are distinguished by several reinforcing traits. The key to identifying communal groups is not the presence of a particular trait or combination of traits, but rather the shared perception that the defining traits, whatever they are, set the group apart.[2]

The salience of communal identifications varies over time. The psychological bases of group identification are reinforced by cultural, economic, and political differentials between the group and others: treat a group differently, by denial or privilege, and its members become more self-conscious about their common bonds and interests. Minimize differences, and communal identification becomes less significant as a unifying principle. It follows that peoples who are distinct at one time may later become virtually indistinguishable from some larger society. The English, for example, no longer make socially meaningful distinctions between Anglo-Saxons and Normans. Other lines of social cleavage, such as the one that divides Protestants and Catholics in western societies, have lost most of what was once a highly charged significance, except in Northern Ireland. The reverse also happens: Sardinians in Italy and the Hurons of Quebec, for example, both began to reassert distinctive group identities in the second half of the twentieth century.[3]

It should be clear that we disagree with observers who (a) think of communal groups as primordial social entities based on biological, cultural, linguistic, and religious givens and (b) regard the states that govern them as inherently artificial entities.[4] This study assumes that all collective identities, whether centered on a communal group or a national state, are to a degree situational and transitory. We also recognize the importance of sharp cleavages within communal groups: identifications with a particular clan, tribe, or faction may be more intense than identification with the larger collectivity. Some collective identities, such as the appelation Indio in Latin American societies, are imposed by powerful outsiders and acquire meaning for members of the labeled groups only as a consequence of their common misfortune. Similarly, it cannot be assumed that immigrant ethnic groups bring their sense of group identity with their baggage. The emergent unity of ethnoclasses such as Asian Americans and Maghrebins is the cumulative consequence of their treatment by dominant groups.[5]

We also disagree with observers who take this argument to the other extreme and regard communal groups as merely one kind of transitory association created to pursue members' material and political interests. Some communal groups in western societies seem to fit such a characterization: they mobilize in response to elites' manipulation of ethnic symbols, they play the political game to maximize benefits, and then they lose their dynamism. But this is a poor characterization of ethnonationalists who are fighting civil wars in Third World countries, or of defenders of indigenous rights in the First World. What is common to all politically active communal groups is the appeal to an underlying sense of collective identity based on a common culture and status.[6] The emotional force and cohesion of communal movements derive from shared cultural values and experiences. On the other hand, the strategies and tactics by which leaders pursue collective interests are a function of a group's status, organization, and political circumstances and the leaders' goals and skills.[7]

From the global perspective taken in this study, the central questions at any given time and place are, What communal identities and interests are most at odds with the structures and policies of existing states, and why? The answers to these questions begin with an analysis of intergroup differentials and discrimination and how they are maintained. This chapter identifies and classifies the relevant communal groups, and chapter 2 summarizes our comparative evidence about their status. The circumstances under which group inequalities lead to grievances, communal protest, and rebellion are dealt with in chapters 3 through 5.

Defining Politicized Communal Groups

No international organization certifies, counts, or records statistics on communal groups, partly because the groups are difficult to define and observe, partly because their existence often is denied or their significance minimized by state elites. Until 1990, for example, the Turkish government referred to the country's Kurdish minority as "Mountain Turks" and banned speaking, writing, and publishing in the Kurdish language. Geographer Bernard Nietschmann estimates that there are three thousand to five thousand "nations" in the world, defined as communities whose shared identity is based on common ancestry, institutions, beliefs, language, and territory.[8] Many of these "nations" are no more than linguistically distinct villages or bands of hunter-gatherers in isolated regions. More stringent criteria are used by political scientists Gunnar Nielsson and Ralph Jones to identify 575 ethnic groups as actual or potential nation-states.[9] The most detailed compendium of information on nonstate communal groups is the Minority Rights Group *World Directory of Minorities*, which includes profiles of 170 peoples.[10]

This study is limited to nonstate communal groups that were politically salient during the post-World War II era, that is, *politicized communal groups*. Communal groups are politically salient, for our purposes, if they meet one or both of two primary criteria: they experience economic or political discrimination, and they have taken political action in support of collective interests. Each criterion needs elaboration.

1. *The group collectively suffers, or benefits from, systematic discriminatory treatment vis-à-vis other groups in a state.* Such differential treatment may be a consequence of widespread social practice or deliberate government policy or both. It also may be the residue of historical circumstances. People of color in the United States know that the malign consequences of past discrimination can persist for generations in spite of remedial government policies designed to eliminate or compensate for it. And legacies of discriminatory treatment and persecution by dominant groups, supposedly dormant, can reemerge with a biting vengeance, as happened with anti-Semitism in Eastern Europe in the early 1950s and in Russia in the late 1980s.

Nearly four-fifths of the groups in this study (183 of 233) were included because of differential status due to economic discrimination (147 groups) or political discrimination (168 groups) or both. (Patterns of discrimination are analyzed in chapter 2). Of the fifty groups that do not now experience any malign effects of discrimination, half are advantaged minorities that benefit from discrimination against other groups. The remainder are included because they meet the second criterion, political mobilization (see below).

By assumption, any communal group or minority that has been subject to political or material discrimination is at risk of collective adversity. Most such groups are impoverished and lack some or most of the economic opportunities open to dominant groups. Most also face collective restrictions on their members' civil and political rights. Such conditions, whether they are current violations of internationally recognized human rights or the residues of past violations, mean that group members are likely to experience material deprivation and have limited political means to protect themselves. In extreme circumstances, systematic discrimination threatens communal groups' most fundamental right, the right to physical survival. Many minorities also face cultural discrimination and the risk of deculturation or so-called cultural genocide in the form of pressures or incentives to adopt a dominant culture, or denial of cultural self-expression. Cultural pressures alone do not warrant a judgment that a group is at risk in the sense intended here. The groups at risk by the first criterion are those whose capacity to defend and promote cultural and other collective interests has been restricted by discrimination.[11]

Ethnies that benefit from positive differentials are *advantaged minorities*, whose special status is discussed later in this chapter. They are at risk in a different way. When they lose power to rebellious subordinate groups, as happened to the Tutsi over-lords of Rwanda in 1971 and as is happening now to white South Africans, they are at risk of being retaliated against and having restrictions imposed on their rights. Note that this study does not include advantaged majorities such as the Malays in Malaysia (who benefit from the economic restrictions placed on the Chinese minority) or U.S. citizens of European descent (in a society that historically has discriminated against African Americans, Asians, Hispanics, and Native Americans). While there is little doubt that the rights and privileges of the Afrikaner and Anglo minorities in South Africa and the rights of the Sunni minority that supports the Ba'thist regime in Iraq are at risk whenever these empowered minorities are displaced by political change, there is little chance that the dominant ethnic majorities of Malaysia or the United States will be displaced by subordinate minorities.

As suggested earlier, many distinct communal groups in the contemporary world are not now affected in any consequential way by differential social treatment, past or present. The Finns coexist amicably with the Swedish minority in Finland. The French-, Romansch-, and Italian-speaking Swiss have long since worked out mutually satisfactory plural institutions with the German speakers. There is little evidence of discrimination or tension among the many peoples—Zigula, Yao, Sukuma, Haya, Chagga, Asians, Arabs, and others—who make up the population of Tanzania. The accommodation or assimilation of such groups makes it likely but does not guarantee that their future relationships will be free of hostility and invidious treatment.

2. *The group was the focus of political mobilization and action in defense or promotion of its self-defined interests at some time between 1945 and 1989.* Most differentially treated peoples have taken some action during the past half-century to assert group interests either in the political arena or against other communal groups. Only 27 of the 233 communal groups have left no record (in our sources) of political organization, protest, rebellion, or intercommunal conflict since 1945. Groups that mobilize in

pursuit of collective interests are at risk because the political pursuit of their goals may escalate into protracted and costly commmunal conflict with other groups, as has happened in Lebanon, Sri Lanka, Burma, and Ethiopia. (The trends and patterns of political action by communal groups are the subject of chapter 4.)

The two general criteria, economic and political discrimination and political mobilization, were used to screen information on a large number of communal groups throughout the world.[12] The following five operational rules then were applied to develop the roster of 233 groups for inclusion in this book.

1. Include only communal groups at risk in countries with a population in 1985 greater than one million.

2. Include only groups that in 1990 numbered at least one hundred thousand or, if fewer, that exceeded 1 percent of the population of at least one country in which they resided.

3. Count and code groups separately in each country in which they meet the general criteria (for example, the Kurds are treated as a separate group in each of four countries).[13] Three exceptions were made to this rule: we analyzed as a single group the Saami of the Nordic countries, the Roma (Gypsies) of Western Europe, and the Roma of Eastern Europe.

4. Count and code advantaged minorities such as the Serbs of Yugoslavia (politically advantaged), the Chinese of Malaysia (economically advantaged), and the Sunni Arabs of Iraq (a dominant minority with both political and economic advantages), because they too mobilize in response to challenges by other groups (as the Serbs have done) and, when not in power, often are subject to discriminatory restrictions (as are the Malaysian Chinese).

5. Count and code groups at the highest within-country level of aggregation. For example, all native peoples in the United States were analyzed as a single group because many of them share a sense of larger, pan-tribal identity and because they usually are regarded and treated by white Americans as one aggregate group. Four exceptions were made to this rule. In the Andean countries there are marked differences between indigenous highland and lowland peoples in group identity, status, political organization, and in their treatment by the dominant society. In Colombia, Ecuador, Peru, and Bolivia, therefore, the native highland and lowland peoples are coded as two separate aggregate groups.

Rule 5 has proved more controversial than any other criterion used to demarcate communal groups for the study, because
it goes to the heart of the question, What is a group? Most Nav-
ajos and Hopis are more antagonistic toward one another than
toward Anglo society; Asians in Britain represent dozens of
southern Asian peoples, each with its own collective identity and
associations. The main theoretical reason for treating such categories of people as single groups is ethnogenesis: when people
of a category are treated by dominant groups as all of a kind,
they come to think of themselves in terms of the larger identity,
even though they usually retain their more localized identity.
The dynamics of ethnopolitical conflict are different for such
fragmented or aggregative groups than they are for strong
identity groups because fragmented groups are more likely to
have competing leaders and movements, and they are more susceptible to divide-and-rule strategies carried out by by the state.
We coded each of the groups on a five-category scale of coherence: more than half are strong (85) or weak (54) identity
groups, about a quarter are dispersed or fragmented but have
some shared values and identities (54), and the remainder have
many local or cross-cutting identities but little or no present evidence of shared identity (35). This information provides a beginning point for the analysis of identity formation and its effects on ethnopolitical conflict.[14]

The roster of 233 groups is an imperfect approximation of
the universe of politically salient communal groups at the beginning of 1990. We know it excludes groups that some regional
specialists think should be included. The Scots, for example,
have aspirations for greater autonomy much like those of Bretons, Basques, and Québecois, though none have used violent
means to emphasize the point. In Belgium there are about
1.2 million French speakers in Brussels, Antwerp, and Ghent
whose civil and political rights have been curtailed since the
1980s as a consequence of regional autonomy granted to
French-speaking Wallonia: the solution to one region's communal grievances created a minority elsewhere that was subject
to discrimination.[15] A third example is the Greek minority in
Albania, about 2.5 percent of the population, whose Greek Orthodox faith made them a special, though not unique, target of
the Albanian government's harsh anti-religious campaign from
the 1960s through the 1980s. An African example is the Krahn
of Liberia, who provided the power base for General Doe's

regime during the 1980s; the advantages they held during his regime prompted retaliation and summary executions after he was overthrown during the 1990 civil war.

All these groups should be added the next time we revise the list of minorities at risk. The list also needs to be continuously updated in response to changing geopolitical circumstances. Following rule 5, we analyzed the southern Sudanese and the Eritreans each as a separate group, despite their cultural diversity and internal cleavages, because each has a common political status and is represented by a broad-based political movement. Now that Eritrea has secured de facto independence from Ethiopia, however, old communal and religious rivalries are likely to reemerge and if they do, new groups will have to be profiled. One such group in Eritrea, the Afars, already are included in the data set, because they have been pursuing separate ethnopolitical objectives since the 1970s. Similar processes are far advanced in the breakaway republics of the former Soviet Union, where independence for the Baltic states has politicized Russian minorities, and independence for Georgia has prompted the attempted secession of 164,000 South Ossetians and 96,000 Abkhazians.

Populations of Politicized Communal Groups

Nearly three-quarters of the 127 largest countries in the world had at least one politicized minority in 1990. The largest numbers are found in Asia and Africa south of the Sahara (table 1.1). The 233 groups in 1990 had an estimated 915 million members, 17.3 percent of the global population. All are listed in the Appendix, tables A.1 to A.6, with information on their approximate populations and other characteristics.

Because communal groups are cultural and psychological entities rather than bounded political communities, it is difficult to estimate their populations. The following account of two problems encountered and procedures used helps illustrate how we dealt with the challenges of developing comparative demographic information on the 233 groups.

First was a conceptual problem: there are inherent social ambiguities in deciding on the boundaries of an identity group. The Bretons of France provide an example of alternative criteria. In 1982 there were 3.7 million people in the five depart-

Table 1.1. Overview of Minorities at Risk in 1990, by Region.

World Region[b]	Number of Countries with Minorities at Risk[c]	Number of Minorities at Risk	Population of Minorities (1990 estimates[a])	
			Total (thousands)	Percentage of Total Regional Population
Western democracies and Japan (21)[d]	15	24	84,023	10.8%
Eastern Europe and the USSR (9)[e]	5	32	153,658	35.0%
Asia (21)[f]	15	43	273,064	10.2%
North Africa and the Middle East[g] (19)	12	31	118,205	28.8%
Africa south of the Sahara (36)[h]	29	74	237,023	42.3%
Latin America and the Caribbean (21)	17	29	49,371	11.0%
Total (127)	93	233	915,344	17.3%[i]

[a] All our population estimates for minorities have been projected to 1990. Many such estimates are imprecise. All country population estimates are 1990 projections listed in *Statistical Abstract of the United States 1989* (Washington, DC: U.S. Bureau of the Census, 1989), 813–815.

[b] Numbers in parentheses are the number of countries and dependent territories in each region whose estimated populations in 1990 exceeded one million. Total regional population (the basis for the percentage in the right-hand column) is for these larger countries only.

[c] The Saami live in three Nordic countries, all of which are counted as having minorities. The Roma (Gypsies) are a dispersed minority throughout Eastern and Western Europe. No European country whose only minority is Roma is counted in this tabulation.

[d] Included in the western democracies are the countries of Western Europe, the United States, Canada, Australia, and New Zealand; Puerto Rico is treated as part of the United States. Turkey and Israel are included in the Middle East; South Africa is included in Africa south of the Sahara.

[e] The Kazakh and Uighur minorities of northwestern China are included in this region because they are extensions (segments) of national peoples who live mainly in the republics of ex-Soviet Central Asia.

[f] Indonesia, Papua New Guinea, and the Philippines are included in the Asia region; Japan is included with the western democracies. China, Taiwan, and Hong Kong are counted as separate countries within the Asia region.

[g] Turkey, Israel, Afghanistan, and Pakistan are included in this grouping. North Africa includes only Libya, Egypt, and the countries of the Maghreb. The Occupied Territories (the West Bank and Gaza) are treated as part of Israel, and their Palestinian populations are coded as a minority within that country.

[h] Including South Africa and Madagascar. Namibia is treated as a separate country. Mauritius, which usually is included in the African region and whose population exceeds one million, was inadvertently omitted from the study.

[i] Percentage of total population (5.30 billion) of all countries and territories whose populations exceeded one million in 1990.

ments that correspond approximately to the historically autonomous region of Brittany (whose boundaries were by no means
fixed). Experts estimate that fewer than one-quarter of the
people in the region now use Breton as a day-to-day language.
But a 1975 survey (not a census) taken during a period of communal activism had shown that one-quarter of the regional population identified themselves as more Breton than French and
half regarded themselves as equally Breton and French. The
luxury of multiple estimates using different criteria is a rarity
among the 233 groups in the Minorities at Risk study.

Second was the problem of lack of reliable data. In some
Third World countries there are no reliable census data for a
country as a whole or for its constituent groups. No census has
ever been taken in independent Lebanon, for example, and
none was reported from Nigeria between 1973 and 1991, in
both instances because precise data on group populations
would be politically inflammatory.[16] A related problem is data
that appear more precise than they actually are. The revolutionary Ethiopian government reported 1980s estimates of populations in regions beset by civil war, estimates based on conjec-
ture and political wish fulfillment in a country where no
complete census has ever been attempted.

Our preferred solution to the conceptual problem is to use
the widest demographic definition of an identity group, for example, all residents of the Breton departments, or all people
who tell census takers they are of Native American descent.
These are the outer bounds of the population that is potentially
affected by group differentials and that might be mobilized on
behalf of group interests.

Our approach to the problem of inaccurate data was to use
the estimate with the greatest prima facie reliability. Estimates
based on people saying they are members of a communal group
or minority in response to census questions come closest to em-
bodying the concept of an identity group. For the former
USSR, which required citizens to carry identity cards specifying
their nationality, there are detailed census data on people's primary language and their nationality registration; we report data
based on formal nationality identification—Armenian, Ukrainian, Lithuanian, and so forth. Census-based group identifications are not completely reliable, because enumerations may be
incomplete and respondents may dissemble. Australia's population of self-identified Aborigines increased dramatically from

the 1950s to the 1970s, evidently because people of part-Aboriginal descent became increasingly likely to self-identify as Aborigines to census takers.[17]

For the 150 groups that are geographically concentrated, the best alternatives to individual-level census data are census or other estimates of the population of their traditional home region. The limitation of this procedure is that members of a group often have dispersed widely from their region of origin, while others have moved in to take their place. Corsicans provide another example from France: nearly half the people born on Corsica now live elsewhere, while many non-Corsicans have migrated to the island. Since the sense of Corsican identity is strong—many people of Corsican birth return to the island for regional elections, for example—we use Corsican birth as the optimal indicator of group size.[18] Offsetting the emigration factor is the fact that some immigrants to a region come to identify with it rather than their place and group of origin. In the Spanish Basque provinces, for example, a substantial and growing number of members of the Euzkadi Ta Azkatasuna (ETA) separatist movement are of Spanish or mixed Spanish and Basque descent.[19]

Where census data were lacking or suspect, we recorded as many estimates as possible from regional experts and advocacy organizations and struck a balance among them. Estimates from advocates were given less weight because their estimates usually were higher than the ones provided by more neutral observers.

Regionally, the most reliable estimates of group size come from the western democracies, Eastern Europe, and the former USSR. Most of these countries have high-quality census data and much supplementary information about constituent groups. The task here was to make informed decisions, such as those about the Bretons and Corsicans, about the outer boundaries of group identity.

In the Third World a number of former British dependencies also have reasonably reliable census data on constituent groups: India, Malaysia, Kenya, and South Africa, for example. For most other African and Asian minorities there are no current, reliable, census-based data, and we had to rely on estimates provided by regional experts. Some such estimates are expressed as percentages of countrywide populations, others are actual numerical values—not always accompanied by a year of reference. Most governments of independent Africa do not collect census data about communal groups because "tribalism" is supposed to be a vestige of the colonial and precolonial past. Colonial regimes did report such estimates, and though they are seldom highly reliable, Africanists continue to rely on them for demographic data. The procedure they use is to calculate a group's proportional size at the last colonial census, then apply that proportion to the most recent population estimate for the country as a whole.[20] The accuracy of the results depend on a number of assumptions: that the last colonial census was accurate, that growth rates among different peoples have been constant, and that current country population estimates are also reasonably accurate.

With the exception of Israel and its Occupied Territories, minority population estimates in North Africa and the Middle East are conjectural. The same is true for most indigenous groups and all Afro-Americans in Latin America. For these regions we relied mainly on expert and advocacy estimates, usually averaging the most plausible numbers.

The population estimates reported in table 1.1 and the Appendix (see the POP90 column in tables A.1 to A.6) were projected forward to 1990 by using the procedure applied to African groups. We decided on the most reliable and valid numerical estimate of a group's size, then expressed it as a percentage of the country's total population for the year of reference. The percentage then was applied to the country's 1990 population to provide a current numerical estimate (table 1.1, footnote a). Most of the comparisons in this book, including those in table 1.1, make use of the percentages (proportions) rather than numerical estimates.

Of special interest are the countries with the largest aggregate proportion of politicized communal groups, shown in the right-hand columns of table 1.2. In five countries that proportion is, effectively, the entire population: Taiwan, Lebanon, Iraq, Burundi, and South Africa. Each is governed by a dominant minority that has been subject to challenge by subordinate groups. In another seven African countries plus Bolivia and Malaysia, the aggregate proportion of groups at risk exceeds 50 percent. High concentrations of politicized minorities do not necessarily translate into high magnitudes of violent conflict, as is illustrated by Taiwan and Malaysia. In these two countries, as in others such as India and Zambia, the political incorporation or cooptation of subordinate groups has moderated the divisive effects of politicized ethnicity. Nonetheless, most countries high on the lists of table 1.2 have had protracted communal conflicts in the past and have high potential for such conflict in future.

Types of Politicized Communal Groups

The 233 politicized communal groups vary so widely in their defining traits, political status, and aspirations that it is useful to make some systematic distinctions among them (table 1.3). The most basic distinction is between *national peoples* and *minority peoples*. National peoples are regionally concentrated groups that have lost their autonomy to expansionist states but still preserve some of their cultural and linguistic distinctiveness and want to protect or reestablish some degree of politically separate existence. Minority peoples have a defined socioeconomic or political status within a larger society—based on some combination of their ethnicity, immigrant origin, economic roles, and religion—and are concerned about protecting or improving that status. To make the distinction most sharply, national peoples seek separation or autonomy from the states that rule them; minority peoples seek greater access or control.

The distinction between national peoples and minority peoples is not absolute because members of minority peoples who are denied equal access and protection may shift strategies and try to exit, as many Soviet Jews did. By contrast, national peoples such as the Tigreans of Ethiopia may decide to seize power at the center rather than secede. Moreover, there are many middle alternatives, such as power sharing and cultural pluralism, within the tripolar extremes of secession, assimilation, and seizure of power. These and other alternatives are considered in chapter 10.

There also are distinctive types of communal groups within each of the two broad divisions. The national peoples comprise *ethnonationalists* and *indigenous peoples*. The types of minority peoples are *ethnoclasses*, *militant sects*, and three subtypes of *communal contenders*: dominant, advantaged, and disadvantaged contenders. The group types are used throughout the book to facilitate comparison and generalizations, but they are not definitive: further analysis may suggest more precise distinctions and revisions in how specific groups are categorized. The types

Table 1.2. Proportional Size of Minorities in 1990.

World Region[a]	Average Group Size[b]	Largest Group in Region[c]	Countries in Region with Largest Aggregate Proportion of Minorities (number of groups in parentheses)	
Western democracies and Japan (21/15)	.049 (24)	French Canadians (.256)	Canada (2)	.279
			USA (3)	.214
Eastern Europe and the USSR (9/5)	.053 (32)	Serbs (.363)	Yugoslavia (3)	.717
			USSR (20)	.402[d]
			Czechoslovakia (2)	.350
Asia (21/15)	.070 (43)	Taiwanese (.85)	Taiwan (3)	1.000
			Malaysia (3)	.502
			Burma (7)	.301
			India (8)	.208
North Africa and the Middle East (19/12)	.144 (31)	Iraqi Shi'is (.52)	Lebanon (5)	1.000
			Iraq (3)	.950
			Iran (7)	.424
			Israel (2)	.394[e]
			Morocco (2)	.376
			Jordan (1)	.350
			Pakistan (5)	.324

Region		Largest group[c]	Country (minorities)[a]	Proportion[b]
Africa south of the Sahara (36/29)	.168 (74)	Burundi Hutu (.83)	Burundi (2)	1.000
			South Africa (4)	1.000
			Guinea (3)	.760
			Niger (3)	.760
			Cameroon (3)	.690
			Ethiopia (6)	.681
			Zambia (3)	.630
			Zaire (5)	.550
			Uganda (9)	.528
Latin America and the Caribbean (21/17)	.092 (29)	Bolivian highlands native peoples (.61)	Bolivia (2)	.630
			Peru (3)	.417
			Guatemala (1)	.360
			Ecuador (3)	.350

[a] The numbers in parentheses are the number of countries and dependent territories in each region whose estimated populations in 1985 exceeded one million (to the left of the slash), and the number of those countries with politicized minorities (to the right of the slash). For countries included in each region see footnotes to table 1.1.

[b] Mean size of groups as a proportion of country population. The numbers in parentheses are the numbers of minorities in the region.

[c] The largest group in proportion to country population.

[d] In 1990 the non-Russian nationalities in the USSR in the aggregate made up slightly less than 50 percent of the country's population. Not all of them met our criteria for inclusion in this study. The minorities of the fifteen successor republics of the USSR make up precisely 25 percent of their aggregate population.

[e] Arab citizens of Israel plus Palestinians in the Occupied Territories as a proportion of the total population of Israel proper plus Gaza and the West Bank.

Table 1.3. Definitions of Types of Politicized Communal Groups.

National peoples	
Ethnonationalists	Large, regionally concentrated peoples with a history of organized political autonomy who have pursued separatist objectives at some time during the last half-century.
Indigenous peoples	Conquered descendants of original inhabitants of a region who typically live in peripheral regions, practice subsistence agriculture or herding, and have cultures sharply distinct from dominant groups.
Minority peoples	
Ethnoclasses	Ethnically or culturally distinct peoples, usually descended from slaves or immigrants, with special economic roles, usually of low status.
Militant sects	Communal groups whose political status and activities are centered on the defense of their religious beliefs.
Communal contenders	Culturally distinct peoples, tribes, or clans in heterogenous societies who hold or seek a share in state power.
Disadvantaged	Communal contenders who are subject to political or economic discrimination or both.
Advantaged	Communal contenders with political advantages over other groups in their society. Advantaged groups with a preponderance of both political and economic power are referred to as dominant minorities.

also are not mutually exclusive: more than a third of all minorities (91 of 233) have characteristics of two group types. We cross-classify such groups rather than forcing them into one category, on the argument that because they have two different statuses, they have a wider range of objectives and strategies and are open to a wider range of accommodations. The types are described below and in table 1.3; the numbers of groups of each type in each world region are shown in table 1.4.

Ethnonationalists

These eighty-one groups are relatively large, regionally concentrated peoples who historically were autonomous and who have

Table 1.4. Types of Politicized Communal Groups by Region, 1990.[a]

World Region	Number of Politicized Groups	Group Type[b]				Communal Contenders[c]	
		Ethno-nationalists	Indigenous Peoples	Ethno-classes	Militant Sects[d]	Disadvantaged	Advantaged
Western democracies and Japan (21)	24	10	5	8	3(1)	0	0
Eastern Europe and the USSR (9)	32	17	11	4	14(1)	0	0
Asia (21)	43	19	25	7	8(2)	3	1
North Africa and the Middle East (19)	31	13	11	5	9(5)	4	4
Africa south of the Sahara (36)	74	21	12	12	5	34	20
Latin America and the Caribbean (21)	29	1	19	9	0(1)	0	0
Totals (127)	233	81	83	45	39(10)	41	25

[a] Regions are defined in footnotes to table 1.1. Numbers in parentheses are numbers of countries in each region with 1985 populations exceeding one million.

[b] See table 1.3 for definitions of types. Since the types are not mutually exclusive, 91 groups are classified under more than one type and the total adds to more than 233. See Appendix, tables A.1 to A.6, variables TYPE1, TYPE2, and ADV80, for categorizations of specific groups.

[c] Advantaged groups are communal contenders with substantial political advantages in the 1980s; i.e. communal contenders coded in Appendix tables A.1 to A.6, variable ADV80, as dominant (DOM) or political (POL). Groups with economic advantages only are classified according to their TYPE1 and TYPE2 categorizations, because almost invariably they are subject to discrimination or restrictive public policies.

[d] Listed first are members of Muslim minorities; numbers in parentheses are non-Muslim minorities: Northern Irish Catholics, Jews (in the ex-USSR and Argentina), Copts in Egypt, Maronites in Lebanon, Hindus (in Pakistan and Bangladesh), Sikhs in India, Baha'is in Iran, and Ahmadis in Pakistan. The latter two have been condemned as non-Muslim heresies in Iran and Pakistan, respectively, which is a warrant for discrimination against their followers. The total number of politicized sects is forty-nine.

pursued separatist objectives at some time in the last fifty years. Some lost their autonomy centuries ago, such as the Bakongo, whose kingdom was subjugated by the Portuguese in the 1660s, and the Québecois, who were conquered by the British in 1760. Others developed the beginnings of national consciousness because they had separate status under colonial rule, such as the Karen of Burma and the people of East Timor, and rebelled when they were absorbed into postcolonial states dominated by other peoples. A few enjoyed brief periods of autonomy during or after World War II, e.g. the Croats, the Kurds of Iran, and the Uighurs of China, and have since fought to regain it. Not all are separatist in the literal sense that they seek their own national states; many of their leaders demand or are willing to settle for greater regional autonomy. Chapter 3 includes a more detailed discussion of the political history of ethnonationalists.

Some ethnonationalist movements have limited public support and mobilization, as is the case among Corsican, Sicilian, and South Tyrolean separatists, for example. We cast a wide net by including in this category all groups that gave rise to autonomy movements that persisted as an active political force (not necessarily in open rebellion) for at least five years between the 1940s and the 1980s. The ability of a movement to remain active for five years in its region of origin suggests that it draws on a significant undercurrent of support.

Indigenous Peoples

Indigenous peoples such as Native Americans, Australian Aborigines, the Masai and San of Africa, Nagas and Santals in India, and Dayaks in northern Borneo also are concerned most fundamentally about issues of group autonomy. They have other traits that distinguish them from ethnonationalists. Culturally these eighty-three groups are more sharply distinct from the centers of state or colonial authority. Most live in peripheral and inaccessible mountain valleys, tropical rainforests, steppes, or deserts. All have lived a preindustrial existence as subsistence cultivators, herders, or hunter-gatherers until quite recently. Until recent decades, most did not have modern political organizations, strong group identity, or a sense of common purpose—and some still lack them. Moreover, their political actions have usually been reactive, aimed at retaining control of what is left of their land and resources, rather than proactive.[21]

The two types of national peoples substantially overlap because some indigenous peoples such as the Kurds, the Nagas, and the Miskitos have developed a sense of nationhood during the past half-century and have supported separatist movements. Twenty-four indigenous groups therefore are cross-classified as ethnonationalists.

Ethnoclasses

Ethnoclasses are forty-five ethnically or culturally distinct minorities, most of them descended from slaves or immigrants, who specialize in distinctive economic activities, usually of low status. The eight ethnoclasses in the advanced industrial societies are at or near the bottom of the economic hierarchy, for example, the Muslim minority in France, people of color in Britain and the United States, and Koreans in Japan. The same is true of Afro-Americans in nine Latin American societies. In Third-World societies ethnoclasses sometimes are economically advantaged but politically restricted merchants and professionals, like the overseas Chinese of Southeast Asia and the residual European and Asian minorities in postcolonial Africa. The Roma of Europe also are categorized here.

Common to most ethnoclasses is the demand for more equitable treatment: more economic opportunities, effective political participation, better public services. Some, such as the Maghrebins and Beurs in France,[22] the Koreans in Japan, and some African Americans, also are concerned about protecting and promoting their own cultural traditions. The ethnoclasses vary widely in political mobilization: in the western democracies they have very actively pursued their interests in the political arena; in Asia their politics are low profile and defensive; in Latin America, Afro-Americans have been unorganized and quiescent, with the exception of Brazilian blacks and Afro-Caribbeans in Panama.

Militant Sects

Most of the forty-nine politicized minority peoples that are defined wholly or substantially by their religious beliefs are Muslims. They include Islamic minorities in societies dominated by other religious traditions, such as the Turks of Germany, the Muslim Albanians of Yugoslavia, the Arab citizens of Israel, and the Malay Muslims of Thailand. They also include the warring Sunni, Shi'i, and Druze communities in Lebanon; and Shi'i communities in Sunni-dominated Iraq and Saudi Arabia. Ten non-Muslim religious groups (see table 1.4, footnote d) also are included in this category. Some of these religiously defined groups, such as the Jews in Argentina, Copts in Egypt, and Baha'is in Iran, are concerned with defending themselves against external threats, not with militant assertion of the group's political interests.

All but eight of the politicized sects are cross-classified in other categories, mainly as indigenous peoples (fifteen groups) and ethnonationalists (eleven groups). Examples of national peoples who define themselves by their religious faith are the Catholics of Northern Ireland, the Central Asian Muslims of the former USSR, and the Kashmiris and Sikhs in India. Another nine are ethnoclasses (for example, Muslim immigrants in France and Germany), and a handful are communal contenders (in Lebanon and countries of the eastern Sudan). For most of these politicized religious minorities, their faith is only one of several traits that define and distinguish them from others. It is a highly salient trait, however, especially around the periphery of the Islamic world where Muslim and non-Muslim peoples often coexist uneasily in the same states.

Communal Contenders

Communal contenders are found in a number of African states and a few other heterogenous societies in the Middle East and Asia, in which political power at the center is based on inter-group coalitions, usually dominated by a powerful minority that uses a mix of concessions, cooptation, and repression to maintain its leading role. This study includes forty-one *disadvantaged* communal contenders, all of which are subject to some kind of economic or political discrimination, and twenty-five *advantaged* contenders that held political advantages in the 1980s. Those politically advantaged minorities that also have economic advantages are dominant minorities, as shown in the Appendix.[23] Elements of a few dominant minorities, such as the Sunni Arabs of Iraq and the Tutsi rulers of Burundi, continue to exercise a virtual monopoly of power. Most other dominant minorities (e.g., the Mainland Chinese of Taiwan, the Maronites of Lebanon, the Creoles of Sierra Leone) have agreed or been pressured to share some power with other groups.

The identity of most communal contenders is based on shared culture, language, and regional origin—they are tribes or clans, playing for power in the state political arena. Fourteen of them also are ethnonationalists. When they find themselves losing position in a coalition, their leaders may opt for exit in the form of separatist movements. The Issaq clan of northern Somalia is a case in point: they were excluded from the governing national coalition in a 1969 coup, organized a so-called liberation movement in the 1980s that triggered severe repression, and, after participating in the civil war that overthrew the General Barre regime in early 1991, declared independence for northern Somalia.[24]

Some governing coalitions have been more effective at managing intergroup conflicts than others. Kenya, Zambia, and Malaysia are examples of states where more- and less-advantaged communal contenders have achieved relatively stable and noncoercive power-sharing arrangements. There always is the risk that conflicts among communal contenders in such countries will escalate into protracted conflict. Intergroup shifts in relative power and prosperity often provoke violent reactions by groups that see themselves losing out—or that see an opportunity to improve their position at the expense of rivals. If institutional restraints are lacking and a dominant group is unwilling or unable to compromise, the results can be full-blown civil or revolutionary war. The failures of power sharing among communal contenders have led to some of the most devastating civil wars of the second half of the twentieth century: in Sudan (on-and-off civil war between north and south since the late 1950s); Nigeria (the Biafran civil war, 1967–70), Pakistan (the 1971 secession of Bangladesh), and Lebanon (internationalized civil war from 1975 through 1990).

Minority Issues in Six World Regions

This chapter concludes with a brief overview of the minorities in each of the six world regions shown in table 1.1. The regions are discussed in descending order of their numbers of minori-

ties at risk, and the industrial democracies and Latin America
are discussed together.

Africa South of the Sahara

The thirty-six countries of this region have seventy-four politicized communal groups, which in the aggregate comprise more
than 40 percent of the region's total population. This high concentration is partly due to the heterogeneous populations and
arbitrary boundaries inherited by most independent African
states and partly a result of intercommunal competition for political dominance in the new states. This kind of conflict flares
up sporadically in individual countries, as it has recently in Liberia and Togo, but rarely spreads beyond them.

There are two larger concentrations of serious communal
conflicts. One centers on the vestiges of European dominance
in southern Africa, involving six ethnoclasses (Europeans in
Zimbabwe and Namibia, and all contending parties in South Africa). The outcomes are uncertain only in South Africa itself.
The most devastating African conflicts are the civil wars of
Chad, Sudan, Ethiopia, and Somalia, whose protagonists include eight ethnonationalists. Similar conflicts may recur along
the cleavage line between Muslim and non-Muslim peoples in
West Africa, from Nigeria to Niger to Guinea. The dozen indigenous peoples of Africa, in contrast, have been politically quiescent. In chapter 9 James R. Scarritt provides a closer analysis of
communal conflicts in Africa, including case studies of governing coalitions in Kenya and Zambia.

Asia

The twenty-one countries of East, Southeast, and South Asia
have the second largest number of minorities at risk, but these
forty-three groups make up barely a tenth of the regional population—the smallest percentage of any world region. More
than half the Asian minorities are indigenous peoples who live
in the hills and jungles on the periphery of states dominated by
urban-centered lowland groups. The political and demographic

expansion of Bengalis, Burmans, Han Chinese, Hindus, and Javanese has prompted organized political resistance by Arakanese, Dayaks, Mizos, Mons, Papuans, Tibetans, and eighteen other indigenous peoples. Thirteen indigenous groups are also ethnonationalists: they have shifted from reactive protest and rebellion to proactive independence movements. Another seven Asian minorities, such as the Indians in Malaysia and Sri Lanka and the overseas Chinese of Southeast Asia, are descendents of economic migrants, and live within restrictions imposed by the dominant peoples of the host society.[25] And ten are religious sects, mainly Muslim minorities in predominantly Hindu, Buddhist, or Christian societies, that have become politicized in defense of their faith, their lifeways, and their lands. They include the Muslims and Sikhs of India, the Malay Muslims of southern Thailand, the Cham in Kampuchea, and the Moros in the Philippines.

Eastern Europe and the USSR

The third largest concentration of politicized communal groups is found in Eastern Europe and the former Soviet Union. Before the breakup of the USSR and Yugoslavia, thirty-two peoples made up 35 percent of the regional population. The heavy concentration in this region is mainly the legacy of Russia's history of imperial expansion; twenty of the USSR's national peoples met one or both our criteria of differential treatment or political mobilization at the beginning of 1990. Yugoslavia has been a tinderbox of communal conflict since it was created in 1919: by 1990, four of its constituent peoples were actively resisting Serbian dominance. Also included in this region for analytic purposes are the Muslim Kazakhs and Uighurs of westernmost China, who are close kindred to groups that live mainly in the former Soviet republics of Central Asia. The identities and status of minorities in this region are changing month by month in the early 1990s. A current assessment is provided by Monty G. Marshall in chapter 7, with an annex that lists the minorities of the fifteen successor republics of the USSR. The aggregate minority population of these republics as of the 1989 census was precisely 25 percent of the USSR's total population.

North Africa and the Middle East

The thirty-one politicized minorities of this region comprise 28.8 percent of its total population. Most numerous and politically active are the Kurds and Palestinians, national peoples who lost out in the twentieth-century process of state formation in the region. The Saharawis, the people of Western Sahara, have fought a long, losing war to resist their forcible incorporation into Morocco, motivated by similar nationalist sentiments. Both Iran and Pakistan have large numbers of politicized regional minorities, some of whom are indigenous tribal peoples such as the Baluchis and Bakthiaris, others of whom are contenders for power at the center such as the Pashtuns and Sindhis of Pakistan. Three of the ten politicized sects are Shi'is: they are a politically restricted and mostly quiescent minority in Saudi Arabia, a militant minority in Lebanon, and a suppressed majority in Iraq. The Middle East also includes several advantaged minorities that hold political power: the Maronites and Sunnis in Lebanon, the Alawis of Syria, and the Sunnis of Iraq. Although the level of communal conflict in the Middle East is proportionally the highest of all regions, some of its largest minorities— the Berbers of North Africa and the Azerbaijanis of Iran—have not been in serious conflict with the state in recent decades. An in-depth analysis of selected Middle Eastern minorities is provided by Barbara Harff in chapter 8.

The Industrial Democracies and Latin America

The world regions with the smallest minority populations are the advanced industrial democracies (twenty-four groups, eighty-four million people) and Latin America (twenty-nine groups, forty-nine million people). Ethnonationalism, the most serious source of communal conflict in Africa and Asia, is rare here. The European countries are long-established nation-states where alternative sources of national identity are mostly the quixotic preoccupation of political hobbyists on the Celtic and Mediterranean fringes. The major exceptions are the Basques and Québecois, some of whom are deadly earnest in the pursuit of regional autonomy and independence. These and other minorities in the industrial democracies are considered in more detail in chapter 6.

The most politically active minorities in the industrial democracies are the eight ethnoclasses of African, Islamic, and Asian origin in Western Europe and the United States. Their organized demands for political and economic equality and cultural self-expression have few parallels among the Afro-American ethnoclasses in nine Latin American countries. The indigenous rights movement, on the other hand, has affected virtually all native peoples in the Americas as well as the European Saami and the Aborigines and Maori of Australia and New Zealand. In Latin America the status of native peoples is by far the most serious of minority problems. Nicaragua's Miskito are among the few who have benefited from recent efforts at accommodation, in a case examined briefly in chapter 10.

Maps showing minority proportions in North America, Latin America, Europe, Africa, the Middle East, and Asia follow on pages 28–33. Maps of the same six regions showing ethnopolitical conflict in the 1980s appear on pages 117–122. Note that these geographic regions do not correspond exactly with the world regions that are listed in table 1.1 and discussed above.

NORTH AMERICA:
MINORITY PROPORTIONS

■ .601 to 1.00
╱ .401 to .600
▦ .201 to .400
▨ .101 to .200
⋰ .051 to .100
⋱ .001 to .050

28

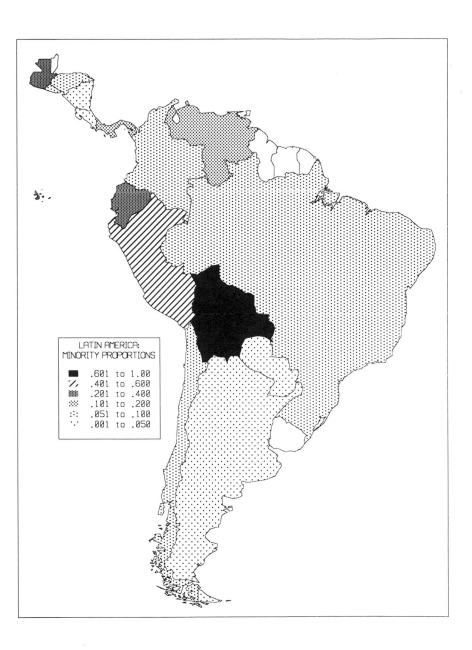

LATIN AMERICA:
MINORITY PROPORTIONS

■	.601 to 1.00
╱	.401 to .600
▧	.201 to .400
░	.101 to .200
∴	.051 to .100
··	.001 to .050

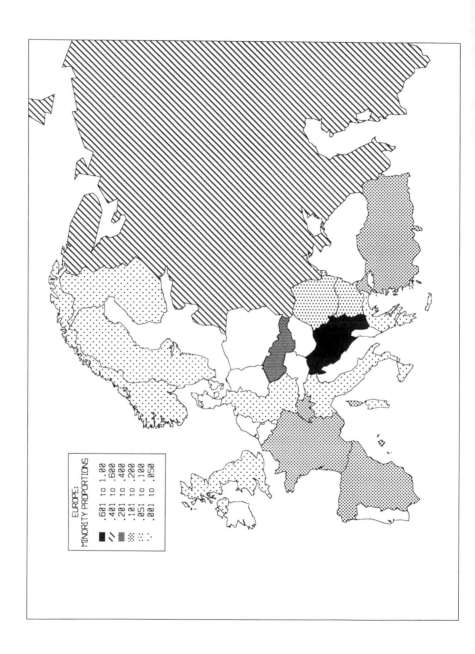

EUROPE:
MINORITY PROPORTIONS

.601 to 1.00
.401 to .600
.201 to .400
.101 to .200
.051 to .100
.001 to .050

30

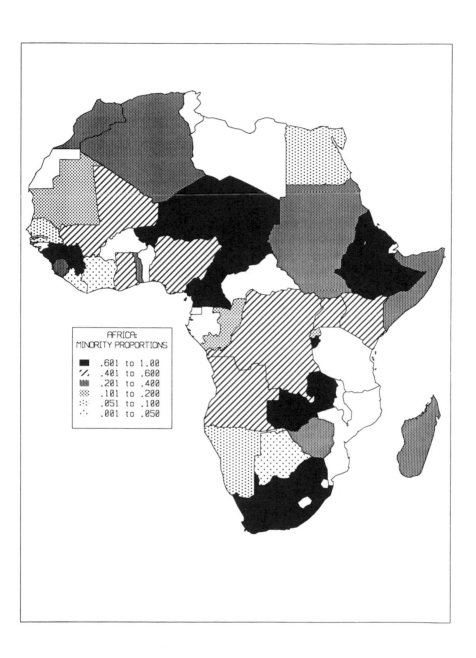

AFRICA:
MINORITY PROPORTIONS

■	.601 to 1.00
⊘	.401 to .600
▓	.201 to .400
░	.101 to .200
∷	.051 to .100
∴	.001 to .050

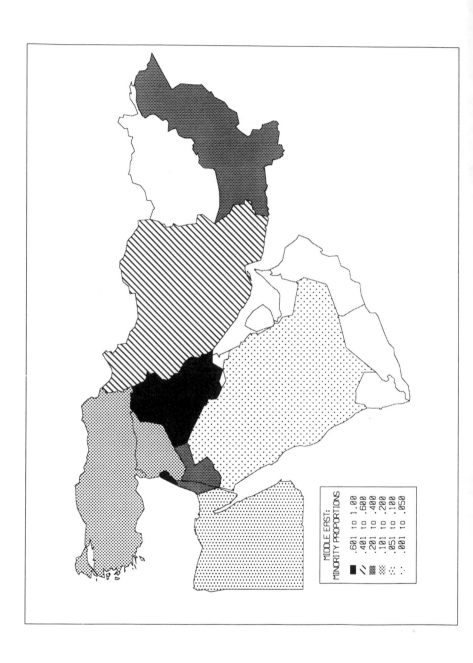

MIDDLE EAST:
MINORITY PROPORTIONS

■ .601 to 1.00
⁄ .401 to .600
▦ .201 to .400
⋮ .101 to .200
⋮ .051 to .100
⋮ .001 to .050

32

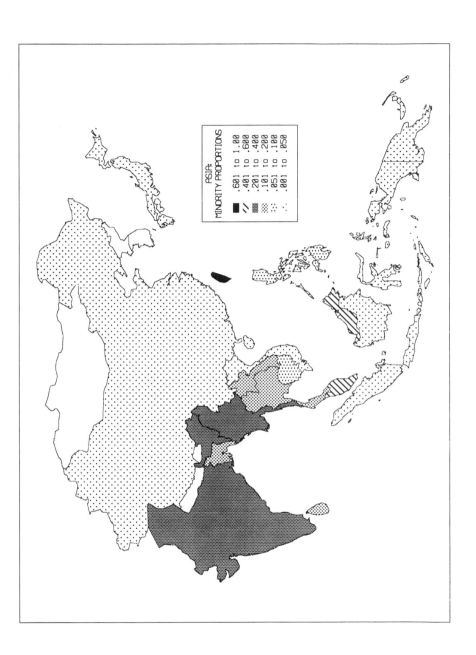

ASIA:
MINORITY PROPORTIONS

.601 to 1.00
.401 to .600
.201 to .400
.101 to .200
.051 to .100
.001 to .050

33

2. The Status of Minorities at Risk
Inequalities and Discrimination

The inequalities that divide disadvantaged minorities from advantaged or dominant groups are the enduring heritage of four major historical processes: conquest, state building, migration, and economic development. Every people who established an empire or settled frontiers, who conquered nonbelievers or civilized natives, who built a modern state, did so at the expense of weaker and less fortunate peoples. Ethnic immigrants have provided functionaries for colonial bureaucracies, labor for plantation economies, workers for industrial revolutions, and menials for the service economies of postindustrial societies. All the common types of minorities at risk had their origins in one or more of these big historical processes.

Imperial expansion by Russia, the Austro-Hungarian Empire, the Ottoman Turks, China, and Ethiopia meant the conquest of a great many autonomous peoples, among whose descendants are nearly thirty of the ethnonationalists and a dozen politically active indigenous peoples of the 1990s. The dominant groups who established modern nation-states in Western Europe and North America forcibly incorporated a number of preexisting polities, from the Iroquois Confederacy to Catalonia. Nine contemporary Western movements seeking the devolution of state power and independence justify their claims on the historical grounds of lost autonomy.

The European conquest of the Americas and Australasia meant massacre, enslavement, and cultural genocide for many ancestors of contemporary indigenous rights activists. Two dozen indigenous groups in this study were subjugated by European settlers of "new lands," and as a set they suffer from the most severe material inequalities identified in the Minorities at Risk study.[1]

Militant Christianity and Islam used the sword to subjugate heretics and infidels who were reluctant to adopt the true faith or to acknowledge the rightful heir of the Prophet. The inheritors of these ancient rivalries among competing faiths and sects are the modern world's embattled religious minorities. Our survey includes twenty-five politicized Muslim minorities in countries that border the Islamic world and eleven politically restricted religious minorities within Islamic countries.

The European colonization of Africa, the Indian subcontinent, and Southeast Asia opened the door for immigrants— European settlers, Chinese and Lebanese traders, Tamil and African laborers. Thirteen of the minorities at risk trace their descent from European-sponsored immigration to colonial territories. European rule also created or reinforced hierarchies among the conquered peoples, because the colonizers almost invariably favored some traditional rulers and tribes over others. Colonial withdrawal after World War II set the stage for the communal rivalries that have riven many new states. In Africa south of the Sahara, for example, we estimate that two dozen of the indigenous communal contenders have been challenged because of political or economic advantages they gained during colonial rule.

The ethnoclasses of the developed democracies and of Latin America are a by-product of planters' and industrialists' need for cheap and reliable labor. The plantation economies of the Americas depended on African slaves, whose descendants constitute ten of this study's ethnoclasses. Analogously, the industrial economies of twentieth-century Europe, North America, and Japan have attracted, and often actively recruited, immigrants willing to do menial work. Six of the politically active minorities in the advanced industrial democracies are economic immigrants and their descendants. There are emergent ethnoclasses of the same kind in the oil-rich Middle Eastern states and in West Africa, though none are included in this study.[2]

Dominance established through any of these processes almost invariably imposed political and economic disadvantages on newly subordinate peoples. For immigrants and indigenous peoples it also created pressures to abandon their own cultures and group identities in favor of the language, beliefs, and lifeways of the dominant groups. Subordinate peoples such as the

Welsh in Britain and Irish Americans in the United States have lost their cohesion and have been assimilated into larger societies. But more than two hundred disadvantaged groups covered in this survey have maintained and reasserted their group identities and are using political means to demand greater rights and redress for historically imposed powerlessness and inequalities. It is a commonplace to say that the intangible quality of cultural identity gives special intensity to their demands. It is less often recognized that these peoples' historical experience of victimization and exploitation also strengthens group identity and contributes to their sense of collective injustice.[3]

This chapter assesses the present-day cultural, economic, and political conditions that differentiate the disadvantaged communal groups from others.[4] In what respects are they disadvantaged, and to what extent are their disadvantages the consequence of deliberate social policy and practice? First we look at intergroup differentials, then at the extent of economic and political discrimination by dominant groups. Third, we examine indicators of demographic and ecological stress—conditions such as rapid population growth, alienation of land, and involuntary population movements that weigh especially heavily on ethnoclasses, indigenous peoples, and some ethnonationalists. Then we examine statistically the interconnections among differentials and discrimination. All of these comparisons use the coded indicators of the Minorities at Risk study; conventional statistical data on intergroup differentials are not available for most minorities. The next chapter begins with a review of the status of each type of minority in each region and then examines the extent to which historical conquest and contemporary inequalities correlate with the grievances voiced by politicized minorities.

First it is useful to spell out some general assumptions that underlie our analysis of differentials, discrimination, and the political conflicts they generate. Some implications of the argument are developed more fully in the next two chapters. Groups that won out in conquest, state building, and economic development established patterns of authority and various kinds of social barriers to protect their advantages, including the policies and practices for which we use the shorthand label of "discrimination." Such barriers are subject to challenge because almost everywhere in the late twentieth century they generate a sense of grievance among members of disadvantaged groups and often a self-righteous defense of privilege among advantaged groups. In the highly interactive modern world, saturated with media information about other peoples' political claims and tactics, disadvantaged groups respond quickly to cues suggesting that they are justified in acting on old grievances. In general, any actions or policies that seem likely to alter the balance of power and well-being among groups provide one or both affected parties with an impetus to conflict, the disadvantaged seeking to improve their lot, the advantaged aiming to consolidate theirs.

Disadvantaged groups seeking to improve their status or regain their autonomy are not the only significant source of pressure for change. Since most of them are weak in comparison with dominant groups, their challenges could ordinarily be suppressed or contained at relatively little cost. That was the fate of politically assertive Afro-Cubans who in 1912 were the victims of a virtually forgotten pogrom, and of guerrilla nationalists in the Baltics who futilely resisted the reimposition of Soviet rule from 1945 to the early 1950s. But in many more recent instances, disadvantaged peoples have won powerful allies, including some members of dominant groups who oppose discriminatory barriers on pragmatic or principled grounds, and public and private international organizations that are committed to the protection and promotion of group rights. Challenges based on coalitions of minorities and their sympathetic supporters have escalated greatly in the past half-century.

Under pressure, the legal underpinnings of discriminatory barriers have been dismantled in many plural societies and politics of accommodation and reform have been adopted, but in the face of great social inertia: formal equality of political and economic opportunity leads with glacial slowness toward power sharing and material well-being. In fact there are two sources of inertia: one is the preference of most communal groups to retain a distinct cultural identity even while they improve their political and economic status, and the other is the resistance of advantaged groups against erosion of their position and privileges. Plural societies in the last decade of the twentieth century are caught up in intense controversies in which dominant groups' ideals of nation building and assimilation contend with subordinate groups' advocacy of autonomy and multiculturalism.

Intergroup Differentials

Groups in plural societies may differ in origin, ethnicity, religion, and lifeways without the differences necessarily being either the cause or the result of invidious treatment. These kinds of traits are intrinsic to group identity and can be powerful sources of group pride and cohesion. They also can provide grounds for disparagement and discriminatory treatment by more advantaged social groups. Among the communal groups surveyed, we find that the more sharply distinct they are culturally from dominant groups, the more they tend to suffer from political and economic inequalities.

Our analysis of differentials is based on information about the traits that distinguish each group from others in the larger society with which it interacts. Group scores on cultural, economic, and political differentials (CULDIF, ECODIF, and POLDIF) for the six world regions and the six types of communal groups are listed in the Appendix, tables A.7 to A.12. Differentials were coded on the basis of conditions in the 1980s. The Appendix codings of differentials are summarized in table 2.1, which lists global distributions for each scale category, global means and totals, and means by region and group type.

Cultural Differentials

The coding of cultural differentials was based on whether the group differed from others in a "socially significant" way with respect to six cultural traits: ethnicity or nationality, language, religion, social customs, historical origin, and urban versus rural residence. Socially significant differences were defined as those that are widely seen, within the minority and the groups with which it interacts, as traits that set the minority apart from others.[5] Each group was coded on the following five-category scale:

Low 0 = No socially significant cultural differences.

     1 = Slight differentials: socially significant differences exist between the minority and the majority or typical group on one or two of the six cultural traits.

     2 = Substantial differentials: socially significant differences on three of the six traits.

     3 = Major differentials: socially significant differences on four of the six traits.

Table 2.1. Cultural, Political, and Economic Differentials in the 1980s, by Scale Category and World Region, with Global Means and Totals.

1. Global Distribution

Scale Categories	Cultural Differentials		Political Differentials		Economic Differentials	
	N	Percent	N	Percent	N	Percent
−2 = Dominant/advantaged	(na)		11	4.9	12	5.6
−1 = Some advantages	(na)		5	2.2	10	4.7
0 = No differences	0	0	32	14.3	41	19.2
1 = Slight differentials	57	24.5	57	25.4	21	9.9
2 = Substantial	51	21.9	59	26.3	39	18.3
3 = Major differentials	57	24.5	35	15.6	32	15.0
4 = Extreme differentials	68	29.2	25	11.2	58	27.2
No data	0	—	9	—	20	—
2. Global Means and Totals[a]	2.58	(233)	1.83	(208)	2.24	(191)
3. Means for World Regions[a]						
Western democracies and Japan	2.8	(24)	1.2	(24)	2.2	(24)
Eastern Europe and the USSR	2.9	(32)	1.2	(30)	1.2	(25)
Asia	3.0	(43)	2.3	(37)	2.6	(30)
North Africa and the Middle East	2.4	(31)	2.5	(26)	2.5	(26)
Africa south of the Sahara	2.1	(74)	1.8	(62)	1.8	(57)
Latin America and the Caribbean	2.9	(29)	2.0	(29)	3.2	(29)
4. Means for Group Types[b]						
Ethnonationalists	2.5	(81)	1.7	(76)	1.9	(67)
Indigenous peoples	3.5	(83)	2.1	(77)	2.9	(73)
Ethnoclasses	2.5	(45)	2.3	(41)	2.9	(36)
Militant sects	2.6	(49)	2.1	(43)	1.8	(42)
Communal contenders[a]	1.8	(66)	1.6	(51)	1.5	(46)

[a] Numbers of groups included in each computation are shown in parentheses. Groups with missing data were deleted from all computations. Politically advantaged communal contenders were deleted from the computation of means for political and economic differentials.

[b] Numbers of group types sum to more than the global totals because some groups were cross-classified.

High 4 = Extreme differentials: socially significant differences on five or more traits.

Comparisons in part 3 of table 2.1 show little variation among the world regions in how greatly minorities differ culturally from dominant groups, except that differences are narrower in

Africa and the Middle East than elsewhere. There are wider variations among the group types, as is evident from part 4: indigenous peoples are nearly twice as distinct culturally from others as are communal contenders.

Political and Economic Differentials

Political and economic inequalities among groups are a consequence of their differential access to scarce positions and resources. Historical processes explain the origin of inequalities, contemporary conditions contribute to maintaining inequalities. Some communal minorities originated in or were pushed into resource-poor regions, as was the case with most indigenous peoples throughout the world, which helps perpetuate their economic disadvantages and makes it more difficult for them to exercise political influence at the center. Groups descended from economic migrants who were recruited as laborers (e.g., East Indian plantation workers in Malaysia and Turks in Germany) often lack skills or access that would help them break class barriers. Cultural differences sometimes play a role in maintaining such disparities, for example, when a group has values and beliefs that discourage participation in the political and economic systems of a dominant group: this evidently is the case for most Roma in Europe. And cultural differences often are invoked by advantaged groups as a rationale for keeping minorities in their place.

Political differentials were coded on the basis of whether members of a communal group, in the aggregate, are significantly different from other groups in their society with regard to these six dimensions:

- Access to positions of political power, national or regional.
- Access to civil service positions.
- Recruitment to military and police service.
- Voting rights.
- Effective right to organized political activity on behalf of group interests.
- Effective right to equal legal protection.

Economic differentials were coded on the basis of these six dimensions:

- Inequalities in income.
- Inequalities in land and other property.
- Access to higher or technical education.
- Presence in commercial activities.
- Presence in professions.
- Presence in official positions (i.e., as a source of income).

Each group's political and economic differentials were then given a summary rating on the following seven-category scale:

-2 = Dominant/advantaged: the group is advantaged on most or all dimensions in comparison with other groups in the larger society.

-1 = Some advantages: the group is advantaged on some dimensions, not disfavored on any.

0 = No differences: the group has no net advantages or disadvantages on these dimensions.

1 = Slight differentials: the group is disadvantaged on one or two dimensions by comparison with the majority or typical group.

2 = Substantial differentials: the group is disadvantaged on three dimensions.

3 = Major differentials: the group is disadvantaged on four dimensions.

4 = Extreme differentials: the group is disadvantaged on five or more dimensions.

One qualification applies to the political and economic codings. As with cultural differentials, coders were asked to take into account only "socially significant" differences, defined as differentials that are salient to the groups concerned. Most native peoples in the United States, for example, neither want nor seek access to positions of national power, instead they exercise political authority at the local or tribal level; hence they were rated 0 on this variable. In most of Latin America, on the other hand, native peoples have no access to power at any level, and their exclusion is a recurrent issue of contention in relations between them and dominant groups, so for them this scale is usually rated 2 or 3.[6]

In the global comparison in table 2.1, part 2, economic differentials are greater than political ones. Our interpretation is that it has been easier for elites to give disadvantaged groups political rights and some access to power than to reduce economic inequalities. Comparison of the means in parts 3 and 4 of table 2.1 also shows that differentials are substantially greater in some world regions and for some group types. The implications of these and other variations are discussed in more detail in the first section of chapter 3.

Economic and Political Discrimination

Economic and political differentials have often but not always been created and reinforced by deliberate social practice and public policy, such as historical patterns of segregation affecting African Americans in the United States and the contemporary restrictions imposed by the Indonesian government on the political and economic activities of the Chinese minority. Since there are no universally accepted scholarly or legal standards about what constitutes discrimination, we use an internal standard for comparison when judging whether discrimination is or has been present: the pertinent question is whether members of a group are, or have been, deliberately restricted in their access to the conditions of material well-being, or political participation and influence, in comparison with other groups in their society. We are not prepared to say, for example, that the Arab minority in Israel proper is free of discrimination because its members have more political rights and are more prosperous than ordinary citizens of Syria. The crucial point is that the Arab citizens of Israel face more political restrictions and economic barriers than either Ashkenazi or Oriental Jews.

One particular difficulty we face when assessing discrimination is deciding what can be inferred from persisting differentials between groups. Some economic and political inequalities in the modern world are the cumulative result of malign or neglectful social practices extended over a long period. Others, as we have suggested, are not the result of deliberate agency at all but simply become salient when isolated groups on the periphery of modernizing societies are drawn, usually against their will, into closer contact with more powerful and technologically proficient groups. Indigenous peoples throughout the Americas are impoverished on virtually all indicators of material well-being in comparison with European-American majorities. Is their economic disadvantage explained by (1) the fact that most live in remote areas lacking in educational or wage-labor job opportunities, (2) their lack of material ambition, (3) debilitating cultural conflict, or (4) pervasive discrimination by the dominant society? The answer lies in the complex interaction of all four factors, whose relative significance varies among countries. We chose to code as discrimination all instances in which groups' objective disadvantage is attributed by knowledgeable observers to deliberate discrimination, in whole or in part, past or present, by dominant groups. On this principle, for example, all native peoples in the Americas are coded on the discrimination scales described in the following section. Appendix tables A.7 to A.12 list group scores on economic and political discrimination (ECODIS and POLDIS). Global summaries are presented in table 2.2.

Economic Discrimination

Groups are subject to economic discrimination to the extent that their members are or have been systematically excluded from access to desirable economic goods, conditions, or positions that are open to other groups in their society. After examining evidence from a great many societies, we focused on two dimensions of economic discrimination: first, the existence of substantial material inequality affecting the group in the 1980s; and second, the general social and political conditions responsible for creating and maintaining these inequalities. We judged the severity of discrimination by examining the general pattern of public policies toward the group in the 1980s. Severity was low if policies aimed at improving the group's condition, intermediate if government and dominant social groups were indifferent toward the minority's disadvantages, and severe if material inequality was a consequence of deliberate social practice or explicit public policy. Examples of deliberate policies of discrimination are the South African government's historical practice of restricting employment opportunities for black workers, and the Zimbabwean government's constitutional amendment, adopted in late 1990, that permits confiscation of land owned by European settlers at a fixed price and without judicial review.

These two dimensions of economic discrimination—the

Table 2.2. Economic and Political Discrimination in the 1980s, with Numbers of Groups by Scale Category and by World Region.

1. Global Distribution

Scale Categories	Economic Discrimination		Political Discrimination	
	N	Percent	N	Percent
0 = None	76	34.1	61	26.6
1 = Neglect, remedial policies	38	17.0	38	16.6
2 = Neglect, no remedial policies	25	11.2	24	10.4
3 = Prevailing social practice	51	22.9	49	21.4
4 = Exclusion/repression	24	10.8	45	19.7
Other[a]	9	4.0	12	5.2
No data	10	—	4	—

2. Groups Subject to Discrimination by World Region

	Low[b]	High[c]	Low[b]	High[c]
Western democracies and Japan (24 groups)	12	7	10	5
Eastern Europe and the USSR (32 groups)	10	3	17	5
Asia (43 groups)	18	14	16	18
North Africa and the Middle East (31 groups)	7	15	5	19
Africa south of the Sahara (74 groups)	15	19	14	33
Latin America and the Caribbean (29 groups)	10	17	12	14
3. Global Totals	72	75	74	94

[a] For correlation analyses these groups were recoded 2.
[b] Including groups coded 1, 2, and "other."
[c] Groups coded 3 and 4.

existence of substantial material inequality, and patterns of social and public policy—were combined in this four-category ordinal scale of the severity of economic discrimination:

Low 1 = Substantial poverty and underrepresentation in desirable occupations due to historical marginality, neglect, or restrictions. Public policies are designed to improve the group's relative material well-being.

2 = Substantial poverty and underrepresentation due to historical marginality, neglect, or restrictions. No social practice of deliberate exclusion. No formal exclu-

sion from economic opportunities. No public policies aimed at improving the group's material well-being.

3 = Substantial poverty and underrepresentation due to prevailing social practice by dominant groups. Formal public policies toward the group are neutral or, if positive, inadequate to offset active and widespread practices of discrimination.

High 4 = Public policies (formal exclusion or recurring repression or both) substantially restrict the group's economic opportunities in contrast with other groups.

Two observations about category 4. First, it includes situations in which neutral or positive public policy toward a minority is contradicted by recurring repressive actions that perpetuate its impoverishment. In Guatemala, for example, the indigenous Maya have legal protections but efforts by activists to organize cooperatives and unions among Mayan agricultural workers lead often to harassment, reprisals, and death squad killings. Second, category 4 includes situations like the one in Malaysia, where public policy systematically restricts the economically advantaged Chinese community in order to promote the well-being of the Bumiputra (Malay) majority. The policies include restrictive quotas on university admissions and government employment for Chinese and requirements that Malays have a substantial share in the ownership and management of larger businesses.

The number of groups subject to each type of economic discrimination in the late 1980s is shown in part 1 of table 2.2: 147 experienced economic discrimination and 76 experienced none (information was insufficient to code 10 groups). The most common coding is 3, the code used for Catholics in Northern Ireland, for example, and immigrant Islamic workers in Western Europe. The second most common category is 1, a pattern of historical discrimination or neglect combined with remedial policies, used for the economic status of African Americans in the United States and the Saami (Lapps) of the Nordic countries. Part 2 of table 2.2 shows that groups which experience active economic discrimination (categories 3 and 4) are disproportionately concentrated in the Middle East, Africa, and Latin America. The comparisons in table 2.3 show that economic discrimination weighs most heavily on indigenous peoples and ethnoclasses.

Table 2.3. Economic and Political Discrimination in the 1980s, by World Region and Group Type, with Global Means and Totals.

	Economic Discrimination		Political Discrimination	
1. Global Means and Totals[a]	1.59	(223)	1.92	(228)
2. Means for World Regions				
Western democracies and Japan	1.5	(24)	1.2	(24)
Eastern Europe and the USSR	0.8	(30)	1.3	(32)
Asia	1.8	(40)	2.1	(41)
North Africa and the Middle East	2.0	(31)	2.5	(31)
Africa south of the Sahara	1.3	(69)	1.9	(71)
Latin America and the Caribbean	2.6	(29)	2.3	(29)
3. Means for Group Types[b]				
Ethnonationalists	1.3	(77)	1.9	(81)
Indigenous peoples	2.1	(80)	2.0	(82)
Ethnoclasses	2.2	(45)	2.4	(43)
Militant sects	1.5	(45)	1.9	(48)
Communal contenders	0.9	(62)	1.6	(65)

[a] Numbers of groups included in each computation are shown in parentheses. Groups with missing data are deleted from all computations. Groups coded "other" were recoded 2.

[b] Numbers of group types sum to more than the global totals because some groups were cross-classified.

Political Discrimination

Political discrimination is identified and coded in the same way as economic discrimination. Political discrimination means that group members are or have been systematically limited in their enjoyment of political rights or access to political positions by comparison with other groups in their society. Again, the standard is an internal one. Until late 1989, for example, the government of Bulgaria suppressed all political dissent; as in other Communist states, political participation, policy preferences, and power could be pursued only through mass organizations controlled by the party. But the playing field was tilted against the country's one million people of Turkic ethnicity. Their collective existence was denied; they were "a fictitious minority"—not Turks but "Islamicized Bulgarians." During the mid-1980s they were forced to take Slavic names on their mandatory identity cards and were fined for speaking Turkish in public. Moreover, if they rejected assimilation, as most did, they were barred from the Party and Party-controlled positions and privileges. The Bulgarian Turks were coded 4 on our scale of political discrimination.[7]

The presence of token or "tame" members of a minority group in visible political positions may be evidence of remedial public policy, but it is not evidence that the group has attained political equality. Most group members must participate on an equal political footing with others to warrant a coding judgment that group members are substantially free from political discrimination. A similar argument applies to economic discrimination. A handful of black South Africans have amassed personal wealth and some are professionals—teachers, physicians, lawyers, engineers. But public policy has sharply restricted who and how many can attain these positions, and the fortunate ones have had to confine their activities almost entirely to black communities.

The four-category ordinal scale of the severity of political discrimination parallels the economic discrimination scale:

Low 1 = Substantial underrepresentation in political office holding or participation or both, due to historical neglect or restrictions. Explicit public policies are designed to protect or improve the group's political status.

2 = Substantial underrepresentation due to historical neglect or restrictions. No social practice of deliberate exclusion. No formal exclusion. No evidence of protective or remedial public policies.

3 = Substantial underrepresentation due to prevailing social practice by dominant groups. Formal public policies toward the group are neutral or, if positive, inadequate to offset discriminatory practices.

High 4 = Public policies (formal exclusion or recurring repression or both) substantially restrict the group's political participation in comparison with other groups.

With regard to category 4, repression aimed at a group because it is engaged in violent opposition is not enough to justify a coding of severe political discrimination. Two contrasting African examples help clarify the coding procedures. In Ethiopia from the 1960s through the 1980s some of the Oromo people in rural Bale and Welega provinces supported harshly repressed Oromo liberation movements against the Amhara-dominated Derg regime; at the same time, assimilated Oromos were present in significant numbers in the Derg government and army. Rural Oromos have long been dominated and exploited by Amhara landowners and officials, assimilated Oromos are not, nor were they targeted for reprisals against rebellion by their rural kindred. We coded political discrimination 3, on the basis of the politically subordinate status of the rural Oromo majority. In Somalia the 1980s rebellion led by the northern Issaq clan (see chapter 1) provoked the army and police to indiscriminately harass and kill thousands of Issaqs, including those living in the south. Political discrimination against the Issaqs is coded 4, because of the reprisal killings.

The changing political status of African Americans in the United States provides a further illustration of categories on this variable. Formal exclusion (legalized discrimination) and recurring repression (lynchings, unequal justice) prevailed until the mid-1940s (code = 4). A period of transition followed, led by the federal executive branch and the U.S. Supreme Court (code = 3), culminating in the legal and political campaigns of the early 1960s that ended restrictions on voting and guaranteed full exercise of civil rights. By the 1970s and 1980s, black voting participation and presence in elective office were substantial but still lagged behind those of whites (code = 1). Note that the discrimination scales are coded for conditions in the 1980s only; the Minorities at Risk data set does not include codes for earlier periods.[8]

A quarter of all communal groups in the study experienced no discernible political discrimination (see table 2.2). Among the others the most common code was 3 (21.4 percent), signifying political discrimination as a result of prevailing social practice. The next most common pattern was 4, deliberate exclusion or patterned repression (19.7 percent). The comparisons in part 2 of table 2.2 show a disproportionate concentration of groups affected by these active forms of political discrimination in the Middle East and Africa. The comparisons of the relative severity of discrimination (see table 2.3) demonstrate that the severity of political discrimination is greatest in the Middle East and among ethnoclasses. Chapter 3 provides a more detailed assessment of the distribution of discrimination among regions and types of groups.

Demographic and Ecological Stress

Descriptions of minorities refer repeatedly to objective indicators of deprivation such as high birth rates and low life expectancies, poor public health conditions, migration motivated by economic privation, and pressures on traditional lands and resources (competition for land, forced development, resettlement schemes). We developed a checklist of nine such conditions, which were coded whenever a group was said in our sources to be adversely affected by them in comparison with other groups in the society. The severity of each reported condition was coded on a three-category scale ranging from minor ($= 1$) to serious ($= 3$).

This information was used to construct indicators of three dimensions of material hardship: demographic stress, ecological stress, and migration—the last usually being a consequence or contributing cause of the first two. Group scores for demographic and ecological stress (DEMSTRESS and ECOSTRESS) are included in the Appendix, tables A.7 to A.12, and the data are summarized in table 2.4.

Demographic stress was measured by coding the presence and severity of three conditions: a high birth rate in relation to other groups, a relatively youthful population (which may be the result of either high birth rates or high adult mortality rates or both), and poor public health conditions. These conditions are particularly common among indigenous peoples and ethnoclasses in western societies. The five million Roma of Eastern and Western Europe have the highest demographic stress ratings of any communal groups in the region. Their birth rates, exceptionally high by European standards, were an estimated 3 percent per year in Western Europe in the 1980s. Their infant mortality rates are reportedly much higher than national averages in a number of countries including Belgium and Britain. Most Roma are itinerant peddlers, craftspeople, scavengers, and seasonal laborers who live in urban slums, shanty towns, and caravan sites where there is little access to the health care and social services provided to settled Europeans. And frequent traveling means that few of their many children attend school regularly, and therefore lack the literacy and skills that would facilitate their incorporation into the modern economy—that is, if they wanted to be.[9]

Table 2.4. Demographic and Ecological Stress in the 1980s, by World
Region and Group Type, with Global Means and Totals.

	Demographic Stress	Ecological Stress
1. Global Means and Totals (195)[a]	1.46	1.14
2. Means for World Regions		
Western democracies/Japan (23)	2.6	0.1
Eastern Europe/USSR (29)	1.6	0.1
Asia (40)	0.8	1.9
North Africa/Middle East (23)	3.1	1.4
Africa south of the Sahara (51)	0.8	0.8
Latin America/Caribbean (29)	1.1	2.5
3. Means for Group Types[b]		
Ethnonationalists (72)	1.0	1.0
Indigenous peoples (77)	1.8	2.1
Ethnoclasses (39)	2.2	0.6
Militant sects (41)	2.1	0.7
Communal contenders (40)	0.6	0.6

[a] Excluding politically advantaged communal contenders and groups with missing data. Numbers of groups included in each computation are shown in parentheses.

[b] Numbers of group types sum to more than the global totals because some groups are cross-classified.

Ecological stress was measured by codings of the presence and severity of three conditions: competition with other groups for settlement of vacant lands, dispossession from land by other groups, and forced internal resettlement. The tribal peoples who traditionally inhabited the Chittagong Hills region in southeastern Bangladesh typify the rural, indigenous peoples throughout the world whose lands and resources have been under escalating pressure from outsiders. In the early 1960s the building of the Kaptai Hydroelectric Dam flooded 40 percent of the arable land in the Hill Tracts and displaced more than a hundred thousand Chakma tribal people, about a quarter of the region's population. In 1964 the Pakistani government revoked the area's special protected status (granted by British authorities in 1900) and thus opened the area to development and alienation (i.e., sale or transfer) of tribal lands. In 1979 a program of the now-independent government of Bangladesh relocated hundreds of thousands of poor Bengalis from the lowlands into the Hill Tracts. The tribal hill peoples formed a self-defense organization in 1972, the Shanti Bahini, which waged communal and guerrilla war throughout the 1980s. One of its attacks on Bengali settlers prompted massive reprisals that precipitated the flight of about 50,000 tribal people into neighboring Tripura state in India. The Chittagong Hills peoples score 8 on the ecological stress indicator.

Migration was measured by codings of the presence and severity of substantial rural-to-urban migration, significant emigration abroad, and influx of kindred groups from abroad, including refugees. Peoples in regions beset by famine and civil war have the highest scores on this indicator. Sudan is an example: during the 1980s hundreds of thousands of southerners, especially people from the Dinka tribe, fled from drought and government reprisals against supporters of the Sudanese People's Liberation Movement. By the end of the decade four hundred thousand reportedly had sought refuge in Khartoum and 1.1 million others had fled to Ethiopia and other neighboring countries. Meanwhile nearly seven hundred thousand refugees from civil war in Ethiopia had gone to Sudan.[10]

Demographic stress is high in the advanced industrial democracies (see table 2.4) because of relatively high birth rates and poor public health among ethnoclasses, and in the Middle East, particularly because of similar conditions among Kurds, Palestinians, and Shi'i minorities. These interpretations are confirmed by the comparisons in part 3 of the table, which show that demographic stress is greatest among ethnoclasses and sects.

Ecological stress is greatest in Asia and Latin America, the regions where the lands and resources of indigenous peoples are most threatened by the demographic and economic expansion of dominant groups. Indigenous peoples have by far the highest ecological stress of any type of group, a mean score of 2.1 versus the global average of 1.14. The low mean scores on both indicators in Africa south of the Sahara are not an anomaly. While a few African groups such as the southern Sudanese, Tigreans, and black South Africans have high stress scores, most are communal contenders who live in demographic and ecological circumstances little different from those of their neighbors. The communal contenders, most of whom are African, have the lowest mean scores on both types of stress.

Connections among Differentials and Discrimination

The issue addressed in this final section concerns the connectedness of differentials and discrimination. Three kinds of connections can be examined with the coded data. The first is descriptive: How closely correlated are minorities' political and economic disadvantages? The second and third connections are causal ones: To what extent do cultural differences between minorities and dominant groups explain their political and economic differentials and discrimination? To what extent does discrimination account for the political and economic differentials among groups? Correlational analyses are summarized in table 2.5.

Previous analyses of these kinds of questions had to depend on case studies and comparisons of a few similar groups. Correlational analysis of our indicators of differentials and discrimination makes it possible to suggest some general answers. For this kind of analysis we must trade away the complexity and precision of case study analysis in the search for general patterns, hoping that the patterns identified will provide a useful baseline for evaluating case study results. We correlated indicators, first for all 233 groups (including advantaged as well as disadvantaged minorities), and then separately for groups in each of the six world regions and each of five group types (ethnonationalists, indigenous peoples, ethnoclasses, militant sects, and communal contenders). Results are summarized in table 2.5. Comparison of the global correlations with the regional and type correlations is a powerful diagnostic tool: it is a test of the universality of relationships, and it pinpoints regions and types of groups where differentials and discrimination most strongly reinforce one another. Reinforcement implies resistance to change.

It is necessary to understand the limitations as well as the strengths of correlation analysis. A correlation coefficient indicates only the probability that a group's score on one variable can be predicted from its score on another variable. For example, table 2.5, part 2, reports that the correlation between cultural differentials and economic differentials is .476. This finding confirms and generalizes the common observation that the more culturally different a minority is from other groups the greater its economic disadvantages. The result is consistent with, but does not prove, the theoretical argument that cultural differentials cause or reinforce economic disadvantage. Moreover, the correlation of .476 is only moderate: it signifies that the extent of economic differentials can be predicted from cultural ones with only 23 percent accuracy.[11] The implication is that many conditions other than cultural differentials contribute to economic inequalities. The correlation also means that many groups deviate from the general pattern: One-third of the 214 groups in the Appendix (data are missing for the other 19) have widely discrepant scores. The other 140 have scores on cultural and economic differentials that are identical or only one point apart. The most common pattern among the discrepant cases is cultural distinctiveness without significant material disadvantage; only a few groups are disadvantaged despite cultural affinity with dominant groups. Other correlates and implications of cultural differentials are discussed below.

The global results of correlation analysis are reported in table 2.5. To avoid statistical overload, we summarized in the right-hand column the evidence about similarities and differences among regions and types of groups, and listed only the correlation coefficients that are markedly different from the global ones.

Correlations between Political and Economic Disadvantages

There is no close or necessary correlation between political and economic differentials and discrimination. In some contemporary democracies we observe a pattern in which minorities are economically disadvantaged yet have effective political equality. In Africa south of the Sahara, on the other hand, political discrimination is often more severe than economic discrimination. Economic determinists might argue that a people's political disadvantages are a consequence of their material disadvantages. From observation of the politics of communal conflict, a different dynamic is more prevalent: disadvantaged groups frequently use political means in attempts to improve their economic well-being.

The empirical results are summarized in part 1 of table 2.5: political and economic differentials are substantially correlated ($r = .634$**) and so are political and economic discrimination ($r = .631$**). The correlations demonstrate only a consistent connection between the two sets of conditions, not causality. In

Table 2.5. Correlations among Differentials and Discrimination.

Pairs of Variables and Their Global Correlations			Differences among World Regions and Group Types

1. Relations between Political and Economic Disadvantages

	POLDIF		
ECODIF	.634**		More weakly related in Asia ($r = .28$) and Eastern Europe ($r = .47*$), more strongly related in the Middle East ($r = .85**$) and among communal contenders ($r = .79**$).
	POLDIS		
ECODIS	.631**		Strongly and significantly related in all types of groups and regions. The relationship is closest in Latin America ($r = .81**$) and among indigenous peoples ($r = .76**$).

2. Effects of Cultural Differentials on Political and Economic Disadvantages

	POLDIF	ECODIF	
CULDIF	.313**	.476**	CULDIF is significantly and more strongly related to ECODIF than POLDIF in all regions except Latin America (where the r with POLDIF is stronger) and among all types of groups except communal contenders (where both r's are near 0).
	POLDIS	ECODIS	
CULDIF	.173*	.415**	CULDIF is more strongly related to ECODIS than to POLDIS in all regions except Latin America, where there is no difference. CULDIF has no significant effects on either kind of discrimination among group types except ethnonationalists (r with POLDIS = .32*, with ECODIS = .69**) and indigenous peoples (r with POLDIS = .33*, with ECODIS = .32*).

3. Effects of Discrimination on Differentials

	POLDIF	
POLDIS	.653**	POLDIS is a strong determinant of POLDIF in all group types and all regions except Asia ($r = .41$) and Eastern Europe ($r = .47*$). The relation is strongest in the Middle East ($r = .81**$).
	ECODIF	
ECODIS	.655**	ECODIS is a strong determinant of ECODIF in all group types and all regions except Asia ($r = .34$) and Eastern Europe ($r = .43$). The relation is strongest in the Middle East ($r = .75**$).

Note: The correlations are Pearson correlation coefficients calculated for all 233 groups, with pairwise deletion for missing-data cases.

POLDIF = political differentials
ECODIF = economic differentials
POLDIS = political discrimination
ECODIS = economic discrimination
CULDIF = cultural differentials

*Significant at $p > .01$, using a two-tailed test.
**Significant at $p > .001$, using a two-tailed test.

four clusters the connections are particularly close: in the Middle East (for differentials) and Latin America (for discrimination); and among communal contenders (for differentials) and indigenous peoples (for discrimination). We interpret these connections as evidence of strong reinforcing relationships between groups' political and economic status, in what might be called "syndromes of inequality." In Asia, however, the relationship between the two dimensions of differentials is very weak, which is consistent with a syndrome of "balanced disparity" in which some groups' political disadvantages are balanced by economic advantages, or vice versa.

We can give more substance to these results by identifying typical and atypical groups. "Typical" groups have the same 1980s scores for both political and economic discrimination on our four-category scales:

- Soviet Central Asian peoples—coded 1 on both.
- Blacks and native peoples in the United States—coded 2 on both.
- Most native peoples in Latin America—coded 2 or 3 on both.
- Communal contenders in Pakistan—coded 3 or 4 on both.
- Communal contenders in South Africa—coded 4 on both.

The most atypical groups are those whose economic and political discrimination scores vary by three points or more. Seventeen such groups face little or no economic discrimination but are subject to severe political discrimination: Twelve are politically restricted communal contenders in independent African countries, such as the Kikiyu of Kenya and the Ashanti of Ghana, who are paying a political price for their previous privileges and abuses. The other five are as follows (the economic discrimination score is to the left of the slash, political discrimination to the right):

- Turks in Germany—1/4.
- Jews in the former USSR—0/3.
- Albanians in Yugoslavia—1/4.
- Taiwanese in Taiwan—0/4.
- Palestinians in Jordan—0/4.

These five groups have been the focus of serious contention over political rights and access to power, and in three instances

there has been substantial recent movement toward accommodation: Jews from former Soviet republics are now free to emigrate, and native Taiwanese and Palestinians in Jordan now participate somewhat more freely and effectively in national
politics. These inherently unstable and conflictual relationships
are not necessarily resolved to the benefit of the minority. Turks
and other Third World residents of Germany were under physical and political attack in 1991–92, and the Serbian government has created the preconditions for civil war in Kosovo
by eliminating almost all vestiges of the Albanians' regional
autonomy.

Very few minorities experience more severe economic discrimination than political discrimination. The Chinese of Malaysia are an exception, with high economic discrimination
(code = 4) but limited barriers to political participation. Examples in which the disparities are less include Afro-Caribbeans,
Asians, and Northern Irish Catholics in the United Kingdom
and native peoples in Canada (economic discrimination = 3,
political discrimination = 1). This pattern is unusual, we conclude, because minorities with political access ordinarily are able
to use it to reduce discriminatory economic barriers. The Malaysian arrangement is a deliberate political design, one that
is applicable in other societies—in southern Africa, for example—where political power is or will be held by an economically disadvantaged majority. Chinese and Malays (and East Indians) are unequal partners to a compact in which the Chinese
have accepted constraints on their economic privileges in exchange for participation in the Malay-dominated democratic
system—on the condition that they do not press divisive ethnic
claims.

Cultural Differentials as Explanations of Political and Economic Disadvantages

Cultural differentials are a function of enduring traits of
groups—their lifeways, language, religion, and traditional region of residence. It can be argued that cultural differences
cause or reinforce political and economic disadvantages because
(a) they make it difficult for minorities to operate effectively in
institutions established by dominant groups and (b) they give
dominant groups rationales for denying access to people who

are "different." The correlations in part 2 of table 2.5 provide
qualified support for these arguments: cultural differentials
have moderate correlations with political and economic differentials, weaker correlations with political and economic discrimination. Two important inferences follow from the results.

First, that the correlations are relatively weak has implications
for policies of multiculturalism: cultural differentials are not
generally antithetical to efforts to reduce inequalities and discrimination. This point is most decidedly true for ethnoclasses:
there is no significant global relationship whatsoever between
these groups' cultural differentials from dominant groups on
the one hand and their political or economic status on the other.
Whatever the sources of ethnoclasses' disadvantages—group
lifeways, social discrimination, public policy—they do not depend in any general way on the extent of cultural differentials.
The same is true for communal contenders, for whom the causality is even clearer: they are treated unequally not because they
are culturally different, but because of the outcomes of competition for power.

It is important to understand what is being claimed here, and
why: Cultural differences may be invoked to explain and justify
the unequal status of particular minorities, but our global evidence shows that there is no statistical relationship whatever between the extent of cultural differentials and inequalities for
ethnoclasses or communal contenders. Thus, there is no general empirical basis for arguing that inequalities affecting these
kinds of groups are a function of cultural differences.[12] The
results for ethnonationalists are different: their cultural differentials *are* a strong influence on economic differentials
($r = .64**$) and discrimination ($r = .69**$). Several reinforcing
factors probably are at work here: the most culturally distinct of
ethnonationalists usually live in resource-poor peripheral regions of Third World countries, were subjugated by modern
states during the twentieth century, and support active autonomy movements. All three conditions helped create or perpetuate their economic disadvantages.

The second major inference follows from the finding that
cultural differentials have a greater effect on economic differentials and discrimination than on political disadvantages. This
contrast is true globally and within each world region except
Latin America. In other words, wide cultural differences contribute more to minorities' poverty than to their lack of empow-

erment. This finding fits with our observations about the politically inclusive policies of most modern states: it has been easier for governments to give minorities political rights than to erase the social practices that are responsible for persisting poverty. Among Latin American minorities and among indigenous peoples, however, the political effects of cultural differences on minority status are equal to or greater than the economic effects. Most of these groups are sharply differentiated culturally and face severe political and especially economic disadvantages (compare the means for group types in table 2.1). Evidently they are caught in a web of reinforcing cultural, economic, and political disadvantages and have not yet achieved the political means to begin breaking out of the web.

Discrimination as Explanation of Political and Economic Differentials

The evidence that has been reviewed showed that, with some exceptions, cultural differentials are not a major source of minorities' current political and economic disadvantages. In comparison past or present discrimination has much greater impact on the extent of minorities' disadvantages. The evidence is summarized in part 3 of table 2.5: the correlation between political discrimination, measured on our four-category scale, and political differentials is .653**; between economic discrimination and economic differentials, .655**. This does not necessarily mean that minorities' political and economic disadvantages had their origins in deliberate discrimination; group histories differ. But it does mean that policies of neglect and deliberate exclusion are substantially responsible for the persistence of contemporary inequalities.

The impact of discrimination on differentials is equally strong among all types of groups, but there are significant differences among world regions. Both kinds of discrimination have relatively weak effects on intergroup differentials in Asia and Eastern Europe, but very strong effects in the Middle East. The explanation, we suggest, lies in the distinctive political cultures of each region. The contrast is particularly sharp between the socialist regimes of the former USSR and Eastern Europe and the nationalist and sectarian regimes of the Middle East. The socialist regimes were committed as a matter of ideological principle to eliminate discrimination and to provide national minorities with opportunities for political and economic advancement within the Communist party and state apparatus. In most Middle Eastern societies, however, strong belief systems justify differential treatment of religious and national minorities. Shi'i, Baha'i, and Jewish minorities are restricted because they do not accept the doctrines of dominant groups, and the exclusion and repression of Palestinians and Kurds are viewed as necessary because they resist subordination to strongly nationalist governments. The status of minorities in these two regions is explored more fully in chapters 7 and 8.

The next chapter begins with an overview of the foregoing findings about the status of politicized minorities in each world region and then matches information on their disadvantages to the kinds of grievances expressed by their leaders and the objectives they pursued during the 1980s.

3. "Give Us the Means to the Future"
The Mobilization of Grievance

Disadvantaged people do not necessarily think that inequalities are unjust, nor does their perception of injustice, once awakened, lead inexorably to political movements demanding redress of grievances. This chapter analyzes the linkages between minorities' objective disadvantages and their political demands. It begins with a brief review of the status of politicized communal groups in each of the world regions, then discusses the role of political movements and leaders in defining and expressing group grievances. The core of the chapter is an analysis of the demands made by politicized minorities in the 1980s, as coded in the Minorities at Risk study, and the correlation of those demands with objective conditions. The analysis is designed to answer this essential question: How closely linked are objective disadvantages to different kinds of expressed demands?[1]

Status of Communal Groups in the World Regions

Policies and practices of discrimination are the conditions most directly responsible for maintaining inequalities between groups, as demonstrated in chapter 2. Discriminatory barriers in 1990 were markedly lower in Eastern Europe and the USSR and in the western democracies than in other world regions. They were somewhat greater in Africa south of the Sahara and in Asia, highest in Latin America and the Middle East. We review the regions in order of increasing severity of discrimination against communal groups.

Eastern Europe and the USSR

Very few of this region's thirty-two politicized minorities in the 1980s experienced deliberate economic discrimination (three) or political discrimination (five). The handful of exceptions included the Turkish minority in Bulgaria, the Albanians of Yugoslavia's Kosovo region, the Roma, and several of the USSR's displaced nationalities. Intergroup differentials between minorities and dominant groups in the socialist states were lower, on average, than in other world regions (see table 2.1), and ecological stress among minorities was negligible (table 2.4). Substantial inequalities existed nonetheless: the Muslim peoples of Central Asia and Eastern Europe were particularly likely to be economically disadvantaged, as is evident from the codings in the Appendix (see tables A.7 through A.12). The most prosperous Soviet republics had more than twice the per capita productivity of the least prosperous; in Yugoslavia industrialized Slovenia had seven times the per capita income of Kosovo.[2]

The relative lack of discrimination in this region was the outcome of Marxist-Leninist doctrine and Communist party practice, which aimed at equalizing the political participation and economic opportunities of all national peoples and minorities. The policies did not eliminate regional inequalities or nationalist aspirations, but it should not be overlooked that socialist policies leveled the playing field for almost all communal groups. Most had the right of cultural self-expression and were encouraged to participate fully in the party and the state apparatus at the local and regional levels, provided they did not pursue nationalistic objectives.

Socialist policies emphasized equality of political and economic opportunity, but not cultural assimilation. On the contrary, most national peoples were encouraged to maintain their own languages and cultural forms, and cultural differentials in this region are among the highest of all the world regions (see table 2.1). Thus it is unsurprising that the communal conflicts that have erupted in this region since the late 1980s rarely have been motivated by grievances over inequalities among groups, but rather by demands for the restoration of group autonomy and desires for revenge against old enemies. It also should be recognized that in the USSR the long-established political access of national peoples to party and bureaucratic positions in the republics and autonomous regions paved the way for the transition to nationalism in the Gorbachev era. Once control weakened at the center, "closet nationalists" were able to take control of regional governments.

Western Democracies and Japan

The advanced industrial democracies have been as effective as the socialist states in reducing political differentials, but less successful in narrowing economic gaps among groups (see table 2.1). Democratic doctrine and public policy emphasize equality of political opportunity for all peoples—except immigrant workers, who are denied full citizenship rights in Japan and some Western European countries. Economic discrimination is more common and severe than political discrimination (see tables 2.2 and 2.3), essentially because it is a consequence of widespread social practices that are resistant to change. Democratic states do not have the capacity or will to redistribute wealth and economic opportunities to the same degree that the socialist states did.

Minorities in western societies include eight ethnoclasses and five indigenous groups, two group types that experience greater political and economic disadvantages than any others, both globally and in the democracies (see table 2.1). The reasons for their disadvantages are different, however: indigenous groups are disadvantaged mainly because of cultural differences and relative isolation, ethnoclasses because of discriminatory treatment based on class and cultural barriers.

There is little contemporary discrimination against the ten ethnonationalist peoples in the democracies. All of them have full citizenship rights and all have benefited from welfare state policies. Most of their political movements began in the 1960s and had regional rather than nationalistic demands, most of which elicited public policies of regional devolution and reallocation of public resources. A few ethnonationalists remain economically disadvantaged (e.g., the Catholics of Northern Ireland, the Corsicans, and the Sardinians), but others, including the Québecois, South Tyroleans, Basques, and Catalans, live in prospering regions.

Cultural differentials between minorities and dominant groups are relatively great in the democratic countries, as they are in the socialist countries. But their causes and implications are very different: in the former USSR and Eastern Europe the most culturally distinct groups have been ethnonationalists such as the Central Asian Muslims, the Baltic peoples, and the Kosovo Albanians, whereas in democracies they are mainly the ethnoclass descendants of immigrants from the Third World, and indigenous peoples. The critical minority problems of the socialist states before and after the breakup of the USSR have been nationalist demands for greater autonomy and independence. The most critical minority problems in democratic states arise from demands of ethnoclasses for equal opportunity and cultural pluralism, issues that are somewhat easier to accommodate than political separatism.

Africa South of the Sahara

When Third World regions are compared we see that cultural, political, and economic differentials among groups are lowest in Africa, owing to the large concentration of communal contenders in that region. There are fifty-four communal contenders among the seventy-four African minorities, twenty of whom were politically advantaged during the 1980s. Most disadvantaged contenders are culturally similar to other African peoples and are adversely affected only because they are excluded or marginalized from ruling coalitions. This kind of political discrimination means that their elites have less access to the power and income that derive from government posts, conditions that have little effect on most group members. Table 2.3 shows that discrimination affecting communal contenders is less severe than for any other type of group.

The most serious communal problems in Africa now are concentrated in South Africa, the Horn, and the countries of the eastern Sudan (northern Nigeria, Chad, Sudan). The greatest intergroup differentials and most severe discrimination on the continent are found in South Africa, where the last and most dramatic stages of conflict between African nationalists and settler minorities are being played out. The likely ascendance of African nationalists to power in South Africa will exacerbate communal conflicts within the black majority and probably lead to the imposition of discriminatory political and economic restrictions on whites.

The civil wars fought by communal contenders in Chad, Sudan, Ethiopia, and Somalia are the result of the breakdown of, or failure to establish, governing coalitions at the center. The intensity of the conflicts has been exacerbated by substantial cultural differentials, especialy the Arab Muslim-versus-Christian (and animist) cleavage that divides contenders in all but Somalia, and also by intervention from other African states and the big powers. Similar communal wars can erupt almost anywhere in Africa if dominant coalitions attempt to increase their advantages at the expense of groups out of power.

Asia

The status of the forty-three minorities in East and Southeast Asia and the Indian subcontinent is too diverse for easy generalization. The severity of both economic and political discrimination in this region is slightly above the global averages, political and economic differentials are substantial, and cultural differentials are the greatest of any world region. The archetypal Asian minority is an indigenous group that has ethnonationalist ambitions for autonomy.[3] Most such groups live on the periphery of modern states: the Moros of the southern Philippine archipelago; Dayaks and Kadazans in the East Malaysian states of northern Borneo; and hill peoples like the Hmong (Meo) of Laos, the Nagas in India, and the Karens in Burma. Some are also differentiated from dominant groups by religion, such as the Kashmiris and Sikhs in India and the Malay Muslims of southern Thailand. Indigenous origins and religious beliefs account for the high cultural differentials that typify the region. These cultural differentials in turn tend to reinforce economic differentials, as we showed in chapter 2.

Discrimination has weaker effects on political and economic differentials in Asia than in any other world region (see table 2.5), for a combination of reasons. There is no predominant "Asian pattern" of relations between minorities and dominant groups analogous to those identified for the regions surveyed above; rather, there are three distinguishable patterns. First, the Communist regimes of the People's Republic of China, Laos, Vietnam, and post Khmer Rouge Cambodia all tried to implement versions of Soviet-style national minority policies, with tolerance for cultural diversity combined with serious efforts to incorporate minorities into party and state structures.[4] Second, the democratic and quasi-democratic regimes of India, Malaysia, the Philippines, and Papua New Guinea—also Thailand and, most recently, Bangladesh—have sought political accommodation with most of their indigenous peoples and ethnonationalists. Governments in India and Malaysia also have designed complex policies to equalize economic opportunities among plural groups. Discriminatory practices remain common, but not for lack of remedial efforts. The third pattern is a traditionally authoritarian and nationalistic reliance on repression to suppress and forcibly assimilate communal minorities. This has been the prevailing response in Burma, Indonesia (in East Timor and Irian Jaya), Pakistan (in Baluchistan and East Bengal), and Sri Lanka. When accommodation failed, repression also has been the response of last resort by the Chinese against the Tibetans and the Indians against the Nagas, the Kashmiris, and the Sikhs.

The range of policies used in attempts to accommodate communal conflicts is examined more fully in chapter 10.

Latin America and the Caribbean

A smaller proportion of this region's population (11 percent) is at risk than in any other Third World region. But that proportion, which includes nineteen aggregate groups of native peoples and nine ethnoclasses descended from African slaves, experiences the greatest economic differentials and most severe economic discrimination to be found in any world region (tables 2.1 and 2.3). Ecological stress is the highest observed in any world region (table 2.4). Cultural differentials also are very wide, especially between Native Americans and the dominant Europeans, while political differentials and discrimination also are above the global averages.

The prevailing pattern of attitudes and policy toward minorities in most Latin American societies is discrimination and denial. Few formal discriminatory barriers exist anywhere in Latin America, and Latins of European descent often express pride that they are "color-blind." But in fact, indigenous peoples and blacks are consistently the poorest and least empowered groups in these societies. The barriers to their upward mobility are inherent in dominant groups' conviction about the cultural superiority of Luso-Hispanic civilization. Pervasive social discrimination is practiced against those who fail to master the language, values, and lifeways of European society. With the exceptions noted below, there is little public effort to encourage acculturation or mobility, and few concessions are offered to assertions of communal rights or cultural pluralism. Mexican policies since the revolution of 1917 acclaim the country's indigenous heritage and attempt to improve opportunities for the rural poor, both indigenous peoples and mestizos. Political accommodation of the collective interests of tribal peoples has been attempted in a few countries, including Costa Rica, Panama, and Ecuador. But the general pattern, even in these countries, is one of serious inequality and pervasive social discrimination against native peoples and others who do not adopt the dominant culture.

North Africa and the Middle East

North Africa aside, most governments in the Middle East are more concerned with limiting minorities' access to political power than accommodating their interests. Groups in this region are subject to more severe political discrimination than those of any other region and are second to Latin America in severity of economic discrimination. In table 2.5, part 3, we reported an unusually strong statistical relationship between discrimination and differentials among groups in this region. Politically, differentials are the highest of any world region. Palestinian and Kurdish ethnonationalists and fundamentalist Shi'is are excluded from political power and participation in a number of states because their demands threaten the state-building ethos of nationalist elites. The Baha'is in Iran and the Ahmadi and Hindu minorities in Pakistan face political restrictions on sectarian grounds. Serious economic discrimination and pronounced economic differentials also are a function of political and religious hostilities. Furthermore, minorities in this region register high to very high on indicators of ecological and demographic stress.

North Africa is an exception to these generalizations. The most active communal groups of the region are the Berbers of Algeria and Morocco. Both countries' governments have made concessions to Berber cultural interests and have followed policies aimed at political incorporation and economic improvement. The North African states also evince greater religious tolerance. The Coptic Christians of Egypt are a prosperous and influential religious minority in a Muslim society, though subject to some political restrictions.[5] Much the same can be said of the Jewish community in Morocco, a group of about fifteen thousand that falls below the size threshold used in this study.

Mobilization of Grievance

Communal grievances are not likely to come to the attention of governments or outside observers until they are given coherent expression by leaders of political movements who claim to represent the group's interests. The authenticity of representatives' claims is difficult to judge, because contending organizations often claim to represent the group, because observers seldom have direct access to a cross-section of group members, and because governments that are challenged by minority-based movements usually try to discredit or minimize the claims. The fact remains that the best evidence we have of the interests and grievances of most communal groups comes from their political movements. Their statements and strategies provide the basis of our coding of group grievances. Four general points should be kept in mind when evaluating all claims and evidence about the interests of communal groups.

1. *Collective interests are not unitary.* There are diverse individual and segmental interests within every communal group. One can assume that there are varying but significant numbers of individuals in every disadvantaged minority who would prefer to accept the status quo, or stay neutral, rather than actively pursue "the just cause of their people." Segments of a group have distinct interests: those who are assimilated or who serve as favored intermediaries with dominant groups have privileges to protect, clans and factions have local interests and clientele to promote. The question is whether there is an irreducible common interest, or collective good, for which members of a group will set aside their more parochial interests.

2. *Political organization is essential to the formulation and expression of collective interest.* Analytically we may decide that conquered and disadvantaged peoples have an objective collective interest in autonomy and equity. Subjectively, journalistic interviews and opinion polls may show that individual victims of

discrimination harbor perceptions of injustice and feelings of alienation. What counts politically is the organized expression of subjective interests. Sustained collective action and political influence depend on the articulation of a believable set of demands and a strategy of action that mobilizes a substantial group of people. Such demands and strategies can be provided only by political organizations that represent and pursue group objectives. The organizational fabric for group mobilization may come from preexisting clan or religious hierarchies, sometimes from economic associations or conventional political parties, but in the modern world it usually is provided by new associational groups such as the American Indian Movement and the Kachin Independence Organization.

3. *Some political expressions of collective interest are more authentic than others.* The early and middle stages of communal mobilization resemble a political bazaar where sellers hawk competing interpretations of group interest and alternative tactics and strategies for promoting them. Among the contenders are traditional authorities, leaders of established political movements, government stooges, militant liberationists, fundamentalist preachers, and many others. Competition and factional fighting among them sometimes continue throughout the course of communal conflict and can wreck efforts at accommodation. In principle, the most authentic movements are those that best represent the group's shared interests. In practice, group members decide what is most in their interest by granting or withholding support for particular leaders and organizations. The only reliable standard for judgment by the outside observer, therefore, is that the most authentic organizations—those whose claims have greatest current validity—are those that are largest and most durable.

4. *Group interests and objectives change during the course of communal conflict.* Consensus on common interests tends to increase during the course of open conflict, according to the well-established sociological principle that conflict with an external enemy increases solidarity within the group. There is, however, no strong tendency for communal movements to become either more radicalized or more moderate during the course of conflict; we have observed examples of both kinds of shifts. What is clear is that shifts in policy by movements and governments cause some individuals and segments to reassess their interests and strategies. Government concessions tend to undercut the

most militant movements, because some group members decide it is less costly to settle for discounted demands than to continue to fight. Government repression, on the other hand, tends to discredit moderate movements because activists decide that they are in an "all or less than nothing" conflict, an assessment that increases support for organizations prepared to use more militant means to pursue more radical objectives.[6]

Patterns of Grievance

Persons belonging to national minorities have the right to exercise fully and effectively their human rights and fundamental freedoms without any discrimination and in full equality before the law.

To belong to a national minority is a matter of a person's individual choice and no disadvantage may arise from the exercise of such choice.

Persons belonging to national minorities have the right freely to express, preserve and develop their ethnic, cultural, linguistic or religious identity and to maintain and develop their culture in all its aspects, free of any attempts at assimilation against their will. In particular, they have the right

—to use freely their mother tongue in private as well as in public;

—to establish and maintain their own educational, cultural and religious institutions, organizations or associations; . . .

—to profess and practise their religion; . . .

—to establish and maintain unimpeded contacts among themselves within their country as well as contacts across frontiers with citizens of other States; . . .

—to disseminate, have access to and exchange information in their mother tongue;

—to establish and maintain organizations or associations within their country and to participate in international non-governmental organizations.

Persons belonging to national minorities can exercise and enjoy their rights individually as well as in community with other members of their group.

Conference on the Human Dimension of the
Conference on Security and Cooperation in Europe (CSCE), June 1990[7]

This statement, agreed to by official representatives of all the states of Eastern and Western Europe plus Canada and the United States, is a fair summary of the cultural and political aspirations of most minorities throughout the world. Many would add two additional dimensions: they also seek greater equity in the distribution of economic resources, and control of regional or national governments through which to defend and pursue their collective interests.

The CSCE statement reflects the contemporary western ideal of cultural pluralism. Turkish law and public policy exemplify an alternative ideal of assimilation. Since the 1920s the aim has been to create a homogeneous Turkish identity and nationalism from all the country's diverse cultural and ethnic groups. Successive constitutions assert that Turkish is the country's exclusive language and "Turk" the only nationality of its citizens, and they forbid any linguistic or political expression of any other group identity.[8] Similar assimilationist goals have been pursued by many western as well as Third World governments, for example, in Australia until the 1950s and in Japan to the present day.

The tension between the communal desire for cultural recognition and government pressures for assimilation reinforces conflicts that arise from political and material inequalities. The coincidence of cultural and material conflicts shapes the grievances and demands expressed on behalf of communal groups. The empirical basis for our analysis of communal grievances is the Minorities at Risk codings of group grievances in the 1980s, which coders were told to derive from "statements of spokesmen, observers, and/or unambiguous actions by the group." An example of action with an unambiguous message is the use of blockades and sabotage to prevent outsiders' development of a group's traditional lands—tactics used recently by indigenous groups in places as distant as Quebec, the Amazon basin, and the forests of northern Borneo. One does not need press releases to conclude that such actions reflect a group's concern for the grievance issue we summarized as "protection of land, jobs, resources from alienation to other groups."

On the basis of observations about the issues raised by the groups surveyed in the Minorities at Risk study, we identified four general dimensions of grievances and a number of more specific issues for each dimension. The dimensions and issues are as follows:

1. *Political autonomy*
   General concern, explicit objectives not clear (coded only
      if more specific categories below cannot be coded)
   Union with kindred groups elsewhere

Independence
Greater regional autonomy

2. *Political rights other than autonomy*
Diffuse political grievances, explicit objectives not clear
Greater political rights in own community or region
Greater participation in politics and decision making at the
   central state level
Equal civil rights, status
Change unpopular local officials or policies
Other grievances about political rights

3. *Economic rights*
Diffuse economic grievances, explicit objectives not clear
Greater share of public funds, services
Greater economic opportunities (better education, access
   to higher status occupations, resources)
Improved working conditions, better wages
Protection of land, jobs, resources from alienation to
   others
Other economic grievances

4. *Social and cultural rights*
Freedom of religious belief and practice
Recognition or toleration of own language, culture
Protection from threats and attacks by other communal
   groups
Other social and cultural grievances

Most politicized communal groups are represented by multiple organizations and spokespersons, as was noted above. And
issues are not of equal salience to the group. Each specific grievance issue was scored on the following scale:

0 = Issue is not significant for the group.
1 = Issue is of lesser or indeterminant salience, or of major
     concern to a segment of the group.
2 = Issue is highly salient to the group.

Grievances were coded for advantaged as well as disadvantaged communal groups because factions of advantaged minorities sometimes express grievances about threats to their
privileges and collective identity. Right-wing Afrikaners have
sharply and sometimes violently opposed the South African

Table 3.1. Grievances in the 1980s, by World Region and Group Type.

	Political Autonomy	Political Rights	Economic Rights	Social Rights
1. Global Means (233)[a]	0.94	2.25	1.96	1.77
2. Means for World Regions				
Western democracies and Japan (24)	1.0	1.9	2.5	1.9
Eastern Europe and USSR (32)	1.1	1.3	0.8	1.9
Asia (43)	1.5	2.7	2.0	2.2
North Africa and the Middle East (31)	1.2	3.2	2.6	2.3
Africa south of the Sahara (74)	0.6	2.1	1.5	1.1
Latin America and the Caribbean (29)	0.6	2.4	3.3	2.1
3. Means for Group Types[b]				
Ethnonationalists (81)	1.8	2.6	1.8	2.0
Indigenous peoples (77)	1.2	2.5	2.5	2.1
Ethnoclasses (45)	0.2	2.7	2.4	1.8
Militant sects (49)	1.1	2.2	1.8	2.6
Disadvantaged contenders (41)	0.6	2.8	1.8	1.4
Politically advantaged contenders (25)	0.4	1.0	0.7	0.7

[a] Numbers in parentheses are the numbers of groups in each cluster. Groups with no reported grievances were coded 0 on all indicators. Advantaged groups are included.

[b] Numbers of groups sum to more than the global totals because some groups were cross-classified.

government's efforts to reach accommodation with African nationalists, for example, and therefore are coded under the dimension of "social and cultural rights" as making highly salient demands for "protection from threats and attacks by other communal groups."

The scores for the issues listed under each dimension were added to provide summary indicators of each group's concerns about political autonomy (AUTGR), political rights (POLRI), economic rights (ECOGR), and social and cultural rights (SOCGR) (see Appendix tables A.13 to A.18). The mean scores for these four indicators are shown in table 3.1 for each world region and each group type. The scores do not have absolute significance, that is, one cannot conclude that economic rights (global mean = 1.96) are twice as salient as autonomy (global mean = 0.94). But we can conclude that economic rights were much more important for minorities in the Middle East (mean = 2.6) and the democracies (mean = 2.5) than in the USSR and Eastern Europe (mean = 0.8).

Thirty groups had no detectable grievances during the 1980s: some were advantaged minorities and others were so marginalized or controlled by dominant groups that they evidently were unable to articulate demands. Examples of the latter include the Karachays, Kurds, and Roma of the USSR; the Muslim Huis of China; and the Bakthiaris of Iran.[9] In other instances, especially for some African groups, our information was too limited for reliable coding. And in some cases the apparent quiescence of the group in the 1980s was belied by an upsurge of activism in 1990–91, for example, among the Kazhaks in the USSR and the Korean minority in Japan.

The world regions differ substantially in their patterns of grievances. Demands for political autonomy were greatest in Asia and in North Africa and the Middle East, least in Africa south of the Sahara and in Latin America. In the socialist states they were only slightly above average: intense and overt nationalism among most Soviet peoples did not surface before 1990–91. The grievance scores in the Appendix, table A.14, show that in the 1980s, demands for greater autonomy in the USSR were openly expressed by the Baltic peoples, the Armenians, the Georgians, and the Ukrainians. Grievances about political and social rights were greatest in the Middle East, paralleling this region's high levels of discrimination and inequalities. Economic grievances, mainly indigenous resentment over alienation of land, were most intense in Latin America. Minorities in the democracies had less than average grievances about political rights but greater than average economic grievances, evidently a reflection of a pattern remarked on at the outset of this chapter: most have won political rights but still experience substantial economic discrimination. Minorities in Eastern Europe and the USSR had the lowest levels of grievance about political and economic rights of any world region. We attribute this finding to two different conditions: authorities' repression of the expression of political demands (including nationalism), and the genuine accomplishments of state socialism in equalizing economic and political opportunities across most national groups (see chapter 7).

The salience of grievances varies by group type, as is shown in part 3 of table 3.1. As expected, ethnonationalists are more concerned about political autonomy than other groups: it is one of the defining properties of that group type. Autonomy is also an issue for indigenous peoples throughout the world, not because most of them seek independent statehood but, rather, because of a shared desire to be shielded from erosion of their culture, economic exploitation, and political domination. Autonomist sentiments are high among militant sects mainly because a number of them are Muslims living in peripheral regions of non-Muslim societies—for example, the Philippine Moros and the Uighurs in China, for whom autonomy is a strategically plausible means for protecting group interests.

Political rights are highly salient for all types of disadvantaged groups. The demand for political rights is a universal theme among them because, in the modern state system, political rights are usually held to be essential to the protection and promotion of all other group interests. The differences among world regions in the assertion of political rights are due mainly to cross-regional differences in human rights policies: democratic states are more likely to protect the civil and political rights of minorities; Marxist-Leninist states, to control their expression; Middle Eastern and Asian regimes, to deny them; and Latin American regimes, to ignore them.

Grievances about economic rights are greatest among indigenous peoples and ethnoclasses, two group types that have experienced the greatest economic disadvantages. The content of economic grievances differ between these two types, however. Indigenous peoples are most often concerned about alienation of lands and resources and only secondarily about the distribution of public resources. Ethnoclass demands focus mainly on more equal access to education and jobs. Social and cultural grievances are most intense among militant sects, a reflection of their defense of the religious beliefs that form the basis of their communities. The relatively high salience of social and cultural grievances for ethnonationalists and indigenous peoples is a function of the threats many of them feel from dominant groups' policies of assimilation and incorporation.

Sources of Group Demands

We turn next to more precise evidence about the connections between minorities' objective situations and the intensity of their demands. Indicators of cultural differentials and political and economic disadvantage (from chapter 2) are correlated with indicators of the four dimensions of grievance. Following the plan of chapter 2, analyses are done for all groups together and separately for groups of each region and type. The tables and discussion emphasize the principal findings, not the underlying mass of statistical detail.

Historical Background of Autonomy Movements

Slightly over half the communal groups in this study (120 of 233) expressed demands for greater autonomy in the 1980s. Included are almost all the groups categorized as ethnonationalists, some indigenous peoples, and a few communal contenders. The common denominator of almost all autonomy demands is the historical fact or belief that the group once governed its own affairs.[10] We have traced the background to separatism in some detail and summarize the results in table 3.2. Sixty-three contemporary separatists justify their claims by descent from ancestors whose long-term autonomy ended when they were conquered by modern states. That is the history of European kingdoms such as Sardinia and Catalonia, of the khanates of Central Asia, of the hill tribes of South and Southeast Asia, of the chieftancies and kingdoms of precolonial Africa, and of the indigenous peoples of the Americas.

The loss of autonomy is historically more distant in some regions than others, as is evident from the "median year(s)" shown in table 3.2. In Western Europe the process of absorption largely ended in the nineteenth century, whereas in Eastern Europe it was associated mainly with the end of the twentieth-century world wars. The republics that seceded from the USSR in 1990–91 had been incorporated into Imperial Russia in a lengthy historical process: eastern Ukraine was absorbed in the 1650s, the conquest of Muslim Central Asia was not completed until the 1880s. Almost all the indigenous peoples of Latin America were conquered before the end of the nineteenth century, whereas in Africa the last rebellions against colonial conquest were not put down until the 1930s. Many of the ethnonationalists of South and Southeast Asia had de facto autonomy under British and French colonial rule, only to lose it when they were absorbed into new postcolonial states.

Table 3.2. Historical Background of Contemporary Demands for Group Autonomy.

Groups with Autonomy Demands in the 1980s[d]	Lost Long-term Autonomy[a]		Lost Temporary Autonomy[b]		Transferred[c]	
	No.	Median Year/s[e]	No.	Median Year/s	No.	Median Year
Western democracies and Japan (15/0)	8	Mid-18th century, mid-19th century	2	1769, 1939	5	1919
Eastern Europe and the USSR (16/1)	6	1918, 1940	6	1921, 1945	3	1944
Asia (33/1)	19	Mid-19th century, early 1950s	3	1949	10	1947
North Africa and the Middle East (16/1)	8	Early 1930s	2	1946	5	1920
Africa south of the Sahara (31/2)	14	About 1900	5	1961	10	1957
Latin America and the Caribbean (9/0)	8	Mid-19th century	1	1979	0	
Total (120/5)	63		19		33	

Note: This table summarizes the last pre-1980 change in political status of groups that expressed demands for greater autonomy during the 1980s.

[a] Groups that were independent states (e.g. khanates, sultanates, kingdoms, republics), autonomous regions (e.g., in empires or indirectly ruled colonial territories), or tribes before being incorporated into the modern state system.

[b] Groups that had independent kingdoms, republics, or autonomous regional governments for a decade or less before being incorporated or reincorporated into the modern state system.

[c] Groups that were transferred from the jurisdiction of one state or colonial territory to another without significant change in autonomy.

[d] The number in parentheses to the left of the slash is the number of groups that sought greater autonomy in the 1980s; to the right is the number of groups with no modern historical experience of loss of autonomy or transfer.

[e] Median year, years, or period during which autonomist groups in a region lost autonomy or were transferred. If losses were clustered in two widely separated periods, two dates are shown.

Nineteen contemporary ethnonationalists briefly broke free from existing states and empires, usually during twentieth-century wars, and then were reincorporated: that was the fate of Slovakia (1939–45), the Kurdish Mahabad Republic (1945–46), and the Chinese Uighurs' East Turkestan Republic (1944–45). Also counted here are the Ukrainians, Georgians, and Armenians, who won brief periods of independence in the aftermath of the revolution of 1917 before being forcibly incorporated into the new Soviet state. Thirty-three modern separatist groups were transferred from one country or colony's rule to another—for example, after the breakup of the Austro-Hungarian and Ottoman Empires, and during decolonization in Africa and Asia. For some, like the Moldavians and the people of East Timor, their arbitrary transfer from one state to another is a direct source of contemporary grievances. Usually, though, transfers and short-lived autonomy are symptomatic of an underlying group identity and a persisting desire for separate status, a desire that is likely to surface whenever external political control is relaxed.

Autonomy and Political Rights

Nearly half the politicized communal groups in this study had no reported demands for autonomy during the 1980s and the salience of autonomist demands varied substantially among the others. The first theoretical question is what mix of historical and contemporary conditions determines the presence and extent of communal demands for greater autonomy. A second question is what conditions led groups to demand political autonomy rather than greater political rights. Table 3.3 summarizes some empirical evidence on these questions.

The effects of historical loss of autonomy on the political demands of disadvantaged groups are shown in part 1 of the table.[11] Information on groups' political history was used to construct a complex indicator of loss of autonomy (AUTLOST; see Appendix tables A.7 to A.12) that gives greatest weight to more recent and substantial political changes in group status.[12] Loss of autonomy has a strong global correlation of .634** with contemporary demands for autonomy but virtually none with demands for greater political rights (see table 3.3, part 1). The regional and type analyses yield two interesting exceptions.

First, loss of autonomy correlates only weakly with the salience of autonomy grievances among ethnonationalists: our interpretation is that greater autonomy is a significant issue for all such groups, and that contemporary conditions are more important than historical ones in determining *how* salient it is. Second, militant sects are the only type of group for whom loss of autonomy translates into demands for greater political rights. The plausible interpretation is that defense of the matters of greatest concern to them (the rights to cultural and religious expression) leads with equal likelihood to demands for greater autonomy from, or for political rights within, the state.

The next question is what contemporary conditions intensify group demands for autonomy. The short answer is that ecological stress and cultural differentials do, but political or economic discrimination do not. Part 2 of table 3.3 shows that ecological stress (pressures on group lands and resources) is the factor of greatest global significance. It is the single strongest correlate of separatism among most of the regionally concentrated minorities, including ethnonationalists, militant sects, and indigenous peoples, but not communal contenders. Demographic stress (part 2) and cultural differentials (part 3) also intensify separatism among ethnonationalists, though not among any other types of groups. The Middle East and Latin America are the world regions where stress and cultural differentials have the greatest effect on separatism.

Our most distinctive finding about separatism is that there is no global or regional correlation between the severity of either kind of discrimination and the intensity of separatist sentiments. This finding needs to be reconciled with the claims of spokespersons for many autonomy movements that their regions are shortchanged in the allocation of public resources and that the political rights and opportunities of group members are restricted by dominant groups. Some Third World ethnonationalists, such as the Palestinians and Kurds, have solid grounds for claiming that their disadvantages are the result of deliberate policy. Others, including the leaders of some regional movements in western societies, use uneven development as the basis for entrepreneural claims for more resources and greater influence at the center.[13]

Other evidence also shows a lack of direct connection between inequalities and ethnonationalism: in chapter 2 we reported evidence that ethnonationalist groups encounter less

Table 3.3. Correlations among Disadvantages and Political Grievances.

Pairs of Variables and Their Global Correlations			Differences among World Regions and Group Types

1. Effects of Lost Autonomy on Political Demands

	AUTGR	POLRI	
AUTLOST	.634**	.125	AUTLOST is the major source of autonomy demands (AUTGR) in all world regions and among all group types, with weakest effects for ethnonationalists (r = .30*). It has weak positive impact on demands for political rights (POLRI) with strongest effects among militant sects (r = .50*).

2. Effects of Ecological and Demographic Stress on Political Demands

	AUTGR	POLRI	
ECOSTRESS	.276**	.288**	ECOSTRESS is a major source of AUTGR in the Middle East (r = .73**) and Latin America (r = .59**), and among ethnonationalists (r = .43**), militant sects (r = .41*), and indigenous peoples (r = .28*). DEMSTRESS has no significant impact on AUTGR except among ethnonationalists (r = .33*). One or both kinds of stress add to POLRI demands in all regions and group types. Their strongest effects are in the Middle East (r's = .60** and .30), among ethnonationalists (r's = .35* and .31*), and among militant sects (r's = .48** and .32).
DEMSTRESS	.021	.224*	

3. Effects of Cultural Differentials on Political Demands

	AUTGR	POLRI
CULDIF	.186*	.116

CULDIF has moderate effects on both kinds of political demands in the Middle East and Latin America and among ethnonationalists (r with AUTGR = .38*, with POLRI = .36*) but not in other regions or group types.

4. Effects of Discrimination on Political Demands

	AUTGR	POLRI
POLDIS	−.060	.331**
ECODIS	−.048	.357**

Neither POLDIS nor ECODIS have significant impact on AUTGR in any world region or in any group type. One or both kinds of discrimination substantially affects POLRI in all world regions except Asia, and among all group types.

Note: The correlations are Pearson correlation coefficients calculated for all disadvantaged groups (n = 208), with pairwise deletion for missing data cases.

AUTLOST = historical loss of group autonomy
AUTGR = autonomy grievances in the 1980s
POLRI = political rights grievances in the 1980s
ECOSTRESS = ecological stress
DEMSTRESS = demographic stress
CULDIF = cultural differentials
POLDIS = political discrimination
ECODIS = economic discrimination

*Significant at $p > .01$, using a two-tailed test.
**Significant at $p > .001$, using a two-tailed test.

economic discrimination than the global mean for all minorities, and only average political discrimination (see table 2.3). An analysis of the correlations between political and economic differentials and separatism, not reported here, also shows no global relationship. On the contrary, it shows that minority separatism in the democracies and the socialist states is greatest among groups with the least differentials. Examples can readily be identified: Spanish Basques, Québecois, Armenians, Ukrainians, and Slovenes all were separatist in the 1980s despite regional prosperity, limited autonomy, and significant national political influence. In sum, the motives for separatism among these and many other peoples are mainly intangible.

Discrimination and stress are the conditions that drive demands for greater political rights. The ecological and demographic stresses that correlate with separatism have equal or stronger impact on demands for equal rights (see part 2 of table 3.3). Discrimination has a significant effect on the salience of political rights globally, in all world regions except Asia, and among all types of groups (see part 4). The correlations are moderate, mostly in the .30 to .50 range, but consistent, and they contrast sharply with the results for separatism.[14]

Economic and Social Rights

Demands for economic rights, whose correlates are summarized in table 3.4, arise from the same kinds of conditions that motivate demands for greater political rights. Economic discrimination is their strongest global correlate ($r = .431$**) followed by demographic and ecological stress, both of which are symptomatic of serious material disadvantages. The connections are closest and most direct among Africa minorities and among disadvantaged communal contenders, two overlapping sets of groups (compare parts 2 and 4 in table 3.4). Economic discrimination is also a major source of economic demands in the democracies (by ethnoclasses)[15] and in Latin America. Political discrimination is a weaker but statistically significant source of economic demands globally ($r = .253$**), probably because in some societies the same social practices and institutional barriers are responsible for both kinds of discrimination.

Cultural differentials correlate significantly ($r = .298$**) with demands for economic rights, more closely and consistently

Table 3.4. Correlations between Disadvantages and Economic and Social Grievances.

Pairs of Variables and Their Global Correlations		Differences among World Regions and Group Types

1. Effects of Lost Autonomy on Economic and Social Grievances

	ECOGR	SOCGR	
AUTLOST	−.028	.165	AUTLOST has no significant effects on economic or social and cultural grievances globally or in any world region or group type, except that it adds to economic grievances by ecoclasses (r = .46*).

2. Effects of Demographic and Ecological Stress on Economic and Social Grievances

	ECOGR	SOCGR	
DEMSTRESS	.415**	.100	One or both kinds of stress have substantial effects on economic grievances in all regions and among all types of groups. Effects are strongest in Africa (r's = .51** and .57**) and among communal contenders (r's = .68** and .59**) and militant sects (r's = .53** and .47**). Neither kind of stress has a substantial and consistent effect on social and cultural grievances in any world region or group type.
ECOSTRESS	.362**	.182*	

3. Effects of Cultural Differences on Economic and Social Grievances

	ECOGR	SOCGR	
CULDIF	.298**	.266**	CULDIF affects economic grievances in all world regions, with strongest impact in democracies (r = .62*), and among all types of groups except indigenous peoples and militant sects. CULDIF affects social and cultural grievances in all regions except Asia and the Middle East, and among all group types except militant sects.

Table 3.4. Disadvantages and Grievances (*cont.*).

Pairs of Variables and Their Global Correlations			Differences among World Regions and Group Types
4. Effects of Economic Discrimination on Economic and Social Grievances			
	ECOGR	SOCGR	
ECODIS	.431**	.279**	ECODIS is most important as a source of economic grievances in Africa ($r = .55*$), Latin America ($r = .51*$), and the democracies ($r = .44$); and among communal contenders ($r = .66**$) and ethnonationalists ($r = .49*$). Its effects are negligible only in Asia and among ethnoclasses. ECODIS has weak to moderate effects on social and cultural grievances in all world regions and among all group types.
5. Effects of Political Discrimination on Economic and Social Grievances			
	ECOGR	SOCGR	
POLDIS	.253**	.116	POLDIS has little impact on economic or social grievances in any world region except Latin America (r's = .44 and .35). It significantly affects economic grievances by indigenous peoples ($r = .43**$) and militant sects ($r = .42*$), and the social and cultural grievances of indigenous peoples ($r = .38*$).

Note: The correlations are Pearson correlation coefficients calculated for all disadvantaged groups (n = 208), with pairwise deletion for missing-data cases.

AUTLOST	= historical loss of group autonomy
ECOGR	= economic grievances in the 1980s
SOCGR	= social and cultural grievances in the 1980s
ECOSTRESS	= ecological stress
DEMSTRESS	= demographic stress
CULDIF	= cultural differentials
POLDIS	= political discrimination
ECODIS	= economic discrimination

*Significant at $p > .01$, using a two-tailed test.
**Significant at $p > .001$, using a two-tailed test.

than they do with either dimension of political demands (compare part 3 in table 3.3 with part 3 in table 3.4). This correlation is another manifestation of a pattern observed in the chapter 2 analysis of differentials: cultural differentials are causally linked to economic disadvantages. The causal sequence, which characterizes especially the ethnoclasses of democracies and the peripheral and indigenous peoples of the Third World, leads from persisting cultural differentials to economic disadvantages to economically motivated protest.

Demands from communal groups for protection of their social and cultural rights are only weakly influenced by indicators of economic disadvantage and affected not at all by the historical loss of autonomy or by political discrimination. Economic discrimination has a weak to moderate impact on the salience of social and cultural demands (global $r = .279**$) and ecological stress has a slight effect ($r = .182*$). Social and cultural grievances arise mainly from conditions less tangible than economic and political disadvantages. Cultural differentials, for example, contribute significantly to demands for protection of social rights (global $r = .266**$) and, in an analysis not reported in table 3.4, we find that a contemporary history (1945–80) of conflict with other communal groups has a greater effect on social demands (global $r = .329**$) than any of the conditions evaluated in table 3.4.

Conclusion: Two Patterns, Three Choices

The global evidence suggests that two different kinds of dynamics drive the political grievances of contemporary minorities. Political and economic disadvantages motivate communal groups to demand greater access to the political system and greater economic opportunities, whereas a history of political autonomy leads groups to attempt secession. Ecological and demographic stress contribute mainly to demands for redress of grievances within the system; only secondarily—in the Middle East and Latin America—do they reinforce demands for autonomy. Cultural differentials are an antecedent condition that contributes substantially to social and cultural demands, but they are not a strong force generating political or economic grievances. These causal patterns are summarized in figure 3.1.

Remote Causes   **Immediate Causes**   **Grievances, Demands**

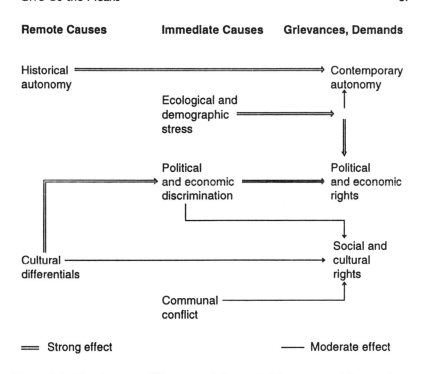

== Strong effect   —— Moderate effect

Figure 3.1. The Sources of Communal Groups' Grievances and Demands.

These conclusions lead to other questions, one of which sets the stage for the subjects of the following two chapters. What strategies are followed by groups that were historically autonomous *and* are disadvantaged? In principle, members of aggrieved communal groups have the choices of three basic alternatives: In terms employed by Albert Hirschman in a different context, their choices are exit, voice, and loyalty.[16] The functional equivalent of "exit" for minorities is, of course, to press for greater autonomy. "Voice" is to protest in hopes of improving their collective status within state and society. "Loyalty" is to accept their situation as given and pursue whatever opportunities may be open to them within the system. The Kurds of Iraq illustrate some of the dilemmas of choice. "Voice" is largely foreclosed, because the Sunni-dominated regime has always used highly repressive tactics against protestors. A minority of Iraqi Kurds, mainly urban dwellers, have opted for loyalty: they have become assimilated into the dominant society as merchants, members of the Ba'thist party, bureaucrats, and military officers. Most rural Kurds, on the other hand, tacitly or openly support rebels who pursue the Kurdish people's historical dream: exit to an autonomous Kurdistan.

The next chapter surveys global and regional patterns of communal protest and rebellion. Examples of their outcomes are documented in the regional analyses in chapters 6 through 9; the entire range of accommodations between contending minorities and states is analyzed in chapter 10.

4. When Minorities Rebel
Patterns and Trends in Ethnopolitical Conflict, 1945–89

Communal identities in all plural societies have a transactional character: they change with time as a result of interactions within the group and between groups. Some groups lose their identities through long-term erosion as individual members become marginalized or are assimilated by other groups. The Viking settlers of eastern Ireland long ago lost their last vestiges of collective identity; so have most Irish Americans. Most important for our understanding of contemporary ethnopolitical conflict, external pressures on a group usually intensify the sense of group identity. The 1980s resurgence of Sudan's civil war was prompted by the northern-dominated regime's retreat from the compromises that ended the 1963–72 hostilities and, most immediately, by a policy of imposing the Shari'a, the Islamic code of justice, on non-Muslim southerners.

Ethnogenesis also can occur in the course of protracted conflict, as has happened in revolutionary Ethiopia. At the time of the 1974 revolution the Amhara-dominated central government was under challenge only by Eritrean nationalists, who had a less than convincing claim to be a distinct nationality. In the next decade at least five other communal groups rebelled against the weakening but increasingly repressive regime in Addis Ababa: the Afars, Anuaks, Oromos, Somalis, and Tigreans. By early 1991, when the Derg regime collapsed under military assault, three decades of civil war had forged a strong sense of identity among Eritreans who supported the Eritrean Liberation Front, one that cut across historically divisive lines of tribal, linguistic, and Christian-versus-Muslim cleavage.

The global processes of economic development and state building and the communications revolution have created a multiplicity of pressures on communal groups everywhere. Increased social interaction means that groups that once occupied isolated social niches are subject to differential treatment and stigmatization by advantaged groups. Members of the increasingly disadvantaged group react with resentment and a sharpened sense of communal identity and common interest. Expansion of the modern economic sector makes inroads on the land and resources of peripheral peoples, draws migrants from minority groups into the pool of unskilled labor, and creates deep-seated feelings of economic injustice among the newly marginalized. Efforts at so-called nation building led by a dominant group almost invariably threaten minorities who regard themselves as separate peoples. The intrusive demands of states dominated by Burmans or Amharas or Serbs makes other peoples ready to mobilize in support of leaders who demand either more power at the center ("voice") or secession ("exit"). All these processes, modernization perhaps most of all, pose threatening alternatives to the cultural values, religious beliefs, language, and lifeways that are the essence of identity in a communal group. These pressures are common throughout the Second World and Third World and everywhere have provided the fuel for political mobilization and action by communal minorities.

Let me amplify parts of this argument. First, the processes that heighten communal awareness and political action in defense of the group are not new. They have occurred wherever and whenever expanding political and economic systems have encountered autonomous peoples. The history of early modern Europe offers a great many instances of distinct peoples and sects swept up into a new social and political order: Welshmen and Burgundians, Albigensians and Anabaptists, Florentines and Ragusans all preceded the modern-day Tibetans and Tamils, Druze and Baha'is, Mapuche and Aborigines, and a hundred other communal groups on the road to forcible subordination or assimilation.

Second, the identities and historical grievances of conquered communal groups can persist and be revived for generations after they seemed to be extinguished, as was shown in chapter 3. In the Third World, many contemporary communal conflicts are merely the latest manifestations of traditional intergroup rivalries. In contemporary Europe and the former Soviet Union dozens of dormant or suppressed communal identities were re-awakened during the past generation. The fact that these resur-gent nationalisms are usually led by modern political entrepre-neurs rather than traditional authorities should not obscure the fact that their success depends on the persistence of deep-rooted sentiments of separate identity that were never com-pletely extinguished by the modern state's policies of national integration.

The last example helps make a third point, that ethnopoliti-cal conflicts are global, not specific to some parts of the Third World. The resurgence of ethnopolitics that became so pro-nounced in the last two decades is a worldwide movement that drew much of its inspiration from the propagation of ideas of intergroup equity and strategies of political action that came to prominence in Western Europe and North America during the 1960s. These ideas and the dramatic impact of strategies like those of the U.S. civil rights movement struck a responsive chord among minorities elsewhere, groups that already were motivated by historic grievances and pressured by contempo-rary change. By the end of the 1980s, protest and rebellion over communal rights had largely run their course in the western democracies but had become the major mode and issue of con-flict in most of Eastern Europe, Asia, Africa, and parts of Latin America.

It also should be obvious that state responses to communal grievances are crucial in shaping the course and outcomes of minority conflicts. Strong states have the capacity both to sup-press rebellions and to make significant concessions to protes-ters, weak states may be unable to do either. Communally based political movements pose a far greater challenge to the newer and poorer countries of the Third World than to states in the developed West, because they have mobilized larger groups, with greater intensity of commitment, against regimes that have fewer political and material resources with which to respond.

A final general point is that there are transnational dimen-sions to most kinds of intrastate conflicts. Regional and global powers have repeatedly intervened on behalf of communal reb-els or the states that they challenge. For example, about one-third of the overt military interventions in the Third World since 1970 have occurred in conflicts being fought along lines of ethnopolitical cleavage.[1] Many of the self-assertive communal groups transcend state boundaries: the Shi'is are a significant, politically active religious minority in eight Islamic states (and a subordinate majority in Iraq and Bahrain). Kurdistan is an ethnocultural region that extends across northern Iraq and four adjoining states. The aspirations and actions of any one segment of such groups are highly contagious among the other segments. And some international conflicts, especially in the contemporary Middle East, are a species of religious communal wars in which one group uses its control of the state apparatus to defend the group's interests against communal enemies. The Lebanese state was the instrument of the Maronite Christians against Islamic contenders, Shi'i clerics have used the powers of the revolutionary Iranian state against Sunni rulers elsewhere, and the state of Israel is the shield of Jews against hostile Palestinians.[2]

Since 1945 more than 200 of the groups in this study have openly resisted the terms of their incorporation in states controlled by other groups. Their grievances about discrimination and threats to group identity have motivated hundreds of protest movements. The same grievances, coupled with historically grounded demands for the restoration of lost autonomy, have triggered rebellions by 79 groups (see the following section). Though some of these rebellions were quickly contained, others escalated into protracted conflicts that have had profound political and humanitarian consequences. In ten instances since 1945, regimes threatened by autonomy movements have resorted to mass political murder in separatist regions. In East Bengal between 1 million and 3 million civilians were massacred in 1971 by the Pakistani army in a vain attempt to halt Bangladesh's secession. In East Timor since 1975, between 60,000 and 200,000 people have been killed by the Indonesian army or have died of privation in an unsuccessful war of independence. At least one-half million southern Sudanese civilians have died in two civil wars since 1963.[3] At the beginning of 1992 more than half the world's 40 million refugees were fleeing from civil wars and repression arising out of communally based conflicts. These included 6.8 million of the 16.6 million transnational refugees in need of protection or assistance and 18 million of an estimated 23 million internally displaced people. The problem was most acute in Africa south of the Sahara, where nearly 3 percent of the total population were refugees from communal conflicts.[4]

Ethnopolitical conflicts also have prompted diverse accommodations and innovations in domestic and international policy.

Democratic states in particular have become adept at accommodating and deflecting the protests of ethnoclasses and ethnonationalists, thereby heading off serious rebellions. In multi-ethnic states such as Malaysia, India, and Nigeria, enormous political energies have been invested in balancing competition among contending communal groups. International and non-governmental actors have attempted, with mixed success, to promote and protect the interests of indigenous peoples throughout the world and to restrain and mediate communal conflicts that have escalated into civil wars.

This chapter reviews the regional patterns and trends in ethnopolitical conflict during the forty-five years that followed the end of World War II. The next chapter offers a more formal and detailed theoretical explanation of the circumstances that lead disadvantaged groups into campaigns of protest (in which they give "voice" to grievances) and rebellion (in which they seek "exit" from or autonomy within the state). Chapter 10 evaluates some of the outcomes of these conflicts.

Profiles of Ethnopolitical Conflict

There are three different forms or strategies of political action by which communal groups pursue their interests: in order of increasing intensity they are *nonviolent protest, violent protest,* and *rebellion.* Protest typically aims at persuading or intimidating officials to change their policies toward the group; rebellion aims directly at more fundamental changes in governments and in power relations among groups. The essential strategy of protest is to mobilize a show of support on behalf of reform; the essential strategy of rebellion is to mobilize enough coercive power that governments are forced to accept change. When protestors use violence it usually occurs in sporadic and unplanned ways, often in reaction to coercive acts by the police and military. The use of violence by rebels, on the other hand, takes the form of concerted campaigns of armed attacks, ranging from political banditry and terrorism to all-out warfare. The distinction between protest and rebellion is not absolute, because the political objectives of peoples with grievances are mixed and their choices of strategies and tactics vary with circumstances, including the responses of their opponents.

In the Minorities at Risk project we developed a profile of each group's history of conflict by using scales of the severity of nonviolent protest (PROT), violent protest (RIOT), and rebellion (REBEL); see Appendix tables A.13 to A.18. The scales (table 4.1) take into account the numbers of people involved and the intensity or destructiveness of their actions. Each group was coded for successive five-year periods from 1945–49 to 1985–89 by means of a Guttman scale scoring procedure: each of the three forms of political action was scored for the most widespread and intense event reported during a period. For example, if an ethnonationalist movement carried out a campaign of urban terrorism (scale value = 2) and fought a large-scale rural guerrilla war (scale value = 4) in the same five-year span, the group was scored 4 on the rebellion scale. The cross-regional comparisons (table 4.2) summarize the scores for each type of political action across the entire forty-five year period.[5]

Four general comments need to be kept in mind about the coding procedure. First, it was limited specifically to actions (a) initiated by members of communal groups on behalf of their interests and (b) directed against state authorities.[6] Government massacres and campaigns to subjugate unresisting peoples are not included in these codings.

Second, the low end of the nonviolent protest scale refers to conventional political activity on behalf of group interests, including the organized expression of grievances and the formation of interest groups, movements, and parties. Such activity is not ordinarily included in most analyses of political conflict, because it does not entail the use or threat of coercion. Yet it is often seen as threatening by officials and is restricted in most authoritarian societies. And it is crucial for understanding the larger dynamics of minority conflicts. When tracing minorities over time, we have repeatedly observed that violent political action follows a period of nonviolent activity that was either ignored or dealt with repressively. Political action by minorities is a continuum; understanding its violent manifestations requires analysis of its nonviolent origins.

Third, the political action profiles are coded for advantaged as well as disadvantaged minorities, because factions of advantaged groups often organize political action to induce governments to defend or reinforce their position. A case in point is political opposition and clandestine violence in the late 1980s and early 1990s by conservative Afrikaners who resisted the government's moves to dismantle apartheid.

Table 4.1. Scales for Coding Communal Political Action.

Nonviolent protest
- 0 = None reported.
- 1 = Verbal opposition (public letters, petitions, posters, clandestine publications, agitation, etc.).
- 2 = Political organizing activity on a substantial scale, including conventional party activity on behalf of group interests.
- 3 = A few demonstrations, strikes, rallies, total participation in the hundreds or low thousands.
- 4 = A number of demonstrations, strikes, rallies, total participation in the 10,000 range or higher.
- 5 = Similar events, total participation over 100,000.
- 6 = Other (specify).[a]

Violent protest
- 0 = None reported.
- 1 = Scattered acts of sabotage, symbolic destruction of property.
- 2 = Limited rioting (one or two small riots or clashes).
- 3 = Substantial rioting.
- 4 = Serious and widespread rioting.
- 5 = Local rebellions: armed attempts to seize power in a locale. (If they develop into sustained guerrilla or civil war, code under rebellion, below.)
- 6 = Other (specify).[a]

Rebellion
- 0 = None reported.
- 1 = Political banditry, sporadic terrorism, unsuccessful coups by or on behalf of the group.
- 2 = Campaigns of terrorism, successful coups by or on behalf of the group.
- 3 = Small-scale guerrilla activity.
- 4 = Large-scale guerrilla activity, distinguished from small-scale by a large number of armed fighters (more than 1000) carrying out frequent armed attacks over a substantial area.
- 5 = Protracted civil war, fought by military units with base areas.
- 6 = Other (specify).[a]
- 7 = Group members are involved in civil or revolutionary war that is not specifically or mainly concerned with group issues.[b]
- 8 = Group members are involved in international warfare that is not specifically or mainly concerned with group issues.[b]

Note: Each group is scored for successive five-year periods from 1945–49 to 1985–89 using a Guttman scale procedure: the score for each dimension is the highest scale value recorded during a period.

[a] Recoded 3 when constructing composite indicators.

[b] Recoded 4 when constructing composite indicators.

Table 4.2. Indicators of Communal Protest and Rebellion, 1945–89.

World Region and Number of Groups	Average Conflict Scores 1945–89			Groups in Each Region with Highest Conflict Scores[a]
	Nonviolent Protest	Violent Protest	Rebellion	
Western democracies and Japan (24)	13.8	3.0	2.8	US: African Americans (28/15/03)
				UK: Catholics (N. Ireland) (15/15/10)
				UK: Blacks (18/11/00)
				Spain: Basques (17/02/10)
Eastern Europe and the USSR (32)	9.3	4.0	1.5	USSR: Lithuanians (17/13/08)
				USSR: Ukrainians (19/02/10)
				USSR: Georgians (18/09/01)
				USSR: Latvians (19/04/04)
Asia (43)	8.9	2.2	9.4	Burma: Karens (18/04/45)
				China: Tibetans (20/14/16)
				India: Nagas (24/09/15)
				Burma: Kachins (12/00/34)

Region				Group	
North Africa and the Middle East	9.9	4.4	9.0	Israel (Occupied Territories): Palestinians	(34/23/15)
				Iraq: Kurds	(18/03/35)
				Jordan: Palestinians	(24/17/09)
				Lebanon: Sunnis	(24/07/18)
Africa south of the Sahara (74)	6.0	2.7	4.6	Zimbabwe: Ndebele	(31/15/17)
				South Africa: Blacks	(30/20/11)
				Sudan: Southerners	(11/07/09)
				Ethiopia: Eritreans	(14/00/26)
Latin America and the Caribbean (29)	5.0	0.5	0.7	Guatemala: Maya	(10/00/10)
				Nicaragua: Miskito	(08/00/11)
				Bolivia: Native highland peoples	(16/02/00)
Global means	8.3	2.8	5.0		

Note: Scores for each group are the aggregate of coded values for all five-year time periods (see text). Means are reported for all groups in each region, both advantaged and disadvantaged.

[a] Listed within each region in descending order of total conflict scores. Numbers from left to right in parentheses are group totals for nonviolent protest, violent protest, and rebellion.

Fourth, the scholarly sources that provided most information for coding other characteristics of communal groups seldom had enough information for the political action profiles. For the remainder we relied substantially on journalistic sources, especially but not only the summaries in *Keesings Contemporary Archives* for the years before the 1980s, and in *Foreign Broadcast Information Service* reports for the 1980s.[7]

Global and Regional Patterns of Protest and Rebellion

Nonviolent protest, by far the most prevalent form of communal political action in the postwar era, was used by 180 of the 233 groups surveyed; many of those that did not protest were advantaged minorities. Violent protest was the least common form of action, used by only ninety-six groups. Just under half of the groups, 114, initiated some form of rebellion. The analysis in table 4.3 shows that terrorism was the only tactic of rebellion used by thirty-five of these groups; the other seventy-nine fought guerrilla and civil wars. Nearly half were protracted communal wars, defined as spanning at least three successive five-year coding periods.[8] These thirty-seven protracted communal conflicts are among the most severe conflicts of the modern world and, as is evident from the table, have been concentrated almost entirely in the Third World.

There are dramatic differences across regions in the forms and magnitudes of communal conflict. Nonviolent protest has been the most common form of communal action in the western democracies, Latin America, and Eastern Europe and the former Soviet Union. Violent protest has been relatively rare globally, but somewhat more likely to occur in Eastern Europe and the Middle East than elsewhere. The violent protests of minorities in western societies are almost exclusively the acts of the first three groups listed in the right-hand column of table 4.2: African Americans in the United States, blacks and Irish Catholics in the United Kingdom. Communal rebellions occur mainly in Asia, the Middle East, and Africa. These regions are the source of all but five of the short-term guerrilla and civil wars in table 4.3, and all but one of the protracted communal wars. Rebellions have been virtually absent from Latin America, where communal groups took part in only two guerrilla wars and one brief terrorist campaign during the entire forty-five

Table 4.3. Communal Groups in Rebellion, by Region, 1945–89.

World Region and Number of Groups	Terrorism Only[a]		Guerrilla and Civil Wars[b]	
	Short-term	Protracted	Short-term	Protracted
Western democracies and Japan (12)	4	8	0	0
Eastern Europe and the USSR (10)	5	1	4	0
Asia (27)	1	0	10	16
North Africa and the Middle East (22)	0	0	11	11
Africa south of the Sahara (40)	12	3	16	9
Latin America and the Caribbean (3)	1	0	1	1
Totals (114)	23	12	42	37

[a] Groups with rebellion codes of 1 or 2 for one or more five-year periods between 1945 and 1989, but no higher codes for any other period. "Short-term" means that the longest episodes coded for the group lasted for one or at most two successive periods; "protracted" means that the group was involved in at least one episode that lasted for three or more successive periods. Note that politically motivated banditry also is included with terrorism.

[b] Groups with codes of 3 to 8 on rebellion for at least one five-year period, "short-term" and "protracted" episodes defined as for terrorism.

year period. The tactics of rebellion also were uncommon in Eastern Europe and the USSR; in nine of the ten instances in which they did occur, they were soon suppressed.[9] Terrorist campaigns were the only kind of rebellion in the western democracies: ethnonationalists such as the Basques, Corsicans, and Puerto Rican Independentistas accounted for all eight protracted terrorist campaigns in these countries.

Trends in Magnitudes of Protest and Rebellion

It is a commonplace observation that communal conflict has increased in the past several decades. The conflict profiles provide solid evidence about what kinds of conflict have increased, in what regions, and among what kinds of communal groups. The evidence is summarized graphically in the accompanying figures. Global trends are depicted in figure 4.1, which was constructed by adding and graphing the scores for each of the three forms of political action for all groups for each five-year period. Figures 4.2 to 4.7 are constructed in the same way for groups in each world region; figures 4.8 to 4.12 show the trends for the six types of communal groups. The magnitudes (summed scores) in each figure have no absolute meaning, because (to use an analogy) they are equivalent to adding the weights of various numbers of apples, lemons, and cantaloupes—very different kinds of fruits. They do show vividly, however, proportional changes over time in each form of communal conflict and differences among regions and group types in the preferred strategies of political action.

Globally, rebellion and violent protest declined in the first decade after World War II, but since the 1950s all forms of communal conflict have increased markedly. Nonviolent protest has more than doubled in magnitude (up 230 percent from 1945–49 to 1985–89) and violent protest has increased fourfold (up 420 percent from its low in 1950–55). Rebellion also has increased almost fourfold (up 360 percent from 1950–55 to 1985–89). Three potential sources of these trends need to be considered: better reporting, escalation of particular conflicts, and contagion, in which conflicts spread from one group to another. No evidence supports the argument that the trends are an artifact of better reporting.[10] But there is ample evidence for escalation: when the seventy-nine groups involved in civil wars and rebellions are examined, we find that forty-three of their conflicts escalated from protest in previous periods and that twenty-eight of them escalated from lower to higher levels of rebellion.[11] It also appears that more groups entered conflict as time passed. Although precise evidence on contagion has not been compiled, our impression is that more new groups entered conflict in the 1960s and 1970s than the 1950s or 1980s.[12]

Regional Trends

The regions vary markedly in conflict trends and typical forms of action. Political action by the twenty-four minorities in the western democracies and Japan increased sharply in the 1960s, peaked in the early 1970s, and has since subsided (see figure 4.2). Case studies suggest that two different contagion processes were responsible for the increase: emulation of the U.S. civil rights movement by ethnoclasses and indigenous minorities

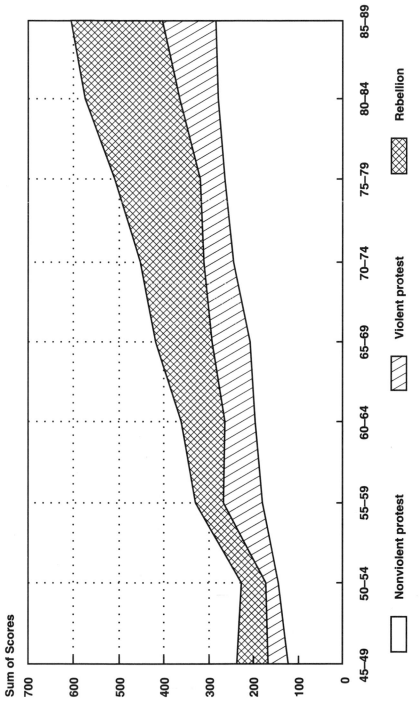

Sum of Scores

Figure 4.1. Global Trends in Minority Conflict, 1945–89.

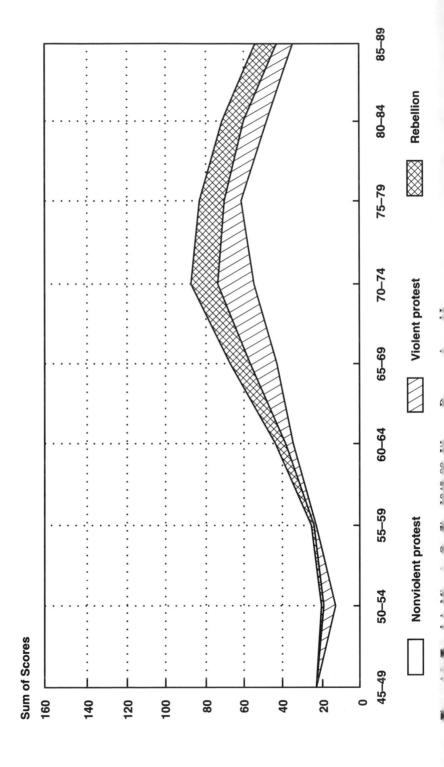

Sum of scores

160

140

120

100

80

60

40

20

0

45–49   50–54   55–59   60–64   65–69   70–74   75–79   80–84   85–89

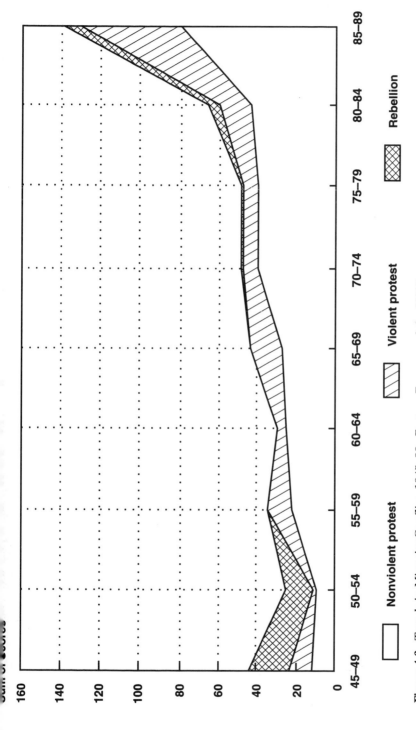

Nonviolent protest   Violent protest   Rebellion

Figure 4.3. Trends in Minority Conflict, 1945–89: Eastern Europe and the USSR.

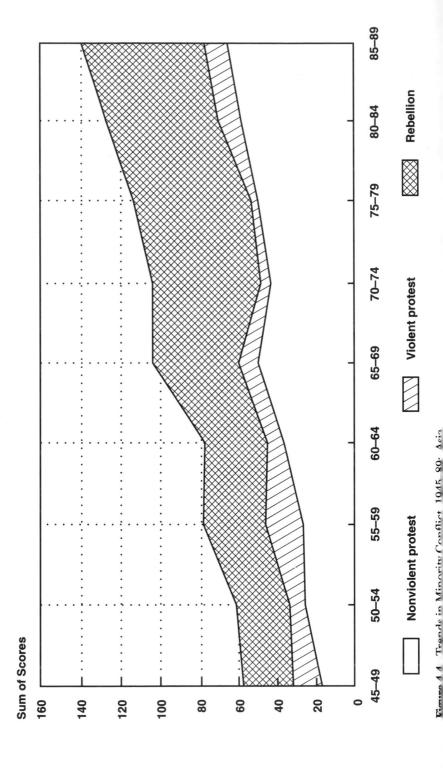

Figure 4.4 Trends in Minority Conflict, 1945–89: Asia

Sum of Scores

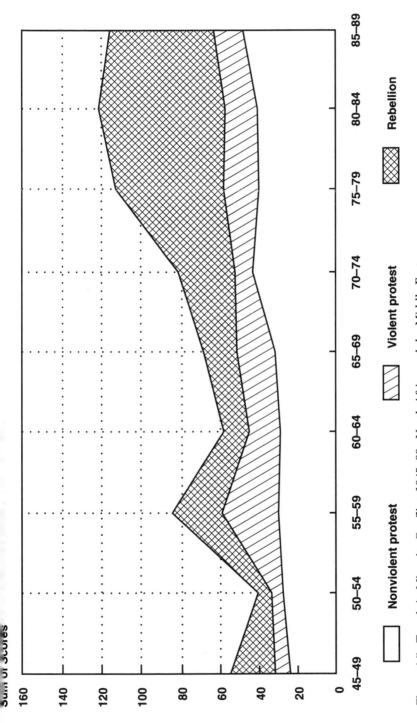

Figure 4.5. Trends in Minority Conflict, 1945–89: North Africa and the Middle East.

Nonviolent protest   Violent protest   Rebellion

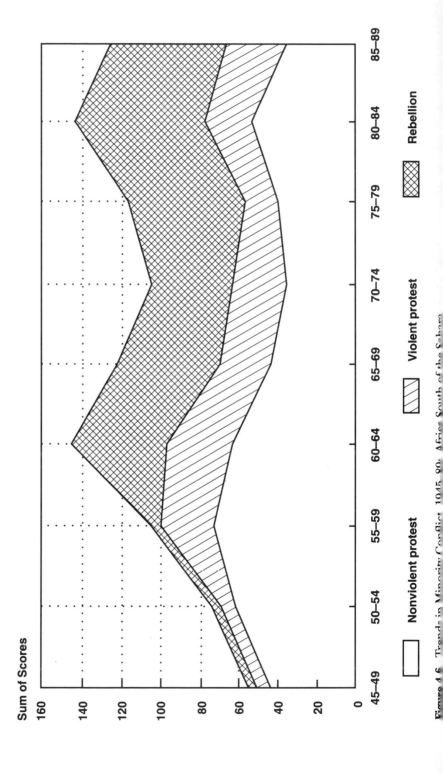

Sum of Scores

Nonviolent protest   Violent protest   Rebellion

Figure 4.6. Trends in Minority Conflict, 1945–90: Africa South of the Sahara

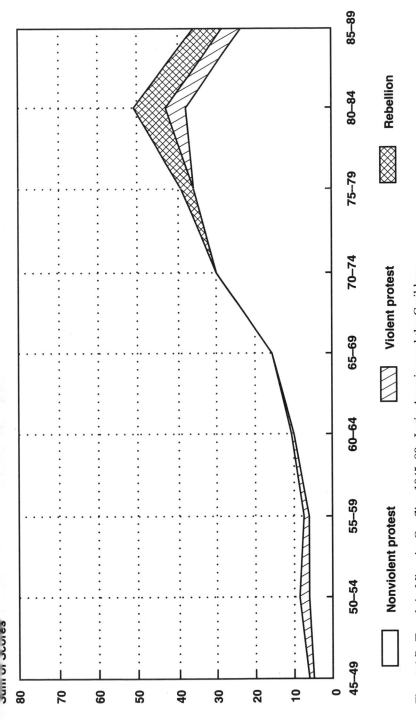

Sum of Scores

80
70
60
50
40
30
20
10
0

45–49   50–54   55–59   60–64   65–69   70–74   75–79   80–84   85–89

Nonviolent protest   Violent protest   Rebellion

Figure 4.7. Trends in Minority Conflict, 1945–89: Latin America and the Caribbean.

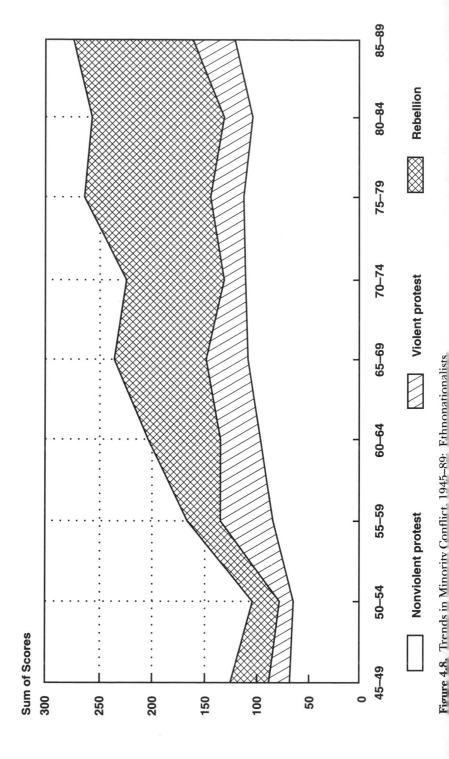

Figure 4.8. Trends in Minority Conflict, 1945–89: Ethnonationalists

Sum of Scores

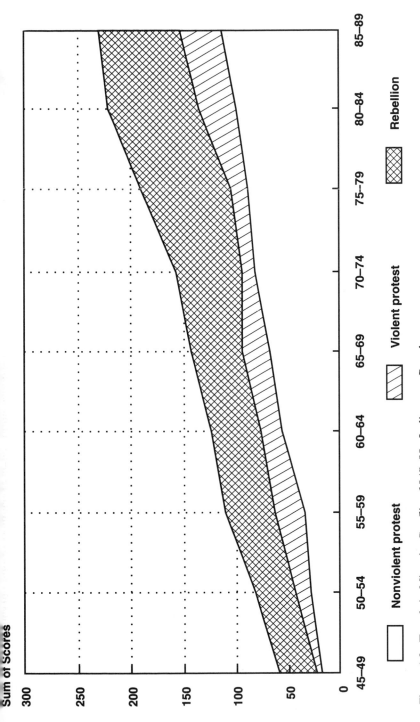

Figure 4.9. Trends in Minority Conflict, 1945–89: Indigenous Peoples.

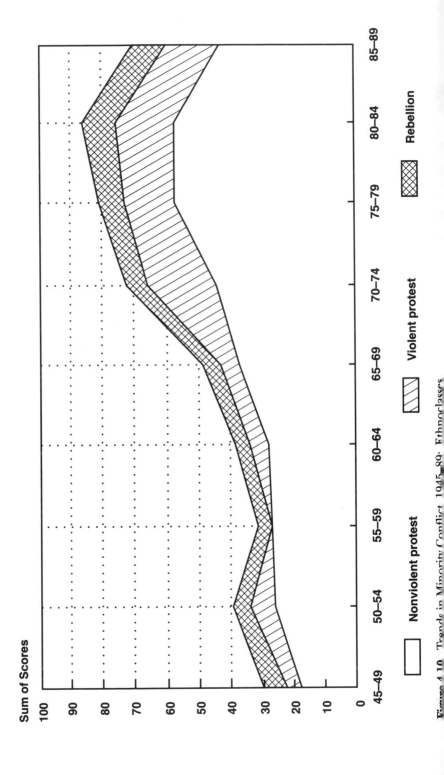

Figure 4.10 Trends in Minority Conflict 1945–89: Ethnoclasses

Sum of Scores

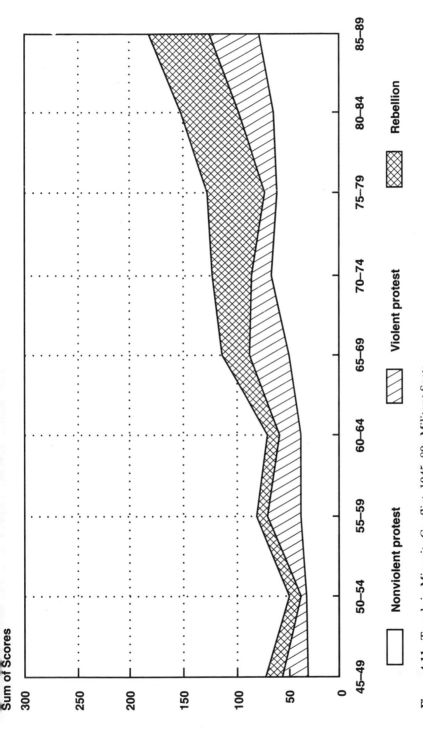

Figure 4.11. Trends in Minority Conflict, 1945–89: Militant Sects.

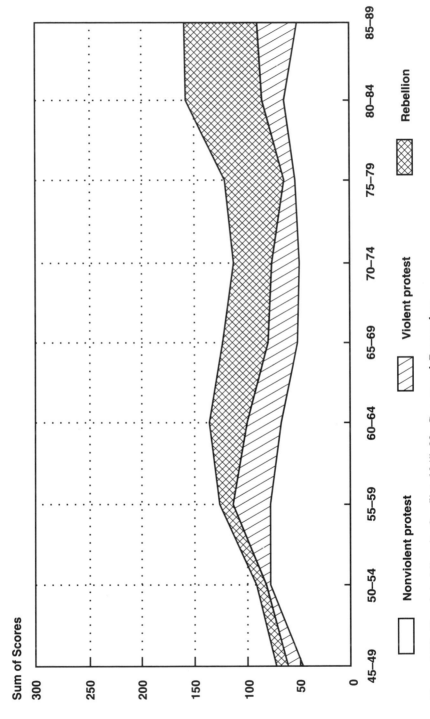

Sum of Scores

☐ Nonviolent protest   ▨ Violent protest   ▧ Rebellion

                                  Communal Contenders.

Figure 4.12. Trends in Minority Conflict, 1945–89: Communal Contenders.

elsewhere, and the resurgence of long-dormant regional autonomy movements in Western Europe and Canada. The reformist policies of democratic governments that contributed to the decline of most of these movements are examined in chapter 6.

Trends among thirty-two politically restive minorities in Eastern Europe and the USSR trace the inverse of the western pattern (see figure 4.3). Postwar resistance was largely suppressed by the early 1950s, except for a susurration of clandestine political activism by small and scattered groups of nationalists in the non-Russian republics and by Croats and Albanians in Yugoslavia. The rebirth of communal political action antedates the Gorbachev era: it began in some regions in the 1970s, escalating rapidly into nonviolent and then violent protest after 1985. Our coding ended with 1989, so it misses the intensification of violent nationalist and communal conflict in 1990–91.

A similarity is evident in preferred forms of political action between the First World and the Second World, especially in comparison with Third World regions: protest far outweighs rebellion. It also is to the credit of the All-Union government of the USSR that from 1989 to 1991 it chose dissolution rather than taking repressive steps that would have transformed nonviolent independence movements into civil wars. On this issue the Russians have thus far followed the western precedent, while the Serbian-dominated government of Yugoslavia has emulated the authoritarian regimes of the Third World.

Asia in our analysis extends from India to Papua New Guinea to Korea and encompasses forty-three politically salient minorities (Japanese minorities are included in the democracies cluster). Ethnopolitical conflict in this megaregion has increased steadily during the postwar era, and rebellion has been the dominant form throughout, with a notable escalation beginning in the late 1960s (see figure 4.4). Asia is home to sixteen of the most protracted communal conflicts of the modern world, including rebellions by the Karen, Kachin, and Shan peoples of the Burmese highlands; Sri Lankan Tamils; the Tibetans; the Nagas and Mizos of India; the people of East Timor; and the Papuans of Irian Jaya. The increase in nonviolent protest in this region since the late 1970s is due mainly to indigenous rights activism among peoples such as the Cordillerans in the Philippines and the Dayaks and Kadazans of northern Borneo.

Communal conflict involving the thirty-one communal minorities in North Africa and the Middle East has varied more irregularly: violent protest and rebellion were particularly wide-spread and intense in the late 1950s (see figure 4.5). This peak resulted mainly from the coincidental upsurge of communal activism in Lebanon and among the Berbers of the Maghreb. The current epoch of transnational conflicts in the region is driven by the national and communal aspirations of the Palestinians, Kurds, and Shi'i Muslims and is reflected in the pronounced increase in rebellion that began in the mid-1970s. If the rebellion profiles were extended to 1990–91 the trend probably would remain flat, because the eruption of Kurdish and Shi'i rebellions in postwar Iraq was balanced by the Syrian-imposed decline of communal hostilities in Lebanon.

In Africa south of the Sahara, nationalism and decolonization have shaped conflict among seventy-four communal groups contending for power in new states and a handful of old ones. Nonviolent protest on behalf of communal ("tribal") interests reached its peak in the decade prior to 1960, the year in which most African colonies gained independence; violent protest was greatest in the immediate aftermath of independence (see figure 4.6). Communal rebellions were very uncommon before independence; in the 1960s the series of regional rebellions and civil wars began that have since devastated the countries of the eastern Sudan and the Horn. Resurgent black nationalism in South Africa shows up in the rising trend of violent protest in the early 1980s. The dominant pattern for Africa as a whole, though, is a long-term shift in the typical mode of communal action from peaceful protest to rebellion.

Latin America and the Caribbean region is anomolous in comparison with all other regions because communal activism there has been limited almost entirely to nonviolent protest by native peoples[13] and remained at a very low level until the 1970s (see figure 4.7). These groups were much influenced by and came to play a key role in the global indigenous rights movement that began in that decade. The apparent decline of communal conflict in the second half of the 1980s reflects a lack of late 1980s information for some of these peoples. There was a substantial upsurge in activism in the early 1990s, including a nationwide uprising, the *levantamiento*, of indigenous Ecuadoreans in June 1990 and a three-hundred-mile protest march to Quito by the same peoples in spring 1992.[14] The only native peoples in open rebellion have been the Maya and Miskito, in both cases because they were caught up in revolutionary conflicts that were tangential to their own interests.[15] Although contagion, in the form of external encouragement, has played a major role in *indiginista* activism in Latin America, the U.S. civil rights movement had virtually no counterpart effect on the Afro-American minorities of nine Latin American countries.[16] They are among the most politically quiescent of all the 233 groups included in this survey. Only Afro-Brazilians and Panamanians of Caribbean descent have been politically active.

Trends among Types of Communal Groups

Comparison of trends in political action among the types of groups provides some additional insights. The dominant features of ethnonationalism are, first, the pronounced upward trend in overall magnitude of political action that began in the late 1950s and, second, the extraordinary upsurge in ethnonationalist rebellion, which increased fivefold between the early 1950s and the 1980s. Indigenous peoples experienced the greatest proportional increase in conflict magnitudes of all the group types, including a sevenfold increase in nonviolent protest and a fivefold increase in violent protest (see figure 4.9). In the Americas these groups ordinarily use nonviolent tactics, whereas in Asia indigenous peoples are much more likely to organize rebellions.

Most ethnonationalists and indigenous peoples aim at what we have called "exit" or greater autonomy from the state. The objective that typifies the other three categories of groups is "voice" or pressure to accommodate their interests within existing political systems. Among ethnoclasses, most of whom live in the western democracies and Latin America, nonviolent protest has consistently been the most common tactic. It increased steadily from the late 1940s through the 1970s, paralleled by an upsurge in violent protest and sporadic campaigns of terrorism from the late 1960s to the early 1980s (see figure 4.10). It is clear from in-depth analysis of particular ethnoclasses, such as African Americans and black South Africans, that violent activism emerges among the most angry and radical followers of nonviolent movements. The lesson learned by most democratic regimes has been that escalation to violence can be preempted by a combination of reform and cooptation of moderate activists. Such responses have contributed to the aggregate decline in political action by ethnoclasses that became apparent in the late 1980s.

A very different pattern of political action is evident among communal contenders, a group type that is heavily concentrated in the least developed African countries and a few Middle Eastern and Asian countries. Contenders have shifted away from reliance on nonviolent protest and toward rebellion, which more than doubled in magnitude between the early 1960s and late 1980s (see figure 4.12). It is easy to infer a general explanation that is the reverse image of political tendencies in the western democracies: in poor, authoritarian regimes there are few resources to satisfy disadvantaged claimaints, and those in power are disposed to think in zero-sum terms and to respond with force rather than compromise. Since few of these states have overwhelming military capacity, the use of force against communal contenders usually engenders greater resistance. The typical result is escalation to protracted communal conflict.

There is finally the upward trend in conflict by militant sects, the most active of which are Muslim minorities in societies dominated by non-Muslim peoples (see figure 4.11). Magnitudes of all three kinds of political action by these groups have gone up since the early 1950s, rebellion most of all. From the late 1960s to the late 1980s the magnitude of rebellion by these groups increased 225 percent, versus 130-percent and 180-percent increases for ethnonationalists and communal contenders, respectively. But the evidence challenges conventional wisdom that religious extremism has become the major source of communal violence of the past decade. First, the average magnitude of rebellion by religiously defined communal groups in the 1980s was roughly the same as that of rebellions by indigenous peoples and communal contenders, and substantially less than that of ethnonationalists. Second, religious groups accounted for only one-quarter of the total magnitude of rebellion by all kinds of groups in the 1980s.

Regional maps showing ethnopolitical conflict in the 1980s appear on pages 117–122. Note that these geographic regions do not correspond exactly with the world regions that are listed in table 1.1 and discussed elsewhere in the text.

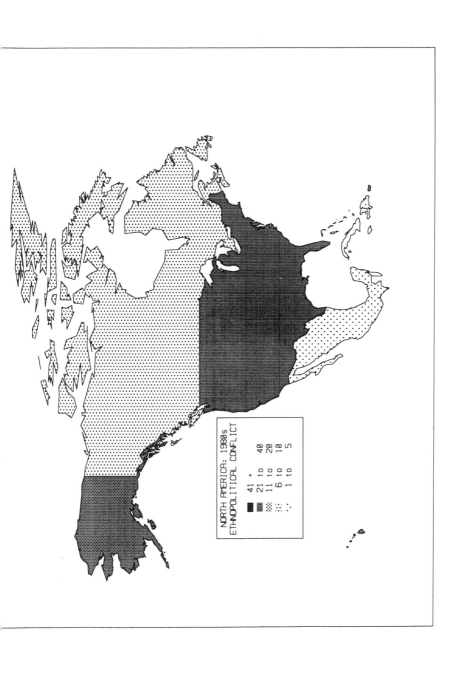

NORTH AMERICA: 1980s
ETHNOPOLITICAL CONFLICT

41 +
21 to 40
11 to 20
6 to 10
1 to 5

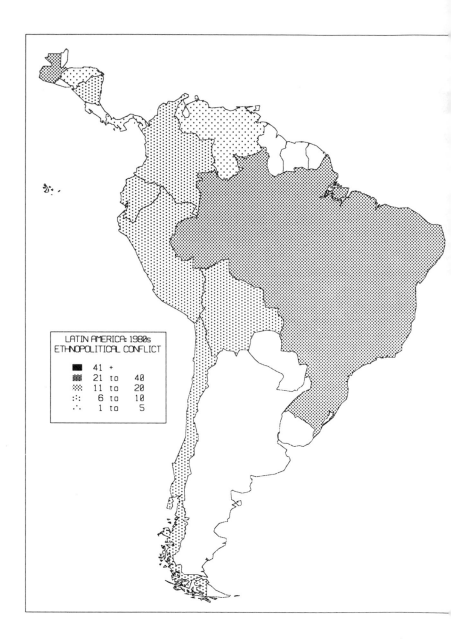

LATIN AMERICA: 1980s
ETHNOPOLITICAL CONFLICT

■ 41 +
▨ 21 to 40
▨ 11 to 20
∴ 6 to 10
∴ 1 to 5

118

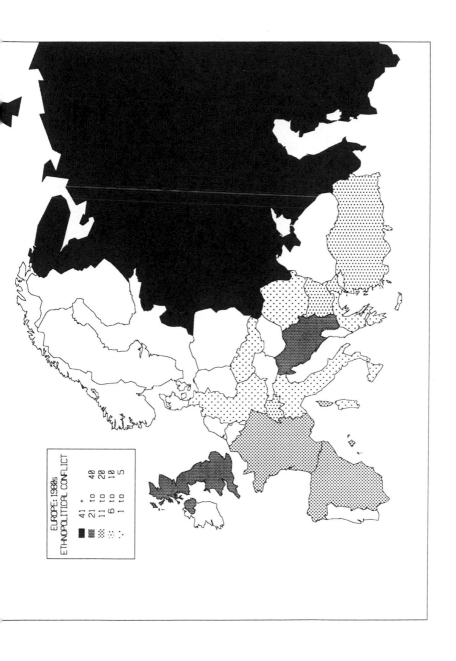

EUROPE: 1990s
ETHNOPOLITICAL CONFLICT

41 +   40
21 to   20
11 to   10
6 to
1 to   5

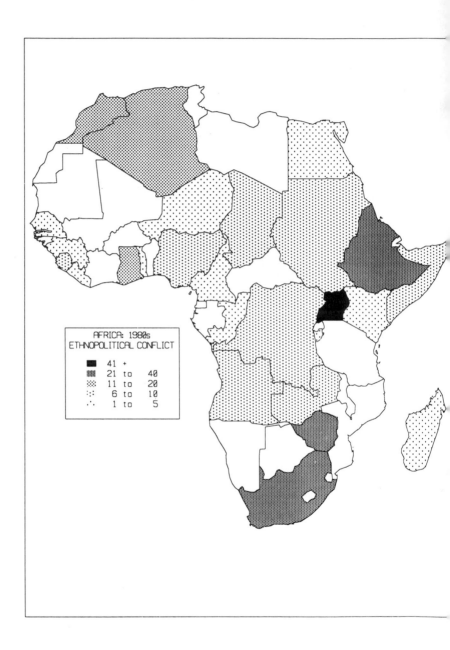

AFRICA: 1980s
ETHNOPOLITICAL CONFLICT

- ■ 41 +
- ▨ 21 to 40
- ▦ 11 to 20
- ⋮ 6 to 10
- ∴ 1 to 5

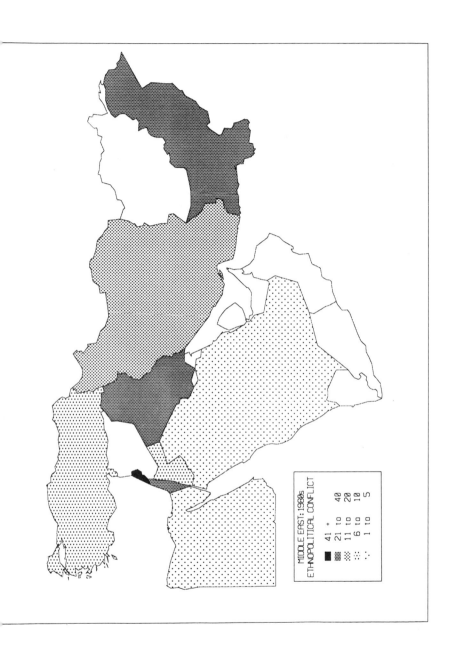

MIDDLE EAST: 1980s
ETHNOPOLITICAL CONFLICT

■ 41 +
▨ 21 to 40
▦ 11 to 20
⋮ 6 to 10
⋰ 1 to 5

ASIA: 1990s
ETHNOPOLITICAL CONFLICT

41 +
21 to 40
11 to 20
6 to 10
1 to 5

5. Why Minorities Rebel
Explaining Ethnopolitical Protest and Rebellion

The review of trends in ethnopolitical action (see chapter 4) highlights the kinds of conditions that have contributed to the political mobilization of communal groups. These conditions include unequal treatment by dominant groups, competition with other groups for access to power in new states, the contagion effect of ethnopolitical activism elsewhere, and patterns of state power and policy that channel communal energies into either protest or rebellion. These factors can be incorporated into a general theory of ethnopolitical action that is applicable to a wide spectrum of groups. The theory sketched in this chapter builds on the empirical evidence of all the preceding chapters and places it in the larger international context. Elements of the theory are tested elsewhere;[1] here it is used to integrate the observations, empirical evidence, and speculations generated by the Minorities at Risk project.

Grievances or Political Calculation?

The most basic assumption of the theory is that ethnopolitical activism is motivated by peoples' deep-seated grievances about their collective status in combination with the situationally determined pursuit of political interests, as articulated by group leaders and political entrepreneurs. In other words, the theory explicitly incorporates two kinds of theoretical assumptions that usually are treated as antithetical. In conflict analysis the competing theoretical perspectives are *relative deprivation* and *group mobilization*: the former contends that peoples' discontent about unjust deprivation is the primary motivation for political action, whereas the latter emphasizes leaders' calculated mobilization of group resources in response to changing political opportunities.[2] In studies of ethnonationalism the competing viewpoints are *primordialist* and *instrumentalist*: the former regards ethnic nationalism as a manifestation of a persisting cultural tradition based on a primordial sense of ethnic identity, whereas the latter interprets ethnicity as "an exercise in boundary maintenance" and assumes that communal movements are an instrumental response to differential treatment.[3]

It is evident from our research on politically active ethnic and communal groups that their mobilization and strategies are based on the interaction of both kinds of factors. Grievances about differential treatment and the sense of group cultural identity provide the essential bases for mobilization and shape the kinds of claims made by the group's leaders. If peoples' grievances and group identity are both weak, there is little chance that they can be mobilized by any political entrepreneurs in response to any external threat or opportunity. On the other hand, the conjunction of shared grievances with a strong sense of group identity and common interest—as among blacks in contemporary South Africa, and Shi'is and Kurds in Iraq— provides highly combustible material that fuels spontaneous action whenever external control weakens. The combination animates powerful political movements and sustained conflict whenever it can be organized and focused by group leaders who give plausible expression to minority peoples' grievances and aspirations.

Group History and Status

Four predisposing traits shape disadvantaged communal groups' sense of grievance and their potential for acting on it. Most of these conditions are the residues of long-term social and political processes and are relatively slow to change. The following arguments are specific to disadvantaged groups, but they are potentially applicable to advantaged minorities whenever they are threatened by the loss of their advantages. The essential difference for advantaged groups is that they ordinarily have more resources, sometimes all the powers of the state, for the organized defense of their interests. The four predisposing traits are listed on the left side of figure 5.1 and described as follows.

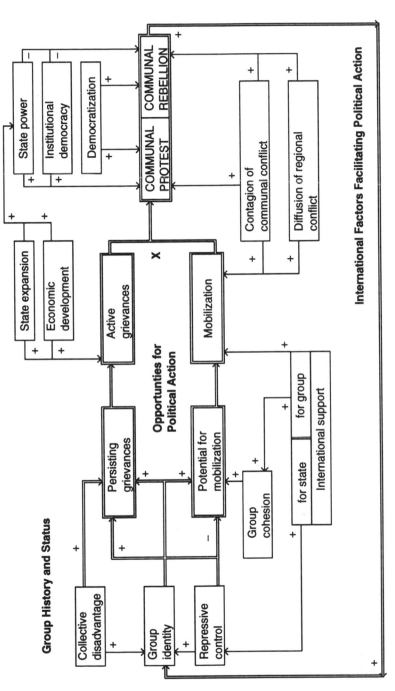

Figure 5.1. Processes of Communal Mobilization for Political Action.

Extent of Collective Disadvantage

The extent of a communal group's collective disadvantage vis-
à-vis other groups is a principal source of its members' grievances and perceptions that they have a common interest in
collective action. "Disadvantage" means socially derived inequalities in group members' material well-being or political access in comparison with other social groups. Three dimensions
of collective disadvantage (analyzed in chapter 2) are political
and economic differentials, group discrimination, and demographic and ecological stress. The analyses of chapter 3 demonstrated conclusively the connections between different kinds
of disadvantage and the kinds of political, economic, and social
grievances of communal groups articulated in the 1980s. These
grievances are the combustible materials around which political
leaders mobilize people for political action.

The general proposition, represented in the upper left quadrant of figure 5.1, is that a group's persisting grievances depend on the extent of its disadvantages and that the extent of
grievances in turn affects the group's potential for political
mobilization.

The Salience of Group Identity

Group identity usually is valued in and of itself but it varies
considerably in salience. Among threatened indigenous peoples
and conquered nations it is usually strong, but among ethnoclasses and some religious sects it is weakened by assimilation
and cross-cutting membership in plural associations. In groups
of all types, identity may be diluted by stratification and seg-
mentation within the group. The issue is whether the sense of
common identity is strong enough to overcome more narrow
loyalties to clans, classes, and communities within the group.

Three external conditions contribute to the salience of group
identity: (1) the severity of the communal group's disadvantages
in relation to other groups, (2) the extent of cultural differences
between a communal group and others with which it interacts,
and (3) the intensity of conflict with other groups and the state.
Disadvantages and cultural differences are slow to change,
whereas conflict with outgroups is more transient. Once a serious episode of conflict occurs, however, it leaves a persistent res-

idue in peoples' memories and for a long time after can be invoked by leaders to justify political action. Serbian nationalists, for example, made effective use of fifty-year-old memories about atrocities committed by the Croatian Ustashi to mobilize Serbian support for their 1991–92 war with breakaway Croatia.

The general proposition is that a group's grievances and potential for political mobilization both are influenced by the strength of group identity. The strength of identity, in turn, depends on intergroup disadvantages, cultural differentials, and the intensity of past and ongoing conflict with other groups and the state. These connections (except for the effects of cultural differentials) are diagrammed in figure 5.1. The linkage from communal protest and communal rebellion back to group identity is a feedback loop, symbolizing one of the essential mechanisms that sustains protracted communal conflicts.

Extent of Group Cohesion and Mobilization

Cohesive groups are held together by dense networks of communication and interaction. Mobilization means the extent to which group members are prepared to commit their energies and resources to collective action on behalf of their common interests. Cohesion is impaired in groups that have competing political movements and organizations (see chapter 3, "Mobilization of Grievance"). Effective mobilization in factionalized groups often depends on the formation of coalitions among diverse segments and contending leaders.[4] Failure to form coalitions reduces the scope and political impact of collective action and makes it easier for states to manage ethnopolitical challenges; for examples see chapter 10.

The extent of cohesion is a function of a group's social, political, and economic organization, past and present.[5] It tends to be greater among groups that are concentrated in a single region (e.g., the Kurds) rather than dispersed (e.g., the Chinese of Malaysia). Groups whose traditional authority structure is intact are relatively cohesive; so are those in command of a quasi-autonomous regional government. Religious movements can provide strong networks that form the basis for political mobilization, as the traditionally black churches did for the U.S. civil rights movement of the 1950s. Economic associations may play the same role: trade unions are the main vehicle for political activism by the Indian Tamil plantation workers of Sri Lanka (see chapter 1, n. 25). Modern political movements and parties are the most common agencies of communal political action, but it is rare for one political organization to incorporate most or all members of the group. The proposition is that a people's potential for political mobilization varies with the scope and strength of its preexisting organizational networks.

Foreign sympathizers can contribute substantially to a communal group's cohesion and political mobilization by providing material, political, and moral support. Indigenous rights organizations such as the American Indian Movement (in the 1970s) and the World Council of Indigenous Peoples (in the 1980s) have promoted the establishment of numerous indigenous peoples' movements. The Palestine Liberation Organization has directly organized and supported oppositional activity by Palestininans in Jordan, Lebanon, and Israel's Occupied Territories. Rebellious Iraqi Kurds have at various times had the diplomatic and material support of the shah of Iran, the Iranian revolutionary regime, Israel, and the United States (1972–75 and since 1991). Figure 5.1 incorporates schematically (in the lower left quadrant) the proposition that these kinds of external support both enhance group cohesion and contribute directly to its mobilization for communal action.

International support for a disadvantaged group may also aim at improving its condition, a relationship not shown in figure 5.1. The countries of origin of Europe's immigrant workers are acutely concerned about the workers' status in the host society. There is ongoing low-key, nonconflictual diplomacy between France and the countries of the Maghreb over these issues, as there has been between the governments of Germany and Turkey. The general tenor of these discussions is constructive; they aim at minimizing individual hardship and reducing the potential for communal and interstate conflict.

Repressive Control by Dominant Groups

Force unjustly applied provokes both anger and caution. Communal groups whose subordinate status is maintained by sustained force usually nurture deep grievances against dominant groups but are hesitant to act on them. The apparent apathy and acquiesence of Southern blacks to white dominance in the

United States before the 1950s, and of native peoples until the 1970s, was based on a hard-learned, culturally transmitted belief that open resistance to discrimination was very risky. Cultural norms of caution and myriad day-to-day calculations based on caution were a heavy drag on those peoples' efforts at mobilizing action on behalf of civil rights and tribal autonomy. Figure 5.1 incorporates this double-edged proposition: To the extent that a group's disadvantages have been established and maintained by force, its grievances and identity are intensified but its potential for political mobilization is reduced.

Military and developmental assistance and political support for states in plural Third World societies contribute to the maintenance of repressive control over communal minorities, as is also shown in figure 5.1. United States military, economic, and diplomatic support has been essential for the maintenance of Israel's continued control over the Palestinians of the West Bank and Gaza; far less well-known are decades of tacit U.S. support for Indonesian campaigns to subdue and incorporate the Papuans of Irian Jaya and the people of East Timor.[6] On the other hand, the United States participated in the international embargo on military and other assistance to South Africa's apartheid regime in the late 1980s. In a less publicized situation, the United States government also suspended military aid to Guatemala from 1977 to 1982 and again in 1983–84 to signal its opposition to the gross human rights violations by which military governments were suppressing Mayan-supported insurgency. In many other instances the support for embattled states has come from other Third World regimes. Examples include Cuban support for Marxist regimes fighting communal wars in Ethiopia (1977–90) and Angola (1975–90) and India's intervention in the Sri Lankan government's war with Tamil rebels (1987–90).[7]

Opportunities for Political Action

The processes by which grievances and the potential for mobilization are translated into protest and rebellion are too complex and contextually specific to be summarized in general propositions. Some episodes are reactive, such as the Los Angeles riots of 1965 and 1992, each of which was precipitated directly or indirectly by police use of force against individuals resisting arrest. But most ethnopolitical conflicts, including all sustained campaigns of protest and rebellion, are shaped by the strategic assessments and tactical decisions of the leaders and activists of communal groups.

The concept of *political opportunity* is useful for analyzing this central issue, because it directs attention to the factors that influence the making of communal decisions. Opportunity factors internal to the group are the extent of common grievances, the salience of group identity, and networks among its members: these are the elements from which leaders build political movements. Large structural factors outside the group also shape its opportunities, including the character of the state and its resources, and whether the group has transnational kindred; these factors are considered in the next two sections. More immediate factors are changes in the group's political environment, such as shifts in state power and policy, the prospects of attracting political allies, and the availability of international political and logistic support. These immediate factors influence the timing of political events, the kinds of claims made, and the choice of particular tactics.[8]

An example gives some substance to these bare-bones generalities. On Australia Day (January 26) in 1972 several young urban Aboriginal activists pitched a tiny tent on the lawn of Parliament House in Canberra, proclaiming it an Aboriginal "embassy" to the government. This event followed nearly a decade of episodic protest over land rights and civil rights issues by local groups; the precipitant of the "embassy" declaration was an announcement by the Liberal party prime minister that Aborigines would not be granted freehold rights to their large reserves in the Northern Territory. The Aboriginal embassy proved to be a brilliant tactical stroke, because it took advantage of two shifts in political opportunity. First, it immediately preceded the campaign for national elections, and second, it coincided with a Southeast Asia Treaty Organization conference in Canberra, with attendant international press coverage. The federal government inadvertently added to the publicity given the Aboriginal demands by staging a six-month-long comic opera of police, political, and legal machinations to get rid of the tent embassy. Aboriginal land rights were taken up as an issue by the Labor party, which won the 1972 elections and instituted major changes in policy toward Aborigines.[9]

It is not clear from their accounts how calculating activists Kevin Gilbert and Tony Corey were about the opportunities facing them when they decided to pitch a tent on Australia Day: they acted initially from a strong sense of collective grievance. But there is no doubt whatever that once they saw the possibilities inherent in the situation, they and their supporters played it for full political effect. The case suggests in microcosm just how complex are the processes that lead from grievances to mobilization to protest.

Global Processes That Intensify Grievances

Returning to the macro level, large changes in the global system since 1945 have intensified the grievances of many communal groups. Two of these, the growth of the modern state system and the global economy, are incorporated in the model. A third, the communications revolution, is not analyzed separately, because it facilitates or enhances almost all other causes: rapid and dense communication networks make communal groups more aware of their disadvantages, bring them in closer contact with supporters elsewhere, and help leaders mobilize mass followings.

Expansion of the State

Virtually all the new and postrevolutionary states in the world system have been committed to consolidating and expanding their power, following the precedents established by the successful states of the industrial North. This objective dictates, among other things, that states subordinate the special interests and relative autonomy of hundreds of ethnic groups to their own conception of national identity and interest. State building almost everywhere in the Third World has meant policies aimed at assimilating communal group members, restraining their historical autonomy, and extracting their resources, revenues, and labor for the use of the state. The building of new Communist states in Eastern Europe after 1945 had the same implications and consequences.

Some communal groups, including most of the overseas Chinese of Southeast Asia, have been able to share power and prosperity at the center of new states. Others—especially in Africa, where the reach of state power is limited—have been able to hold on to de facto local autonomy. But the net effect of state building in most parts of the world has been to substantially increase grievances of the majority of ethnic and communal groups that have not been able either to protect their autonomy or to participate meaningfully in governing coalitions.

The Development of a Global Economic System

The worldwide impetus to industrialize and to exploit underutilized human and natural resources has benefited some ethnic and communal groups and harmed others. Ethnoclasses in developing societies have often benefited from expanding economic opportunities; some also have mobilized in efforts to overcome discriminatory barriers that restricted their access to new wealth. Indigenous peoples have been most adversely affected. Like it or not, their resources and labor are being absorbed into national and international networks of economic activity. They are almost always disadvantaged by the terms of their incorporation. Their reactions have been especially sharp in response to the alienation of the lands, forests, and natural resources on which they are culturally as well as materially dependent.

The effects of state expansion and global economic development on communal grievances are shown schematically in the upper middle part of figure 5.1 The effects of state power on the political context and strategies of communal action are assessed in the last section of this chapter.

International Diffusion and Contagion of Conflict

The political and economic dimensions of modernization have inadvertently added to the grievances of many communal groups and have pushed some of them into reactive or defensive communal protest and rebellion. Two other international factors have facilitated their mobilization by increasing the opportunities and incentives for political action: the diffusion and contagion of communal conflict elsewhere (see the lower right quadrant of figure 5.1).

Diffusion of Political Action among Transnational Kindred

Diffusion refers to the "spillover" processes by which conflict in one country directly affects political organization and action in adjoining countries. The most important spillover effects in communal conflict occur among groups that straddle interstate boundaries. Political activists in one country often find sanctuary with and get support from their transnational kindred; generations of Kurdish leaders and fighters in Turkey, Syria, Iraq, and Iran have sustained one another's political movements in these ways. If a disadvantaged group's kindred are a favored or dominant group in a neighboring state, they often can count on their diplomatic, political, and sometimes military support. The Philippine Moros had the political and material support of the Malaysian government during the early phase of their 1970s civil war against the Marcos regime, partly because Malaysians sympathized with their Muslim coreligionists, partly because Malaysia wanted a counter to Philippine claims to the Malaysian province of Sabah.

Communal groups also may be able to take risky advantage of interstate warfare to pursue their own interests. At the end of World War II, Soviet help enabled the Kurds to establish the Mahabad Republic in northwestern Iran; it was soon suppressed by the Iranian government. Various Kurdish factions continued to pursue autonomy during the Iran-Iraq War and in the aftermath of the 1991 Gulf War. In this and most other examples we have identified, spillover effects contribute to communal rebellion, not protest. Of the groups in the Minorities at Risk study nearly two-thirds (159 of 233) have kindred in one or more adjacent countries. The general proposition is that a disadvantaged group's potential for mobilization and communal rebellion is increased by the number of segments of the group in adjoining countries, by the extent to which those segments are mobilized (whether as disadvantaged minorities or as a dominant group in control of the state), and by their involvement in open conflict (including civil and interstate war).

Contagion of Communal Activism

Contagion refers to the processes by which one group's actions provide inspiration and strategic and tactical guidance for groups elsewhere: the diffusion of conflict is direct, contagion is indirect. While there is some evidence that internal conflict is generally contagious, we think the strongest force of communal contagion occurs within networks of similar groups.[10] Informal connections have developed among communal groups, especially since the 1960s, so that, for example, one finds New South Wales Aborigines in the early 1960s organizing freedom rides, and Dayaks in northern Borneo in the 1980s resisting commercial logging of their forests with rhetoric and tactics remarkably like those used by native Canadian peoples in 1990.

More precisely, networks of communication, political support, and material assistance have developed among similar groups that face similar circumstances. The two most dense and well-organized networks, discussed below, link Islamic minorities and indigenous peoples. Groups that are tied into these networks acquire better techniques for effective mobilization: plausible appeals, good leadership, and organizational skills. Equally or more important, they benefit from the inspiration of successful movements elsewhere, successes that provide the images and moral incentives that motivate activists.

Around the periphery of the Islamic world are three faultlines—in Africa, Central Asia, and Southeast Asia—across which Islamic and non-Islamic peoples confront one another. The reassertion of traditional religious and political values throughout the Islamic world has encouraged self-assertion by Islamic minorities among states straddling the fault lines that are governed by Christian, Marxist, and Buddhist majorities. In a number of instances moral encouragement for Muslim minorities has been accompanied by material and diplomatic support. Malaysian support for the Moros was a relatively early example. Libya also provided assistance for the Moros, as it has for politically radical Muslim movements in a number of other countries. Since 1979, Iran's revolutionary Islamic government has encouraged resistance by Shi'is in Lebanon and the Gulf region. Meetings of the Organization of the Islamic Conference provide a forum for the exchange of ideas and encouragement among activists and officials of Islamic states.

The global indigenous rights movement stems from the coalescence in the 1970s of regional groups like the American Indian Movement and the Circumpolar Arctic People's Conference. They soon established contact with indigenous peoples throughout the world. Since the early 1980s the World Council of Indigenous Peoples has provided one of several global foci for discussions, publicity, and joint action. Conferences, newsletters, personal visits, and representations to United Nations bodies have communicated a common vocabulary of grievances and demands, rationales for action, models of political organization, and examples of successful strategies and tactics for the defense of group interests.[11]

Networks of more limited scope connect the Roma minorities of Europe and North America and regional autonomists in Europe's "Celtic fringe"—Brittany, Wales, Scotland, and Ireland. And temporary alliances developed during the 1980s among ethnonationalists facing a common opponent, for example, the mountain tribes of Burma, the ethnonational rebels of Ethiopia, and the Baltic peoples.

Effects of State Power and Democracy on Political Action

The political context of communal action is set by the state's political institutions and capabilities. Political systems shape the opportunity structures that guide communal choices among exit, loyalty, and voice. If the choice is voice, then the openness and resources of the state influence what groups demand and their strategic choices about protest or rebellion. Our observations in the Minorities at Risk study point to the special significance of three factors: the scope of state power, the political values and practices of institutionalized democracy, and the destabilizing effects of democratization. Some of the connections among these variables and communal political action are shown in the upper right quadrant of figure 5.1.

Uses of State Power

In virtually all postcolonial and postrevolutionary states, state building has meant policies aimed at assimilating communal group members, restraining their collective autonomy, and extracting their resources and labor for the use of the state. The end result of this process is powerful, resource-rich states with the capacity both to accommodate and to suppress communal minorities at relatively low cost, depending on the preferences of their elites. Rulers of weaker states face more stark, zero-sum choices. They can expand the governing coalition at risk to their own positions, or they can devote scarce resources to all-out warfare against communal rebels. The alternative of letting ethnonationalists secede has rarely been chosen voluntarily. The example provided by the breakup of the Soviet Union, in a process that was largely peaceful, may prove to be a historical fluke or the beginning of a reverse trend.[12]

The growth of state power is likely to have cross-cutting effects on communal action: increased grievances, increased costs of acting on them, and increased payoffs of cooperating with and assimilating to dominant groups. It follows that communal political action in the most powerful states is likely to be limited in scope and to take the form of protest, whereas protracted communal conflict will typify weak states that are attempting to extend their reach.

There is substantial evidence in support of these two propositions. In a correlational study using the Minorities at Risk data, we find a weak positive correlation of .180 between an indicator of the extent of state power and the magnitude of communal protest in the 1980s, but no correlation with communal rebellion. The process of expanding state power, however, shifted communal action away from protest ($r = -.242$) and provoked rebellion ($r = +.230$).[13] Examination of states scoring highest on the indicator of expanding state power shows that most were activist Third World regimes, a number of which sought to establish state socialism during the 1960s and 1970s: Burma, Laos, Algeria, Guinea, Ethiopia, and Nicaragua.

In these and nonsocialist countries such as the Philippines, Sri Lanka, Mali, Sudan, and Zambia, the expansion of state efforts to control resources and socioeconomic activity more or less directly stimulated resistance by adversely affected communal groups. Most of the negative impact of state expansion was felt among ethnonationalists and indigenous peoples whose autonomy and resources were being subjected to central control. Given their situations, regional rebellion was a more feasible and promising strategy than urban-based protest.

Institutionalized Democracies

The resolution of ethnopolitical conflicts in institutionalized democracies depends most fundamentally on the implemention of universalistic norms of equal rights and opportunities for all citizens, including ethnoclasses, and pluralistic accommodation of indigenous and regional peoples' desires for separate collective status.[14] Empirical comparisons have shown that communal minorities in the advanced industrial democracies face few political barriers (chapter 2, tables 2.1 and 2.3) and are more likely to use the tactics of protest than rebellion (chapter 4, table 4.2). The reasons are inherent in the political cultures and policies of contemporary democratic societies. In the past half-century the political leaders of these societies have become relatively responsive to the interests of politicized communal groups, in particular to groups able to mobilize large constituencies and allies in persistent campaigns of protest. Groups using violent protest and terrorism, on the other hand, have risked backlash and loss of public support. Thus, the calculus of communal action in democracies favors protest over rebellion.

The advanced industrial democracies also score high among the activist and powerful states, which means that they have the resources to respond favorably to grievances expressed within the democratic framework. On this count again, the opportunity structure for communal groups provides incentives for protest and disincentives for rebellion.

Democratizing Autocracies

Democratization is the process whereby many formerly autocratic states in the Second World and Third World are attempting to establish more participatory and responsive political systems. The success of democratization in general and its effects on communal conflict are problematic.[15] The Soviet and Eastern European regimes relaxed coercive restraints on nationalism and intergroup hostilities at a time when the institutionalized means for their expression and accommodation did not yet exist, or were fragile and distrusted. The successor republics of the USSR face the same uncertainties. The result has been a resurgence of communal activism, both protest and rebellion.[16] Similar consequences can be expected to follow from democratization in multiethnic Third World autocracies. The most dubious expectation of all is that authoritarian states such as Sudan, Iraq, and Burma might be able to defuse ethnopolitical wars by moving toward democracy.

Two general propositions about the effects of state institutions and power on political action by communal groups are incorporated in figure 5.1. In long-established democracies the opportunities for ethnic mobilization are substantial and the potential payoffs are significant—for cohesive groups that rely largely on nonviolent tactics. The proposition is that institutionalized democracy facilitates nonviolent communal protest and inhibits communal rebellion. This tendency is reinforced in strong states, those that have ample power and resources to respond to pluralist interests. The relative lack of state resources is one of the reasons why democracy in a weak multiethnic state such as Lebanon had little staying power.

In democratizing autocracies, by contrast, the opportunities for communal groups to mobilize are substantial, but states usually lack the resources or institutional means to reach the kinds of accommodations that typify the established democracies. In these states, democratization is likely to facilitate both protest and communal rebellion. The serious risk is that the rejection of accommodation by one or all contenders will lead to civil war and the reimposition of coercive rule.

It is worth pointing out again that both the USSR and the Federal Republic of Yugoslavia faced this situation in 1990–91. The majority of Soviet and Russian leaders chose democracy and decentralization; Serbian nationalists chose to fight rather than switch, with devastating short-term consequences. Ethiopia is a state that has reached the same choice point by a different path: protracted communal conflicts culminated early in 1991 in the seizure of power at the center by a coalition of contending groups. The question is whether the contenders will continue to act on the principles that brought them victory. If they do so, the independence of Eritrea will have to be accepted, along with the right of all other communal contenders to some combination of regional autonomy and shared power in Addis Ababa. In mid-1992 it appeared that Ethiopia's new leaders were following the Soviet precedent toward democracy and decentralization. But there will be for a long time the risk that those who inherit the wreckage of multinational empires will attempt to recreate them.

6. Minorities in the Western Democracies and Japan

From a global viewpoint, minorities in the western democracies and Japan have two distinctive traits. Their grievances usually are expressed in protest, rarely in rebellion, and the most common response by governments in the late twentieth century is to accommodate their interests rather than forcibly subordinate or incorporate them. There are two plausible and reinforcing reasons. First, individual members of most minorities in contemporary democracies in principle enjoy the same civil and political rights and benefit from the same social and economic programs as other citizens. Thus they seldom experience the severe forms of discrimination and repression practiced in many authoritarian and Third World societies, and they usually have opportunities to move into the dominant society if they choose to do so. These conditions tend to reduce the intensity of individual and collective grievances about communal issues.[1]

Second, the cost-benefit calculus of collective action strongly favors protest over rebellion. Minorities in late twentieth-century democracies have both the right and the opportunities to mobilize for political action aimed at protecting and promoting their collective interests, whether they define those interests as cultural recognition, affirmative action, or regional autonomy. Moreover, the political cultures of western democracies encourage the accommodation of contending interests, so that campaigns of minority protest prompt elites to devise and apply strategies of concessions and incorporation like those used to manage other conflicts. On the other hand, mass publics in western societies resent and react against the use of disruptive and violent tactics on behalf of any political or communal minority, which means that terrorism and rebellion are high-risk strategies that are much more likely to lead to publicly supported repression than to accommodation.[2]

Nonetheless, there is considerable variation among democracies in the status and claims of minorities, in their modes of political action, and in political outcomes. Jurg Steiner suggests, for example, that the Swiss have perfected power-sharing arrangements that minimize conflict among their country's four major communal groups, whereas the prevailing model in the United States is winner-take-all power competition among ethnic groups.[3] Some of the differences on the continuum from Swiss-style power sharing to American-style power competition can be traced to different historical experiences of intergroup conflict and state consolidation, which we will consider in the following case studies. A more basic source of variation is a consequence of the traits of the minorities themselves: it is politically more difficult to share power with ethnoclasses than to devolve power to indigenous peoples and regionally concentrated communal groups.

The early stages of political mobilization of ethnoclasses in democracies typically has been motivated by desires for equal opportunity and incorporation, as in the U.S. civil rights movement during the 1950s. These claims typically impinge directly on members of the dominant group—on their job opportunities, their housing and schools, and their political influence in local and national affairs. The result may not be incorporation of the minority but, rather, countermobilization based on intergroup animosities, followed by the institutionalization of competitive but unequal ethnic politics. Switzerland is not immune to this kind of problem, because it is home to one million immigrant workers, mainly of Southern European origin, who are denied full political rights. Though it is widely recognized that most are by now permanent settlers, the native Swiss have defeated initiatives to liberalize immigrants' status (for example, in 1981 and 1982), and even the Swiss-born children of foreigners are ordinarily denied citizenship.

In contrast, regional peoples in democratic societies usually have better chances of accommodation because they can win (or in the Swiss case, retain) substantial local autonomy and control of their own resources without seriously threatening the political or economic interests of other groups. The situation is similar for indigenous peoples such as Native Americans: it usually is politically feasible for officials to accommodate the demands of indigenous peoples for local autonomy, because doing so threatens few other societal interests. Thus a paradox arises: ethnoclasses, even if they are large and empowered, seem to have poorer prospects of making substantial gains in democracies than regionally concentrated communal and indigenous groups have. The plausibility of this general thesis will be examined in the case studies that form the core of this chapter. First, though, we survey the minorities at risk in the twenty-one advanced industrial democracies.

Comparative Overview of Minorities at Risk

Almost all the advanced industrial democracies have one or more distinct ethnic or communal minorities, from the Ainu and Koreans in Japan to the French-speaking Walloons of Belgium and the Inuits of Canada and Alaska. All of them also have resident immigrants and refugees from other continents who thus far lack the numbers, status, and coherence to qualify for inclusion. We identified twenty-four groups in these countries that were at risk in the 1980s because of differential treatment and persistent political mobilization.[4] We evaluated other communal groups but concluded that they did not meet the criteria. Among them were the Walloons in Belgium and the Swedish minority in Finland, both of whom enjoy full rights and collective power sharing; and Scottish and Welsh nationalists, who have pursued their regional interests exclusively through conventional politics. These judgments are timebound. In the 1960s the Walloons were at risk, and other French-speaking Belgians arguably are at risk now.[5] Scottish nationalism was intense in the 1960s and is in the ascendant in the early 1990s. Regional groups that decisively fail to meet our criteria include the Galicians of Spain, the Frisians of the Netherlands and northern Germany, and the Danish and German minorities in Germany and Denmark, respectively. These groups have benefited from public policies aimed at assimilation or accommodation and their cultural identities are vestigial, their communal grievances minor, and their political activism limited. Of much greater concern are emerging ethnoclasses among Second World and Third World immigrants and refugees in a number of western societies.

The twenty-four minorities at risk in democratic societies numbered an estimated eighty-four million people in 1990 and made up 10.7 percent of the total regional population. All are listed in Appendix table A.1 with data on their size, status, and involvement in political action. Eight are ethnoclasses, ten are ethnonationalists, five are indigenous people, and one (the Turkish Muslims of Greece) is a religious minority.[6]

By comparison with other regions, minorities in democracies are relatively small in both numbers and proportions. Individually they have an average of 3.5 million members (less than the mean for all other regions except Latin America) and average less than 5 percent of their country populations (the lowest of all five regions).[7] Only Canada and the United States have more than one-fifth of their populations at risk, while Switzerland, Spain, France, and New Zealand range between 10 and 20 percent, as shown in table 6.1.

These percentages suggest another reason why minority conflicts are relatively muted in western societies: it is easier for the political leaders of prosperous democracies to accommodate or control groups that make up 2 percent or even 10 percent of the population than it is for leaders of poorer countries to accommodate the more intense grievances of proportionally larger groups—for example the Ndebele of Zimbabwe (one-fifth the country's population) and the Shi'is of Lebanon (one-third).

Objective ethnocultural differences in language, customs, religion, and physical appearance between the twenty-four minorities and dominant social groups are less than those in any other world region.[8] Minorities in western democracies and Japan also tend to be geographically more widely dispersed than groups in any other region (according to our group concentration indicator, CONCEN; see Appendix tables A.1 to A.6) and have fewer transnational segments (0.6 per group, which is half the global mean). These patterns are due partly to the personal mobility and tendencies toward assimilation that characterize most democratic societies. They also imply that social and cultural barriers to accommodation of minority interests should be less obstructive than in other world regions.

When we compare intergroup differentials and inequalities (see Appendix table A.7), the problems and grievances of minorities in democratic societies come into sharper focus. Except for immigrant workers from outside the European Community,

Table 6.1. Minorities as Proportion of Total Population in Some of the Western Democracies.

Country	Minorities at Risk	Proportion of Population
Canada	French Canadians	.256
	Native peoples	.023
United States	African Americans	.123
	Hispanics	.084
	Native peoples	.007
Switzerland	Foreign workers	.145
	Jurassiens	.022
Spain	Catalans	.101
	Basques	.045
France	Bretons	.068
	Afro-Arabs	.034
	Corsicans	.006
	Basques	.004
New Zealand	Maori	.100

minorities' political rights and status are not badly impaired. Our indicator of political differentials (POLDIF) shows that, on average, minorities in democracies have a mean score of 1.2 (1 = slight differentials in political positions and rights, 2 = substantial differentials), which is significantly below the global mean of 1.6. On the political discrimination indicator (POLDIS) they also fare better than most groups elsewhere: nine minorities in democracies experience none, ten others are low (defined as substantial underrepreresentation in politics due to historical neglect or restrictions), and only five encounter deliberate political discrimination.[9] On both these indicators, democratic minorities faced fewer political liabilities in the 1980s than minorities in any other region except Eastern Europe and the USSR.

Material inequalities are the crux of most communal grievances in democratic societies, as was shown in chapters 2 and 3. They are sharply differentiated from majority groups and also score high on demographic stress: fourteen have younger populations and poorer public health than dominant groups. But few of these material differentials are deliberately maintained; in only seven cases is inequality the result of prevailing social practice or public policy.[10]

There is thus a particular kind of dissonance in the status of many minorities in western democracies: they are culturally differentiated and materially deprived but are politically empowered. The dissonance is evident in the patterns of grievance expressed by communal leaders in the 1980s: their economic grievances were greater and more salient than political and social grievances. In other regions, in contrast, political or social demands, or both, outweigh economic ones. Communal leaders and political entrepreneurs in democracies also are relatively free to build political movements and to use a wide repertoire of techniques of conventional and unconventional action to pursue their material interests. One index of their success in political mobilization is the 3.8 mean score of democratic minorities on the group coherence indicator (COHERE; see Appendix table A.1), which is second only to groups in Africa, where the basis for cohesion is cultural tradition rather than modern associations.

Another prominent feature of ethnopolitics in western democracies is the quest of regional and indigenous peoples for greater autonomy. Fifteen of the groups expressed demands for greater autonomy and eleven of them had active separatist or autonomy movements in the 1980s, on a par with the Middle East and Asia and proportionally far more than in Latin America, Africa, or even Eastern Europe and the USSR, where widespread but latent separatism exploded in 1990–91 (see chapter 7). Autonomists almost always invoke the desire to preserve their culture and identity; grievances about regional poverty and demands for greater allocations of public funds are usually a secondary theme in advanced industrial democracies, in part because some ethnonationalist regions are relatively prosperous.

The democratic framework facilitates mobilization around minorities' grievances: every one of the twenty-four groups used nonviolent political tactics at some time between 1945 and 1989, while half of them gave rise to violent protest and half had militant factions that used terrorism. No minority conflicts in democratic societies escalated from terrorism to guerrilla or civil wars, though the conflict in Northern Ireland came close. The comparison in table 6.2 shows that rebellion is distinctively associated with ethnonationalist groups, all but one of which used terrorist tactics at some time during the 1970s and 1980s.[11] Three radical ethnoclass organizations also used terror tactics:

Table 6.2. Strategies of Political Action by Minorities in Democratic
Societies in 1970–89.

Group Type (and number)	Number of Groups Using Each Strategy		
	Nonviolent Protest	Violent Protest	Terrorism
Ethnoclasses (8)	8	4	3
Ethnonationalists (10)*	9	4	9
Indigenous peoples (5)	5	1	0
Religious sects (1)	1	0	0

*The only ethnonationalists who did not use nonviolent protest in the 1970s and 1980s were the Germans of South Tyrol; they did so in the previous decades. The only ethnonationalists who did not use terrorism during the period were the Jurassiens in Switzerland; they did employ terrorism in the 1960s.

the Black Liberation Army in the United States (early 1970s), militant Puerto Rican nationalists (from 1950 to the present), and the Black Liberation Front in Britain (late 1980s). The ethnoclasses that protested violently in the past two decades were Afro-Caribbeans in Britain, African Americans in the United States, Maghrebins in France, and the Roma (in one isolated incident in Spain). Native Americans, mainly supporters of the American Indian Movement, were responsible for localized acts of violent protest in the 1970s. The violent protests of summer 1990 by Mohawks in Quebec began after our survey was completed.

There is another important observation to be made about the sequences of political action by minorities in the democracies. Virtually all of the eighteen groups that used violent protest or terrorism, or both, did so only after varying periods of nonviolent activism. Setting aside two exceptions, an average of thirteen years elapsed between the establishment of political movements representing communal interests and the first occurrence of violence.[12] Historical context explains the two apparent exceptions. In Northern Ireland the Irish Republic Army (IRA) carried out a few bombings in the late 1950s, but the current episode of protracted conflict began with a nonviolent Catholic civil rights movement in 1968, followed by counterrioting that provided an opportunity for the IRA to reengage. The other exception is the Puerto Rican nationalist movement: a nationalist party was active on the island from the 1920s onward, but the first overt act of nationalists after 1945 was the attempted assassination of President Truman in 1950.

We can put some meat on the bare bones of these comparisons by examining the three group types separately and illustrating each with several brief case studies.

Ethnoclasses

There are eight distinct ethnoclasses in the democracies and many others in the process of formation. The eight are Afro-Caribbeans and Asians in Britain (counted as one aggregate group); African Americans and Hispanics in the United States; immigrant workers in France, Germany, and Switzerland; Koreans in Japan; and the Roma of Western Europe. Except for African Americans, most members of these ethnoclasses are descendants of twentieth-century immigrants who took low-paying factory and service jobs in expanding industrial societies. Racial hostility and discrimination have a much longer history in the United States but were considerably reduced by active public policy in the second half of the twentieth century. The Roma and other travelers are the odd group out in this set: "odd" because most prefer their centuries-long seminomadic existence to permanent settlement and assimilation, "out" because they are widely regarded with suspicion and denied rights and services by the Europeans with whom they uneasily coexist.[13]

The at-risk status of these ethnoclasses is due to racial enmity by dominant groups, informal but widespread economic discrimination, and (in continental Europe) denial of citizenship and full political rights to many immigrant workers and their families who originate outside the European Community. These conditions are increasing throughout Western Europe in response to the fact and fear of a new influx of immigrants and refugees from the Third World and Eastern Europe. Surveys in 1990–91 show public antipathy to the new immigrants among nearly 80 percent of (West) Germans, more than two-thirds of the British, and more than 70 percent of the French.[14] Discrimination and hostility are primary causes of ethnogenesis: shared identity, grievances, and political activism among emergent ethnoclasses like Maghrebins in France and Afro-Canadians are the cumulative consequences of malign treatment by dominant groups.[15] Some democracies, the Netherlands and Sweden among them, have incorporated Third World immigrants into their respective societies with little overt conflict. Elsewhere, for instance in Germany and Italy, anti-immigrant hostility is palpable and often violent.[16]

We examine the status and mobilization of two major ethnoclasses in greater detail: the Afro-Caribbeans and Asians of Britain, and the Afro-Arabs in France.

Afro-Caribbeans and Asians in Great Britain

Britain's 2.3 million people of color, or blacks, include a number of distinct immigrant groups from the New (i.e. non-European) Commonwealth countries. On our indicator of group coherence they are coded as a fragmented group with sharp subgroup divisions. About half are Afro-Caribbeans from Jamaica, Trinidad, and other Caribbean countries (plus some Africans), most of whom originated in an immigrant flow that began immediately after World War II. Most others are Asians from India and Pakistan, East Africa, and East Indian communities in the Caribbean who immigrated somewhat later, most heavily in the 1960s. Although of different ethnicity, regional origin, and religion (most Asians are Muslims or Hindus), blacks are defined in British political discourse and social policy as a single group. Moreover, though they have somewhat different social positions and occupations, they are heavily concentrated in the same inner-city districts of London and old industrial cities in the Midlands, and they face similar discriminatory barriers. There also are emergent tensions between the two groups, arising mainly from the growing relative affluence of Asians.[17]

Differential Status

Both groups have faced discriminatory barriers in housing and access to most middle and higher status occupations, partly because of racist and class attitudes among white Britons, partly because of cultural differences. Afro-Caribbeans have had chronic difficulties in schooling and a long history of antagonistic

relations with the police. They are concentrated in service occupations and have very high unemployment rates. In contrast,
first-generation Asians often speak English poorly, but their
children do well in school. They once worked mainly in low-
skilled industrial jobs but have become increasingly successful
in family-owned businesses. Their unemployment rates are now
near the national average.

In addition to facing substantial economic discrimination,
both groups have been targets of sporadic violence since the late
1950s by gangs of white youths engaged in what they called
"nigger hunting" and "pakibashing." Serious riots against Afro-
Caribbeans took place in 1948 and 1958. In the mid-1980s
there were hundreds of arson attacks on Asian homes, especially in London's East End, some of them fatal. And a 1988
survey of Asians in Glasgow found that more than a third had
recently experienced racial violence, threats, or harassment in
their neighborhoods.[18]

Mobilization and Political Action

There are a great many local organizations concerned with
communal issues, including at least 160 Muslim groups that are
represented by an umbrella group, the Union of Muslim Organizations. Most leaders of the separate ethnic communities have
cooperated with one another in the pursuit of common interests, and a number of joint organizations encompass both Afro-
Caribbeans and Asians at local and national levels. Their national organizations have never had influence like that of the
National Association for the Advancement of Colored People in
the 1950s or the Southern Christian Leadership Conference in
the 1960s, however.[19]

Collective action, while widespread, has been largely local
and spontaneous. Moreover, blacks in Britain did not use demonstrations and riots until a decade or more after the first major
episodes of collection action by African Americans. Urban demonstrations by Afro-Caribbean protestors in Britain became increasingly common during the 1970s, often leading to confrontations with police. Waves of deadly and protracted urban riots
erupted in 1980–81 and again in 1985–86. These episodes
were precipitated by racially loaded encounters with police but

quickly assumed a general antiestablishment character. Afro-Caribbeans were the main actors; some Asian and white youths also took part. Throughout the 1980s, small-scale demonstrations and clashes with police were common. A group called the Black Liberation Army began a series of mail bombings in 1987 after a black man suffocated during a struggle with police in Wolverhampton and they continued in 1988, with the avowed purpose of protecting the black community from police harassment.

Policies and Prospects

The liberal British for a long time favored assimilation, a preference reflected in their praising some Afro-Caribbeans as "black Englishmen." But there are sharp limits on the feasibility of assimilation in an economically static and class-conscious society, which Britain was for most of the postwar period. Thus, in response to intense political pressure from white Britons concerned about economic competition and racial tensions, a succession of British governments restricted, then virtually prohibited, further Third World immigration through acts passed in 1962, 1968, 1971, and 1981. Public authorities deserve credit for making persistent and thoroughgoing legal efforts to reduce discriminatory barriers by passing a series of race relations acts between 1965 and 1976, the last of which provided effective means of redress for individual victims. There also has been a noticeable shift away from assimilation and integration toward multiculturalism in public discourse about racialism. But few public funds have been provided for remedial and economic programs either by Labour governments of the 1970s or Conservative governments of the 1980s.

On the political front, the energies of many blacks are being absorbed in party politics, with the Labour party taking the lead. Many have been elected to local councils, and the first four black members of Parliament (three Afro-Caribbeans, one Asian) were elected from pro-Labour constituencies in the 1987 general election. The first black Conservative member of Parliament, a barrister, was elected in 1992. The balance sheet, therefore, shows some economic mobility for people of color, especially Asians; a shift from assimilation toward acceptance of multiculturalism; substantial legal efforts to guarantee the civil and political rights of minorities; and the beginnings of political incorporation.

Afro-Arabs in France[20]

The status and prospects of Afro-Asian immigrants to Britain resemble those of African Americans in the United States: they have full civil and political rights but are subject to racial harassment (more so in Britain than the United States) and face mainly class barriers to economic advancement. Their situation is somewhat better than that of France's Maghrebins and other African immigrants: the Afro-Arabs face serious cultural as well as class obstacles to acceptance and have limited access to higher education and better jobs, and the political rights of those who are immigrants are restricted as a matter of public policy.[21]

The 1990 census showed a total of 3.6 million foreign residents in France, about 7 percent of the total population. Most were immigrant workers who came to France after World War II to meet the growing demand in the lower levels of the labor market, where wages and working conditions were too poor to attract citizens. The new immigrants followed a pattern established in the 1920s, when three million foreign workers entered France in a government-sponsored flood. These immigrants, past and present, have more or less voluntarily accepted the conditions that apply to migrant workers throughout Europe: government regulation of employment, lack of citizenship and the right to vote or hold public office, and restrictions on collective bargaining rights. Unlike the Germans and the Swiss, however, the French regard themselves as a "society of immigration" and do not discourage naturalization. Thus many foreigners have become citizens and their children are encouraged to integrate into French society, in much the same way the children of immigrants have been assimilated into mainstream U.S. and Canadian society.

Differential Status

The most impoverished and maligned immigrant workers are the Maghrebins and black Africans from former French colonies, especially Senegal. These Afro-Arab workers numbered about 1.9 million in 1990; sharply distinct in culture and religion from the French and from European immigrants, they thus face the greatest obstacles to integration or to acceptance of the right to be different. Among them are several hundred thousand undocumented foreigners who are not counted in official enumerations; most work for minimum, often exploitative wages. Only 60 percent of Afro-Arab workers hold full-time jobs; during the 1980s, French business reduced the hiring of immigrants by some 40 percent, despite continued immigration.[22]

Politically the Maghrebins are the object of the openly racist policies of the National Front party, which advocates their repatriation, and whose leader, Jean-Marie Le Pen, polled 14 percent of the first-round vote in the 1988 presidential elections. Socially they usually are separated from families (about 70 percent of Maghrebins in France are males), they face increasing restrictions on family immigration, and many live in shanty towns or *foyers* (improvised barracks).

Political Mobilization and Action

Afro-Arab workers have been politically volatile for the past two decades. They have formed many cultural, political, and self-help associations—at least 850 of them, according to one expert.[23] They have initiated frequent wildcat strikes and intense protests over inadequate housing, tightened government controls, and the politically inspired murders of Maghrebins and Africans by white racists. Most strikes and demonstrations have been localized rather than nationally coordinated events. The exceptions include coordinated demonstrations against racism in which French sympathizers have joined Afro-Arabs. In addition to workplace organizations, often linked to leftist unions, the Afro-Arab workers have countrywide associations based on their countries of origin. The Algerian, Moroccan, and Tunisian workers' organizations have been particularly active.

Protection and promotion of Arab identity was the binding force of countrywide Maghrebin political associations such as SOS-Racisme during the early 1980s. A shift toward mainstreaming and ethnic politics was evident by the late 1980s, exemplified by France-Plus, founded in 1985 to mobilize the one million or more Beurs, the citizen-descendants of North African immigrants.[24] The aim of such groups now is to make of the Franco-Maghrebins an ethnic voting bloc and lobbying group, politically incorporated in French society but pursuing Muslims' particular cultural and religious interests.

Policies and Prospects

There are two distinct thrusts to government policy toward the Afro-Arabs: regulation of immigrant labor and promotion of cultural pluralism. Workers' status is regulated through a system of residence permits and legal restrictions on naturalization. These restrictions are offset, to a degree, by legislation enacted in the early 1980s that gave noncitizen workers collective bargaining rights as well as the right to vote in union and labor tribunal elections. Policies of cultural pluralism, initiated by Socialist governments during the 1980s, are a departure from the traditional French emphasis on assimilation. For Afro-Arabs, citizens and noncitizens alike, the policies mean representation on regional and national commissions concerned with Maghrebin affairs, encouragement for voluntary associations, public funds for teaching Arabic and promoting Islamic culture, and government responses, albeit grudging, to Afro-Arab political pressures. These policies may be less relevant to immigrant workers than for Franco-Maghrebin citizens.

The limits of multiculturalism were highlighted in a controversy that erupted late in 1989 when a junior high school principal prohibited three Muslim girls from wearing the *chador* (scarf or foulard) in school. Afro-Arab resistance on this and related issues was seen by both the political left and the right as evidence of Muslims' rejection of the secular principles of French society. The immediate controversy was managed by an administrative rule from the Conseil d'Etat, which permitted the "nonprovocative" wearing of religious symbols but also gave local authorities license to decide whether wearing the *chador* or other religiously dictated practices were "provocative." It is a reflection of mainstream French antipathy to Afro-Arabs that a number of public institutions, not just schools, then proceeded to sanction and expel Muslim women for observing religious precepts.[25]

France's Afro-Arabs continue to face greater social and economic barriers than people of color in Britain and the United States, but fewer political restrictions than their counterparts in Germany and Switzerland. The Afro-Arabs and their children can and often do become full citizens, and they are using political means to defend and assert their interests. Turks in Germany and immigrant workers in Switzerland, on the other hand, face greater restrictions on the right to organize, move, and choose occupations, and they rarely meet the demanding requirements for citizenship. Moreover the racial animosities that have led to harassment and violence against Third World immigrants in Britain and France became increasingly common in Germany in 1991–92.

Ethnonationalists

In 1950 a careful observer probably would have concluded that there was virtually no potential for ethnonationalism in the European democracies or Canada. Although some historically autonomous regions were poor in comparison with the center, economic and political discrimination were virtually nonexistent for all but the Catholics of Northern Ireland, and no concerted demands for political or cultural rights had been heard for decades—none, at least, that politicians at the center took seriously. Yet ethnonationalism exploded in the borderlands of the European democracies during the 1960s, among such culturally distinct peoples as the Bretons and Corsicans in France, the Sardinians and South Tyroleans in Italy, the Scots and Welsh in Britain, and the French-speaking Jurassiens in Switzerland's Berne canton.[26]

The 1960s wave of ethnonationalism in Europe and Canada focused mainly on cultural and economic issues, and it has commonly been attributed to entrepreneurship on the part of a more radical generation of political activists who came of age in the 1960s. These activists built new political movements that evoked old sentiments of cultural identity, stirred up old and new grievances, and pressed for greater regional autonomy, reallocation of public resources to favor their regions, or (in the case of Quebec) outright independence. Rogowski makes the case that these movements were mainly regional forms of competition for power and resources at the center, not reactions to deprivation or the pressures of uneven modernization.[27] It is equally important to note that most had limited political support even within the regional population, as is evident from voting patterns.

All these movements prompted shifts in national and local policy that satisfied most, not necessarily all, plaintiffs, and most of the regional conflicts abated during the 1980s. The three exceptions to the latter generalization include the Québecois and the protagonists of the two most persistent and deadly separatist movements in western democracies: the Catholics of Northern Ireland (the current episode began in 1968) and the Spanish Basques (since the mid-1950s).

Although the latter two rebellions have ancient historical roots, in their current phase they are inheritances from authoritarian, not democratic, regimes and practices. The Ulster Protestants began in 1923 to exercise a majoritarian tyranny over the impoverished Catholic minority. After more than two decades of IRA terrorism and countermobilization by the Protestant majority in which more than two thousand people have died, only two visible accomplishments can be cited. First, the political instrument of Protestant domination, the Stormont Parliament, was replaced in 1972 by direct rule from London. Anti-Catholic discrimination in politics and public services thus was halted, but all subsequent British efforts to establish more equitable power-sharing arrangements have been thwarted, mainly by Protestant intransigence. Second, the 1985 Hillsborough Accord between the governments of the United Kingdom and the Republic of Ireland gives the latter an advisory role on policies in the North. Dismissed by most Catholics as too little, the arrangement is rejected by Protestant Unionists as the entering wedge of "Roman rule." The conflict thus is stalemated, and civil peace is maintained only through the presence of some ten thousand British troops.

The Spanish Basques, who were briefly autonomous under the Spanish Republic in the 1930s, were subordinated to a highly centralized and authoritarian state and denied all manifestations of cultural or political identity from 1939 until Franco's death in 1975. In 1978–81 the new democratic government of Spain instituted an autonomous community system for the Basque provinces (also for those of Catalonia and Galicia, and later for fourteen other regions as well), which was welcomed by most politically active Basques. A radical faction of the Basque independence movement, Euzkadi Ta Azkatasuna

(ETA), rejected the compromise and continued a terrorist campaign for complete independence until the late 1980s. Arrests of ETA leaders by French police in spring 1992 showed that it still maintained an extensive underground network in France and Spain with serious potential for future violence.[28]

The following cases below are more typical of the course and resolution of ethnonationalism in democracies.

Bretons in France

The 3.7 million people (1982) of the five departments of Brittany have since 1898 given birth to a succession of regionalist political movements. These movements are rooted in the Bretons' history of political autonomy—which they surrendered to the French revolutionary government in 1789—and their distinct Celtic language and customs.[29]

Group Identity and Status

Cultural and economic differences are at the root of contemporary ethnonationalism in Brittany. A 1975 poll showed that half of all Bretons defined themselves as being as much Breton as French, and one-quarter felt more Breton than French. Their language and customs had gradually eroded under pressure from the Paris government, which since the 1880s had required that only French be taught in the public school system. Local efforts to maintain the Breton culture and language had little impact until the late 1960s. Now Breton is understood by less than a quarter of the regional population and used on a daily basis by only a few of them, mainly in the rural west (estimates range from fifty thousand to four hundred thousand). The historical poverty and isolation of Brittany vis-à-vis the rest of France provided the more immediate impetus for regional political movements and separatist action after 1945.

Political Mobilization and Action

The first significant collective action in postwar Brittany was a wave of strikes among workers in maritime industries in the late

1940s, a reflection of economic, not political, grievances. There also were mass demonstrations by Breton farmers in 1960–61 over low prices. Until the early 1960s, ethnonationalism was limited to cautious advocacy of regionalism and cultural revival by conservative and socialist political organizations. Then, in the mid-1960s, a new generation of activists issued increasingly militant demands for economic, cultural, and (ultimately) political independence. The most radical group was the tiny Front pour la Liberation de Bretagne (FLB), which demanded "decolonization" and carried out sustained campaigns of bombings against property targets from 1966 to 1979. In 1980 government plans to build a giant nuclear reactor complex in Finistère prompted serious demonstrations that capitalized partly on autonomy sentiments, partly on the new environmentalism.

Policies and Prospects

Central government policies since the late 1940s have been to promote regional economic development, though more slowly and with fewer resources than regional activists sought. Investment in infrastructure, industry, and modernization of Breton agriculture accelerated in the 1970s. In 1975 the Paris government grudgingly acquiesced to demands for the promotion of the Breton language. In 1981, under Socialist president Mitterand, the central government shifted to a policy of regional decentralization throughout France and adopted policies that aimed at "a flowering of regional languages and cultures."[30] Brittany was one of twenty-two regions to gain partial self-government in 1982 under the direction of a popularly elected regional council. By the early 1990s the economic gap between Brittany and the center had closed and the more extreme manifestations of Breton nationalism had vanished. Politically the energies of ethnonationalists were directed into conventional party activities, principally the Union Dèmocratique Bretonne, the only Breton party that has done well in local elections.

    In retrospect, Breton nationalism proved to be little more than an expression of Breton regional interests, some of whose advocates used nationalist rhetoric and bombs to make their point. Similar rhetoric and tactics were used in the 1970s on behalf of the quarter-million French Basques. They too benefited from increased regional autonomy and a modest influx of public funds for cultural activities. Similar responses have failed to dampen the more persistent and violent movement of some Corsican nationalists. Autonomist sentiments on the island have prompted thirty years of demonstrations, a few riots, and terrorist campaigns—two hundred to eight hundred bombings annually—from the late 1970s to the present by the Front de la Liberation Nationale de la Corse.[31] The majority of native-born Corsicans have migrated to the mainland, and autonomist candidates for Corsica's regional assembly (established after the 1982 reforms) have never received more than 15 percent of the vote. These facts suggest strongly that Corsican nationalism, like other regional nationalisms in France, is the preoccupation of a minority of a minority and that the use of terrorist tactics has very little support.

Germans (Tyroleans) in Italy

The three hundred thousand German speakers of the northern Italian region of South Tyrol, centered on Bolzano, are a politically conservative group with a strong sense of ethnic self-identity. Once part of the Austro-Hungarian Empire, the region was transferred to Italian control at the end of World War I. After 1922 the Fascist government followed a systematic policy of Italianization, abetted after 1939 by the Nazi government, which agreed to accept all South Tyroleans who would not accept complete assimilation. About a third were in fact transferred north of the Alps (seventy-five thousand, of whom one-third returned after 1945), and substantial numbers of Italians migrated into the region.[32]

Differential Status

In the early postwar period South Tyrol was relatively poor and rural. An autonomy statute in 1948 allowed for preservation of German cultural identity but left political and economic affairs in the hands of the Italian majority in the larger Trentino-Alto Adige region. Continued Italian immigration into the towns of South Tyrol further angered the German-speaking population.

Political Mobilization and Action

The Südtiroler Volkspartei has actively asserted the interests of the German community since 1945 and has enjoyed its overwhelming support. Resentment over the limited rights provided in the 1948 statute led in the 1950s to appeals for greater autonomy by the South Tyroleans to the Italian state, the United Nations, and the new Austrian government. It then escalated to mass rallies (1957) and prompted a terrorist campaign by a handful of individuals, which peaked in the early 1960s. Due in part to active diplomatic initiatives by Austria, the Italian government agreed in 1969 to a major overhaul of the 1948 statute.

Policies and Prospects

Since implementation of the new autonomy pact, beginning in 1972, the German minority has gained effective control of public administration, educational and cultural affairs, and economic development in South Tyrol, financed by a guaranteed percentage of government spending in relevant sectors. A quota system gives preference in hiring to German speakers in public and quasi-public sectors. These policies, and a tourist boom, have made South Tyrol one of the most prosperous Italian regions. A few ethnic Germans have been concerned about a possible retreat by the Rome government from full implementation of the autonomy pact, and a few others still seek union with Austria. A new autonomy agreement was reached in May 1988 and prompted a new rash of bombings by Ein Tyrol separatists.

A potentially more serious issue is the resentment of the region's Italian minority over preferential treatment being given to the ethnic Germans, which has been expressed in electoral support for a neo-Fascist party in provincial elections. This kind of conservative reaction to concessions for minorities has many parallels in other western democracies: support in Britain for the racial exclusion policies advocated by renegade Conservative Member of Parliament Enoch Powell in the 1960s, French electoral support for the xenophobic National Party in the 1980s, and white Louisianans' enthusiasm for ex-Klansman David Duke's political career in the early 1990s.

French Canadians

The group identity of the Bretons, and knowledge of their language, was eroded by generations of assimilation into mainstream French society, whereas the French Canadians have a very strong sense of group identity and have had little desire or opportunity for assimilation into the Anglo-Canadian majority. Cultural identity among the ethnic Germans of South Tyrol is comparably strong, but they are a minuscule proportion of Italy's population; the French Canadians, by contrast, are numerically and proportionally the largest of all ethnonationalist groups in democratic societies (6.8 million in 1990, 27 percent of Canada's population). The high salience of French Canadian identity, their numbers, and their control of a large and economically strategic province make ethnonationalism among the Québecois qualitatively different from ethnonationalism in other western societies. The Québecois have not been satisfied by the Canadian federal government's policies of accommodation and now appear headed toward full sovereignty.[33]

The French Canadians are descended from the original European settlers of Canada but were conquered by the British in 1760—an event recalled even on Quebec auto license plates.[34] Cut off from France, they remained a majority until a surge of British-sponsored immigration in the 1840s. They have vigorously maintained their language, culture, and Catholicism throughout. The British North America Act of 1867, which united the Canadian provinces in a confederation, gave the Québecois legal and language rights but in effect subordinated them politically to the dominant Anglo-Canadians. They also lagged economically: predominantly a rural, farming people, they were ill equipped to take part in the Anglo-led commercial and industrial growth of the late nineteenth and first half of the twentieth century.

Differential Status

The cultural differences between French Canadians and Anglo-Canadians have been sharpened by the once-pervasive view among Anglo-Canadians that the French are an inferior people, and by enduring French resentment against their historical defeat and subordination. The former prejudice has justified informal economic and political discrimination against the French, the latter has strengthened the French resolve to preserve their own language and lifeways.

The "Quiet Revolution" of the early 1960s fundamentally changed the conservative and rural nature of Quebec society. A new generation of urban intellectuals promoted the development of a progressive and secular society modeled on Ontario and the United States. The provincial government of Quebec took responsibility from the Roman Catholic Church for education and health and welfare programs and followed the French model of active intervention in and direction of the economy. Rapid urbanization and economic development followed, so that by the 1970s the economic gap between Quebec and Anglo Canada had been largely eliminated. The modernization of Quebec did not eliminate tensions between the two communities, however. Prejudice and discrimination against the one million French Canadians who live in other provinces is a continuing problem. In Quebec itself the language policies of the provincial government are regarded by Anglo-Canadians as a form of reverse discrimination.

Political Mobilization and Action

The quiet social, economic, and intellectual revolution prompted some members of Quebec's growing urban working and professional classes to attempt a noisier revolution on behalf of autonomy. Nationalist movements were established in the mid- to late 1960s, including the Parti Québecois (PQ). Its commitment to the slow and uncertain electoral pursuit of Quebec's independence led a number of its most militant supporters to establish more radical and clandestine organizations, the most extreme of which was the Front de Liberation de Quebec (FLQ). One of the FLQ's loose alliance of cells kidnapped and murdered the Quebec minister of labor in October 1970, precipitating a government crisis and crackdown. A campaign of FLQ bombings persisted for several years, but the tactic of violence was widely condemned by virtually all Québecois, including the PQ. The decline of violence was paralleled by rising support for the PQ, which won an unexpected electoral victory in the 1976 provincial elections. In 1980, however, 52 percent of

French-speaking Quebec voters rejected a PQ referendum calling for "sovereignty-association" as a way station on the road to
complete independence. In 1985 the PQ repudiated its commitment to Quebec independence and lost the 1986 provincial
elections to the conservative Liberal party, which it had defeated
a decade earlier.

Policies and Prospects

The Ottawa government began moving politically to accommodate Quebec interests, especially on the language issue, in the
1960s. Since the late 1960s the federal government has promoted bilingualism throughout Canada. It has also given Quebec officials wide latitude in designing and administering some
programs and functions that in principle were under federal
control. (Other provinces also have benefited from devolution
of federal authority that was initiated to meet Quebec interests.)
Nor was there effective federal opposition when in the 1970s
Quebec made French the official language of the province and
restricted the use of English in schools and public places, to the
consternation of Quebec's anglophone minority.

By the early 1980s it appeared that Canada provided a model
for the successful accommodation of communal conflicts. Quebec was prosperous, it had acquired greater control of provincial affairs, 90 percent of its population seemed assured of the
preservation of their language and culture, and popular support for independence was declining. The adoption of a new
Canadian consitution in 1982 was expected to confirm the new
arrangements. Instead it was initially rejected by the Quebec
government on grounds that it gave too much power to the federal government on matters of language and centralization.
The Meech Lake accord, hammered out in 1987 by provincial
and federal officials, met Quebec objections, but when the time
came to ratify the accord in 1990 two other provinces rejected
it, essentially because of public resentment about Quebec's special status.

By 1992, therefore, Quebec nationalism was once again ascendant and chances are that the province will proclaim its sovereignty in the next several years while hoping to negotiate economic association with the rest of Canada. The Quebec case
illustrates the limits of accommodation to ethnonationalism in

democratic societies. The objective economic and political inequalities between the two communities have been eliminated and Quebec cultural rights are assured of expression, but the Canadian federation is foundering on irreconcilable symbolic differences.

Quebec's potential secession may resolve one set of communal problems but exacerbate others. About one million French Canadians live outside Quebec. Their status and political influence, which have improved somewhat in recent decades, are likely to decline if Quebec secedes. Independence for Quebec also will create a new minority at risk, the 706,000 (1981 census) English-speaking inhabitants of Quebec, who already are subject to provincial restrictions with respect to language and schooling.

There is one positive conclusion about the norms and practice of Canadian democracy. They may not be able to forestall Quebec's eventual secession, but they virtually ensure that the impending divorce will be peaceful: very few Canadians are prepared to go to war for either a free Quebec or a united Canada.

Indigenous Peoples

Seven western democracies are home to descendants of peoples who occupied the land at the time of European conquest: the Inuit and other native peoples of Canada and the United States, the Maori of New Zealand, the Aborigines of Australia, and the Saami of northern Scandinavia.[35] The Ainu of Japan and the fifty thousand Inuit of Denmark's autonomous province of Greenland have a similar origin and status, but they fall below this study's population threshold. All indigenous peoples have been adversely affected by one-sided cultural conflict with dominant societies and, except for the Inuits of Greenland, all have lost most of their historical lands and autonomy.

The indigenous people who fared best are those that had complex societies and a high degree of political organization at the time of European conquest. These groups, especially the Maori and the Navaho, have been politically and culturally more resilient than most others. The Maori, by sheer numbers and military resistance, were able to keep much of their land and were given representation in the settlers' parliament in

1867. All other indigenous peoples in the democracies had to endure poverty and powerlessness for another century before achieving significant collective gains. Three factors have contributed to recent reforms. First is the indigenous rights movement itself, led almost everywhere by young activists—more familiar through education and residence with the dominant society, more militant than their elders, and very much aware of civil rights and indigenous movements elsewhere. The new activism among Native Americans began in the early 1960s; the first civil rights and land rights protests among the Australian Aborigines occurred in 1963; a new Maori protest movement emerged in the early 1970s.

Second is the political support for indigenous rights among significant parts of the mass public in democratic societies. In Australia, for example, the nascent Aboriginal rights movement got substantial support from the Uniting Church and the Australian Congress of Trade Unions, and in the heat of the 1972 national election campaign, the Labor party took up the cause of land rights. Mixed sentiments and motives account for this support, including liberal sympathies for the poverty and social distress of many indigenous communities, which have been given ample publicity—not least by activists. Closely allied is the sense of guilt felt by many Europeans about the peoples they have conquered ("Custer died for your sins") and the romanticism of many city people who regret the loss of mythic lifeways that were more elemental, more environmentally correct ("Dances with Wolves").

Third is the fact that a number of political leaders have taken principled or expedient stands in favor of indigenous rights. In the United States, President Nixon, motivated by his belief in decentralization of the federal government, initiated in 1970 the Indian self-determination policy that has remained in effect for three decades. In Australia the Labor party's platform of improving Aborigines' welfare contributed to Gough Whitlam's 1972 electoral victory. His government actively promoted socioeconomic development and land rights, in part because Whitlam drew an explicit linkage between Aboriginal rights and his policies of reorienting Australian foreign policy toward the Third World. Both federal governments, the Australian more than the U.S., have qualified their support for indigenous rights and autonomy by pressuring tribes and land councils to permit private corporations to exploit their natural resources.[36]

Democratic politics means compromises. As a result the reforms and land rights won or strengthened during the 1960s and 1970s have generally fallen short of what the most outspoken activists sought. There also has been something of a backlash from whites who resent restraints imposed by indigenous peoples on the development of resource-rich areas from Quebec to Western Australia. The native peoples of North America and the Saami of the Nordic countries provide more detailed illustrations of the changing status of indigenous peoples.

Native Peoples in North America

Differential Status

Slightly over half of the 1.8 million Native Americans in the United States (1990 estimate) live on the 283 reservations in the lower forty-eight states or in some 200 Inuit, Aleut, and Amerindian communities in Alaska.[37] The others are town and city dwellers, most of whom maintain tribal affiliations but are not eligible, because of urban residence, for the extensive services provided by the federal Bureau of Indian Affairs. Native Americans on average have much higher unemployment, lower incomes, lower levels of schooling, higher rates of violent crime and imprisonment, and higher incidence of serious diseases and alcoholism than the national averages. Some whites who live near Native American communities still harbor prejudices against them, but by the global criteria used in the Minorities at Risk study the group ranks in the lowest category of economic and political discrimination: their poverty and lack of political influence outside their reservations are the legacy of historical conquest and oppression, not of contemporary social practice or public policy.[38]

Political Mobilization and Action

The major political issues for native peoples in the United States during the past half-century have been protection of their cultural and political autonomy, and improved material conditions for those living on tribal lands. Their principal pan-tribal associations are the National Congress of American Indians (NCAI, founded in 1944, increasingly influenced in the 1960s by urban activists) and the National Tribal Chairmen's Association (founded in 1970, in part to counteract NCAI). More militant action groups were the National Indian Youth Council (founded in 1961) and the American Indian Movement (AIM, founded in 1969), led mainly by young urban activists. These groups carried out a series of dramatic protests that culminated in AIM's 1973 occupation of the village of Wounded Knee, South Dakota. Hostile reactions by whites and tribal leaders to the violence attendant on the occupation contributed to a decline in confrontational politics and a shift toward reliance on legal tactics.

Policies and Prospects

Federal policy since the Nixon administration has supported political self-determination for the tribes and entrepreneurial development, with widely varying effects. The Navahos, the largest and one of the most successful tribes, are an autonomous nation within U.S. boundaries, with their own representative council and flag, administrative system, schools and colleges, and police force. Other large tribes have many of the same attributes. A number have succeeded, after long court battles, in reestablishing their rights to land and resources that had been alienated or compromised. Reliance on legal proceedings, and political mobilization in response to threats to native rights and status, are considerably more likely in the future than is the 1960s style of militancy. It is doubtful, though, that most tribes have the resources, capital, and skills for up-by-the-bootstrap improvement of their economic situation. Economic progress for most tribes will continue to be dependent on outside assistance and investment.

A Canadian Contrast

Canada's 610,000 native peoples (1990 estimate) include about 325,000 "status" Amerindians, 70 percent of whom live on 2,242 reserves; 25,000 Inuit who live north of the tree line, from James Bay to the High Arctic; and more than a quarter-million "nonstatus" native people, mainly Metis of mixed descent, who live in predominantly white urban and rural areas throughout the country. "Status" peoples have special legal-standing as members of bands (tribes), which gives them some privileges but also reserves control of their land, schooling, and economic enterprises to the provincial governments and the Canadian federal Department of Indian and Northern Affairs. Status peoples have the same economic and social problems of indigenous peoples in the United States but significantly less political autonomy to define and pursue their own interests. They are subject to provincial social and economic programs and regulations in ways unknown in the United States. Nor have they gained self-government or land rights equivalent to those achieved by most tribes south of the U.S.-Canada border, and thus they are coded 3 on our political discrimination scale (POLDIS; see Appendix table A.7).

Some Canadian tribes resisted efforts to subordinate them to federal control until the 1890s. Contemporary activism began in the 1960s and has included conventional politics, legal efforts to secure land rights, and local demonstrations over specific issues. For status peoples, represented by the Assembly of First Nations and the National Indian Brotherhood (founded in 1967), the major concerns have been preserving their treaty rights, securing land rights, and obtaining resources for self-sustaining development on the reserves. The Inuit, represented by the Tungavik Federation, have pressed since the early 1980s for establishment of their own territory of Nunavut, encompassing all the area of the Northwest Territories beyond the tree line (a region that does not include the Quebec or Labrador Inuit, who have their own associations). The nonstatus peoples, working through the Native Council of Canada (founded in 1967), are especially concerned with issues of economic opportunity and the pervasive discrimination against native peoples that pervades white Canadian society.

The Canadian federal and provincial governments' paternalistic approach to indigenous peoples began to erode in the early 1990s. A catalytic role seems to have been played by serious, sometimes violent local confrontations that became increasingly common in the late 1980s. The immediate issues included resistance to alienation of tribal land (the Mohawk in Quebec), logging on indigenous land (the Algonquin in Quebec, the Haida of British Columbia), mineral exploration (the Cree in

Alberta), and water resource development (the Cree in Quebec). Two indicative political agreements were reached in 1991. In August the Ontario government formally recognized the inherent right of 140,000 native peoples in that province to be self-governing. In December the federal government agreed to grant political domain, including self-government and limited land rights, to the 17,500 Inuit of the Northwest Territories, one-fifth of all Canadian territory. The effect of both agreements, once implemented, will be to give indigenous peoples status and rights comparable to those of the provincial governments. Indeed, the expectation is that once the territory of Nunavut is established in 1999 it will become a province in its own right.[39]

The Saami (Lapps) in the Nordic Countries

The 62,000 Saami who inhabit northern Norway (30,000 to 40,000), Sweden (17,000 to 20,000), Finland (5,000 to 8,000) and the northeastern extremity of the former USSR (2,000) are the indigenous people of all of upper Scandinavia. Their traditional lands have been subject to centuries of gradual expropriation and colonization from the south, with the result that the Saami are now a relatively small minority even in the northernmost forest, coastal, and mountain regions where they are most heavily concentrated. In Norway about half of them live in the province of Finnmark, where they make up less than one-quarter of the population. No more than a tenth rely mainly on reindeer herding for their livelihood; most Saami have diverse sources of income as fishermen, small farmers, and part-time wage earners. Some are civil servants, teachers, and professionals, and some live and work outside Saamiland.[40]

Differential Status

While the Saami historically were subject to pressures to assimilate, especially in Norway, they were never systematically persecuted, killed, or forcibly evicted from their lands as other indigenous peoples have been. Acts of Saami resistance, which peaked in Norway in 1851–52, were checked with little bloodshed. Nor is there any significant political or economic discrimination against the Saami, though many of their Scandinavian neighbors have a stereotypical view of them as lazy and sloppy.

Political Mobilization and Action

The Saami are at risk in two senses. First, there is growing pressure on their ecologically fragile environment. Their first modern political confrontation occurred in Norway in 1979–81 in opposition to a dam and hydroelectric scheme in the heart of reindeer country and led to modifications in the project's implementation. Also, fallout from the Chernobyl nuclear disaster in April 1986 was especially heavy in Saamiland and has contaminated the food chain for years to come, with serious effects on traditional means of livelihood. Second, some Saami have increasing political aspirations similar to those of indigenous people elsewhere, which have not been fully met. Members of the Saami political associations (not parties) that were established in all the Nordic countries between 1945 and the 1970s have pressed for establishment of Saami parliaments in each country (Finland has had such a parliament since 1976, Norway since 1989), for recognition of the Saami as national minorities, for protection and promotion of Saami language and culture, and for a decisive say about development projects in their regions.

Policies and Prospects

The principle of consultation with corporate groups is well established in the Nordic countries. The Nordic Saami Council (founded in 1956) is consulted by all three Nordic governments on matters of interest to the Saami. But granting the Saami formal recognition as a separate people with special political rights and veto powers not enjoyed by other groups runs against the grain of Nordic political culture. While recognizing that full autonomy is out of the question, militant Saami groups in all three countries will continue to press for special political rights and status.

Prospects for Minorities in the Democracies

Almost every one of the twenty-four minorities considered in this chapter, including those mentioned in passing, has benefited from some public effort to come to grips with the group's differential status and its demands. The Turkish minority of eastern Greece is the only exception: since the 1960s the Greek government has used all political and administrative means to restrict Turks' political and cultural expression. The reasons lie in the historical enmity between the Greeks and Turks and the exigencies of the Cyprus conflict, not in some special failing of Greek democracy.

Elsewhere the policies of accommodation have varied widely in scope and significance. At the narrow and symbolic end of the spectrum was the Japanese government's accreditation of a Korean university in Tokyo, a small but telling concession to an ethnoclass that has been principally concerned about cultural self-expression. More substantial are the democratic responses to ethnonationalism: the economic and political status of virtually every politically assertive region in the democracies has improved in the past two decades. The United States affords two examples of substantive reforms for indigenous peoples and ethnoclasses: the federal policy of granting self-determination to tribal peoples, and the legal, political, and economic reforms of the 1960s and 1970s that aimed at incorporating African Americans more fully into American society. Dissatisfaction with the imperfect consequences of these reforms has given impetus to emergent policies of multiculturalism. As happened in the 1960s, reformers and activists in the United States play a leading role in redefining the issues and in proposing ways of dealing with them.

Conclusion

This chapter concludes with an overview of the gains and potential future problems of each of the three group types. The indigenous rights movement is relatively easy to accommodate within the framework of democratic pluralism once the political decision is made to abandon paternalism. Canadian governments have been particularly slow in this regard. There is considerable latent sympathy in democratic publics for the status and claims of indigenous peoples—sympathies on which indigenous activists and their mainstream supporters have capitalized. Moreover, most indigenous peoples live in peripheral and sparsely populated areas, so relatively few members of the dominant society are adversely affected or offended when central governments follow policies of accommodation. The most potent resistance comes from proponents of resource development: mining and oil corporations, utility companies (public and private), and forest industries. These interests enjoy considerable influence over state, provincial, and national decision making because they provide jobs and tax revenues, and thus they have been the main source of political restraint on accommodation of indigenous interests.

Concessions to indigenous interests have not led to a rapid narrowing of social and economic deficits. Empowerment, when and where it has occurred, has usually meant giving indigenous people the right to manage their own poverty problems and programs. Few of them have acquired enough public funds or private capital to begin to build modern economies, an objective about which many are skeptical anyway. Their most fundamental and pervasive problem is the cultural legacy of subordination to European societies. It probably will take as many generations for newly empowered indigenous peoples to work out their own solutions as it took to create the problem.

The demands of ethnonational movements also have been largely resolved by increasing the resources and autonomy of regional governments. The French government's concessions to regionalism and demands for cultural expression in the 1980s were an especially dramatic reversal of nearly two centuries of political centralization and cultural hegemony directed from Paris. The governments of Spain, Italy, the United Kingdom, and Canada have all taken similar paths. Such accommodations have not been enough to resolve conflict in Northern Ireland, for the obvious reason that the region is not homogenous: accommodation of Catholic interests antagonizes Protestants and vice versa. The conflict appears less susceptible to resolution than any other ethnoconflict in the western democracies. On the other hand, the British and the Republic of Ireland have developed some skills at managing the conflict, and the long-term trend in deadly violence is distinctly downward.

Quebec nationalism also has proved very difficult to resolve within the Canadian federal system. Mutual resentment by some politicians (and publics) over symbolic issues has led to an impasse. There is little potential for violence in the impasse, however, and if not resolved it will probably culminate in negotiated sovereignty for Quebec in economic association with Canada.

The demands of ethnoclasses are less tractable than those of indigenous peoples and ethnonationalists. Historically, dominant groups defined ethnoclasses as inferior peoples, which helped justify the discriminatory practices that kept them at the bottom of the class ladder. Such attitudes are still widespread among Europeans and North Americans and provide support for xenophobic and racist political movements.[41] The liberal alternative, integration, coupled with policies designed to overcome disadvantage, has had mixed success: some ethnoclass members have chosen assimilation (some Franco-Maghrebins, some blacks in Britain, many Hispanics and African Americans in the United States), others have not. Preferences now seem to be shifting toward multiculturalism, in which ethnoclasses (and indigenous peoples) maintain distinct identities in plural societies that guarantee all peoples equality of status and treatment. These alternative strategies are discussed more fully in chapter 10.

The escalation of the international movement of peoples within Europe, and of Third Worlders into the advanced industrial democracies everywhere, will put policies of integration and pluralism to a severe test. The settler societies, the United States and Canada most of all, historically have incorporated large and diverse groups of immigrant peoples and thus are more open to experiments with pluralism and multiculturalism than the more homogeneous European societies are. There also are relative success stories in Europe of the accommodation of immigrants: the Netherlands, Belgium, and Sweden all have significant numbers of economic migrants and political refugees from the Third World and have incorporated them at some public cost but thus far with relatively little popular hostility.

The larger countries of Europe face the greatest challenges. The steps toward integration in 1993 have brought free movement of labor within the European Community (EC). In practice, free movement (or movement subject to ineffectual restraints) is implied for all the Third World immigrants who now are legally or illegally resident in the EC. It was estimated in 1991 that non-Europeans accounted for about one-tenth of all new births in Europe, and Muslims are characterized by a French historian as "a sort of thirteenth nation of the European Community."[42] Although France and Britain have a history of incorporating immigrants from other western societies, neither has found it easy to come to terms with Third World immigrants. Public policies of multiculturalism in Britain and tolerance of ethnic diversity in France are given the lie by private antagonism and violent harassment against Africans, Arabs, and Asians. Germanic Europe is even more restrictive for Third World immigrants, most of whom are discouraged from citizenship and assimilation even if they seek it, and is experiencing an upsurge of xenophobic reaction. One likely outcome throughout Europe is ever-tighter restrictions on immigration from outside the EC. More problematic is whether the immigrants who are already within the gates can be incorporated and accommodated without provoking greater public backlash.

7. States at Risk
Ethnopolitics in the Multinational States of Eastern Europe

Monty G. Marshall

Perhaps no political transformation has caught western social scientists so completely off guard as the recent events in Eastern Europe and the Soviet Union. The full course of those events was equally unforeseen by those leaders most responsible for setting them in motion. There has been a dramatic change in ethnic relations and the status of minorities in this region since 1985, when a little-known figure in Soviet politics, Mikhail Gorbachev, ascended to the helm to steer the Soviet Union along a route mapped only by "new thinking."

The very concepts *ethnic* and *minority* take on special meaning in the East European context. Every ethnic identity group is potentially a minority in some relational sense. Even a dominant majority can become a minority in the face of a concerted opposition (a coalition of disaffected minorities), thereby putting the majority state itself at risk. Ethnic groups that inhabit a defined territory can come together to act as a nation and demand their own state. All the nations of Eastern Europe have been conquered and absorbed by other states at some time in this millennium—some, several times and by different regional powers.

The use of the term minority in this social context can shift just as often and as suddenly as political borders. This problem of definition emphasizes the relational nature of the concept. A minority can exist only in relation to some majority; to be considered at risk, it must be either subordinate to a majority or dominant over a potential majority. When political borders shift, the distinction among social identity, or ethnic, markers; territorial boundaries; and political borders can become either more definitive or more blurred. Nations can become minorities in their relations to a regional suzerain and, when that power wanes, find themselves either suzerain or sovereign in relation to their own (subnational) minority groups.

The political changes in Eastern Europe and the former Soviet Union remain transitory in early 1993, awaiting coalescence. What is clear is that, in the short course of six years, groups that had been designated minorities at risk have become politically empowered to the extent that now the formerly omnipotent states themselves may be considered most at risk. Three of the federated, multinational states of this region, the USSR, Yugoslavia, and Czechoslovakia, have disintegrated as a result of their constituent republics exercising the constitutional right to secede from the political union.

The downside of the changes is that these "states at risk" are now countries at risk of massive disruptions in normative social relations and, in the worst case, of civil warfare. Even though minority ethnic groups that were formerly considered at risk of detrimental, differential relations within the political system of which they were a part may gain state sovereignty and express the right of self-determination through political independence, the relational character of the group is not changed nor are all the issues of contention resolved between them and the group with whom they experienced difficulties. What this change does is elevate those tensions to a higher level of abstraction; further intergroup conflict will be played out between a larger state and a smaller state in the international arena. Thus "minorities at risk" become, themselves, "states at risk."

The Stalinist authoritarian state systems that have governed the Socialist bloc countries since World War II are most certainly at risk. Most of these states, old and new, have instituted broad reform programs designed to disassemble (or delink) the firmly entrenched organizational apparatuses of the authoritarian Communist states.[1] Intergroup relations also are being redefined in the 1990s, concurrent with a restructuring of the institutions of governance and both the formal and informal rules, or norms, of social group interaction. Symptoms of these concurrent processes are evident throughout the region as the myriad affected groups hammer out new positions and systems of relations in response to unfolding conflict issues. In the interim, uncertainty and insecurity will rise, because old methods of conflict management are no longer operative and new ones are yet to be devised and instituted. Under these conditions, it must be assumed that all people will feel increased personal risk in an increasingly unfamiliar social landscape. All social and political cleavages are likely to become energized as groups and individuals jockey for position and influence. In the confusion, it is possible that the proverbial "baby" of civil society may be thrown out with the "bath" of the coercive state, making every social group in the region individually and communally at risk.

The symptoms of systemic change have played out differently in different societal contexts. They already range from violent civil warfare (e.g., between Croats and Serbs, Armenians and Azerbaijanis) to the initially peaceful yet profound transformations taking place among most of the constituent minorities of the many republics that formerly composed the USSR. Between these extremes lies a continuum of dyadic relations exhibiting more or less hostility and better or worse prospects for cooperation. The pockets of violent interethnic warfare remind us at once of the potential volatility of ethnic rivalries and the incredible resilience of historical animosities. Even more frightening, they attest that the Eurasian landmass has not developed an immunity to the pathologies of war, despite nearly a half-century of reconstruction and "peaceful" coexistence among its ethnic, religious, and national identity groups.

How will social group relations eventually be redefined? Some trends and guiding principles can be discerned. Recent systemic changes have transformed many former minorities at risk into the governing majorities of more or less independent political administrations and nations. Other minorities, such as the Uzbeks of Tajikistan and the Chechens and Ingushes of Russia, have gained political leverage in their relations with their governing states. For many other groups, such as the Russian and Ukrainian minorities living outside their home republics, official relations with their governments have changed substantially with the transformation of authoritarian client regimes to more liberal agent regimes.[2] In many cases, the recent empowerment of national ethnic groups has placed those former minorities at odds with subnational minority groups caught in the process of systemic transformation. The prospects of political autonomization, atomization, and administrative re-alignment have stimulated ever more ethnic groups to become active players in the unfolding political process. At the same time, the salience of ethnicity has become more pronounced, thus energizing social cleavages with vital political interests and highly regarded moral and ethical considerations.

Yet even the most profound social changes take place within a more or less stable environment and in terms of a defined historical context. What will be is, for the most part, a function of what has been, slightly modified by what is now; even profound and radical political changes must eventually contend with the same socioeconomic constraints and historical traditions that affected their predecessors. The general history of this region has two sides, one of which has been very dark and profoundly disturbing. The return to normalcy in Europe may be a harbinger of renewed hope, or it may reveal that nothing really has changed; the same problems of interethnic contention that precipitated the two great continental wars in the twentieth century and contributed to the massive, revolutionary dislocations that characterized the "great Socialist experiment" are still at work.

Both the Soviet Union and the Yugoslavian union ceased to exist at the beginning of 1992.[3] It seems likely that some sort of union, confederation, or commonwealth will be retained or reforged with some or most of the constituent republics of both former countries, although the level of violence involved in the Yugoslavian dissolution will surely hinder the establishment of amicable relations among the formerly federated republics for a long time to come.[4] It is clear that many administrative boundaries are being realigned and that some political borders may eventually be redrawn. Disputed territorial claims, while presently being downplayed by most parties, loom just beyond the pale of civil relations and involve nearly all the states of the region. The treatment of foreign nationals such as the Serbs in Croatia and in Bosnia and Hercegovina has already become a major issue of contention in the new international relations of this area. Corollaries to this issue are the problems of ethnic polarization and compression due to mass refugee movements and population transfers from areas that previously had seen various degrees of ethnic intermingling but now are embroiled in communal conflict.

The study of emerging states is a prerequisite to the study of the status of their minorities. The statuses of all groups in a given society are defined by the legal and conventional normative structures of the political state. In view of the rapid social changes now taking place, establishing the referential role of the state in the social relations that make up the political system has become difficult. Thus, the general focus on identifying the specific character and status of minorities becomes fused with a broader and more fundamental focus on the changing nature of the state in this region.

Three of the nine countries of Eastern Europe that existed in 1990 were characterized as multinational states, states that govern more than one culturally, linguistically, territorially, and politically distinct ethnic identity group or nation: the USSR, Yugoslavia, and Czechoslovakia. All but three of the groups considered at risk in Eastern Europe prior to 1990 were situated in these countries. Of the thirty minorities identified at risk in the period of the study, twenty-six were either coded as ethnonationalist (seventeen) or dual coded as both indigenous people and militant sect (nine).[5] The other four were coded as ethnoclasses. The mean on the group concentration scale for the twenty-six ethnonationalist and indigenous/sect groups was 5.12 (6.00 indicates the highest group concentration) versus a global mean of 4.70. By 1992, these nine countries had become at least twenty-five separate states, the majority of which may be considered multiethnic states (see annexes 1 and 2 at the end of this chapter for the ethnic compositions of the populations of these polities). Many of the minority groups in these new, smaller states are also regionally or territorially concentrated.

For most of this century the status of minorities in the socialist multinational states has been defined by a distinctive structure of political administration that has, sometimes directly and sometimes indirectly, promoted social or political stratification or both on the basis of ethnic identity. The coincidence of cultural and political boundaries makes ascriptive ethnic distinctions especially salient in the constitutional provisions of the multinational states.[6] These countries have remained true ethnic mosaics; the central state has acted officially to foster and maintain unique linguistic, religious, and cultural forms in its constituent groups, in contrast to the melting pot philosophy of the United States. This fact, perhaps more than any other, makes minority relations in Eastern Europe distinct from those in most other parts of the world.

The remainder of this chapter is organized in four sections. The first describes group cleavages in the region and puts them into a comparative context. The second section presents a brief contemporary history of intergroup relations, in the form of an argument posing a political tension between theories of Leninist national self-determination and Stalinist cultural autonomy solutions to the "national question" in multinational states. Theory has had a pronounced influence on the political structures and policies that define the status of minorities in Eastern Europe. The third section details current relations among minority groups in the region. Differences are noted among subregional clusters of ethnonationalists and indigenous sects, as are differences that distinguish the nationalists from ethnoclasses.[7] The concluding section speculates on the future of minority group relations.

Group-State Relations in Eastern Europe

In the period covered by the Minorities at Risk project, the Eastern Europe region included nine countries, five of which had minorities that met the basic criteria for inclusion in the study. After the project period ended in 1989, the two Germanies merged (in 1990) and the three Baltic states regained their former independence (in 1991), changing the total number of countries from nine to eleven in late 1991. By mid-1992, the Soviet Union had dissolved into twelve independent republics, and three republics had seceded from the Yugoslavian federation, bringing the total number of globally recognized countries in the region to twenty-five. Twelve of these successor states are small, with populations ranging from 1.6 million in Estonia to 5.4 million in Georgia. In January 1993 one more state was added when the Czech and Slovak republics separated.

The thirty minorities identified as at risk in this region in 1990 numbered together about 143 million people and accounted for about 35 percent of the region's population; of those minorities, sixteen are now the governing majorities in new states. In 1993 the number of minorities that must be considered at risk in the twenty-six successor states (assuming that all minorities are at risk under conditions of systemic disruption and high uncertainty) total about 93 million people (20 to 25 percent).

The multinational character of the socialist states of Eastern Europe has almost completely disappeared with the recent political transformations. The successor states are, for the most part, multiethnic nation-states. The dominant trend toward political disaggregation may or may not be punctuated by economic and social disintegration; if not, then the noted political trend may eventually be reversed, just as the contemporary trend toward unity in Western Europe has been stalled.

Of the twenty-six countries that comprised this region in early 1993, fifteen are relatively homogeneous uninational states (Albania, Armenia, Azerbaijan, Belarus, Bulgaria, the Czech and Slovak republics, Hungary, Lithuania, Poland, Romania, Russia, Slovenia, Turkmenistan, and Uzbekistan) in which the majority ethnic group accounts for more than 70 percent of the population with no major minority contenders.[8] Of the remainder, Kazakhstan is a binational state composed of two major national groups.[9] One is trinational (Bosnia and Hercegovina) with three major groups actively contending for political influence.[10] Eight are tentative national states (Croatia, Estonia, Georgia, Kyrgyzstan, Latvia, Moldova, Tajikistan, and Ukraine) in which the majority group has between one-half and three-quarters of the population with at least one contending minority group; these states are experiencing serious challenges based on legitimacy, citizenship, or sovereignty (boundaries). One still claims to be a multinational state (the truncated Yugoslavia).[11] The Commonwealth of Independent States (CIS), the successor to the Soviet Union, is best considered an international organization under the conditions that obtained in early 1993, although it could provide the nucleus for a resurgent multinational state in the future.[12]

The Eastern Europe region was dominated by the politics of the Soviet Union from 1945 to 1989. Stalinist authoritarian regimes were installed in all its countries after the collapse of the Nazi occupations of World War II and maintained through the threat of Soviet or Warsaw Pact intervention. Several of the states retained or reestablished some autonomy in spite of the preponderant power of the USSR: Yugoslavia, Romania, Albania, and Bulgaria developed their own variations on the Socialist-Communist theme.

What was common to the regimes in all these countries was their rigid intolerance of political cleavages and their immediate, harsh responses to any and all forms of protest and dissent.

This stance did not prevent occasional limited acts of defiance, but it was highly effective in preventing sustained protest. At the same time, the regime's total control of the legal organs of communication ensured that what sporadic activity did occur remained mostly unreported and unnoticed. Interethnic conflict and other overt "manifestations of bourgeois nationalism" were effectively suppressed, at least at the level of collective consciousness, in the Socialist communities from 1955 to 1985. These regimes' strategy of conflict suppression was so deceptively effective that by 1975 the national question was considered by the Communist leadership to have been resolved.

Liberalization of the regimes of the Socialist bloc after 1985 provided the forum for reopening the social debate over the national question. The opening (*glasnost*) of the Communist systems to legal expressions of opposition and political protest soon provided proof that the national question was not resolved. Ethnic-based protest and communal conflict between ethnic groups quickly became the preeminent political issue of the late 1980s. The ethnic republics within the multinational states, beginning with the Baltic republics, pressed ever stronger demands for greater autonomy from the central authorities. Historic rivalries and feuds between neighboring ethnic groups began to flare up, especially in the Soviet Caucasus, Soviet Central Asia, and Yugoslavia.

How could interethnic conflicts suddenly explode to rend the harmonious relations among Socialist peoples? The explanation advanced here is that the process of reform in the Communist states necessarily involved the decentralization of authoritarian power. Because political associations continued to be outlawed even after the onset of systemic liberalization, much oppositional mobilization was channeled into the only alternative organizational vehicles available in those systems: the networks of legal or semilegal cultural organizations and the formal structures of nationality-based regional administration.

Soviet-style nationalities policy thus provided the framework for political challenges to the hegemony of the central state. The paradox in the state's structure of political hegemony arose with the formation of an accommodative cultural policy and the implementation of an administrative policy of *korenizatsiya* (indigenization), which counterposed the general assimilationist thrust of authoritarian public policy.[13] This nationality paradox is the product of an ongoing theoretical rift between adherents of Lenin's and Stalin's prescriptions for dealing with the nationality problem. What resulted was a mixture of Stalinist policies of cultural autonomy overlaid on a federal administrative structure based on Leninist policies of national self-determination. This duplicitous inconsistency and its social effects will be examined in the next section.

Not all East European states were affected equally by this policy paradox. The six uninational states of that period either were effectively homogeneous or had relatively small and inconsequential problem minorities. In these states, policies of accommodation were not deemed necessary, because the minorities were small or dispersed and had little or no political or economic leverage. Bulgaria has implemented heavy-handed policies at different times, ultimately unsuccessfully, either to assimilate their 10-percent minority population of Turks into the dominant culture or to force them to emigrate. The Romanian regime seems to have preferred to ignore the minorities (8 percent Hungarian and less than 2 percent German) inhabiting the mountainous areas of Transylvania—at least until the 1980s, when the Ceausescu government attempted to extend and consolidate central control in those areas.

The status of minorities in the multinational states of Eastern Europe was quite different. For the most part, politicized minorities in Czechoslovakia, USSR, and Yugoslavia were relatively large groups of geographically concentrated, long-term inhabitants of territories that are clearly demarcated by administrative boundaries associated with the groups' ethnic identifications: cultural, historical, religious, and, especially, linguistic distinctions. The members of each ethnic group were allowed, if not encouraged, to retain ethnic distinctions, including their own language. The multinational states thus fostered the development of bilingual urban cultures in the minority regions.[14] The majority group's language served as the medium of between-group communication and the indigenous language often remained the primary medium of within-group communication.[15]

The multinational states of Eastern Europe have had common ethnic-federal political systems. Czechoslovakia was composed of two ethnic republics: Czech and Slovak. Yugoslavia comprised five major ethnic republics (Croatia, Serbia, Slovenia, Macedonia, and Montenegro) and one mixed ethnic republic, Bosnia and Hercegovina (Serbs, Croats, and Bosnia

Muslims).[16] The Soviet Union was at least nominally a federated union of fifteen major ethnic republics, thirteen of which are coded in the Minorities at Risk study, and myriad lesser ethnic administrations—thirty-eight in all, seven of which are coded.

Religion is a major issue of ethnic differentiation and divisiveness in this region despite the Communists' secular ideology and their suppression of organized religion. The core religious culture is Eastern Orthodox Christianity with subdivisions based on the autocephalous nature of the eastern national churches. A major sectarian division is between Christian and Muslim religions and cultures. Other divisions exist between the eastern Christian heritage of many of the major ethnies and the professions by smaller groups of western Christian religions— Protestant, Catholic, and Uniate. The Jewish minority in the USSR, after lengthy debates among the Bolshevik leaders in the early 1900s, was officially defined as an ethnic group rather than a religious group, although the religious dimension has become increasingly politicized in recent years.[17]

The de facto political status of minorities in Eastern Europe seems most similar to the status of minorities in Western Europe and the other advanced industrialized democracies, despite the characteristic de jure differences. Ethnic differences among the constituent ethnic groups of Eastern Europe are as diverse as those in any other region of the globe. Official policy in these states has been to protect the rights of minorities under the law and to promote the status of minorities that are relatively disadvantaged on account of historical conditions or discrimination; actual practices have been more or less successful in guaranteeing disadvantaged minorities equal access and treatment. East European minorities in the aggregate have many of the lowest coded means on variables measuring political differentials (1.2 versus the global mean of 1.8 and the western regional mean of 1.2); economic differentials (1.2 versus 2.2 and 2.2, respectively); political discrimination (1.3 compared to 1.9 and 1.2); and economic discrimination (0.8 compared to 1.6 and 1.5) (see chapter 2, tables 2.1 and 2.2). Soviet-style nationalities policies do appear to have been relatively effective in mitigating political and economic inequalities among ethnic identity groups.

How successful these policies have been in subordinating communal identities to a common, superordinate group identity remains open to debate, however. Many, perhaps most, ethnic group members in this region have resisted the kind of systemic intermixture and more or less voluntary assimilation to the dominant culture that characterizes most ethnic relations in the United States. In fact, systemic disintegration seemed to be the prevalent norm as the major ethnic groups of the Soviet multinational state successfully pressed their demands for national independence, which led to the dissolution of the Soviet Union in December 1991. The current warfare of Serbs against Croats in Croatia and against Muslims and Croats in Bosnia and Hercegovina followed closely upon the declarations of independence by those former Yugoslavian republics from what they perceived as a Serb-dominated federal system. The Slovaks' demands for greater autonomy or independence from the Czechs culminated in a peaceful divorce of the two republics on January 1, 1993.[18]

Descriptions of current ethnic minority relations in the multinational states of Eastern Europe will follow a brief discussion of historical and theoretical factors that contributed to the definition of ethnic identities and to the development of interethnic relations in this region.

History and Theory

The contrast in cultural profiles between Eastern Europe and Western Europe is both dramatic and essential to comparative analysis. Whereas most countries of Western Europe are relatively culturally homogeneous uninational states, those in Eastern Europe were culturally and ethnically heterogeneous multinational states.

Cultural diversity is the norm not only in many areas of Eastern Europe but also in most other regions of the Old World. Cultural cleavages and social stratification often become intertwined in multinational states, leading to political mobilization and further complicating social group conflict. State boundaries, drawn for the most part according to the preeminent interests of the European Great Powers (including Imperial Russia and the Ottomans) with little regard to the political interests of the indigenous populations, are often arbitrarily drawn across existing social cleavages, making the identification and definition of jurisdiction and sovereignty issues complex and problematic. The concomitant lack of systemic development in most

of these societies confounds the problems of establishing societal consensus and regime legitimacy.

Much of East European territory skirts the borderlands between empires of the ancient, medieval, and modern eras;
among them the Roman-Byzantine, Tatar, Ottoman, Russian,
Austro-Hungarian, and various Western European imperial
powers such as Napoleonic France, Fascist Italy, and Nazi Germany. For centuries the changes in the relative strength of
neighboring imperial powers have led to periodic shifts in the
borders dividing competing suzerainties. These border shifts
contributed to the complexity of cultural and religious distinctions among the peoples of this region.

The border shifts between secular and religious authorities
also contributed to the intermixing of ethnic groups due to
transmigrations of alien peoples to occupied territories for administrative and economic reasons. Hungarians and Turks (the
so-called Rumelian Turks) migrated into conquered areas in the
Balkans and established ethnic enclaves in Romania, Bulgaria,
Czechoslovakia, and Yugoslavia.[19] Similarly, Russians and
Ukrainians migrated to the Baltic region, Siberia, the Transcaucasus, and Central Asia. The shifting tides of the Ottoman
Empire dispersed Turkic enclaves in the Balkans and resulted
in the propagation of Islam among many Balkan peoples, including the Albanians, the Bosnian Muslims, and the Pomaks.

Also contributing to the cultural diversity in this region are
the dispersed urban minority populations, nomadic pastoralists,
and vagabond groups. Examples of these relatively dispersed
social-migratory peoples are the Roma (Gypsies) resident in
nearly all countries of the European continent (vagabond
groups), the Tatars and Jews of the Soviet Union (modern, urban migrants), and the mixed Turkic-Mongol pastoralist
peoples of the steppes in Central Asia (e.g., Uzbeks, Kazakhs,
Kyrgyz).

Many of the ethnic distinctions among the southern Slavs of
modern Yugoslavia can be traced to the arbitrary nature of imperial boundaries: Croats and Serbs of Yugoslavia and Czechs
and Slovaks of Czechoslovakia are much like twins separated at
birth. The Czechs fell under the more civil Austrian suzerainty,
whereas the Croats and Slovaks were subjected to harsher Hungarian suzerainty and the Serbs most often found themselves at
the mercy of the Ottomans. The Balkans were subject to intermittent Ottoman and Russian military dominance.

The most dynamic empire of the modern era in Eastern Europe was that of the imperial Russian czars. The expansionism of the Russian state that began in the fifteenth century eventually led to the incorporation of vast territories inhabited by many diverse, indigenous peoples. Continued political domination of conquered territories and subject peoples by the autocratic Russian state led many intellectuals of the times to regard Imperial Russia as a "prison of nations." [20] The oppression of indigenous populations was especially apparent in the empire's treatment of the Muslims. Of the twenty minority groups at risk in the Soviet Union in the 1980s, ten are indigenous Muslim peoples inhabiting traditional homelands in the Caucasus and in Central Asia, areas that are among the most economically disadvantaged in the former Soviet Union. [21]

In the early years of the twentieth century a political debate raged among Marxist and socialist activists and intellectuals over the nature of the differences in the political processes between the societies of Western Europe, most of them ethnically homogeneous and relatively well developed, and those of Eastern Europe, which were ethnically heterogeneous and developmentally backward. [22] The debates centered on identifying the barriers to systemic development in the heterogeneous states so that they might realize the prosperity and civility that was so evident in the West and so absent in the East. Prosperity was seen as a function of industrialization, specialization, and an efficient division of labor. Systemic backwardness was viewed as the result of a lack of societal coordination, consensus, and cohesion due to the multiplicity of national identities and rivalries within the political society. Lenin argued that these rivalries were the consequence of national competition, the striving for sectarian dominance, and the consequential oppression of minor nationalities by regional "bully" nationalities. [23] That is, the imperial dominance and oppression of smaller and more backward social identity groups by larger and more powerful groups was seen as both the cause of underdevelopment in the oppressed groups and as a serious constraint on the further development of the oppressor groups.

The central concept of the debate was Lenin's insistence on national (ethnic) self-determination (and its policy expression in the right of secession) as the basis of political relations in the multinational state and as the only humane solution to the national problem. [24] Lenin prevailed in the debate on the national question in the fledgling Soviet state, but his theories and policies were constantly challenged within the Communist party leadership. As the conditions of civil society in the Soviet state worsened in the early 1920s as a result of the civil war, the calls within the collective leadership for tighter central control became ever more appealing and compelling.[25]

Many of the countries that now comprise Eastern Europe came into being as a result of border realignments in the former Russian Empire during the civil war period and the dismantling of the Austro-Hungarian and Ottoman Empires after their defeat in World War I. The states of Estonia, Latvia, Lithuania, Poland, Czechoslovakia, and Yugoslavia were created by treaty from former territories carved out of those empires; Poland and Lithuania, of course, had been states before their forced incorporation into the Russian Empire. Lenin himself was not concerned about the absolute losses of territory; he had conceded far more territory in unilaterally suing for peace with the Germans at Brest-Litovsk. Stalin, on the other hand, seemed to be particularly anguished at the thought of losing ground to the capitalists.

While Lenin was undeniably the theoretical architect of the fledgling Soviet state that grew from the Bolshevik Revolution of 1917, his untimely death left the vital principle of national self-determination defenseless in the face of heavy, pragmatic opposition. Lenin made a plea to Trotsky to take the initiative in defending the principle in a confrontation with Stalin, Dzerzhinsky, and Ordzhonikidze concerning their heavy-handed methods in "negotiating" for the (re)incorporation of Georgia into the Soviet fold in 1922. He again asked agents within the leadership to defend the principle during the drafting of the Union Treaty, this time appealing to Kamenev and Zinoviev.[26] It remains unclear to what extent these agents followed his urgings; what is clear is that without the living force of Lenin's will, the effective constitutional principle of national self-determination was lost. Lenin seems to eulogize its demise himself in one of his last articles, dictated from his deathbed:

> I have committed, I think, a great offense against the workers of Russia because I have not intervened with sufficient energy and sharpness in the notorious question of "autonomization," which is, it seems, officially called the U.S.S.R.
>
> It is said that we need a single unified apparatus. But where do these assertions come from? Is it not from the same Russian appa-

ratus, which, as I observed in one of the previous numbers of my diary, was taken over from Tsarism and only thinly anointed with Soviet holy oil?

Undoubtedly we should have waited to take this measure until we could vouch for the apparatus as being our very own. At present, we must in all conscience state the opposite: what we call ours is an apparatus that is still thoroughly alien to us, representing a bourgeois Tsarist mechanism which we have had no chance to conquer during the past five years, in the absence of help from other countries, and in view of the overriding pressures of the "business" of war and the struggle against famine.

Under the circumstances it is quite obvious that the "freedom to withdraw from the Union," with which we justify ourselves, will prove to be nothing but a scrap of paper, incapable of defending the minorities in Russia from the incursions of that hundred percent Russian, the Great-Russian, the chauvinist, in reality, the scoundrel and despoiler which the typical Russian bureaucrat is. There can be no doubt that the insignificant percentage of Soviet and sovietized workers will drown in this Great-Russian sea of chauvinist riff-raff like a fly in milk.[27]

Stalin had originally been commissioned by Lenin in 1913 to devise a Marxist policy statement on the national question for the Bolsheviks. In that early statement can be seen the fundamental rift that divided these leaders after the 1917 seizure of state power. Stalin was named the first commissar of nationalities in the fledgling Bolshevik government. He came out strongly in favor of Soviet nationalities policies that sacrificed political autonomy (inherent in the concept of national self-determination) in favor of cultural autonomy, policies promoted by Austrian Marxists such as Karl Renner and Otto Bauer.[28] Stalin and Lenin continued to butt heads over these issues until Lenin's death in January 1924. Thereafter, Stalin was able to subvert many of Lenin's federalist and democratic policies and consolidate central (Russian) control of the Soviet state.[29] He proceeded, essentially, to reinstate a czarist bureaucratic-authoritarian regime with the intention of forcing through the industrialization of the inherited Soviet or Russian imperial state.

The duplicitous aspects of the Soviet nationalities policy were institutionalized under Stalin's leadership. Perhaps nothing symbolizes this duplicitousness more than the right of secession, which has been written into every Soviet constitution but which has remained a legal sham, because until April 1990 no provision was ever made to allow the exercise of that right. The interests of the central authority and the problem of social control were supreme in the Stalinist state, subordinating all other political considerations. The republics' governments were not empowered to be the balancing institutions envisioned by Lenin but simply became client states that acted as extensions of central authority; their leaders were an ethnic mixture of regents appointed by the central authorities, including loyal members of the indigenous party cadres and their ethnic Russian overseers. Another aspect of the Stalinist nationalities policy that seems to display a dual character is the *propiska* (internal passport), which every Soviet citizen was required to carry at all times and which prominently displayed the citizen's ethnic identity. In a system that claimed to be the birthplace of "the new Soviet man," no legal provision was made for transforming subordinate ethnic identity to supraordinate Soviet identity.[30] Another major example is Soviet language policy and its emphasis on bilingualism in Russian and the native language, a policy that has failed miserably in accomplishing its professed goal of linguistic integration.[31]

Lenin's pronouncements of self-determination and the right of secession could not be abandoned, because Stalin's authority—that is, his perceived legitimacy—depended on the mantle of mythic authority, which was a legacy from the charismatic Bolshevik leader. The promulgation of the Union Treaty of 1922 was Lenin's last official act in establishing the Soviet system of governance. To bypass the inherent limitations of central power embodied in the federal treaty, Stalin emphasized the "preeminent role" of the highly centralized, nonsectarian Communist Party of the Soviet Union (CPSU) and used it as the vehicle for his own designs for political administration. Thus, the essentially decentralized federal administrative structure of the USSR, based on a balance of power among independent ethnic republics, was subordinated to the monolithic CPSU. The ethnic republican structure of the Union was not, however, disengaged completely; it continued to preserve aspirations for national self-determination by supplying a focal point for cultural symbolism and ethnic group identifications.

Throughout the contemporary era, Soviet-like nationalities policies in the multinational states of Eastern Europe have alternated in their policy foci between accommodation and assimilation (e.g., policies of Russification in the USSR and Bulgarian-ization in Bulgaria). National (i.e., political) self-determination was replaced by varying forms of cultural self-determination—cultural or social autonomy—combined with a more or less formal and strictly enforced political subordination. Rigidly enforced CPSU party discipline provided the glue that kept the state together.

Stalin's primary goals of rapid industrialization and consolidation of a centralized, authoritarian regime exacerbated ethnic relations in two primary ways: centralization of the regime emphasized Russia's central, dominant role in the administration, and rapid economic modernization disrupted traditional social patterns. Foremost in determining the strength of the relationship between center and periphery were the effects of security considerations based on real and exaggerated perceptions of substantial antiregime hostility and credible threat from both internal sources (i.e., counterrevolutionaries, Trotskyites, and other "enemies of the people") and external sources ("capitalist encirclement" and the rise of European fascism). Moscow's attention was fixed on the potential vulnerability posed by the non-Russian peoples inhabiting the state's borderlands. Social control was an essential issue in these areas, especially in consideration of the internal dissatisfactions that accompanied the dramatic social disruptions associated with industrialization and collectivization. Stalin's ambitions to regain the western territories lost in the early years led to his "complicity with the devil" (Hitler) in illicit treaties, such as the infamous Molotov-Ribbentrop Pact of 1939, which led to the forcible reoccupation of the lost territories. It is certainly not a coincidence that the minorities that were most vociferous in their opposition or aversion to the Soviet state were those dwelling in the areas of greatest historic vulnerability: Europe and the Middle East.

Several of the minorities designated at risk in this study are included as a result of their treatment after the German occupation of vast territories in Eastern Europe and in the western and southwestern Soviet Union. The Soviet Union reestablished its pre–World War I boundaries in the West in connivance with Nazi Germany. Control in many of these areas was imposed only at great cost in the face of determined armed resistance. Estonia, Latvia, Lithuania, western Ukraine, and Moldova (Moldavia) all supported insurgencies that survived for up to a decade after the war. Mass deportations from these border areas occurred as an immediate result of the acts of incorporation and reincorporation and, later, because of accusations of collaboration with the enemy during the Nazi occupation. Massive population transfers occurred after the war; many inhabitants of these border regions who retreated with the defeated German armies were forcibly repatriated to the USSR after the war, many continued to resist Soviet hegemony after the war and were deported from their native lands, and many ethnic Russians were enticed to relocate to the border areas.

In the south, several smaller ethnic groups were forcibly relocated after being accused of collaboration with the Germans: the Crimean Tatars, the Balkars, the Chechens, the Ingushes, and the Karachays were summarily rounded up and deported en masse under the most inhumane conditions to undeveloped exile camps in Central Asia. The ethnic Germans had already been removed from their homes and relocated to less hospitable interior climes.[32] In Yugoslavia, intervention by Fascist Italy in Croatia led to the creation of a Croat state during the war years led by the Ustashi party; Nazi involvement contributed to the mass internment of "problem" populations and the institutionalization of atrocities. The result was a systematic, reciprocal fratricide accomplished by armed bands of Serbian Chetniks and Croat Ustashis.

The repressive regimes that were imposed in Eastern Europe in the aftermath of the war were eventually able to reimpose social order in these war-ravaged countries. Reconstruction was accomplished very slowly in these demolished economies. During the years of the Cold War and the Iron Curtain, the nations of the Warsaw Pact enjoyed a de facto political status very similar to that of the ethnic republics in the Soviet Union. Policies similar to *korenizatsiya* and cultural autonomy were instituted between Moscow and its client states in Eastern Europe; self-determination remained a symbolic myth within the Warsaw Pact. One advantage of this system was the virtual prevention of the transmigration of peoples from the more disadvantaged regions of Eastern Europe to the more advantaged West. One consequence of the return to normalcy in Europe in the 1990s is the issue of just such population movements.

Ethnic relations in the Soviet Union and in the Soviet client states of Eastern Europe remained stagnant throughout the contemporary period of detente between the nuclear superpowers. Gorbachev, it appears, attempted to regain systemic legitimacy in the USSR by reviving Lenin's theory and policy pronouncements and by following Lenin's political strategies almost verbatim. He stood as the agent for the principle of national self-determination and gambled heavily that Stalin's centrally planned economy, or "command capitalism," and the resulting public policies had allowed sufficient development of the economic base of the Soviet state and strengthened the industrial proletariat to the point that the institutionalization of the social democratic revolution that had been thwarted in Lenin's time was now possible.[33]

The success of Gorbachev's "new Bolshevik revolution" and its "democratic" successors depends on the abilities of the political leadership to maintain some form of systemic coordination and cohesion without resorting to coercion or force until a new systemic consensus can be constructed and institutionalized. As Lenin argued earlier, the peaceful union of peoples in a multinational state may be ensured only through voluntary association based on mutual political trust and mutual economic benefit. The multiethnic successor states of the Yeltsin-led Commonwealth of Independent States are faced with the same social dilemma. The apparent gains from dismantling the central government apparatus are threefold: the disempowerment of the entrenched reactionary forces of the CPSU *apparat* (bureaucracy), which seemed intent on thwarting substantive structural change in the system; the removal of the spectre of Stalin and the potential return of the repressive state, which stymied individual innovation and initiative; and the "one step backwards" to a lower order of administrative organization, which should make it easier to restructure and democratize the political system.

The return to political normalcy in Eastern Europe was a prerequisite to the return to political normalcy within the Union itself for three reasons. First, reform of the moribund administrative command, or centrally planned, economy meant adopting capitalist practices of self-management and cost accountability. Rapprochement with the West was a necessary precondition for economic reform. Second, reform of the economy meant reform of the central bureaucracy, which would not be possible without the existence of a countervailing political force and alternative authority structure to pressure and persuade the stagnant administrative agencies and lethargic functionaries of the very real necessity of reform.[34] To avert complete structural disintegration and systemic breakdown during the transformation period, it was also necessary to have a viable alternative for public administration that was compatible with the decentralization of power from the ineffectual bureaucracy and the inefficient party apparatuses.

Third, these potential countervailing forces could not be empowered without reviving Lenin's theories of the right of self-determination and democratization. These theories would be seen as hypocritical, the policies of decentralization as cynical, and the reform intentions of the central authorities as illegitimate while Soviet troops continued to prop up Communist proxy governments in Eastern Europe. Without the credible perception of real systemic legitimacy, the natural centrifugal forces of ethnic assertiveness that would be unleashed would not be moderated by the theorized natural centripetal forces of systemic convenience and efficiency. Polarization would have been the more likely result, thus providing real systemic disintegration rather than the credible threat thereof, and probably would have triggered a conservative reaction in the center to enforce the union and thus effectively abrogate the reforms.[35]

The strategy of reform in the international arena, then, comes full circle with reforms in the domestic arena. Subject nations and national ethnic groups have been freed by an elite-led social revolution to redefine themselves and their relations with one another on an equal political footing and, it is hoped, through peaceful negotiation. Thus, in a few short years, minorities at risk have in many instances become governing majorities, putting to political task a whole new set of subject, sub-regional minorities. In many cases, however, the newfound assertiveness of ethnic minorities has put them at even greater risk of communal or interethnic conflict.

In the next section are discussions of some specific cases: Eastern Europe, the Transcaucasus, Central Asia, and the dispersed communal minorities.

The Current Situation

The basic distinction between national peoples and minority peoples (see chapter 1) is especially appropriate for analysis of the minorities in Eastern Europe and the Soviet Union. But there are important differences in general levels of development between the two subcategories of national peoples, ethnonationalists and indigenous peoples. That is, groups classified as ethnonationalists, such as the Slovenes in Yugoslavia or the Estonians and Georgians in the former USSR, often enjoy a better than average standard of living within the suprasociety; those classified as indigenous peoples are relatively disadvantaged, falling below the systemic mean.[36] Ethnonationalist groups seem to want out of the system that rules over them more to protect their relative prosperity or categorical advantages than to protect their collective group identity. On the other hand, the indigenous peoples, such as the Tajiks, Turkmens, and Uzbeks of the former Soviet Union, are living in relatively underdeveloped regions and with much lower standards of living; these groups tend to want in so that they can gain access to the resources they need to improve their collective conditions. Seen in this way, the ethnonationalist-indigenous distinction may derive more from national egoistic considerations of protecting material advantages or seeking developmental assistance than from perceived cultural encroachments or rivalries. This economic function of nationalist exclusiveness and the pursuit of particularist interests was termed "bourgeois nationalism" by Lenin.

It has been noted elsewhere that the ethnic separatism in the Soviet Union did not follow the pattern generally found in the multinational states of the Third World.[37] Ethnic separatism in the developing states of the Third World tends to be most intense among the least integrated ethnic groups—which are also, generally speaking, the poorest peoples living in the least developed areas of those countries. These groups are actively engaged in resisting the increasing encroachments of the state on their cultural autonomy and the imposition of external authority.

In Eastern Europe as well as the Soviet Union, ethnic separatism seems to be most active among groups that enjoy a relatively high standard of living and that live in the most highly developed areas of the country; it seems to be least active among groups who are relatively less mobilized, least integrated, and most disadvantaged.[38] Of the eleven minorities coded as ethnonationalists in this study and that enjoy formal-legal recognition and designation as a separate administrative unit, all are Christian cultures.[39] The mean score of these ethnonationalist groups on the economic differentials scale is a negative value, -0.18, indicating a slight net advantage in economic status. These groups have been the most active and legalistic in their expressions of political independence from the authority of the central state. The only positive scores coded, signifying economic disadvantages, were for the Moldavians in the USSR (3.0) and the Serbs in Yugoslavia (1.0). But of the nine minorities coded as indigenous peoples that enjoy a similar, separate political status, all are Muslim cultures; the mean value of their economic differentials scores is a positive 1.54.[40] Separatism in the USSR has, however, followed a general pattern noted in this study in that groups that have a historical identity or a history of independence or autonomy are most active in seeking greater autonomy or separation from central political authority.

The issues and dynamics of ethnic conflict vary substantially within the larger region. In the following sections the relations of ethnic groups to the state are examined according to their geopolitical context.

Eastern Europe

Regional integration opportunities and group security considerations (i.e., political context) are paramount issues both in ethnic demands and aspirations and in interethnic negotiations. Western Europe has been far more prosperous than Eastern Europe throughout the modern era, and as a consequence it stands as the most attractive alternative for regional political integration. Unfortunately, integration opportunities with the dynamic economies of the developed West are not available or accessible to all. The maintenance of regional prosperity in the West depends, in part, on the limitation of wealth redistributions from the dynamic core countries to less prosperous or productive regions.[41]

The East European nations have remained on the semiperiphery of the world capitalist system in the modern era; as a direct result of World War II, they have also remained on the semiperiphery of the world socialist system through the current period. The East European areas have historically possessed neither the material nor the human resources commensurate with advanced industrial development. As a result, they have not experienced the competitive advantages that might allow them to compete and prosper under general free trade arrangements.

The nation-state system in Europe served national self-interests well in preventing capital transfers among states and income redistributions from the more prosperous areas to disadvantaged regions; the Cold War system worked to prevent labor migrations and economic refugeeism. The issue here, however, is not to analyze *why* Eastern Europe came to be and continues to be economically disadvantaged; it is enough for the present argument simply to recognize that the region is disadvantaged and that the general situation has not changed in relative terms.

One major factor in the decision by the Soviet Union to divest itself of its obligations in Eastern Europe—that is, to effectively abdicate its suzerainty over this region—involves this economic consideration. The political-security value of suzerainty as a buffer zone to protect the highly vulnerable Soviet core gradually decreased considerably as the Soviet system recovered, was rebuilt, and stabilized. The perceived cost-benefit ratio of that relationship eventually eroded into an economic liability as the Soviet system became relatively less vulnerable and the subjugated national populations became more restive. It seems unlikely that the USSR could have retained its grip on Eastern Europe without either a significant rise in authoritarian repression or a massive influx of investment capital to these countries. In either case, the long-term situation of dominance in Eastern Europe represented an increasing fiscal drain on the limited resources of the Soviet Union.[42] The recent liberalization in the East may pose a similar problem for the advantaged West.

Minority status and relations in the present East European context reflect the systemic attributes of economic and political competition. Relatively prosperous ethnic minority regions feel that they can improve their economic condition and their political bargaining position by establishing sovereign control over their territorial and human resources. This assumption is surely true if security considerations are discounted. However, many states are incapable of functioning as viable social systems without the resource capacities of these more prosperous areas. This relationship of economic dependence can worsen (or pose a threat of worsening) the already precarious economic conditions in the poorer abandoned states, thus heightening domestic tensions within the affected areas and focusing animosities on the economic rift, which is often symbolized by concomitant ethnic or national cleavages. Many people are willing to engage in warfare to prevent the loss of access to valuable resources and the lessening of international status and prestige that accompanies such a loss of political power.

If advantaged regions are forced to defend themselves against less fortunate but more militant neighboring ethnic groups, their relative economic advantages may be quickly consumed by military outlays to the point of a severe net economic disadvantage. On the other hand, establishing security agreements with other powerful neighbors may lend these regions security at a lower net economic cost but possibly at a higher cost of credible deterrence—that is, the ally may decide not to respond to a provocation against its security client—and at a certain risk of perpetuating their political subordination to a different hegemon. This security arrangement also runs the risk of escalating and spreading the scope of otherwise narrowly confined interethnic conflicts beyond their original issue-related boundaries.

Most of the minorities at risk in Eastern Europe were ethnonationalists: the Slovaks, formerly of Czechoslovakia; the Estonians, Latvians, Lithuanians, Ukrainians, formerly of the USSR; and the Croats, Serbs, and Slovenes, formerly of Yugoslavia. The present civil war between Serbs who still see themselves as part of Yugoslavia and Croats and Bosnia Muslims who do not, illustrates the disastrous potential of severing political ties between ethnic groups. The declaration of ethnic (national) independence is meaningless unless it is acquiesced to by all significantly affected parties or unless it can be defended by force. Separation does not in itself resolve ethnic hostilities; it simply transfers them to a higher level of abstraction.

The smaller transmigrant communal groups of Eastern Europe run into a sort of double jeopardy: they are often used as hostage populations and "bargaining chips" in negotiations between the nation-states with which they identify ethnically and their sovereign nation-state, and they are often subjected to substandard treatment by their immediate governments. The Turks in Bulgaria, the Hungarians of the former Czechoslovakia, the Albanians of Yugoslavia, and the Germans and Hungarians of Romania are examples of this problem. These peoples are truly disadvantaged and at the mercy of their state governments because these minority groups, unlike their republican counterparts, are not legally armed and have been granted little or no participation in public administration. Another problem has surfaced in the Baltic states as they hammer out political relations in the context of economic reform, that is, citizenship and its attendant privileges with regard to property ownership. Debate has raged in the new states of Estonia and Latvia over how, or indeed whether, to limit the citizenship rights and thereby limit the political and economic influence of nonindigenous, usually Russian, interlopers.

Irredentist claims have an ignoble past in this area. Several of the minorities in this study inhabit areas that lie across interstate borders: the Hungarians of the former Czechoslovakia, the Moldavians (ethnic Romanians) of the former USSR, and the Albanians of Yugoslavia. The Hungarians of Transylvania in Romania may also be included here; in addition, many of the ethnonational group areas have resident minority populations that may be subject to irredentist claims, such as the Serbs living in Croatia and in Bosnia and Hercegovina, and the Russians living in neighboring republics. Relations between such minority groups and the state are inextricably linked to relations between the host country and the neighboring country with which the minority identifies ethnically. States historically have been more willing to rid themselves of problematic sections of their resident populations—by forced emigration, as in the case of the Turks in Bulgaria, or by more deadly options, as occurred in Croatia under the leadership of the Ustashi—than they are to transfer portions of their territory to another state.

Transcaucasus

The Transcaucasus region consists of the Georgian, Armenian, and Azerbaijani republics of the former USSR and the northern Caucasus region of the Russian republic.[43] In addition, there are twelve ethnic administrative divisions: the Nakhichevan and Nagorno-Karabakh units in Azerbaijan; the Abkhaz, Adzhar, and South Ossetian units in Georgia; and the Chechen-Ingush, Dagestan, Kabardin-Balkar, Kalmyk, North Ossetian, Adyge, and Karachay-Cherkess units in Russia. Groups included in the study from this area are the Armenians and Georgians (ethnonationalists) and the Azerbaijanis, Chechens-Ingushes, and Karachays-Balkars (indigenous peoples and militant sects).

This region was the first to witness significant outbreaks of ethnopolitical conflict in the reform era, beginning with the dispute over the treatment of Armenians in the Nagorno-Karabakh Autonomous Oblast (NKAO), which surfaced in 1987. It is also the locale of most of the violent interethnic confrontations, beginning with the anti-Armenian riots in Sumgait, Azerbaijan, on February 28, 1988. In 1989, violent communal confrontations between ethnic Georgians and resident enclaves of Abkhaz and Ossetians came to the forefront. The confrontation between Armenia and Azerbaijan over the jurisdiction of the Nagorno-Karabakh enclave inside the Azerbaijani republic and the treatment of the Armenian minority in that neighboring republic quickly escalated into an internecine struggle, which has involved reciprocal pogroms, mass population transfers, and serious clashes between armed bands of irregular ethnic militias. Soviet interventions, both military and diplomatic, failed to defuse the communal conflicts. After the breakdown of central authority that followed the August 1991 coup, these communal conflicts escalated even further as republic-based armed forces were formed with personnel and weapons inherited from the former Soviet armed forces.

The withdrawal of former Soviet Interior Ministry troops from the Nagorno-Karabakh enclave in late December 1991 (completed by CIS authorities) placed Armenia and Azerbaijan at the brink of all-out international war. On November 23, 1991, the government of independent Azerbaijan voted to dissolve the special status of the NKAO within its territory. On December 10, the people of the NKAO held an independence referendum and, as a result, the Nagorno-Karabakh leadership declared it an independent republic. Azerbaijan countered with legislation declaring the independence referendum null and void (Azerbaijan had previously negated the NKAO's special administrative status). Since then the battle over control of territory has raged and spilled over to include the strip of land dividing the Nagorno-Karabakh from Armenia (an area known as Lechinskaya *raion*).[44] In May 1992 the Armenian-Azeri violence spread to include attacks on the Azeri enclave that is similarly geographically separated from Azerbaijan, the Nakhichevan. This political push and pull between the new, independent republics and their ethnic minorities is currently being played out in similar ways throughout the territories of the former Soviet Union.

Since political liberalization in the Soviet Union and the successful first wave of ethnic assertiveness in the republics that

began in 1988, many of the Transcaucasus region's smaller ethnic groups have become more vocal in advancing their grievances against the republic administrations, signaling a second
wave of ethnic assertiveness and unrest in the region. In neighboring independent Georgia (which is still experiencing violent
civil unrest over the issue of Georgian nationalism, symbolized
by the deposition of president Zviad Gamsakhurdia) a confrontation between ethnic militias has taken place as a result of the
political maneuverings of the leaders of the South Ossetian and
Abkhaz ethnic regions in their desire to remove these areas
from Georgian jurisdiction. Ethnic assertiveness in the Caucasus region of the Russian federation is also rising and has broken into violence; for example, in November 1991 mass protests
were staged by the Chechens and Ingushes and an independent
Chechniya was declared.

The Azerbaijanis (or Azeri Turks) are the only major ethnic
group of the former USSR that professes the Shi'i branch of
Islam. The oil fields of Baku make Azerbaijan the most prosperous and the most modernized of the Soviet Muslim republics. There are about seven million Azeris living in the Transcaucasus. Another fifteen million Azeris dwell across the border in
Iran under far less advantageous conditions and with no special
legal recognition or status.[45] The Azeris are culturally and linguistically, but not religiously, similar to the Anatolian Turks of
Turkey, who have a long history of animosity with the Armenian
population of this region. The 1894–1915 genocide of the Armenian population at the hands of the Anatolian (Ottoman)
Turks is deeply embedded in the ethnic identity of the Armenian people, making relations between Armenians and Turks
extremely sensitive and political accommodations particularly
problematic.

The situation in Georgia is an even more complex mixture of
communal conflicts. Violence has been a characteristic of these
conflicts, but because of the size and capability discrepancies between the antagonists, the communal incidents have generally
been of lesser magnitude. Georgia itself is a multiethnic state.
The transformation of the ethnic Georgians from a subordinate
minority within the USSR to an empowered majority within
their republic has shifted the focus of minority relations to the
situation of the several ethnic minorities living within the borders of Georgia. Ethnic assertiveness among the 70-percent
Georgian majority in the republic produced anxieties in the

smaller ethnic enclaves of the Abkhaz, Adzhars, Armenians, and South Ossetians. Demands for administrative separation have been advanced since 1989 by both the Abkhaz and the South Ossetians. Communal confrontations between Georgians and the minorities have often resulted in violence, and tensions remain very high.

Ethnopolitical conflict in the Transcaucasus region has taken on special characteristics because of its close proximity to the war-torn Middle East region. Perceptions of insecurity diffuse geopolitically, rippling out in concentric rings from the sites of protracted social conflicts and having serious effects on how social conflicts are played out in adjacent areas.[46] Especially influential in this regard are (a) the proliferation of weapons in regions that experience high levels of social tensions for long periods, punctuated by sporadic outbursts of political violence, and (b) the effects that the consequent availability of weaponry has on the character of indigenous social conflict. Another major factor in regional insecurity is the inculcated disposition to perceive conflicts as *vital* threats; to assume threatened, defensive, group-exclusive, and group-protective postures; and to engage in the rapid, aggressive, or preemptive escalation of conflict interactions.

The association of the ethnic republics in the Transcaucasus with first the Russian and then the Soviet state is itself unique in comparison with the other republics. Georgia is an ancient society that has historically experienced persecution at the hands of its more powerful Islamic neighbors, the Turks and Persians. As a result, the kingdom of Georgia voluntarily recognized Russian suzerainty in 1801 and joined the empire as a protectorate. The Armenians have suffered terribly at the hands of the Ottoman Turks in the twentieth century and were effectively driven out of their ancestral lands in eastern Turkey; Azerbaijanis have long been persecuted by the Iranians (Persians). The Armenians and the Azeri Turks can be said to have experienced a more symbiotic relationship with the Soviet suzerain; the modern states of Armenia and Azerbaijan are both Soviet creations.

For both of the Christian regional minorities, their association with the Soviet state was a marriage of convenience. The viability of their recent national independence depends as much in the present as it has in the past on these groups' perceptions of their own security in this volatile region. That the Azerbaijanis appear to have opted to maintain their association with the Soviet successor state, the CIS, complicates matters for the Armenians. Georgia and Armenia are unlikely to form any meaningful collective security alliance, for even these two groups have historical animosities that would be difficult to overcome. Geopolitical realities are likely, as they were in the early years of the Soviet state, to persuade both groups to seek some sort of security (i.e., political) arrangements with the CIS or any other possible Soviet successor state.[47]

Since the contraction of Soviet power and the dissolution of the Soviet Union, outside regional powers such as Turkey and Iran have provided assistance, signed agreements, and made various other overtures to the republic governments of the Caucasus. Turkey has provided a large amount of humanitarian assistance to the Nakhichevan enclave since its only rail link with its nominal republic, Azerbaijan, was cut by Armenian militias in 1991. (The Armenians were retaliating against the Azerbaijanis for cutting off their oil supplies. Such reciprocal sanctions accent interdependence.) Iran has agreed to allow the construction of a new rail link between Azerbaijan and the Nakhichevan district through its territory. More recent agreements have detailed economic assistance, trade, and investments. Iran especially has shown great interest in helping to open new mosques in this region. Recent escalations in the Armenian-Azeri conflict, especially the clashes close to the Turkish border in the Nakhichevan enclave, have made Turkey increasingly attentive to affairs in the region.

Central Asia

The Central Asian region comprises the Kazakh, Kyrgyz, Tajik, Turkmen, and Uzbek republics, which together account for 18 percent of the total territory of the former Soviet Union.[48] There are two autonomous ethnic areas in this region: the Karakalpak unit in Uzbekistan and the Gorno-Badakhshan unit in Tajikistan. Although there was considerable ethnic unrest within the republics of Soviet Central Asia in recent years, the leaderships of these states have been most supportive of continued association with the Soviet central government and, presently, with the CIS.

Kazakhstan is the largest territorial unit in the former Soviet Union after Russia. The indigenous Kazakh population (about

40 percent) is nearly equaled by that of the ethnic Russians
(38 percent); the territory itself is relatively segregated, with
Russians predominating in the north and Kazakhs concentrated
in the south. The Kazakh leader of Kazakhstan, Nursultan Na-
zarbaev, has been a major proponent in the proceedings for
reforming the Soviet system. The Kazakhs, like most of the
other Central Asian ethnic groups, are former transhumant-
pastoralists who have retained a largely rural and traditional
Muslim culture. The Kazakh republic saw a great deal of investment and infrastructural development in the Soviet period, especially because World War II had devastated industry in the
western part of the Soviet Union and necessitated the relocation
of industrial capacity to less vulnerable regions. Treatment of
the indigenous population in this area has been exemplary, so
much so that when ethnic Kazakhs in neighboring China experienced heightened repression by that state in 1962, some sixty
thousand sought asylum in the USSR. There has been little evidence of communal conflict in the Kazakh republic either during the Soviet period or in the reform era.[49]

The situation of minorities in the other Central Asian republics has not been so quiescent. Communal clashes between the
majority ethnic groups and the smaller ethnic enclaves in these
areas have become quite common, such as the incidents between
Uzbeks and Tajiks in the Samarkand *oblast* in Uzbekistan in
1988, between Tajiks and Kyrgyz in the Isfara *raion* in Tajikistan
in mid-1989, and between Uzbeks and Kyrgyz in the Osh *oblast*
in Uzbekistan in mid-1990. The least developed areas of the
Soviet Union, the Central Asian republics are also the least urbanized. Even though these republics are relatively economically disadvantaged in comparison with the European and
Slavic republics, they are relatively advantaged in comparison
with regional neighbors such as Afghanistan, Iran, and the
northwestern provinces of China.

These areas were mainly unorganized politically in the pre-
Soviet era, except for the khanates of Kokand, Khiva, Bukhara,
and Samarkand, and they remain relatively underorganized today. The Uzbeks were traditionally dominant in south central
Asia; the Tajiks seem to have had the most advanced civil culture. The Basmachi resistance to the imposition of Soviet authority in the 1920s is well known, but it appears to have been
limited to roving bands of brigands without much political
coordination.[50]

The ethnic composition of Central Asia was complicated considerably during Stalin's regime as many of the ethnic groups deported during and after World War II were relocated to these areas (e.g., Germans, Crimean Tatars, and the Transcaucasus groups such as the Meskhetians, Balkars, and Chechens). Communal riots, which have become more frequent in the reform era, have often been instigated by roving bands of youths targeting immigrant minorities, such as the pogroms against Meskhetians in the Ferghana valley in Uzbekistan in mid-1989. Riots in Dushanbe (capital of Tajikistan) in February 1990 were reported to have started in response to a rumor that Armenians, relocated from the civil unrest in Transcaucasia, were being given access to scarce housing. These riots quickly took on an antioutsider, antiregime character. Small-scale communal clashes between members of major ethnic groups and republic minorities are not uncommon and are probably best explained as resulting from tensions caused by poor economic conditions and high rates of unemployment, especially among youth.

The recent promulgation of language laws in these republics that make the language(s) of the indigenous population the official language of the republic has caused friction between the indigenous ethnic groups and Russian-speaking groups. As a result, Russian speakers have been emigrating out of these republics at an increasing rate, leaving many of them with a critical shortage of technicians, trained professionals, and other specialists. This problem has caused considerable consternation among the more urbanized and modernized portions of the indigenous populations and has heightened political competition between their modernizing and traditional sectors.

Islam, of course, is a major factor in Central Asia. The liberalization and decentralization of the Soviet regime has been followed by a meteoric rise in the visibility and influence of Islam in Central Asian republic politics. Since official toleration of religion-based political activity is a very recent phenomenon, its eventual impact is difficult to assess. Islamic Movement parties began to appear in many of the Asian republics in late 1991. Mosques are being reopened, rebuilt, and constructed at an increasing rate. What is known is that, despite Soviet-era official policies aimed at suppressing overt religious activity and systematic campaigns of anti-religious propaganda and education, Islam has remained an integral part of the indigenous culture, especially in the more traditional rural areas.

Two issues are likely to be paramount in the definition of Central Asian politics in the future: the burgeoning role of Islam and the political economy of Central Asia. Islam is likely to aggravate a political schism between the urban, modernizing elites and the traditional, rural masses. This pattern is evident in many Islamic countries such as Afghanistan and Pakistan. Pakistan has shown some interest in expanding its influence in this region, but the high mountains separating these areas present a formidable barrier to significant economic and exchange relationships. Iran also borders this region but has expressed few common interests with the Central Asian peoples until recently; China presents the least attractive alternative. The demands of economic development and the geopolitical circumstances of Central Asia leave the peoples of this region few options other than maintaining economic ties with Russia, the CIS, or some Soviet successor state.

As in the Transcaucasus, outside regional powers have shown increased interest in establishing relations with the republics of Central Asia. In the final weeks of 1991 and the first weeks of 1992, Iran, Turkey, Pakistan, India, and Afghanistan all sent delegations to confer and negotiate agreements with the republic governments. Like the situation in the Transcaucasus, the complexion of violence in intergroup relations that has characterized the neighboring regions for many years (in this case, the civil war in Afghanistan) threatens to spill over into Central Asia. Several accusations have been made recently by the government of Tajikistan that agents from Pakistan and the Afghan rebels have been conducting covert destabilization activities and recruiting and supplying armed provocateurs. The ongoing governmental crisis, which has plagued Tajikistan since independence, broke out in violence in May 1992. As a result, the Tajik government requested CIS assistance in closing the border with Afghanistan to prevent any further smuggling of armaments.

Dispersed Communal Minorities

The dispersed communal minorities of the former Soviet Union are diverse groups of ethnic peoples who are either dispersed, living in small enclaves with or without distinctive political status, or living outside their home republics. Gorbachev has stated that some sixty million people (20 percent of the total population) in the former Soviet Union live outside of their home ethnic administrations or are members of groups without home administrations. Many of these are Russians; the Russians are the largest minority in nearly all the successor states of the Soviet Union (outside Russia). The recent devolution of central power and authority in the Soviet Union and the rising assertiveness of the non-Russian groups have put these trans-migrant and communal minorities in a precarious and possibly vulnerable position. Similar trends in Eastern Europe also may be expected to endanger such communal groups, especially economic migrants. The minority peoples coded at risk by the Minorities at Risk project are the Turks of Bulgaria; the Hungarians of Czechoslovakia; the Germans and Hungarians of Romania; the Germans, Jews, and Tatars of the USSR; and the Roma, who are resident in all countries of the region.

Without the protection of the central state and under conditions of severe economic hardship, all dispersed minorities must be considered to be at risk in the present era. It has already been evident in Central Asia and the Transcaucasus that small enclaves of outsiders make convenient scapegoats for economic frustrations and convenient targets for pogroms. It is also evident that a number of these people are feeling increasingly insecure in their alien surroundings and are migrating out of troubled areas when doing so is feasible; many ethnic Germans and Jews, as well as increasing numbers from other groups, have been emigrating abroad. According to official data, about 235,000 people emigrated in 1989, up from 108,000 in 1988 and 39,000 in 1987. Minorities living in regions experiencing violent conflict in recent years such as those in Armenia and Azerbaijan are relocating to safe havens in large numbers.[51]

The status of such minorities in the future will depend primarily, as it has in the past, on the people's proclivities and abilities to adapt, accommodate, or be assimilated by the host culture. Culturally recalcitrant minorities (i.e., ethnic minorities who collectively reject the host culture in favor of retaining exclusivist, isolationist, or traditionalist rationales) are likely to face increasing difficulties under the new commonwealth arrangements being forged. The most immediate consequence of the collapse of the Soviet state has been that the lesser minorities have lost the potential protection afforded by the central state authority in their relations with regional governments. These groups will continue to be the least likely to be able to organize effectively for their own defense and political promotion—except those, such as the Russians, who can count on support from their home states. Even then, these peoples are likely to become political pawns, bargaining chips, and the rationale for irredentist claims and border disputes.

Conclusion

As Gregory Gleason pointed out in a recent article, the CPSU party program adopted in 1986 "reflects the deep-seated ambivalence of the Soviet leadership regarding the problems of contemporary national relations in the USSR. The Program asserts that 'the nationality question, *as it has been inherited from the past,* has been successfully solved.'"[52] Within the short span of two years, deteriorating social relations in the Soviet Union had prompted the CPSU leadership to call a special Central Committee plenum to reexamine the nationality question and to devise a special party platform to address the escalating problems of interethnic conflict; the "Draft Nationalities Policy of the Party Under Present Conditions (CPSU Platform)" was adopted in September 1989. In much of the Soviet thinking on the problem, it has been convenient to place blame for the extent of the current problems on the vagaries, distortions, and arbitrariness imposed by the Stalinist system. This chapter has accepted many of these premises.

The high degree of concurrent or reinforcing cleavages in ethnic markers (language, culture, religion, and territory) among the major ethnies has made for sharp ethnic boundaries in the East European region. This interethnic distinctiveness has contributed to these social groups' perennial stability, resilience, and resistance to assimilation. The policies of the Soviet-type governments have also contributed significantly to the maintenance of interethnic distinctiveness, in spite of discernible and moderately successful yet highly inconsistent efforts by central authorities to effect some form of cultural assimilation across ethnic divisions, either by promoting a composite culture or by imposing policies directed at the coerced assimilation of minority groups. An identifiable division of intent in the Soviet central administrations has worked both to promote, by collective compulsion, and prevent, by individual choice, cultural assimilation in these countries. This dichotomy of interethnic policy may be seen as consistent with a strategy of balancing centripetal and centrifugal ethnic processes. It is not clear, however, whether this dichotomy has been the result of a conscious strategy or is simply attributable to unconscious interethnic competition, or whether it represents inconsistencies in how various Soviet regimes have implemented nationality policies.

The logical outcomes of ethnic conflicts in multinational states can then be seen simply as a reaffirmation of the social dynamics; that is, the separate ethnic identities are reinforced, rather than constrained, by their political interaction. A mutual accommodation and rapprochement of ethnic differences and interests (*sblizhenia*) effects the formation of compatible and complementary, common identifications and a superordinate systemic unity (*sliiania*).[53] Rather than resulting in a process of complete assimilation into a dominant or composite culture with the attendant loss of primordial ties, ethnic processes in multinational societies tend to counterpoise equally vibrant sectarian (i.e., ethnic, religious, linguistic, or cultural) and secular identifications.

The question posed by Alexander Motyl in the title of his 1987 book *Will the Non-Russians Rebel?* may be better posed, then, "Are the non-Russians rebellious?"[54] The answer to that question is certainly yes. But the meaning of that answer is obscured considerably when the corollary question is posed, "Are the Russians rebellious?" The answer to that question is also yes. Will, then, the non-Russians or the Russians or both rebel? They *are* rebelling, but they are rebelling against the past and a system of repressive governance that one hopes no longer actually exists; they are essentially responding to memories and myths of oppression, the accumulated shadows, specters, symbols, and relics of the past. They are left to rebel against regimes that are themselves the product of a rebellion. And they are rebelling in ways that are principally democratic, that is, through mass mobilization, civil disobedience, and civil protest—usually not through the uncivil methods of armed rebellion and violent resistance. In short, the citizens of the East European region, for the most part, are acting as though they are living in and reacting to modern, civil states, not coercive empires. The real question for the future of this region might be best stated, "Can the existing systems be reformed in ways that will mitigate the existing levels of systemic disaffection and social rebellion and prevent the situation from degenerating into political fratricide and violent revolt?"

At the beginning of 1993, the political disintegration of the states of Eastern Europe seems to have reached a plateau. Although the formal structure of the post-Communist order appears to be coalescing, the reality of this new order is still in serious contention everywhere. Ethnic tensions and divisions continue to intensify and deepen, and the scattered pockets of interethnic violence and warfare continue to escalate and spread. The region as a whole seems poised on the brink of civil paralysis or even self-destruction; quite an ironic denouement for a reform movement that originally proposed general disarmament, the demilitarization of political relations, national self-determination, and an end to the repression of human rights. Yet repressed populations usually begin to rebel only after an authoritarian system has been partially liberalized. Mass public opinion lags considerably behind significant political developments. This observation lends some hope to the present situation, depending on the immediate performance of the new states in attending to social needs and demands.

It is especially disturbing, however, to note that the diverse ethnic groups of this region are failing to reach any meaningful agreements regarding the reformation, reconstruction, or replacement of the superordinate political state as the primary institutional instrument of intergroup conflict management. Without some supragovernmental organization that can be a forum for voicing particularist grievances and negotiating and implementing generally acceptable solutions to common problems, the peoples of this region will find themselves left with few alternatives other than unilateral displays of relative power for mitigating intercommunal conflicts.[55] Under such conditions, civil warfare becomes increasingly likely and peaceful conflict resolution becomes increasingly unlikely. As in all such cases, it is the relatively powerless minorities who become the immediate victims of unfavorable social conditions.

In the western press much has been made recently of the prospects for democratic reform since the breakup of the Soviet Union and the dissolution of the Communist party. If one accepts the premise that democratic process begins when the leaders of a political system declare that force and violence can no longer be accepted in political relations, then a most loyal and powerful proponent of democracy was lost with the resignation of President Gorbachev. If one agrees with Giovanni Sartori that "the working principle of democracy is the principle of limited (restrained) majority rule"; with J. Burnham that "the fundamental characteristic of democracy . . . is the concession of the right of political expression to minorities"; and with Lord Acton that "the most certain test by which we judge whether a country is really free is the amount of security enjoyed by minorities," then the new governments of the CIS republics, the former Yugoslavian republics, and Eastern Europe have a long way to go to prove that they are even as democratic and free (in respect to the status and security of systemic minorities) as the systems they have replaced.[56] The political bargaining leverage of minorities in general, it may be argued, has decreased considerably as a function of the disintegration of the multinational states into their much more ethnically homogeneous national components. Minorities were almost a political majority in the former Soviet Union and Yugoslavian federation.

Should this region devolve into chaos, it is unlikely that the neighboring regions could remain unaffected or uninvolved for long. The world can only hope that the peoples of this region will retain, or regain, their sensibilities and recognize the ultimate futility of violence and warfare before it escalates out of control. It is quite seductively appealing for the western world to stand by and watch its long-time enemies writhing in existential angst. Yet history shows that the pain of our neighbors is soon visited on us in our highly interconnected and interdependent world system.

I am reminded of the powerful closing scene from the classic movie "Greed."[57] The two long-term antagonists, Marcus and McTeague, finally confront each other in the middle of Death Valley, where, after a long struggle, McTeague bludgeons his enemy to death with an unloaded pistol. The ecstasy of McTeague's stunning victory turns immediately to despair when he realizes that he is handcuffed to the corpse and has thus sealed their destinies to die in desolation together.

Annex 1

Ethnic Composition of the
Former Republics of the Soviet Union

Note: All population figures are in thousands (× 1000). Ethnic minorities listed are the ones that meet the minimum population criterion set for the Minorities at Risk project (i.e., one hundred thousand population or more than 1 percent of the total population).

Source: Statistics for ethnic populations are from the 1989 USSR All-Union census: Joint Publications Research Service, "Nationality Composition by Union Republics," *Soviet Union: Political Affairs* JPRS-UPA-90-066 (December 4, 1990):16–23.

Russia

Preeminent Ethnic Group: Russians
Ethnic Population/Total Population: 119,866 / 147,022 (81.5 %)

Ethnic Group	Population	Ethnic Group	Population
Tatars	5,543	Komis	336
Ukrainians	4,363	Azerbaijanis	336
Chuvash	1,774	Kumyks	277
Bashkirs	1,345	Lezghins	257
Belarussians	1,206	Ingushes	215
Mordovians	1,073	Tuvins	206
Chechens	899	Moldavians	173
Germans	842	Kalmyks	166
Udmurts	715	Tsygans	153
Maris	644	Karachays	150
Kazakhs	636	Komi-	
Avars	544	Peremyaks	147
Jews	537	Georgians	131
Armenians	532	Uzbeks	127
Buryats	417	Adygeys	125
Ossetians	402	Karelians	123
Kabardinians	386	Koreans	107
Yakuts	380	Laks	106
Dargins	353		

Ukraine

Preeminent Ethnic Group: Ukrainians
Ethnic Population/Total Population: 37,419/51,471 (72.7 %)

Ethnic Group	Population	Ethnic Group	Population
Russians	11,356	Bulgarians	234
Jews	486	Poles	215
Belarussians	440	Hungarians	163
Moldavians	325	Romanians	135

Belarus

Preeminent Ethnic Group: Belarussians
Ethnic Population/Total Population 7,905/10,152 (77.9 %)

Ethnic Group	Population	Ethnic Group	Population
Russians	1,342	Ukrainians	291
Poles	418	Jews	112

Uzbekistan

Preeminent Ethnic Group: Uzbeks
Ethnic Population/Total Population: 14,142/19,810 (71.4 %)

Ethnic Group	Population	Ethnic Group	Population
Russians	1,653	Koreans	183
Tajiks	934	Kyrgyz	175
Kazakhs	808	Ukrainians	153
Tatars	468	Turkmens	122
Karakalpaks	412	Turks	106
Crimean Tatars	189		

Kazakhstan

Preeminent Ethnic Group: Kazakhs
Ethnic Population/Total Population: 6,535/16,464 (39.7 %)

Ethnic Group	Population	Ethnic Group	Population
Russians	6,228	Tatars	328
Germans	958	Uighurs	185
Ukrainians	896	Belarussians	183
Uzbeks	332	Koreans	103

Tajikistan

Preeminent Ethnic Group: Tajiks
Ethnic Population/Total Population: 3,172/5,092 (62.3 %)

Ethnic Group	Population	Ethnic Group	Population
Uzbeks	1,198	Tatars	72
Russians	388	Kyrgyz	64

Kyrgyzstan

Preeminent Ethnic Group: Kyrgyz
Ethnic Population/Total Population: 2,230/4,258 (52.4 %)

Ethnic Group	Population	Ethnic Group	Population
Russians	917	Germans	101
Uzbeks	550	Tatars	70
Ukrainians	108		

Turkmenistan

Preeminent Ethnic Group: Turkmens
Ethnic Population/Total Population: 2,537/3,523 (72.0%)

Ethnic Group	Population	Ethnic Group	Population
Russians	334	Tatars	39
Uzbeks	317	Ukrainians	36
Kazakhs	88		

Azerbaijan

Preeminent Ethnic Group: Azerbaijanis
Ethnic Population/Total Population: 5,805/7,021 (82.7 %)

Ethnic Group	Population	Ethnic Group	Population
Russians	392	Lezghins	171
Armenians	391		

Georgia

Preeminent Ethnic Group: Georgians
Ethnic Population/Total Population: 3,787/5,401 (70.1 %)

Ethnic Group	Population	Ethnic Group	Population
Armenians	437	Ossetians	164
Russians	341	Greeks	100
Azerbaijanis	308	Abkhaz	96

Armenia

Preeminent Ethnic Group: Armenians
Ethnic Population/Total Population: 3,084/3,305 (93.3 %)

Ethnic Group	Population	Ethnic Group	Population
Azerbaijanis	85	Russians	52
Kurds	56		

Moldova

Preeminent Ethnic Group: Moldavians
Ethnic Population/Total Population: 2,795/4,335 (64.5 %)

Ethnic Group	Population	Ethnic Group	Population
Ukrainians	600	Bulgarians	88
Russians	562	Jews	66
Gagauz	153		

Lithuania

Preeminent Ethnic Group: Lithuanians
Ethnic Population/Total Population: 2,924/3,675 (79.6 %)

Ethnic Group	Population	Ethnic Group	Population
Russians	344	Belarussians	63
Poles	258	Ukrainians	45

Latvia

Preeminent Ethnic Group: Latvians
Ethnic Population/Total Population: 1,388/2,667 (52.0 %)

Ethnic Group	Population	Ethnic Group	Population
Russians	906	Poles	60
Belarussians	120	Lithuanians	34
Ukrainians	92		

Estonia

Preeminent Ethnic Group: Estonians
Ethnic Population/Total Population: 963/1,566 (61.5 %)

Ethnic Group	Population	Ethnic Group	Population
Russians	475	Belarussians	28
Ukrainians	48		

Annex 2

Ethnic Composition of the
Former Republics of Yugoslavia

Note: All population figures are in thousands (× 1000). Ethnic minorities listed are the ones that meet the minimum population criterion set for the Minorities at Risk project (i.e., one hundred thousand population or more than 1 percent of the total population).

Source: Statistics for ethnic populations are from the 1981 Yugoslavian census: United Nations, Committee on the Elimination of Racial Discrimination, *Yugoslavia,* CERD/C/118/Add. 23, Annex II.

Serbia

Preeminent Ethnic Group: Serbs
Ethnic Population/Total Population: 6,182/9,334 (66.2 %)

Ethnic Group	Population	Ethnic Group	Population
Albanians	1,303	Croats	150
Hungarians	390	Montenegrins	148
Bosnia Muslims	216	Roma (Gypsies)	111
Yugoslavians (or no nationality) 471			

Croatia

Preeminent Ethnic Group: Croats
Ethnic Population/Total Population: 3,455/4,601 (75.1 %)

Ethnic Group	Population	Ethnic Group	Population
Serbs	632		
Yugoslavians (or no nationality) 396			

Bosnia-Hercegovina

Preeminent Ethnic Group: Bosnia Muslims
Ethnic Population/Total Population: 1,630/4,124 (39.5 %)

Ethnic Group	Population	Ethnic Group	Population
Serbs	1,321	Croats	758

Yugoslavians (or no nationality) 344

Macedonia

Preeminent Ethnic Group: Macedonians
Ethnic Population/Total Population: 1,281/1,912 (67.0 %)

Ethnic Group	Population	Ethnic Group	Population
Albanians	378	Roma (Gypsies)	43
Turks	87	Bosnia Muslims	40
Serbs	45		

Yugoslavians (or no nationality) 15

Slovenia

Preeminent Ethnic Group: Slovenes
Ethnic Population/Total Population: 1,712/1,892 (90.5 %)

Ethnic Group	Population	Ethnic Group	Population
Croats	56	Serbs	42

Yugoslavians (or no nationality) 29

Montenegro

Preeminent Ethnic Group: Montenegrins
Ethnic Population/Total Population: 400/584 (68.5 %)

Ethnic Group	Population	Ethnic Group	Population
Bosnia Muslims	78	Serbs	19
Albanians	38	Croats	7

Yugoslavians (or no nationality) 32

8. Minorities, Rebellion, and Repression in North Africa and the Middle East

Barbara Harff

In the half-century since World War II the thirty-one politically active minorities of North Africa and the Middle East have initiated greater magnitudes of communal protest and rebellion than groups in virtually any other world regions.[1] Communal hostilities also have been the main cause of, or a contributing factor to, most interstate wars in the region. Comparative evidence in chapters 2 and 3 showed that minorities in this region experience greater political inequalities than groups in other regions. Problems are most severe in the core of the Arab world; there is less inequality and greater accommodation among communal groups in North Africa and Pakistan.[2]

Sources of communal inequalities, conflict, and repression in the Middle East are highlighted in the seven case studies of this chapter. One is the denial of the national aspirations of the Palestinians and Kurds, both of which are consequences of large political processes in this century: the disintegration of the Ottoman Empire, foreign intervention in the region, and state building by new nationalist elites. Muslim dominance over the subordinate confessional communities (i.e., Christians and Jews) and the schismatic divisions within Islam have added to the conflict helix.

All six types of communal groups are represented in the region. Most numerous are thirteen ethnonationalist groups, most of whom are cross-classified in other types: the Kurds, for example, are classified as both ethnonationalists and indigenous peoples in each of three Middle Eastern countries.[3] In addition to the Kurds, the eleven groups classified as indigenous people include the Berbers in the Maghreb and the Baluch in Pakistan and Iran. Fourteen minorities are defined in whole or part by their religious beliefs; the Baha'is in Iran are distinguished only by their faith, whereas the Palestinians in Lebanon and in Israel's Occupied Territories are separated from dominant groups by their ethnonationalism as well as their religion. The Arabs in Israel and the Shi'is in Iraq are examples of the region's five ethnoclasses; their class status is reinforced by differences in religious belief between them and dominant groups. Eight groups are classified as communal contenders, most of them in Lebanon (four groups) and Pakistan (two groups). The Shi'is in Lebanon and the Sindhis in Pakistan are disadvantaged contenders (the former more so than the latter), while the Sunni Arabs of Iraq and the Alawis of Syria are among the region's advantaged contenders.

This chapter traces the political mobilization of seven of these groups, examines their claims and patterns of discrimination, and assesses regimes' responses to communal protest and rebellion. The first case is the Palestinians, a stateless people with a strong sense of national identity, dispersed among a multitude of countries; in Israel's Occupied Territories the Palestinians actively oppose a democratic state for redress of their territorial ambitions and deprivations of rights. The second case is the Kurds in Iraq, who are representative of ethnically distinct groups that are dispersed across international boundaries, seek greater autonomy or independence, and are mobilized into active rebellion against oppressive regimes. The Berbers of Morocco are the third case, also a transnational people but one whose aspirations are mainly cultural and economic and capable of being managed within existing state structures. The Arabs in Israel, the fourth case, identify more with Palestinians than with the state of Israel, but many have focused their political efforts on improving their status within the Israeli polity.

Lebanon provides two cases, the Shi'is (communal contenders) and Palestinians (immigrant ethnonationalists). Both have been involved in a civil war that is temporarily on hold, but against different antagonists: the Shi'is have opposed the Maronite-dominated political elite, whereas the Palestinians fought their Lebanese oppressors and the occupying Israeli forces. Finally, the Baha'is are a religious minority repressed by a theocratic regime. They lack the ability and organization to counteract discriminatory measures, but their status has improved partly because of international pressures on the Iranian government.

I begin with a brief overview of each group's political history and persistent conflicts with other groups. The analysis follows the theoretical model of ethnic and communal mobilization developed in chapter 5, and is designed to assess the model's plausibility.

The first block of variables in the model refers to group status. The general argument is that endemic discrimination increases the latent sense of grievances among a communal group and increases its potential for political mobilization. Ethnopolitical mobilization further depends on the salience of the group's identity, its cohesiveness, and the degree to which the group's subordinate status has been maintained with coercion. Of course a neat linear process cannot be assumed by which the above traits develop simultaneously, increase to equal strength, or are present at all times. It could equally well be argued that only some discriminatory actions of a dominant group precipitate ethnic mobilization and are confined to particular polities.

The second block of variables in the model is concerned with national and international conditions that may intensify communal grievances. State expansion by dominant elites, democratization, and an expanding global economy all are said to have potentially adverse effects. The model also identifies three other international factors that facilitate the proactive mobilization of ethnic groups: international support, transnational kindred, and contagion of communal activism elsewhere. Obviously not all states expand; neither is the process of democratization significantly advanced in more than a few Middle Eastern societies. Most are autocracies, a political condition distinctly associated with ethnic rebellion.

Dispersed Groups Seeking Greater Autonomy and Independence

Palestinians in Israel's Occupied Territories

Palestinians are a national people who are dispersed throughout the world, with politically active segments—using the criteria of the Minority at Risk project—in Jordan, Israel, and Lebanon as well as the West Bank and Gaza. Their hopes for their own state were set back by their leadership's inability to control popular sympathies with Iraq during the 1991 Gulf War. Widespread Palestinian support for the Saddam Hussein regime was ammunition in the hands of an increasingly right-wing Israeli polity.

The losers in Kuwait were not just the Kuwaitis but foremost the resident Palestinians, who were deprived of jobs, homes, and a country that in the past had supported their political aspirations with money and long-term residency. Since March 1991, Kuwait has closed its borders to those wanting to return and persecuted others suspected of collaboration with the Iraqi regime. The last stronghold of Palestinian support now is the Jordanian monarchy, which in the past has played a dubious role in Palestinian national aspirations. This support has cost Jordan dearly. Between September 1990 and February 1991 its economy plunged to Third World status and its political credibility reached an all-time low in the eyes of the United States.

There is some hope for Palestinian aspirations, however. The United States, by charting a more evenhanded course in its treatment of security issues and national self-determination in the Middle East, was able to pressure all sides to join multilateral negotiations that began in Madrid in November 1991. Continuation of these initiatives may further the cause of peace in the region, in which the Palestinian issue is the thorniest.[4]

Background

Palestinians in the West Bank and Gaza are largely Sunni Arabs; less than a tenth are Christians. In the Ottoman Empire confessional groups were organized into millets (relatively autonomous communities responsible for many social and administrative functions). Ethnicity—in the contemporary sense of bonds that are created by a common religion, culture, race, language, and history—was treated as a nonissue; only religion was recognized as a factor separating peoples. Thus, Christian and Jewish communities enjoyed internal autonomy but little political clout and were treated generally as inferiors. (Arab Shi'is were not formally recognized as a millet.) Sunni Muslims in principle had access to political power as long as they recognized the Ottoman Empire as the heir of the Arab empires and were sufficiently Turkified. This does not mean, however, that today's Palestinians could not be distinguished from other citizens of the Ottoman Empire. First, they were Arabs, not Turkomans, and their point of origin was in the Arabian peninsula and the Fertile Crescent rather than the steppes of Asia. Their language was part of the Semitic family of languages in contrast to the Indo-Germanic origin of Turkish. Arabic dialects are distinct and often identify place of origin. Many peoples in the Arab world were sedentary, although tribal migration continued well into the twentieth century, coinciding with the emergence of modern states. Despite some claims to the contrary, Palestine during the British Mandate period (1919–20 to 1947) was a relatively well-settled, agriculturally productive land. But religiously based communal identity was nevertheless fragmented, pitting Sunni oligarchs against landless peasants, Christian Arabs against Muslim Arabs, Jews against Muslims, and Shi'is against Sunnis. The scope of sectarian rivalries further extended to Alawis, Druze, and other Shi'a sects.

In general, ethnic solidarity tends to increase as a result of adversity. When competition for land became part of Arab political experience in the twentieth century, Palestinians failed to secure a territorial base for their political aspirations. The Jewish diaspora, combined with external intervention by former colonialists and later the superpowers (the United States and the Soviet Union), lack of a unified leadership among the Palestinians, and class and religious divisions among them combined to prevent a territorial compromise.

Consequences of Mobilization

The Intifada is the latest expression of communal frustration that began in 1919 and escalated in 1929 and 1936 to large-scale clashes between Jews and Arabs in Jerusalem and other parts of Palestine. Few Palestinians can see themselves as members of a binational, Israeli-dominated state in which Jews and Palestinians live in harmony. The mainstream Fatah within the PLO has overall the strongest support, while other groups such as Hamas (Islamic fundamentalists), the Popular Front for the Liberation of Palestine, and the Democratic Front for the Liberation of Palestine enjoy some support. The last two organizations have left the PLO, while Hamas was never under the PLO umbrella. Insofar as these organizations incorporate most Palestinians, they are the functional equivalent of political parties or movements within the structure of the state of Palestine that was unilaterally declared by the PLO on November 14, 1988.

Recent Events

The Intifada erupted spontaneously on December 8, 1987, and soon created its own leadership; the PLO was surprised by a rebellion that was neither initiated nor led by PLO activists. However, the PLO Council attempted to seize the initiative with the historic statement (on the first anniversary of the Intifada) that the PLO would recognize Israel's right to exist. Simultaneously it advocated a two-state solution and accepted United Nations Resolutions 242 and 338: the former (passed on November 22, 1967) called on Israel to withdraw from the territories occupied in the June 1967 war; the latter (passed October 22, 1973) called for a cease-fire to halt the October 1973 war and for the implementation of UN Resolution 242.

Current Status

West Bankers and Gazaens are noncitizens and subject to severe discriminatory treatment. They have been killed, maimed, and deported; they have had their houses demolished or sealed, are at risk of physical mistreatment, are under curfew, are detained without trial, experience censorship, and have had their institutions of higher learning closed for months at a time. Many West Bankers and Gazaens worked as menial laborers in Israel, at least until the beginning of the Intifada. Since then their movement has been severely restricted. Work is available only to those deemed trustworthy by Israeli officials, and those allowed to work in Israel often are the target of discrimination and harassment at home by fellow Palestinians.

Since the beginning of the Intifada, economic conditions have deteriorated for the Palestinians. Frequent strikes and curfews, a decline in tourism, and a dramatic drop in foreign remittances have taken their toll. In the aftermath of the Gulf War many Palestinians were expelled from Kuwait and Saudi Arabia, the PLO lost major financial supporters (such as Saudi Arabia and Kuwait), and many potential wage earners were put in Israeli jails or put out of work in Jordan, the West Bank, and Gaza. Between December 8, 1987, and October 31, 1991, a total of 802 Palestinians were killed as a direct result of the uprising and an additional 462 Palestinians suspected of collaboration with Israelis died at the hand of other Palestinians; estimates of serious injuries range from thousands to tens of thousands. In contrast 31 Israelis were killed in the territories and 47 inside the Green Line (Israeli territory prior to 1967).[5] Israelis also suffered a slight loss in income because of declining tourism and for want of Palestinian labor in the construction industry.

The reduction of remittances caused by the Gulf War and the limited support forthcoming from the PLO further increased economic hardship in the territories. The UN Relief and Works Agency for Palestine Refugees in the Near East has supported large numbers of Palestinians since 1948, but the support is barely adequate. Demographic stress also is high, partly because Palestinian birthrates are higher than those of Israelis. Most Palestinians emphasize the positive aspects of high birthrates, arguing that in the early twenty-first century Arab Palestinians will outnumber Jews in Israel, and may therefore acquire more political clout. On the downside, the demographic stress in a region that suffers from lack of arable land is enormous, and there are few economic opportunities for an educated people. Since few options exist in Israel for West Bankers and Gazaens, and only a few are able to leave to find work abroad, Palestinians are likely to become increasingly impoverished.

The Palestinians' collective disadvantages vis-à-vis Israelis are very high and are likely to remain high until a political settlement can be reached. The Intifada is an active expression of ethnic conflict that includes elements of both protest and rebellion. An increase in any of the underlying conditions is likely to intensify conflict and may precipitate a return to terrorist incidents.

Role of the State

In the late twentieth century the long-established democratic states seldom practice patterns of discrimination that intensify ethnic conflict. Israel, however, is still a new state. State building typically involves the subordination of special interest groups and restraints on ethnic autonomy to fit the ideals of the dominant group. Few new states have been able to successfully integrate different ethnies; the democratic pluralistic state in post-colonial societies is rare.

Democratic Israel is no exception. Israel is a multiparty democracy for Jewish Israelis. Minorities can vote for various parties representing their interests, but they lack access to high-level decision making. Israeli rule in the Occupied Territories is authoritarian with limited provisions for democratic participation. It is proposed in chapter 5 that when autocratic control is lessened, communal mobilization increases, with high potential costs. This situation appears to exist in the territories. On one hand, Israel's policy of continuing expansion in the form of new settlements on the West Bank and continuing reliance on coercion to maintain the inferior status of Palestinians in the territories helps to reinforce open resistance against an expanding Jewish presence. On the other, a total crackdown on the Intifada, one that would involve increased imprisonment, killings, and mass expulsions, is unthinkable for many Israeli citizens and policymakers.

The communal basis of the Israeli state complicates efforts to reach political accommodation. Shifts in the Israeli electorate due to immigration of Jews from Muslim societies have led to a greater emphasis on the religious nature of the state and a blurring of the divide between secular and religious matters. In the initial phase of state building, infighting between secular and Orthodox Jews was less serious than it is now. Efforts to define Jewishness narrowly have led to widespread protest among Israelis and American supporters of Israel. The Law of Return grants every Jew the right to immigrate to Israel and enjoy full citizenship. Non-Jews married to Jews, and their children and grandchildren, enjoy the same rights: thus the question of what constitutes Jewishness becomes a matter of rights.

Palestinians in the West Bank and Gaza whose ancestors lived for centuries in the area enjoy such rights in principle if they were living in the territories on the day of occupation in September 1967. Palestinians residing outside the territories for work or study were refused reentry, and so many families were separated. In practice, residency for Palestinians is not a right but a privilege. Family reunification requests are often denied, and residents married to nonresidents are subject to harassment or spouse removal. The sacredness of the family and its unity are protected in most societies and considered a fundamental right in the Universal Declaration of Human Rights (1948); any denial of such rights constitutes discrimination and oppression.

Israeli society and its political establishment have experienced political polarization on account of the growth of an ideological block in the Knesset consisting of ultranationalists, ethnocentrists, religious Zionists, and fundamentalists dreaming of a rebirth of the kingdom of Israel. Democratically minded Israelis have clamored for electoral reforms as a result of what they see as a dangerous collaboration between religious and right-wing parties sharing similar platforms (especially Tehiya, Tzomet, Moledet, and the National Religious party). These parties have inordinate power and, despite their limited membership, are able to influence important decisions. Not only does this situation impede the building of effective governing coalitions, it has prevented a meaningful dialogue with the Palestinians and the peace camp. The above parties are united as the "Eretz Yisrael Front" and, along with the charismatic social movement Gush Emunim, are representative of the religious nationalist hard-liners' unwillingness to yield on Palestinian demands to stop building settlements in the West Bank. Prior to the June 1992 elections that brought a new Labor-dominated coalition to power, they had effectively blocked territorial compromise.

International Environment

The dispersion of a people across international boundaries facilitates political mobilization. The Palestinians are part of a diaspora. Nearly three million Palestinians live in other Arab countries, Europe, the Americas, and elsewhere. Showing formidable political and economic support for their brethren living in Israel and the territories, they have formed lobby groups and support the PLO morally and financially. They have been able to exert considerable pressures on Arab policymakers, and until the Gulf War they had considerable political leverage in the countries of the Arabian peninsula. They also can sway public opinion in Jordan at will.

Since 1988, Yasir Arafat, representing the mainstream of the

PLO and accepted as the legitimate spokesman for the Palestinians, has often included in his messages a public disavowal of terrorism. Terrorist networks exist nonetheless. In Lebanon, where linkages with other disaffected groups have been easy to establish, Palestinian groups have taken actions under the organizational umbrella of the Islamic Jihad. Since 1985–86, Palestinian terrorist activity has diffused primarily among newer and less-established organizations outside the Arafat camp. Although Palestinian terrorist activity tapered off in the late 1980s, disaffected groups operating with the tacit support of Libya or Syria still are active.

The support of international actors also facilitates communal mobilization. The Palestinians traditionally enjoyed strong support among members of the Organization of the Islamic Conference, the Arab League, and the Organization of Petroleum-Exporting Countries. Most Asian and African states have traditionally supported the Palestinian cause in the UN General Assembly, where they consistently have voted in favor of Palestinian demands and against the interests of Israel, to the degree of conferring observer status on the PLO and equating Zionism with racism (since rescinded). This atmosphere has led Israel to question the objectivity of the United Nations and further led to its insistence on a diminished UN role in any peacemaking effort.

Kurds in the Middle East

Background

The Kurds are a dispersed national people, but their situation differs in many respects from that of Palestinians. They are a non-Arab, mostly Sunni Muslim people who number about twenty million and live in Turkey, Iraq, Iran, Syria, and the former USSR. Most Kurds are reluctant to be assimilated into dominant groups; instead they promote their own culture, preserve their own customs and language, and are determined to win regional autonomy, if not independence. Relatively cohesive, they have agitated for self-rule since the early twentieth century. Pawns of British colonialists, various independence and liberation movements, nationalist leaders, and monarchs, they were only briefly able to pursue their own political destiny. The

Treaty of Sèvres (1920) called for the establishment of an independent Kurdistan, a hope realized only for a few months in 1945–46 when the Soviet-backed Mahabad Republic was established in northwestern Iran. It was overthrown when Iranian troops entered in 1946.

Although the Kurds in Turkey number about ten million, their existence was officially denied and they were referred to, if at all, as Mountain Turks. Many individuals subordinated their Kurdish identity to that of the Turkish nation, and some have played an active role in political life: for example, an ethnic Kurd, Hikmet Cetin, was appointed foreign minister in late 1991 and became head of the government's Committee of Ministers in May 1992. The Turkish government changed its policy in 1990 by publicly acknowledging the Kurds' collective existence, accepting expressions of Kurdish identity and language, and permitting limited political activity by Kurdish activists.

The leaders of Turkey, a country traditionally on the crossroads between the Middle East and Europe, prefer cordial but distant relations with their Muslim brethren and close cooperation with Western Europe and the United States. Turkey's recent concessions to the Kurds may be motivated partly by a desire to win greater western acceptance, but they also seem to reflect the desire of leaders of a quasi-democratic state to reach accommodation with its largest minority. However, the Kurdish Workers' party (known by its Turkish initials as PKK) has used guerrilla and terrorist tactics to pursue independence and in 1991–92 was the target of bombings and reprisals both in Turkey and in villages and camps in northern Iraq.

Iranian Kurds, numbering about five million, were first supported by the late Muhammad Reza Shah in the late 1960s but abandoned in 1975, when the shah reached agreement with Iraq on sharing the Shatt al Arab waterway. The Khomeini regime actively supported the Iraqi Kurds against Saddam Hussein's regime but simultaneously imposed restrictions on its own Kurds, on grounds that the Sunni Kurds were "only one level above heretics."[6] Kurds clamoring for greater autonomy since the beginning of the revolution faced periods when open aggression alternated with promises of economic support. At no time was the Khomeini regime willing to support greater self-rule for the Kurds. The fortunes of Iranian Kurds are closely tied to whether the states with the largest number of Kurds— Iran, Iraq, and Turkey—cooperate with or oppose one another in trying to respond to the Kurds' demands. The western stance has shifted from hostility to support depending on the Kurds' changing political rhetoric. Their sometimes anti-imperialist posturing has not helped their cause in the West.

The Kurds of Syria and the former USSR are relatively small and nonvocal minorities. Estimates of the number of Kurds in Syria range from fewer than one hundred thousand to more than one million. The Kurds in the USSR were given their own national district in Azerbaijan in 1923 but were forcibly dispersed in 1937 and 1944 among nine Soviet republics. The 1989 Soviet census tallied 153,000 Kurds.[7]

Iraqi Kurds

Current Situation. The Kurdish Resistance (Pesh Merga) has fought an on-again, off-again guerrilla war against the Iraqi regime since the early 1960s. Iraqi Kurds' demands for greater autonomy, cultural self-determination, and a greater share in oil revenues were to be honored in 1970, when a new constitution formally granted them greater autonomy. None of the pledges were fulfilled, however. The Kurds living in the oil-rich northern mountains have yet to achieve the kind of prosperity enjoyed by other Iraqis.

Rebellions have repeatedly been suppressed militarily, and villagers have been forcefully relocated. In March 1988, during the Iran-Iraq War, Saddam Hussein's regime was responsible for gassing an estimated five thousand people in the Kurdish town of Halabja. This genocidal act resulted in a refugee stream to neighboring Turkey and Iran. In addition, more than one hundred thousand Kurds were forcibly relocated from oil-rich areas to the Saudi border.

Although there had been sharp and sometimes violent hostilities between the Kurdish Democratic party, led by the Barzanis, and the Patriotic Union of Kurdistan (PUK), formed in 1976 by Jalal Talabani, the Gulf War prompted closer cooperation among groups; in March 1991 they rebelled against the Saddam Hussein regime but were unable to persevere. Whole villages again were eradicated, and by the beginning of 1992 about two hundred thousand Iraqi Kurds were refugees in neigboring countries. Active financial assistance from western private and public relief organizations and the promulgation of a general amnesty (March 1991) by the Iraqi regime led to the return of some refugees and the rebuilding of some of the devastated villages. Amnesty International claims that hundreds of Kurds disappeared and were executed after returning to Iraq, despite Saddam Hussein's general amnesty offer. As of late 1992 the situation was extremely unstable. An uneasy truce existed between Saddam Hussein's regime and the Kurds, reinforced by the coalition's ban on Iraqi military flights over the Kurdish zone.[8]

Consequences of Mobilization. The previously fractious leadership has combined efforts: Massoud Barzani, leader of the Kurdish Democratic party, and Jalal Talabani of the PUK appear united in their quest for Kurdish autonomy. Iraqi Kurds now as always depend substantially on the goodwill of outside powers. Though negotiations with the Saddam Hussein regime continue, in the aftermath of the economic devastation inflicted on Iraq the Kurdish provinces are not likely to gain greater autonomy, especially not in the oil-rich Kirkuk region, nor are the Kurds likely to be invited to share political power in Baghdad. The more likely outcome, even without Saddam Hussein, is a return to the status quo ante bellum, in which cooperative Kurds are not actively persecuted but are neither allowed greater political participation at the center nor given regional autonomy. The destiny of Kurdish aspirations is now more than ever closely allied with regional realignment.

International Environment. Recent international support for the Iraqi Kurds has been in the form of foodstuffs, medicine and symbolic support, complemented by shows of military force. For the time being, Turkey appears to support the Kurdish struggle in Iraq, but it is simultaneously fighting rebels among its own Kurds. Turkish Kurds have in the past been supported by Syria, but at other times Syria has cooperated with Turkey (e.g., in 1987) in efforts to deal with the Kurdish problem.

In the past the Kurds had no significant international support. Their status and rebellions were usually perceived as local matters, falling within the jurisdiction of each sovereign state. Potentially sympathetic Third World leaders were careful not to take sides in situations too close to those at home. Many new states face the problem of rebellions by minorities against the dominant group in the quest for internal autonomy or independence (for example, by Biafrans in Nigeria and the East Timorese in Indonesia).

In May 1992 the Iraqi Kurds held formal elections to constitute a representative body that was to deal with internal issues on a more official basis. Outside observers helped assure fair elections, Saddam Hussein declared the process illegal, and Barzani and Talabani received nearly equal shares of the votes, with minor candidates receiving negligible percentages. Once again Kurdish fortunes are tied to the cooperation between the Talabani and Barzani forces and their ability to influence the Ba'thists in Baghdad.

Moroccan Berbers

Background

The Berbers, descendants of the original indigenous tribes of North Africa, are Sunni Muslims located in Morocco, Mauritania, Algeria, Tunisia, and the western Sahel. Of these countries Morocco has the highest concentration of Berbers, about 9.7 million or 37 percent of the population, most of whom have maintained their own language and culture. They are also a sizeable and politically significant minority in Algeria (5.4 million, 21 percent of the population).

Ancestors of the Berbers are thought to have lived in the area for four thousand years. Under the Umayyad caliphate (661–750), Islam spread across North Africa to Spain. Early Arab conquerers and merchants typically lived separately from their subjects and forced conversions were rare; more important was the collection of taxes from subjects. Over time, some pagans adopted Islam as a means to obtaining equitable treatment from their Arab overlords. Christianity did not reach the Berbers.

Even Berbers who adopted Islam retained rituals reminiscent of their ancient past, such as cults of holy men. Over the centuries local dynasties ruled in relative autonomy from the caliphate, which governed first from Damascus and later from Baghdad. At first the Berbers' sense of nationhood did not extend beyond their tribes, but in the eleventh century two federations, the Almohads and the Almovarids, brought Berber dynasties to power. The Almohads were the first to unite all of North Africa and Spain under one rule.

Berbers' sense of identity is rooted in Islam and to a lesser degree in a web of kinship. With the advance of secular culture brought by the colonizing Europeans, Islamic civilization and kinship ties were profoundly altered. Eventually all local peoples, including Berbers, were strongly affected.

Whereas Islam establishes precise rules of conduct, European ideas challenged Qur'anic and tribal traditions. Western secular thought questioned the compatibility of faith and reason. The challenges posed were immense. Autocratic Islamic regimes were confronted with the western doctrine of popular sovereignty, secular codes of law, and political structures designed to implement the popular will. The Shari'a (Islamic law), which traditionally dominated the lives of citizens and rulers, gave way to French maritime, civil, and commercial law. Where once the ulema (Muslim scholars) transmitted knowledge, that knowledge was now deemed irrelevant or inadequate for the purposes of a modern state and society.

After European settlement began in 1830, Morocco fared better than Algeria, which came under full occupation by France. At the height of French colonial power some one million Frenchmen lived in Algeria, versus only two hundred thousand in Morocco. Algerian culture and education were dominated by French-Arab schools. Islamic schools received no financial support, and French civil law was imposed in 1850. In Morocco Islamic law and the traditional systems remained largely intact, and traditional Muslim life thus had some continuity.

In the seventeenth century the current dynasty of Morocco, known as the Alawis, came to power. Unlike Berbers, they originated in Arabia and claim descent from the prophet Muhammad. From 1912 to 1956 Morocco came under French and Spanish rule as a protectorate. Berbers revolted against Spanish rule in the Rif mountains in 1921, and were brought under control through combined Spanish and French efforts in 1927.

The Berbers were favored by the French authorities, and some Berber chiefs became wealthy. The non-Berber sultan became a figurehead in his own country. The situation changed after World War II, when an active independence party, the Istiqlal, emerged. This party was led by Sultan Mohamed V, who became the symbol of the movement for freedom from colonial rule and independence. In a concrete example of Muslim resistance and Arab-Berber cooperation, Berbers joined with Arabs to fight the European colonizers in the Rif insurrection in the 1920s, led by former Muslim judge Abd al-Karim. Although Berber leaders briefly cooperated with French authorities and actively supported the deposal of Mohamed V in 1953, they joined non-Berbers and rallied to rescue Mohamed from exile in 1955.[9]

Consequences of Mobilization

Moroccan society is divided by class, urban-rural, and intercity rivalries. That rural Berbers are geographically concentrated in the mountains adds to their sense of isolation, and no political party can claim the group's exclusive loyalty. The Berbers are only partially integrated into the general society. The king's role as patron of some powerful Berber clan leaders contributes to inter-Berber rivalries.

The Berbers under European rule experienced neglect and poverty. After independence, they demanded increased expenditures in their region to raise the standard of living. In addition, the Berbers asked to have their own schools and to run their own local administrative apparatus. The central government was slow to respond, which led to local rebellions and some guerrilla activity. The 1960s and 1970s were relatively peaceful, but cultural awareness increased. Educated young Berbers resisted arabicization efforts by the government and demanded that their language be taught in separate schools and become a choice in all other schools, and they further demanded that institutes be set up for the study of Berber culture. In the recent past the government has attempted to accommodate Berber cultural interests.

Role of the State

Berbers are essentially part of the Islamic culture of the Maghreb. Whatever historical grievances they may have had against the dominant Arab culture did not lead them to challenge Muslim rule. The present dynasty's legitimacy rests on its uninterrupted rule and descendence from the prophet Muhammad. I suggest that Berber identity, although always a factor in tribal traditions, was more profoundly influenced by the advance of the Europeans than by conflict with the Islamic state.

Current Status

Pan-Berber consciousness of the past few decades seems the work of a new generation of university educated Berbers, reacting against what they perceive as arabicization efforts. Some have returned to their tribal lands to mobilize their people, others have joined Islamic revivalist movements that emphasize the common bonds of the Maghrebins. Mostly, they are quietly agitating for greater recognition of Berber identity and culture within the bounds of the existing Moroccan state. The group's cultural demands are largely met; hence there has been no widespread rebellion or regional diffusion of conflict.

Suppressed Ethnoclasses

Arabs in Israel

Background

Israel's eight hundred thousand Arab citizens make up about 17 percent of the total population. Most Arabs in Israel are descendants of the original inhabitants of pre–World War II Palestine, who remained after the establishment of the state of Israel in 1948. Although heavily concentrated in the Galilee, some live virtually in all regions and cities. Arabs in Israel are largely Sunnis, but 12.8 percent are Christians and 9.5 percent are Druze. Here I am explicitly concerned with Sunni and Christian Arabs, since the Druze have a somewhat different, slightly more privileged status in Israel; they are conscripted into the armed forces and are recognized as an autonomous religious community. Bedouins, another small segment of the Arabs in Israel, typically volunteer for service in the armed forces.

Theoretically, Arabs in Israel are full citizens, but in practice they are second-class citizens. Despite increasing prosperity during the 1980s, more than 40 percent of Arab households now live below Israel's poverty line. More than a quarter of all Arab families live in crowded conditions versus 1.1 percent of Jewish families; Arab infant mortality is 2.5 times that of Jewish Israelis. There is discrimination in mortgage assistance, schoolrooms are overcrowded, and employment prospects for educated Arab Israelis are dismal. Since army service is not compulsory for Arabs in Israel and they rarely join, they are deprived of many benefits. There are numerous surveys dealing with the attitudes of Arabs in Israel toward the state of Israel, showing that the majority accept the state of Israel in principle, assuming that they can achieve equal citizenship through some form of accommodation or by changing the Zionist-religious character of the state. Only about a tenth deny Israel's right to exist and want it replaced by a democratic secular Palestinian state within the old mandate territory.[10]

Consequences of Mobilization

Although collective disadvantages are severe and reinforced by state policies, ethnopolitical mobilization has been hindered by the divisions within the Arab communities in Israel. However, the impetus for mobilization increased with the use of coercion and violent measures against Palestinians in the Occupied Territories. Hence, Arab Israelis' sense of dissatisfaction with their status has increased. As a result, more have been willing to join in open protests and strikes (for example, the Land Day strikes of March 30, 1988, 1989, and 1990). Traditional Arab electoral support for the Labor party dropped from 31 percent in the 1984 Knesset elections to 17 percent in 1988, more people voted (some 80 percent), and many gave their votes to parties perceived as pro-Arab, such as the Arab Democratic party, the Democratic Front for Peace and Equality, and the Progressive List for Peace. Demands for equality as full-fledged Israeli citizens have steadily increased.

Role of the State

Throughout the twentieth century, Jewish organizations have acquired territory from Arabs. With the physical expansion of the Jewish settlements came policies to control and incorporate territories into what in 1948 became the state of Israel. The current Israeli government follows the tradition by sometimes buying and sometimes expropiating land, especially in the Occupied Territories but also in the Galilee. These policies have led to a significant decline in the number of Palestinians able to determine their own economic and political future. With high birthrates—2.8 percent for Arab citizens of Israel versus 1.3 percent for Jewish Israelis—land and resources are shrinking exponentially for the Arab population. Demographic stress has led to some migration to other countries.

International Environment

The fate of Arab citizens in Israel is closely linked with that of their brethren in the Occupied Territories beyond the Green Line—the border separating Jordan from Israel prior to 1967. Many have relatives in the territories and are therefore affected in many ways by the ongoing Intifada and the uncertainties of the occupation. Some have actively supported the uprising, others have contributed food or money. This support has diminished the Arabs' already marginal status in the eyes of many Jewish Israelis.

Palestinians in the Occupied Territories enjoy significant support from various governments and groups abroad, support that seldom reaches Arabs in Israel. More often, Arabs in Israel are treated with disdain by West Bankers and Gazaens, who consider them sellouts or outright traitors. Most Arabs in Israel believe Jews and Arabs can live together in peace in the same state and view Arab regimes as nondemocratic and unreliable. But a substantial majority would like to see a more secular Israel. Such views are quite unpopular in the Arab world.

The situation of Arabs in Israel is similar to that of other dispersed ethnic groups living in heterogeneous societies throughout the world. To a certain degree, their status is reminiscent of that of Native Americans, who, dispossessed of their lands and autonomy, faced three choices: to separate from mainstream American life by establishing their own nations within the United States; to give up their separate identity through assimilation; or to participate in a heterogeneous culture while trying to preserve some degree of group identity.

Palestinians in Lebanon

Lebanon is a worst-case example of protracted communal conflict. Communal rivalries, exacerbated by external interference, have made Lebanon a battleground involving competing confessional groups—Shi'is, Druze, Christians, and Sunnis—compounded by infighting between family clans, armed militias, and Islamic fundamentalists. It also involves outside powers such as Syria, Israel, and (indirectly) Iran.

Background

Among the many immigrant communities that make up what later became the modern state of Lebanon, the Palestinians are the latest arrivals. After the establishment of Israel in 1948 some one hundred thousand refugees arrived, among them many professionals and intellectuals who easily blended into the upper and middle strata of Lebanese society. The majority, however, were villagers who were unable to return to Israel and became permanent refugees settled in camps outside major urban centers. Refugees became sources of cheap labor. Most were denied citizenship and thus became stateless people. Impoverished and resented, they made easy recruits for Palestinian guerrilla movements.

After the 1967 war a few more refugees entered Lebanon from the West Bank, but most went to the East Bank of Jordan. Many others arrived after Black September (when the Jordanian regime suppressed a Palestinian uprising in 1970–71). Currently 250,000 to 400,000 Palestinians reside in Lebanon— estimates are unreliable. Palestinian fighters and civilians left during and after the Israeli invasions of 1978 and 1982, and most of the PLO leadership left after the U.S.-sponsored truce in 1982.

Status and Grievances

Most Palestinians are stateless, either by choice or by design. The PLO uses the "stateless" argument to good political effect by arguing that since Palestinians have nowhere to go, they need a state of their own. In Lebanon, statelessness has undoubtedly added to the second-class status of Palestinians; they are denied basic state benefits, cannot vote, and have no passports. In the past, harassment of Palestinians by Lebanon's security and defense forces was common. Occasional battles began occurring in the late 1960s, largely between Christian Phalangists and Palestinian guerrillas, especially after Israeli reprisals. Christians protested against Palestinians in 1975. Palestinians backed by leftist Muslims soon were fighting Phalangists. What had started as clashes between Palestinians, sympathetic Shi'is, and the urban and rural poor against the Maronite establishment developed into a full-fledged civil war pitting Muslim against Christian, Sunnis against Shi'is, Palestinian factions against each other, militias against one another, and Syrians competing with Israelis to establish hegemony over parts of Lebanon. In September 1982, Phalangist militiamen entered the Sabra and Shatilla refugee camps and under the eyes of the Israeli Defense Force troops massacred hundreds of Palestinian men, women, and children.[11]

Consequences of Mobilization

Palestinians are fighting not for acceptance in Lebanon, but rather for a permanent home, preferably in what is now Israel and the Occupied Territories. Thus, they oppose the further extension of the Israeli security zone in southern Lebanon and agitate for better treatment of their people in the Occupied Territories. The Israeli-backed Christian South Lebanon Army under the leadership of Antoine Lahad and the Christian Phalangists (the largest and most important Maronite political party) are the Palestinians' foremost enemies in Lebanon proper. Both are seen as representing Maronite interests and thus as the successors of those responsible for massacring the Palestinians' brethren at Sabra and Shatilla.

The Palestinian experience has been one of disillusionment with the ability of other Arab states to regain Palestine. Many Arab states used the Palestinians as pawns to further their own interests. As a result of the disastrous Arab showing in the 1967 war, the PLO took active control of Palestinians in Lebanon and elsewhere. Their usual policy was noninterference in the internal affairs of their host countries, but the decision to use Lebanon as a guerrilla base for PLO raids into Israel brought Israeli retaliation and led to many casualties among the Lebanese. The Lebanese government was unable to control Palestinian activities. After 1970, the PLO (expelled from Jordan) made its headquarters in Beirut, and the raids against Israel increased. In 1975, the ambush by militant Maronites of a bus carrying Palestinians triggered the first civil war of 1975–76. The second civil war started with the Israeli invasion of Lebanon in 1982, which forced PLO fighters into Syria, the Biqa' valley, and elsewhere. Although Israel established control over Beirut, many PLO fighters returned under the protection of the Syrians. Israel, eager to escape the increasingly anarchic situation in Lebanon, retreated in 1985 and established a security zone in the South. President Assad's use of the Shi'is in the late 1980s to oust returning PLO fighters from Palestinian camps was followed by serious fighting between Syrian-backed Palestinians and Arafat's forces.

Recent Events

The PLO continues to enjoy widespread support among the Palestinians of Lebanon, yet it has lost control in Lebanon to the Syrians. Lebanese Palestinians are among the most desperate of those awaiting a solution of the Palestinian problem. The ongoing Middle East Peace Conference may yet reshape the destiny of the Palestinians. The least likely outcome, an independent Palestinian state on the West Bank and Gaza, would absorb all Palestinians willing to return. Given Syria's continued hegemony in most of Lebanon, not much can be hoped for the Palestinians there other than an end to overt persecution. The 1980s civil war effectively ended Maronite control of the government. President Harawi, a Maronite, is seen as a Syrian puppet. A Lebanese leadership committed to overcome its segmental cleavages and willing to agree to representation based on actual numbers of citizens may be ready to share political power with the Palestinians, or at least give permanent status to those Palestinians willing to make Lebanon their home.

Shi'is in Lebanon

Background

In contrast to the Palestinians, the Shi'is, although impoverished and repressed, were an integral part of the Lebanese political landscape. The Shi'i presence dates back to the original split between Sunnis and Shi'is in the seventh century. Over the years the Shi'is further split into Twelvers, also called Imamis (in the ninth century A.D.) and the Seveners, from whom emanated the Isma'ilis who, in the tenth century A.D., established the Fatimid caliphate to rule Egypt. The original split centered on the matter of the legitimate successor to the prophet Muhammad. The Shi'is trace the succession to Ali, son-in-law and cousin of Muhammad. Isma'ilis agree with the Twelvers only on the first six imams but believe that Isma'il was the true successor of the sixth iman, Abu Abdullah Ja'far al-Sadiq. Other sects that evolved from Shi'ism include the Zaidis of Yemen, the Alawis of Syria, the Druze of Lebanon, the Ahmadis of Pakistan, and the Baha'is—the latter sufficiently removed in doctrine to qualify as a new religion. Most Lebanese Shi'is are Twelvers; the Druze, considered Shi'is by some, more often are considered a heterodox sect of Islam. In Lebanon they are not considered part of mainstream Shi'ism.

The dominant Maronites and Sunnis are challenged by a coalition of Shi'is, Druze, and some disaffected Sunnis, the most vociferous of whom are the Shi'is. From the twelfth century onward, the Shi'is were considered outsiders or heretics by the majority Sunnis and were treated with disdain. They were geographically concentrated in two areas, the southern mountains and the northern reaches of the Biqa' valley. The northerners were mostly tenant farmers, led by feudal landlords, while the southerners were a seminomadic people.

The twentieth century witnessed the rapid descent of the Shi'is into poverty and powerlessness. Reaching about 17 percent of the population by the time of the French Mandate (1920), they were badly represented and exploited by their clan leaders, some of whom enjoyed French support. In 1943 Sunnis and Maronites agreed on power sharing and established Lebanon as an independent state in which the Shi'is, having lost their French connections, were given only a symbolic share of political power. Where Maronites dominated the presidency and the armed forces and the Sunnis the premiership, the Shi'is received the speaker of the house position, a relatively minor role that seldom yielded significant power. Even in the 1950s, when the personal powers of the southern Shi'i Assad clan and its northern counterpart the Shi'i Hamadeh clan grew, personal power did little to improve the social or economic standing of the Shi'i community at large. By the 1980s the Shi'is had grown into the largest minority (about a third of the population) in Lebanon. Yet under the old political system they were allocated only nineteen of ninety-nine seats in the legislature, reflective of a reality long gone. They were underrepresented in all important branches of government (the bureaucracy, diplomatic corps, and armed forces) and equally underrepresented in the business sector.

During the 1950s and early 1960s Lebanon successfully modernized and built an economic infrastructure, a process interrupted by the 1967 war. This modernization led to opportunities for young Shi'is, who with increased free education sought liberation from the power of their traditional leaders. The process of social mobilization had begun. Whole families escaped the grip of feudal landlords and clan leaders to move to the economic centers, mainly Beirut. Urbanization and increased contacts among Shi'is from different parts of the country led to an increased awareness of their limited shares of wealth and political power. The politicization of urban Shi'is grew, as witnessed by their membership in movements largely made up of Arab Socialists, Communists, and other disaffected members of society.[12]

Consequences of Mobilization

The contemporary solidarity of the Shi'is is based on shared grievances against advantaged groups and their own *zaims* (political bosses), who have exploited their people in the traditions of medieval feudal landlords. The first major crisis in 1958 united formerly opposed *zaims* to fight President Chamoun. However, it had only limited appeal to the urban dispossessed, who saw it mainly as a fight within the traditional elite to retain personal powers. With the influx of Palestinians, Shi'is joined their fight against injustice and dispossession. Thus, large numbers of Shi'is joined anti-establishment parties and under the leadership of Kamal Jumblatt, a Druze, the Shi'is did much of the fighting in the 1975–76 civil war, which challenged Maronite and Sunni dominance. Backed by the Syrians and with Israeli acquiescence, the Maronites were able to crush Jumblatt's forces. The Shi'is were the main losers; as many as forty thousand died in the fighting.

From the 1960s Musa al-Sadr (Imam Musa) was the preeminent leader of the Shi'is. An Iranian by birth (he was given Lebanese citizenship in 1963), he tried to reform the political system without alienating Maronite leaders. Under his leadership the Shi'is organized into the "Movement of the Deprived" and formed their own militia, a force soon to be reckoned with. Amal (Hope), as it became known, evolved into the leading fighting force of Shi'is in Lebanon.

The spirit of the Iranian revolution, combined with the disappearance of Imam Musa in Libya—he is believed to have been murdered there in 1978—and the first Israeli invasion, intensified the zeal of the Shi'is. Imam Musa, a reformer rather than a revolutionary figure, became the symbol of Shi'i dissent and is still recognized by all Shi'i leaders as their spiritual guide. The movement he founded has split into secular and revolutionary Islamic factions.

International Environment

The revolution in Iran unquestionably contributed to the radicalization of Lebanese Shi'is. Encouraged by the success of their brethren in Iran, Lebanese Shi'is grew impatient with the lack of progress in achieving political and economic equality, and readily abandoned the moderate strategies advocated by the imam. For some time Iran's revolutionary regime actively backed Lebanese Shi'is, and at present there is little doubt that it has considerable influence over the Shi'i Hizbollah (Party of God).

The expansionist policies of Syria and Israel have reshaped the political landscape of Lebanon. Syrian ambitions in Lebanon date back to the Ottoman period, when all of Lebanon was part of Greater Syria. The notable exception was the Maronite area of Mount Lebanon, an autonomous Christian region as of 1860. Syria's President Assad has taken up the role of power broker in Lebanon's internal affairs. As of 1992 Syria effectively controls most of Lebanon, and President Harawi has little independent authority. The Israelis, in fighting Palestinian guerrillas across the border, have twice invaded and twice withdrawn from Lebanon. They partially succeeded in rooting out Palestinian resistance and, with the implicit recognition of Syria, have established a permanent security zone in the South.

With the help of Syria and friendly Arab states, efforts are under way to work out a comprehensive peace plan that would give the Shi'is greater access to political power, an essential element in any enduring solution to Lebanon's chronic anarchy.

An Embattled Sect: Baha'is in Iran

The Baha'is are a nineteenth-century offshoot of Shi'ism. The majority Twelvers believe that the twelfth imam went into hiding in 878 and will return as the Mahdi on the day of resurrection. A nineteenth-century Iranian merchant, Sayyed Ali Mohammed, claimed to be an intermediary of the Hidden Imam. This proclamation, though unusual, was accepted as within the bounds of Twelver Shi'ism. Others before him known as Bab (gate) claimed to have communicated with the Hidden Imam. Calling himself the Bab, Sayyed Ali Mohammed was imprisoned in 1848 and executed for heresy in 1850. During his imprisonment he wrote *The Bayan*, which became the basis for the Baha'i faith. In it, he claimed to be the Mahdi and later to be an independent prophet. He also proclaimed "that another manifestation of God would one day appear" by the name of Baha'ullah.

After the Bab's death two brothers (one designated heir apparent by the Bab) claimed the followership of the faithful. Of the two, Mirza Hosain Ali proclaimed himself Baha'ullah and was accepted by the majority of his followers—henceforth the name Baha'is. The universalistic appeal of the religion is based on its teachings of equality and opposition to prejudice based on religion, race, wealth, and class. Baha'is also oppose consumption of alcohol and drugs, homosexuality, gambling, and all forms of crime, and they strive for a universal language. They strongly believe in the virtues of education (especially for women), charity, and loyalty to government, but participation in partisan politics is not permitted.[13]

Background

Only four religions are officially recognized in Iran: Islam, Christianity, Judaism, and Zoroastrianism. The Baha'is, considered heretics by religious and governmental authorities since the death of the Bab, have never been accepted as a legitimate religion. Exiled to Turkey, Syria, and Cyprus in the nineteenth century, they converted thousands of people to the new faith and now number about three million worldwide. Modern Baha'is are a transnational group bound by a common religion. An administrative network connects the faithful in many countries. Its headquarters, the Universal House of Justice, has been in Haifa since the time of the British Mandate; there a Spiritual Assembly, its members periodically elected by many national assemblies, exercises supreme authority.

About three hundred thousand Baha'is lived in Iran prior to the Revolution of 1978, some of whom since have fled the country. During the shah's regime the Iranian Baha'is were not persecuted as long as they did not seek official recognition as Baha'is. Thus, a marriage between Baha'is had to be sanctioned by a civil court or performed by an authority belonging to one of the recognized religions.

From 1978 to 1985 the revolutionary government of Iran actively persecuted members of the sect. In 1983 it became a crime to be a Baha'i, and Baha'i-owned enterprises were confiscated. Children born of a union of Baha'is were considered illegitimate, which had serious repercussions. Considered a secular, political movement by religious authorities and harassed by civil authorities, the Baha'is thus became a convenient scapegoat. The Israeli connection of Baha'is—many have visited Haifa and send money to support the Universal House of Justice and its mission—were used to discredit many as Zionist agents and to charge them with espionage or treason.

Consequences of Mobilization

The Iranian Baha'is have never mobilized politically, not even in the face of government persecution. Rather, they follow the doctrine of political quiescence.

International Environment

From 1978 to the mid-1980s the Iranian government was widely accused by individuals, governments, and international bodies such as the European Parliament of having violated the basic human rights of Baha'is. The charges included economic persecution, imprisonment of hundreds of people, disappearances, torture, and the killing of more than two hundred people. Some scholars argued that this was genocide, albeit on a small scale.

By the late 1980s the Iranian government had curbed some of the abuses. Persistent pressure by coreligionists and governments, including such states as Germany (with a large expatriate Iranian and Baha'i community) and appeals by organizations as Amnesty International and the UN Commission on Human Rights evidently contributed to the improvement in the status of the Baha'is.

The outcome of the Gulf War evidently has reinforced the trend. Since Iraq's defeat by the coalition forces, Iran again seeks a greater role in the Middle East. It also needs western support and customers to rebuild after its own costly war against Iraq. Thus, the government is in the process of revamping its image. The release of western hostages in Lebanon, undoubtedly due to Iranian pressure, is one manifestation of moderation; so is better treatment of Iran's beleaguered minorities.

Nonetheless, there is little hope that the situation of the Baha'is will ever be fully normalized. Given the status of Iran as an Islamic republic, and the status of Baha'is as heretics, they are likely to be denied equal rights indefinitely.

Comparative Analysis

The process model of ethnic and communal mobilization, which explains the extent of communal protest and rebellion as a joint function of the extent and intensity of grievances and the group's mobilization (chapter 5), provides a general explanation for why Palestinians, Kurds, and to a lesser degree Lebanese Shi'is extended their political activities to embrace armed struggle. Furthermore, it explains relatively well why Arabs in Israel are intensely disaffected with that state. It also provides an interpretation of why the Berbers of North Africa have used nonviolent means to pursue their communal objectives. The model is of little value in explaining Baha'i quiescence in the face of severe persecution.

Extent and Intensity of Grievances

Palestinians in the Occupied Territories and Iraqi Kurds share intense grievances due to long-standing discrimination and recurrent persecution by their respective governments. West Bank and Gazaen Palestinians are noncitizens and are closely restricted in their movements, whereas Arabs in Israel enjoy citizenship but have fewer political and economic privileges than their Jewish counterparts. Kurds have been actively persecuted by the various Iraqi regimes, have little political clout, and have paid for oppositional activity with privation and dislocation.

In contrast, Berber grievances historically were first directed against European colonizers and sometimes against other tribes or their clan leaders; similarly, the Shi'is resented their own *zaims*. At present, Berber demands are limited to cultural issues, such as the preservation of their language and customs, and the Moroccan government has responded favorably to Berber protests by making curricular changes to fit Berber educational needs.

Kurds, Palestinians in the Occupied Territories, and Baha'is have been victims of extreme repression in the form of torture, killings, prolonged detainment without due process, extradition, and forced resettlement. Both Palestinians and Kurds have actively rebelled, whereas the Baha'is are passive in the face of overwhelming pressures. Whereas Arabs in Israel protest political and economic discrimination, Lebanese Shi'is shifted from protest to open rebellion for political rights and a greater share of the economic pie. The Baha'is enjoy full citizenship and protection in most states; only in postrevolutionary Iran were they persecuted as a heretical minority. Berbers enjoy full citizenship and political participation, and their protests are aimed at preserving their cultural identity.

Mobilization Factors

Group identity, although strong in all these groups, is sometimes hampered by infighting. Kurds have a history of factional fighting. Kurds are predominantly Sunni Muslims but about a quarter are Shi'is. Unity is further impeded by their distribution among five states. Iraqi Kurds have further been factionalized along political and clan lines; some have been willing to work for autonomy within Ba'thist Iraq, whereas others adamantly demand an independent Kurdistan. The unity of Shi'is in Lebanon is a relatively recent phenomenon, inspired by the success of the Iranian revolution and the leadership of the late Imam Musa. Both the Palestinians and Shi'is of Lebanon have an image of themselves as segments of larger disposessed, impoverished peoples fighting neocolonialists (local elites) and western influence.

Relatively cohesive, the Shi'is, the Berbers, and the Arab citizens of Israel resemble functional alliances that seek redress for specific grievances. Palestinians, a stateless people in diaspora, are united in their quest for a territorial state of their own but are nevertheless divided along political, social, and religious lines. Christian Palestinians often enjoy a higher socioeconomic status than their Muslim brethren; Gazaens are poorer than West Bankers. Thus it is not surprising that Hamas, the Palestinian equivalent of an Islamic fundamentalist movement, enjoys stronger support in Gaza. Although the PLO appears to enjoy the broadest support, local leaders have sometimes demonstrated their independence since the Intifada. Renegade Palestinian guerrilla groups still operate with the tacit support of Syria and Libya.

Role of the State

State expansionism and consolidation deprived Palestinians, Arabs in Israel, Kurds, and to a lesser degree Shi'is and some Berbers of their autonomy, or of meaningful participation in governing coalitions. The situation for the Baha'is deteriorated with the advent of Iran's Islamic revolution.

Israel, the one functioning democracy in the region, experiences the highest degree of communal protest but less rebellion than Iraq, Lebanon, or Iran. Its Arab citizens use protest and political activism in seeking redress of grievances. Palestinians in the Occupied Territories engage in both protest and rebellion, sometimes using guerrilla tactics in their quest for autonomy and eventual independence. In Morocco, a constitutional monarchy with democratizing tendencies since 1972, the Berbers' demands have been largely met. Authoritarian and repressive systems clearly promote revolutionary fervor in contrast to democratic regimes, in which various forms of protest are the most likely manifestations of long-standing grievances.

Syria and Iran are examples of autocratic states where dissenters are dealt with harshly, and communal grievances are vented in sporadic rebellion. Lebanon's feeble democracy was unable or unwilling to muster effective civil authority to address the multitude of grievances affecting its communal groups, though as of 1992 some agreements are within reach. Iraqi president Saddam Hussein has wavered between conciliation and repression to deal with Kurdish demands. From 1983 to 1987 relations between Talabani's followers and the Hussein regime were relatively benign, but efforts in 1991–92 to achieve promised internal autonomy and economic parity have not been realized.

International Factors

Oil-rich "Kurdistan" is vital to Iraq's war-ravaged economy. Once UN-mandated sanctions against the Iraqi regime are lifted, international demand for oil will undermine claims of Kurdish autonomists on the oil-producing areas of Kirkuk and Khanaqin. On the other hand, the western powers and some Middle Eastern regimes (e.g., Syria) have actively backed the formation of a coalition of Iraqi opposition groups, including the Kurds. This development may prompt Saddam Hussein to attempt to divide his opponents by moving quickly to a limited autonomy agreement with the more compromise-minded Kurdish Democratic party.

Shi'is were to some degree victims of unequal development and international economic penetration in Lebanon. Prior to the civil war, Lebanon was the banking and investment center of the Middle East. Largely unskilled and rural, the Shi'is were unable to compete with urbanized Sunnis and Maronites for white collar jobs.

The establishment of Israel led to the Palestinian diaspora. Forcible resettlement, restrictive economic policies, and expulsions led the remaining Arabs to take up arms. Supported by anti-West regimes in the Middle East, Palestinian guerrillas wrecked havoc on Israel, destabilized Lebanon and Jordan, but gained the attention of the international community, which eventually legitimized the Palestinian leadership.

All the groups examined here have been encouraged by, and sometimes received financial and military support from, their transnational brethren and sympathetic groups. Such support clearly aided mobilization among the Kurds, Shi'is, and Palestinians.

Berbers' mobilization was more limited. A new generation of Berber intellectuals in Morocco and Algeria evidently influenced one another's demands and strategies, but support for rebellion was not included.

Baha'is in Iran did not mobilize. Their passivity can be explained by their limited numbers, persecution of their leaders (killed by Iranian mobs, imprisoned, or executed), and their religious doctrine, which requires political neutrality. On the other hand, there was active international mobilization on behalf of the Baha'is, which evidently prompted changes in regime policies toward them.

International support, although diminished since the Gulf War, remains strong for Palestinians, as is shown by the recent efforts sponsored by the United States for a comprehensive Middle East settlement. At the same time, Kurdish demands are being given little attention in the design of a Middle Eastern peace plan.

Shi'is in Lebanon for the time being are pawns between Syrian aspirations in Lebanon and Iranian efforts to mend fences with the western world. The release of western hostages in 1992 showed the strength of Iranian influence.

Prospects for Ethnopolitical Accommodation

The Shi'is in Lebanon, seeking broader access to political participation and prosperity, have a somewhat better chance than Palestinians to gain some concessions, provided Lebanese Maronite, Sunni, and competing Shi'i leaders accept a united Lebanon under Syrian supervision. Palestinians who arrived in the late 1940s and 1950s enjoy a somewhat better status than their brethren who live in the refugee camps of a war-ravaged country. The former have been largely absorbed, whereas the latter are a perennial irritant to Lebanese citizens. Palestinian destiny in Lebanon hinges more than ever on the political ambitions of Syria's Assad and the willingness of Israel to negotiate with its Arab neighbors and vice versa.

Some Kurds apparently would settle for greater autonomy; Palestinians in the Occupied Territories, however, appear less willing to compromise their goal of formal independence. Kurdish concentration in areas that overlap the boundaries of well-established states in the region significantly hampers the establishment of an independent entity. Syria, Iran, Iraq, and Turkey have at times cooperated to curb Kurdish nationalism and will continue to do so, because it poses a common threat to their territorial integrity.

The Palestinians, in contrast, are concentrated in disputed territory, the West Bank and Gaza—territories not yet formally annexed by Israel. East Bank Palestinians also are now nearly a majority in Jordan, which is both a handicap and an advantage in advancing their claim to form an independent state. Israel argues that the Palestinians already have a state, namely Jordan, and Jordanians fear a Palestinian takeover if an independent state is declared on the West Bank and Gaza. Arabs in Israel also identify with other Palestinians and would have divided loyalties toward a new Palestine entity. An autonomous Palestinian region will transform ethnonationalist conflict among the people of the diaspora but not end it.

Conclusion: Multiculturalism and Islam

Relations among communal groups in the Middle East are shaped in a fundamental way by Islamic doctrine and practice. Whereas Christianity provides a means to salvation for individual believers, Islam stresses the importance of correct action and gives specific instructions about all aspects of social life. Where the Shari'a (Islam's sacred law) reigns supreme, there is no separation of state and religion. Although many Middle Eastern countries adhere to dual systems of law dealing with civil, criminal, and commercial matters, tensions are ever present. The Shari'a stresses rigid adherence to the desired mode of behavior, giving pious Muslims much less discretion in responding to changing circumstances or in basing their actions on the utility of a given course.

The tension between secular forces and pious Muslims in the Middle East is the result of the inability of modernizers to reduce a religious culture to a personalized path to salvation. Sadat the modernizer, a pious man, was unable to satisfy fundamentalists. Saddam Hussein, an autocratic socialist, distorts Islamic principles by asking Muslims to fight a holy war against infidels. In the eyes of pious Muslims, Islam is a complete code regulating all civil and public affairs, while for the aspiring politician it is the greatest obstacle to emulating western examples.

Ayatollah Khomeini's treatment of the Baha'is was not an exception, because Muslims have traditionally treated renegade Muslims more harshly than Christians or Jews, whom they gave second-class status as dhimmis (monotheistic peoples subject to Islamic rule). This episode may serve as an example of what to expect from Islamic revivalist forces, who in Iran were able to defeat a secular and westernized, albeit autocratic and oppressive, modernizer. Pakistan's Bhutto similarly catered to fundamentalist wishes when he decreed in 1974 that the Ahmadis, a Shi'i splinter group that follows the nineteenth-century prophet Ghulam Ahmad, were non-Muslims.

With the democratic gains of the Islamic revivalist movement in Algeria at the beginning of 1992, the challenges increased for the Muslim modernizers. If revivalists eventually achieve electoral victory in Algeria, Jordan, Egypt, or elsewhere, can they possibly build a modern nation based on Islamic principles? Or is modernity in the western sense incompatible with Islamic principles? Can an Islamic polity produce a prosperous society in which citizens enjoy equality and freedom from oppression? And furthermore, how compatible is the ever-increasing separation among ethnic or national groups with the doctrinally prescribed unity of the religious community: should one supersede the other? What then is the role of the state vis-à-vis the institutions of Islam?

I think a western type of multicultural society in which ethnies of different beliefs are treated as equals is essentially incompatible with Islam. The often-cited status of dhimmis in the Islamic empires provides the example. Members of dhimmis were treated as second-class citizens who seldom could hold public office or build new churches and temples. There was never true coexistence where Islamic institutions and the Shari'a prevailed. Whereas monotheists were treated relatively benignly, polytheism had no place. There are modern corollaries. Christians cannot gain citizenship in many Middle Eastern states, and the avowedly Jewish state of Israel makes it extremely difficult for non-Jews to receive full citizenship. In that sense the Arabs in Israel are the dhimmis of Israel.[14]

No analysis of ethnopolitics is complete without an assessment of the tensions produced by two competing strands of religiopolitical doctrine among Islamic scholars and politicians, that is, between supranational ideals represented in pan-Arabism and pan-Islamism versus modern nationalism. The resurgence of radical Islamic movements has brought about a reassessment of the role of Islam in the modern state. Critics of secular modernism have long argued that when allegiance is pledged to the nation, loyalties to God are replaced by adherence to secular standards, reducing Islam essentially to ritualistic formalism. Whereas reformers differ from traditionalists or conservatives, all agree that since Islamic law (Shari'a) is divinely inspired, it ideally should serve as a blueprint for modern society: "It is not Islamic law that must change to modernize but society which must return to Islam, to conform to God's Will." [15] If Islam is true to its universal, eternally valid message, pan-Arabism and nationalism, including the nationalism of Palestinians and Kurds, should be strictly subordinate as a means to political and social reform. Islamic movements such as Hamas have resurrected this message. But history provides little guidance as to what the ideal Islamic state should look like in the twentieth century. Lack of consensus among Islamic practioners is evident in the existence of a multitude of sects and varying interpretations of the Shari'a. Islamic traditions have always favored the strong leader in the role of either the caliph or the imam—it is this yearning for divinely guided authority that testifies to the alienation of modern people, and not only in Islamic societies. The ideal Islamic state resembles in its utopian vision a model United Nations with a caliph as the ultimate arbiter of sociopolitical conflict. Realization of this ideal may well have to await the second coming of the Messiah.

9. Communal Conflict and Contention for Power in Africa South of the Sahara

James R. Scarritt

This chapter summarizes the findings of the Minorities at Risk project on ethnopolitical conflict in Africa south of the Sahara, or black Africa, starting with the special traits of African ethnopolitical groups that predispose these groups toward certain patterns of conflict, proceeding to the causes of group grievances and the interaction of grievances and mobilization in the determination of political action in the 1980s, and concluding with the prospects for the containment of various types of ethnopolitical conflict in the African context. Comparisons based on coded data are made among types of black African minorities and between minorities in this region and those in other regions. Three country case studies—Zambia, Kenya, and Ethiopia—illustrate some of the variations in conflict patterns among African countries south of the Sahara, although no three cases can be representative of the full range of variation. Prospects for mitigating African communal conflicts are assessed in the conclusion.

All six types of politicized communal groups exist in black Africa, and all types of ethnopolitical conflict have occurred there since 1945, but the most common group type is communal contenders. The prevalent form of conflict, almost always involving this group type, is competition over political power and economic distribution in the context of unstable multiethnic coalitions—often existing within a single governing party or among officers in a military regime. Leaders of specific ethnopolitical groups move in and out of these coalitions, and there is always some concern that defections will deprive the coalition of power. Any group whose leaders are presently in the coalition but were in opposition for a substantial period in the past will probably be suspected by other coalition members of having oppositional tendencies. The actual opposition, in turn, may be viewed as dangerous, even if its numbers are few, because it is a potential magnet for defectors from the governing coalition.[1] But such competition tends to be less intense than in other regions (although not in comparison with ethnopolitical conflict in established democracies) and less strongly influenced by the primordial roots of ethnicity than most ethnopolitical conflicts in other areas of the world. Although this prevalent type of African ethnopolitical conflict is no more likely than other types of such conflict to disappear as a consequence of modernization—which in fact stimulates it[2]—its intensity can more easily be reduced to manageable levels by appropriate policy measures because it tends to be based on a favorable combination of minimal cultural differences among larger groups, relatively low levels of inequality and grievances, a history of nonviolent mobilization and limited repression, and limited external influences.

Black African examples of more intense and violent ethnopolitical conflict along relatively stable and primordial lines usually involve ethnonationalist groups, ethnoclasses, and militant sects; some are long term (Burundi, Chad, Ethiopia, Sudan, and apartheid South Africa) and others are short term (the civil wars in Angola, Liberia, Nigeria, Uganda, and Zaire). On the other hand, conflicts that involve smaller scale violence but are along even more fixed, primordial lines tend to occur between indigenous peoples who are excluded from governing multiethnic coalitions, or who only wish to be left alone, and governments that are (a) dominated by agricultural groups and opposed by pastoralist minorities, or (b) dominated by traditionally pastoral groups and opposed by hunter-gatherer minorities. These types of conflict are more difficult, although not impossible, to ameliorate.

The prevalence of communal contenders in black Africa in combination with the existence of other types of minorities raises the questions of the distinctive nature of ethnicity in this region and its relation to other social forces, especially class. In the literature on ethnicity and ethnopolitical conflict in Africa and around the globe there is a long-standing debate between primordialists and situationalists. As ideal types, these theoretical positions are alleged to portray ethnicity in entirely different ways. In the primordialist view, ethnicity is an immutable set of emotionally charged biological, cultural, linguistic, and religious givens that are the primary sources of identity. In the situationalist view, ethnicity is an almost totally flexible set of identities that (a) varies from situation to situation depending on rational calculations of advantage, primarily material and political, and (b) is stimulated by political mobilization under the leadership of actors whose primary identities and motives are nonethnic.[3]

Since most scholars realize that the primordialist and situationalist approaches are not really the polar opposites specified in these ideal types, it is not surprising that most studies, including the Minorities at Risk project, take an intermediate position between them and sometimes seek to synthesize them.[4] Ethnic groups are based in shared cultural identities (information) that are changed or maintained, respectively, by diverse or common political, class, and economic interests (energy), and that in turn weaken or reinforce these interests. The flexibility of identities in response to changing interests is limited by the finite number of available persistent identities, so that communal contenders are ethnic even though the situational component of their ethnicity is stronger and the primordial component is weaker than is the case for other types of minorities.

Characteristics of Ethnopolitical Groups

The more and less intense patterns of black African ethnopolitical conflict are based on the following ten characteristics of minorities in the region.

1. *Large number of groups.* There are far more minorities at risk in Africa south of the Sahara, comprising a larger share of the regional population and the population of many countries, than in any other region of the world. There are seventy-four black African minorities in the data set versus forty-three in Asia, where the total population is much larger, and somewhere between twenty-four and thirty-two for the other world regions. Many additional minorities would certainly be coded if we lowered the minimum population limits or eliminated the coding rule excluding subgroups of an identified group (see chapter 2). Black African minorities comprise 42 percent of the region's

population versus the global average of 17 percent. In three countries all of the population is at risk, in eight over half, and in four over 40 percent. Minorities at risk are found in twenty-nine of the thirty-six countries in the region having a population of more than one million, the second highest percentage among world regions. The seventy-four minorities and the data on them are listed in Appendix table A.5.

The African states south of the Sahara are more ethnically diverse than those in other regions because most of their geographical boundaries were drawn by the European colonial powers at the 1885 Berlin Conference without regard for, or in many cases knowledge of, existing African political or cultural boundaries. With the primary objective of avoiding a European war over Africa, borders were drawn in terms of the territory already occupied by various powers and "logical" extensions of the borders between occupied areas into unoccupied areas. Occupation was sometimes demonstrated by treaties with African chiefs, who often were willing to get more compensation by signing away areas they did not control or whose people were not culturally similar to their own. Colonial administration tended to preserve diversity by severely limiting the process by which smaller, decentralized groups were assimilated by larger, more centralized ones, which had been a common characteristic of many areas in the precolonial period.

2. *Predominance of "cultural contender" traits.* Thirty black African minorities are exclusively or primarily communal contenders, twenty-one are classified as ethnonationalists, twelve are ethnoclasses, eight are indigenous peoples, and three are militant sects (see table A.5). Of the thirty groups that are cross-classified in two categories, twenty-four have a secondary classification as communal contenders; thus fifty-four of the seventy-four groups have some of the traits of communal contenders. Evidently communal contenders are becoming more common: most of the groups that are cross-classified as communal contenders would have been classified as belonging exclusively to this group type on the basis of circumstances in the late 1980s and 1990s alone, and the changes that are under way in South Africa are likely to transform ethnoclasses there into communal contenders. Moreover, black African communal contenders account for slightly more than 80 percent of the world's communal contenders. The ethnic demography described above goes a long way toward explaining the prevalence of this group

type in black Africa, and this prevalence goes a long way toward explaining the existence of unstable multiethnic coalitions in many African countries. Moreover, there is feedback in these relationships, so that the politics of unstable multiethnic coalitions helps to preserve a large number of groups and encourages them to act as communal contenders. By retaining their group's separate existence, each group's leaders hope to maximize payoffs through competitive bargaining with governing and opposing coalitions that are seeking the group's support.[5] But the existence of transnational segments may predispose the leaders of groups to ignore the tactical advantages of communal contention and to be ethnonationalists committed to uniting their groups across national boundaries.[6]

3. *Relative insignificance of cultural differences.* Objective cultural differences (CULDIF; see table A.11) between dominant groups and minorities are smaller in black Africa, on the average, than in all other world regions, and these differences are not highly correlated with political and economic differences (POLDIF and ECODIF; see table A.11), especially in the case of communal contenders. Thus cultural differences do not discourage the formation of multiethnic coalitions in most countries, and it is the dynamics of these coalitions rather than the presence of cultural differences that most effectively explains the persistence of large numbers of minorities in this region. Parallel to the global finding reported in chapter 2, greater cultural differences among groups in black African countries predispose those groups toward patterns of political action other than communal contention, in which cultural differences are more important in explaining group persistence.

4. *Geographical concentration.* Because land in most rural areas of Africa south of the Sahara is owned by ethnically defined communities and is not available to outsiders, African minorities are more highly concentrated in single contiguous geographical areas than are minorities in other regions. Nearly 70 percent of black African minorities were coded as concentrated in one region in comparison to 61 percent in Latin America (where indigenous communities tend to be concentrated in peripheral areas) and 48 percent in the rest of the world. When various degrees of geographical concentration were combined in a group concentration indicator (CONCEN; see table A.5), African minorities were found to be more concentrated than those in any other region except Latin America. Because of

rural-to-urban migration, especially migration to large, multi-ethnic capital cities, concentration has weakened considerably in absolute terms in recent decades, but such migration has been even higher in other world regions, preserving and perhaps strengthening black Africa's relatively high level of concentration. Concentration strengthens the tendency toward multiethnic coalitions in many countries, because it guarantees that many electoral constituencies and informal local power bases will be controlled by a single ethnopolitical group.

5. *Sense of group identity.* On average, African ethnopolitical groups have a stronger sense of group identity than groups in other regions. Fifty-seven percent of black African minorities on which data are available are strong identity groups (the highest coding category) versus the global mean of 37 percent. It must be emphasized that this identity is ethnopolitical rather than primordial: a substantial majority of black African groups had little if any coherence in the precolonial period, but they developed higher levels under the impact of colonial administrative practices and anticolonial and postindependence political competition. Strong identity leads to substantial ethnopolitical activity in all black African countries that contain minorities, but the forms of that activity are determined by the interaction of identity with the other variables discussed in this chapter. A strong sense of identity tends to stimulate communal contention among African groups even in the absence of high levels of other action-predisposing variables.

6. *Low incidence of economic discrimination.* A smaller percentage of black African minorities experience economic discrimination (ECODIS; see table A.11) than groups in most other regions, and the resulting economic differentials in Africa are low by world standards. This region is closer to the global mean on political discrimination (POLDIS) and differentials (POLDIF). Sixty-five percent of black African minorities experience some degree of political discrimination versus 78 percent of the groups in other world regions; 47 percent of African groups experience some degree of economic discrimination while 73 percent of minorities in other world regions do so. As explained in chapter 2, discrimination that is due to deliberate public policies or prevailing social practices is considered more severe than discrimination that is due to historical neglect or historical restrictions. A much greater percentage of the political discrimination and a slightly greater percentage of the

economic discrimination that does occur in black Africa is severe according to this definition: 70 percent of the political discrimination is severe versus 48 percent for other world regions. When the percentage of minorities experiencing severe discrimination (versus mild and none) is examined, African groups are found to experience relatively little severe economic discrimination by global standards and about average severe political discrimination (the lowest of Third World regions but substantially above the First World and former Second World). Like group coherence, discrimination in black Africa is largely the product of colonial and postindependence public policies and social practices. Political discrimination is lower and economic discrimination is substantially lower for (disadvantaged) communal contenders than for other types of groups in black Africa as well as other regions.

Political and economic differentials are essentially the products of discrimination, past or present. Economic differentials are lower in black Africa than in any other world region except Eastern Europe and the USSR, where long-established socialist policies worked effectively to keep those differentials small. Such policies have been implemented in only a few African countries for relatively short periods and have been only partially effective. Relative demographic and ecological stress (DEMSTRESS and ECOSTRESS; see table A.11) are closely related to economic differentials; black Africa has among the lowest scores of any world region on these indicators. African minorities (and nonminority groups) are certainly subject to the stresses of high population growth, poor health, migration, and competition for land, but they are relatively equally affected by them. Economic differentials and both types of stress tend to be low among communal contenders in Africa and elsewhere, because the dynamics of unstable multiethnic coalitions dictate that most groups participate to some degree in the distribution of valued goods and opportunities in order to acquire or maintain their loyalty to the governing coalition. Potential opponents are also potential allies, but differential treatment weakens the latter potential.

Black Africa also is very close to the global mean on political differentials; it is again the lowest of the four Third World regions, although higher than the First World and former Second World. Once again, disadvantaged communal contenders are less adversely affected than other disadvantaged minorities, but the differences between them and ethnonationalists are very small. Being outside the governing coalition in Africa, whether or not it is multiethnic, results in greater political differentials than in the western democracies and Japan, because democratic political access is less fully institutionalized.

7. *Nonpursuit of autonomy.* The percentage of black African minorities that currently are pursuing independence or regional autonomy is substantially lower than the percentage in any other region except Latin America and the Caribbean. In striking contrast, the percentage of minorities that formerly sought independence or autonomy for at least five years but have given up on that pursuit is the highest of any world region. In the years immediately following independence, the weakness of many black African states combined with surprisingly (in the thinking of both participants and observers) intense conflict within unstable multiethnic coalitions to generate a number of separatist movements. In the absence of significant foreign support in recent years, as both African neighbors and major powers have recalculated the costs of supporting separatist movements, many groups have switched back to a strategy of maximizing the strength of their positions within governing coalitions, especially since many of these have become more stable. This change is a major cause of the trend toward more minorities becoming communal contenders.

8. *Mild grievances.* Levels of grievances among black African minorities are among the lowest in all world regions, as shown in chapter 3, table 3.1. Grievances about political rights are the most substantial (although less than in any other Third World region), while grievances about autonomy and social rights are very low. This pattern is consistent with findings reported above on the relatively low levels of discrimination and differentials. All types of grievances are substantially lower among communal contenders than among other types of minorities. In the politics of unstable multiethnic coalitions, however, high levels of conflict can occur in the absence of large differentials or long-standing and deeply felt grievances if minorities fear that they will lose power and economic privilege if they fall—or are pushed—out of the governing coalition, or if other members of their coalition defect, causing it to be defeated by the opposition. Thus it is not surprising that political rights grievances are stronger than other grievances for these groups.

9. *Frequent conflicts among communal groups.* Conflicts among

communal groups that do not involve the state were more wide-spread and severe in black Africa than in any other region during the 1945–89 period, although Asia and the Middle East are not far behind. The large number of black African minorities, the weakness of African states, the insecurity of unstable multi-ethnic coalitions, and the machinations of colonial rulers and dominant postindependence majorities or minorities all help to account for this finding. Primordial differences and the types of differentials discussed above play a smaller role.

10. *Infrequent conflicts with the state.* Rebellions by communal groups against the state from 1945 to 1989 are slightly below the global mean in frequency and intensity, while levels of non-violent protest and riot are lower than in any region except Latin America and the Caribbean. The pattern for the 1980s alone is very similar, except that nonviolent protest in black Africa is the lowest of all world regions during this period on account of an increase in this form of political action in Latin America in the early 1980s and a decrease in Africa in the late 1980s. Approximately 60 percent of black African minorities engaged in nonviolent protest between 1945 and 1989, approximately 35 percent engaged in riot, and approximately 45 percent engaged in rebellion. These findings suggest that the journalistic image of most black African countries as rent by severe ethnic conflict is inaccurate. In reality, all forms of antistate political action are relatively infrequent by global standards, although this is least true for rebellion, largely because of the presence of competing ethnonationalisms in weak authoritarian states. The relative frequency of communal conflicts not involving the state is more in accord with the journalistic image.

Nonviolent protest reached its peak in the final years of the anticolonial struggle in the late 1950s and early 1960s and has been declining ever since except for a slight increase in the 1970s, while rebellion is essentially a postindependence phenomenon that has increased slightly since 1960 (see chapter 4, figure 4.6). Although there are examples of all types of protest among all group types, nonviolent protest has been most common among communal contenders, while rebellion has been most common among other group types. In contrast to the pattern found in Western Europe, in which nonviolent protest tends to escalate to violence after a number of years (see chapter 6, table 6.2), African minorities tended to participate in the same form or forms of political action throughout the postindependence period. Overall changes in the volume of protest were accounted for in large part by the increasing authoritarianism of regimes, which led to decreased nonviolent protest, especially among communal contenders, and increased rebellion among ethnonationalists and indigenous peoples.

Causes of Group Grievances, Mobilization, and Political Action

Further conclusions about patterns of conflict in black Africa can be drawn from analysis of relationships among the variables that have been discussed in the preceding section. These results parallel the global results reported in chapter 3.

First, economic variables—demographic and ecological stress, economic differentials, and especially economic discrimination—are even more important than political differentials and political discrimination in explaining grievances about political rights in black Africa. Although the levels of most of these variables are low in this region by global standards, they are sufficiently high to produce at least some articulation of grievances among those minorities who experience them and for whom global comparisons are irrelevant. In the politics of unstable multiethnic coalitions, as we have seen, even relatively small economic disadvantages can lead to moderately high political grievances. Group identity or coherence is the only internal group trait that is related to political rights grievances in black Africa. Thus the causes of political rights grievances in this region are similar to those in the global population of minorities.

Second, in black Africa, only political differentials are strongly related to political autonomy grievances, while economic and cultural differentials are very weakly related. Globally, cultural differences and identity are strongly related to this type of grievance, but in Africa, demands for autonomy are much more the product of colonial policies of divide-and-rule and postindependence conflicts than of group characteristics.

Third, economic differentials and discrimination and cultural differences are the variables that are most strongly related to economic grievances in black Africa. Major differences between the determinants of economic grievances in the global and black African samples are the significance of demographic and ecological stress in the global set of cases and the significance of cultural differences in the black African cases. The relatively low variation in stress among African groups probably accounts for the failure of this variable to explain economic grievances in this region. On the other hand, cultural differences in Africa are greatest between demographic majorities and groups that are either indigenous peoples or colonially privileged ethnoclasses, both of which—for different reasons— have relatively strong economic grievances.

Fourth, economic differentials and discrimination, cultural differences, and communal conflict not involving the state are significant determinants of social grievances both globally and in black Africa. Demands for cultural freedom and tolerance are maximized by this combination of economic and social factors, and demands for protection from attack by other groups are obviously intensified by a history of communal conflict. In black Africa, political discrimination and coherence also are significant factors, because groups with strong social grievances are either indigenous peoples or have been involved in extensive violent conflict.

Fifth, forms of political action in the 1980s are less fully explained by grievances and their causes in black Africa than they are in the global population of minorities. All types of grievances and most of the variables that have been used above to explain them fail to have significant relationships with any form of political action in the 1980s. It is very likely that (a) protest in the anticolonial nationalist and immediate postindependence periods occurred more directly in response to grievances felt at those times and that (b) this relationship was attenuated in the 1970s and 1980s by the dynamics of mobilization and repression discussed below, although we do not have systematic data on this point. Anticolonial nationalism was the organized response to the many political, economic, and social grievances felt by virtually all Africans under colonial rule. Nationalists promised to rectify these grievances after independence but did not have the financial or organizational resources to satisfy all the grievances of every group in the society, even in periods of rapid state expansion and economic growth. Leaders of various ethnic groups began to mobilize their followers to secure higher priority for their group grievances, usually at the expense of other groups. Most grievances remained wholly or partially unsatisfied because no group was able to attain all its goals in a situation of competitive mobilization and increasing economic decline. By the 1980s some formerly intense grievances had become less important because they now appeared so unrealistic, but the mobilization that had originally been based on them continued.

Sixth, mobilization for nonviolent protest in the 1960s and 1970s is strongly related to the actual occurrence of this form of protest in the 1980s, and the same is true of mobilization for rebellion. This pattern is consistent with the tendency of African groups to engage in the same forms of protest for extended periods rather than shift to more violent protest when less violent forms do not alleviate grievances. The strong relationship of mobilization for nonviolent protest in the 1960s and 1970s to actual nonviolent protest in the 1980s points once again to the importance in this region of communal contention within unstable multiethnic coalitions, a situation in which nonviolent protest—which occasionally turns violent—is stimulated by prior mobilization even when differentials, differences in stress, discrimination, and grievances are relatively low. Repression does not eliminate conflict, but it prevents conflict from taking other forms. Zambia and Kenya exemplify this pattern. The strong relationship of mobilization for rebellion in the 1960s and 1970s to actual rebellion in the 1980s points to the reverse dynamic in black African countries populated mainly by ethnonationalists, in which strong grievances are unresolved during long periods of partially successful rebellion that do not significantly change the status of minorities. In this case, repression cannot end rebellion but limits its effectiveness as a vehicle for change. Ethiopia exemplifies this pattern.

Case Studies of Political Action by Communal Groups

Political action by black African minorities—especially communal contenders, the most common type of minority in this region—can best be understood in the context of their interaction with other groups. Thus the following three case studies focus on intergroup relations. Zambia represents countries in which minorities are exclusively communal contenders (although there are European and Asian ethnoclasses in that country that are too small to be included in our population of minorities) and conflict is relatively mild. Kenya typifies countries in which most types of minorities are found (although the European and Asian ethnoclasses are again too small to be included in our data) and, partly as a consequence, relations among communal contenders striving for dominance and between communal contenders and other types of minorities are more highly conflictual. Finally, Ethiopia represents the alternative pattern of conflict in African countries, in which most groups are ethnonationalists or indigenous peoples rather than communal contenders and conflict is most severe. The impacts of colonialism, the strength of nationalist movements and political parties, and foreign intervention on the status, grievances, and mobilization of various groups will be considered for each case.

Zambia

Addressing the primordial-situational distinction described in the first section of this chapter, Robert Molteno suggests that *sectionalism* is a more accurate term for describing competing political groups in Zambia than *tribalism* or even *ethnicity*, because the latter terms tend "to assume that kinship links or long-standing political ties are the paramount solidarity bond, when in fact geographical propinquity and linguistic unity may be more important factors . . ."[7] These terms, according to Molteno, also imply the irrelevance of rational economic motives, coincidence in boundaries between precolonial and contemporary groups, and the absence of urban-rural differences, all of which are untrue in the Zambian case. I argue that, while Molteno's points have considerable validity, they do not eliminate the strong element of ethnicity that remains in group conflicts and that is essentially denied by the term *sectionalism*.[8] Language, which Molteno calls a defining characteristic of sectionalism, is an important element of ethnicity, and ethnic identities are sufficiently flexible to eventually expand or contract their scope in response to (a) differentials, discrimination, and grievances created by economic development, urbanization, class formation, and (especially) to (b) the possibility of attaining or maintaining a position in the ruling multiethnic coalition through participation in political competition. What Molteno sees as sectional movements are exactly what we call communal contenders, and their ethnicity is primarily situational.

In Zambia, where there are more than seventy "primordial" or "tribal" ethnic groups, this process of group expansion (and occasionally contraction) through colonial policies, social change, and communal contention has resulted in the emergence of four to eight ethnopolitical groups (depending on the issue and the point in time examined) with strong identities, each of which has at various times played a major political role. The most important ethnopolitical groups, each encompassing more than one primordial group, are the Bemba, Tonga, Nyanja (Eastern Province), and Lozi, comprising approximately 37, 19, 15, and 8 percent, respectively, of the country's population of more than eight million. Unlike the others, the Nyanja-speaking group does not appear in our population of minorities, because it was never outside the ruling coalition before the end of the 1980s; as we will see below, however, its turn has come in the 1990s. Smaller groups sometimes act independently of these large groups, but they more commonly join coalitions led by one or more of the large groups.

Cultural differences among these groups are small and have little political significance. Economic and political differentials and differences in demographic and ecological stress are not large, and discrimination has not been extensive, because all groups have had some access to the more developed parts of the country through migration to towns or employment on primarily European commercial farms. The Zambian population is almost half urban, and the towns are located on the boundaries between areas inhabited by major groups. The rural areas inhabited by all groups (apart from the commercial farms, which are mainly in the Tonga area) are underdeveloped. Communal conflict and both nonviolent and violent protest (although not rebellion) have occurred because the process of political mobilization and competition has magnified political and especially economic grievances in spite of limited differentials and discrimination and has directly produced conflict through its own dynamic. Only the Lozi have ever pursued separatism, and that was some years ago; they were responding to their traditionalist leaders' weak position in political competition, and were under the influence of colonial officials and white settler politicians.

Zambia became independent from Britain in 1964, after a short but intense struggle to escape domination by white settlers who came to the country to participate in mining and, in smaller numbers, farming. The interparty and intraparty competition of the multiparty First Republic (1964–72)—which was the predominant form of minority-versus-state conflict during that period—was rather complex.[9] The unity of the anticolonial nationalist movement, established a decade earlier, was broken in 1958 when the United National Independence party (UNIP) split off from the African National Congress (ANC) over tactics for the conduct of the independence struggle, and competition between the two parties was intense from then until the imposition of the one-party system at the beginning of 1973. This competition frequently involved localized urban violence. In the 1964 elections, the first under universal franchise, UNIP won an overwhelming victory but, given ANC's organizational disarray, some UNIP leaders were disappointed not to have done better. ANC had its strongest support among the Tonga groups of Southern and Central Provinces and the emergent African farmers who were concentrated in that area, while UNIP had greater support in the remainder of the country, although its organization was weak in the Lozi areas because of conflict with traditionalist-separatist leaders.

At the party's 1967 general conference, competitive elections were held for the UNIP Central Committee for the first (and last) time, changing the previous practice of electing by acclamation an ethnically balanced state of candidates selected by President Kenneth Kaunda (who was to some degree above communal contention because of his joint Bemba-Nyanja ancestry). The slate of candidates put forth by an alliance of Bemba party activists from Northern, Copperbelt, and Luapula Provinces and Tonga party activists from Central and Southern Provinces—uniting the areas of the party's best organization and strongest support with the areas of its weakest support, to the tactical advantage of the former—won all but one of the contested seats. As a result, charges of tribalism were raised, and party officials from the Nyanja-speaking Eastern Province and Lozi-speaking Western (then Barotse) Province, who tended to come more from the bourgeoisie, were alienated. Some of the Lozi leaders soon left UNIP to form the United party (UP), in alliance with more traditionalist and formerly separatist Lozi who had long been in conflict with UNIP; when the UP was banned, they joined ANC. As a result of these defections from UNIP, ANC was able to win the majority of parliamentary seats from Western Province—as well as from its traditional stronghold—in the 1968 elections and disappoint UNIP's hopes that it would disappear.

Between 1968 and 1971, conflict within UNIP shifted toward a pattern of Northern and Copperbelt Bemba activists versus the rest of the country because of widespread resentment against the increased influence of these activists. Even Bemba-speaking leaders from Luapula Province shared this resentment, because they felt they were not receiving their fair share of high government and party positions. The Bemba group gradually lost power through a variety of events, but especially through changes in the party constitution, and in 1971 some of them—although few from the higher levels of the bourgeoisie—also left UNIP to form the United Progressive party (UPP). Considerable violence took place around the December 1971 by-elections, in which UPP captured one seat from UNIP and UNIP captured two seats from ANC. A few weeks later, UPP was banned and the president announced his intention to establish a one-party state. UPP was the most dangerous opposition party for UNIP because it attempted to create a coalition of unionized workers and private sector bourgeoisie as well as (in alliance with ANC) a coalition of a majority of ethnopolitical groups.

Intraparty competition during the one-party Second Republic (1973–91) involved a continuation of many multiparty First Republic conflicts, although there were also significant differences. Bornwell Chikulo states: "Since the establishment of the one-party system, the level of violence, intimidation, sectional and factional conflict has been considerably reduced. This is not surprising because . . . the introduction of the one-party system limits sharply the range of activities open to the various factions to express political opposition."[10] This evaluation is quite reasonable, although it does not take into account either the high level of conflict that surrounded the establishment of the one-party system or the increased class conflict that occurred subsequently.

The prohibition on opposition parties enacted in 1972 and put into effect at the beginning of 1973 engendered extensive nonviolent protest, but little violence. ANC leaders unsuccessfully petitioned the courts to stop it, and those former UPP leaders who were not in detention unsuccessfully attempted to form a new party. Members of the bureaucracy, the private sector bourgeoisie, the petite bourgeoisie, and the unionized workers voiced objections. Many of the recommendations of the commission established to investigate the possible structure of the one-party system were rejected by UNIP and the president and were replaced by provisions incorporating a greater centralization of power in the party, the executive, and especially the president and reducing the amount of intraparty competition. Debate was particularly intense over the provisions of a leadership code to limit the ownership of private property by state officials, and resolution of this issue was postponed. ANC signed an agreement at Choma in Southern Province in June 1973 to integrate into UNIP, but its ex-UP wing did not join in this agreement, and conflict over its implementation soon arose. Former UPP members were not invited to join UNIP at that time, although they were selectively readmitted a few years later.[11]

Conflict took place primarily along class lines in subsequent years, but with overtones of the ethnically based factionalism of the First Republic.[12] Both the emerging business class and the workers increasingly engaged in conflict with the ruling party and the state after the onset of economic decline in 1975. Factional conflict was largely localized by the system of competitive legislative elections within the single party framework. But the unsuccessful attempt by the former ANC and UPP presidents to contest the 1978 presidential election from within UNIP, and various forms of oppositional activity by former UPP leaders over the years, provoked strong negative reactions from those in control of the governing party-state reminiscent of their reaction to earlier ethnic factionalism. Popular Bemba-speaking legislative candidates were frequently rejected by the UNIP Central Committee because of the suspicion that they were UPP sympathizers.

In summary, the combined changes that took place in Zambia beginning in the early 1970s—dramatic economic decline, increased class formation, and the institution of the one-party system—sharply reduced the intensity of conflicts between ethnic minorities and the state in the 1980s but probably did not deeply alter the conflicts' underlying shape. Forcing all elements of the ruling multiethnic coalition into UNIP did not entirely eliminate instability in that coalition, given the substantial history of communal contention. Thus the Bemba were coded in the Minorities at Risk study as the minority most at risk in the late 1980s for two reasons: because of the state's continued, and

partially justified, fear of an overt or disguised resurrection of
the UPP, and because the first food riots that occurred in response to measures introduced at the insistence of the International Monetary Fund to combat economic decline took place in
towns with predominantly Bemba populations. The Tonga and
the Lozi were also coded as at risk because of their historical
opposition, even though members of these groups were actively
promoted to high positions under the one-party state. The level
of active risk was, however, quite low for all ethnopolitical
groups as such—although not for their members who were
peasants or were unemployed in the towns.

In August 1990 the UNIP National Council agreed to hold
multiparty elections in October 1991, the Zambian constitution
was amended by Parliament in December 1990 to legalize opposition parties, and a new multiparty constitution for the
Third Republic was adopted in July 1991. The major opposition group that organized to push for these changes—the
Movement for a Multiparty Democracy (MMD), which became
a party in March 1991—won an overwhelming victory in the
October legislative and presidential elections. Frederick Chiluba—leader of the Zambia Congress of Trade Unions
(ZCTU)—was the MMD's successful presidential candidate, de-
feating Kaunda by 81 to 19 percent. MMD represents an alliance of the bourgeois and labor oppositions that have been active for the entire duration of the Second Republic, combined
with the somewhat more recent opposition of the Christian
churches and some elements of First Republic opposition parties and tendencies.[13] UNIP won seats in the 1991 election only
in Nyanja-speaking Eastern Province where no former opposition party existed, and MMD received support from the very
ethnopolitical and class coalition that the one-party system had
been instituted in 1973 to prevent.

The alliance between organized labor and capital in MMD
makes sense only in terms of mutual opposition to the former
UNIP government and is thus unlikely to last very long now
that a party representing both of these classes is in power.
ZCTU is large and relatively well-organized and has been relatively free of ethnic factionalism under Chiluba's leadership.
But he is a Bemba and is sometimes referred to somewhat in-
accurately as having assumed the mantle of Simon Kapwepwe,
the late UPP leader. Former UPP leaders are not prominent at
the higher levels of the MMD government, which is dominated

by people with business and civil service backgrounds who tended to remain in UNIP during the former period of inter-party competition, rather than by long-time political activists such as those who led UPP. Given its small size, both absolute and in relation to the unionized workers, the most logical way for the Zambian capitalist class to obtain majority support in a multiparty system would be through the use of ethnic faction-alism. Several minor opposition parties have formed, most of which are splinter groups from MMD that accuse it of being Bemba dominated, and there are increasing rumors of a more serious split in the poorly organized MMD.

Although it is easy to understand why more than 80 percent of the Zambian voters supported a change in the ruling party, the danger of reviving the intense ethnopolitical factionalism of the late 1960s and early 1970s is real, and steps need to be taken to avoid it. Several weak parties competing for support along ethnic lines, but each fostering privileged-class interests, would exemplify the politics of unstable multiethnic coalitions at its worst and would be an excellent recipe for a military coup, es-pecially if no party develops effective policy proposals for re-versing the country's economic decline. Only if one or two rela-tively cohesive and broad-based transethnic parties emerge and formulate economic policies that produce both growth and equity will democratization offer Zambia the opportunity to minimize ethnopolitical factionalism and forestall a return to authoritarian rule.

Kenya

Kenya's total population of more than twenty-five million com-prises more than forty ethnic groups, but the largest five—Kikuyu (21 percent), Luo and Luhya (each 13 percent), and Kalenjin and Kamba (each 11 percent)—comprise more than two-thirds of this population. These five and a few others are the communal contenders of Kenyan politics. Some smaller groups such as the Masai and the Somali (each 2 percent) have had disproportionate political significance. In addition to these groups, which (with the exception of the Luhya) have strong identities, there exist mosaic groupings with multiple local or cross-cutting identities based on shared ascriptive traits but with little or no broader sense of identity within the group; examples include the Turkana and Pokot (3 percent) and the Rendille, Boran, and Gabbra (1 percent). These seminomadic pastoralists, including the Masai, are classified as indigenous peoples. All Kenyan groups have specific geographic locations: for example, the Kikuyu inhabit Central Province and the multiethnic city of Nairobi, although they have moved into a number of other areas—especially Rift Valley Province—both under colonial rule and since independence; the Luo are concentrated in southwestern Nyanza Province; the Kalenjin (whose identity as such is relatively recent and politically induced) live in central Rift Valley Province; the Luhya live in the Western Province and adjacent areas of Rift Valley Province; the Masai live in southern Rift Valley Province and in northern Tanzania; the Somali are found in North-Eastern Province and in the Somali Republic; and the mosaic groupings inhabit the northern part of the country.

Cultural and physical differences among ethnopolitical groups are greater in Kenya than in Zambia, and as a result the process of expansion of ethnopolitical identities to unite different "primordial" groups has not gone as far, although the identities of extremely decentralized pre-colonial groups such as the Kalenjin and the Masai are products of social change and communal contention, and the identities of other groups have been strengthened by these processes. The two most significant cultural differences among Kenyan groups, which overlap to a considerable extent, are those between speakers of Bantu and Nilotic or Cushitic languages (which correspond to some physical differences), and those between agriculturalists and pastoralists. The pastoralists—particularly the Masai, but also the Somali, the Turkana and Pokot grouping, and the Rendille, Boran, and Gabbra grouping—have been the object of discrimination by both the colonial and postindependence governments, which have thought them to be generally inferior and have limited their roaming and fighting by placing heavy restrictions on them. Unlike the other pastoralists, the Somali are classified as ethnonationalists rather than indigenous peoples because of their desire to unite with the Somali Republic. The decision to make English and Swahili official languages has come at the expense of the Somali, who speak neither of these languages.

Economic and political differentials and discrimination, as well as variations in demographic and ecological stress, are also

greater in Kenya than in Zambia. Foremost among the advantaged groups are the Kikuyu, who were advantaged both politically and economically until 1978, and who still maintain their
economic advantage and have relieved their earlier demographic and ecological stress by settling outside their traditional
areas. Some other agricultural groups are moderately advantaged economically, while pastoralists are severely disadvantaged. The Luo were politically advantaged for a few years
before and after independence; even while they were disadvantaged later, they retained special political significance. Since
1978 the Kalenjin have been gaining political advantage and
using it to improve their previously disadvantaged economic
position. The Somali, the Masai, and the two groups of northern pastoralists have long suffered from substantial political as
well as economic underrepresentation due to historical neglect
and continuing restrictions. Thus grievances of all group types
are on the average higher in Kenya than in Zambia, and there
has been more violent protest; in the 1950s there was an anticolonial rebellion.

Like Zambia, Kenya became independent from Britain (in
1963) as a result of intense conflict between Africans and a colonial state controlled largely by white settlers. In Kenya the settlers were mostly farmers who took advantage of the fertile
highlands region to produce export crops after the previously
landed African peasantry had been forcibly removed onto inferior land or into the urban labor market. Kenya's ethnic
groups were not equally affected by this process; most of the
land taken came from the Kikuyu, and smaller amounts came
from the Kamba and Rift Valley Province groups, causing great
ecological and demographic stress. Other groups were only
marginally affected.

In 1944 the first territorywide nationalist movement, the
Kenya African Union (KAU), was formed. That members and
leaders were disproportionately Kikuyu was not suprising, for
the Kikuyu had been the most politically organized group in
Kenya for more than twenty years.[14] Kenya's most violent conflict between the state and a communal group erupted in the
early 1950s, when the more militant Kikuyu leaders in KAU
began using traditional oathtaking to build strong solidarity
among their followers and to prepare them for more radical
actions, including violence. The colonial government called this

movement "Mau Mau." Its alleged goal was to physically drive European settlers off African land. Localized violence led the colonial regime to declare a state of emergency in 1952 that lasted until 1960. KAU president Jomo Kenyatta and other top leaders were detained even though their relation to the oathing movement was unclear, more than one hundred thousand Kikuyu were relocated under harsh conditions, and perhaps fifteen thousand men went to the forests of Central Province to conduct loosely organized guerrilla activities, mainly against Kikuyu loyal to the government. Although the Mau Mau uprising was militarily defeated, it shortened colonial rule.

The turning point in Kenya Africans' struggle for independence came in 1960 when the British agreed to set a prospective date for the transition to majority rule. This step led to a resurgence of nationalistic activity, particularly by the newly named Kenya African National Union (KANU), descended from KAU.[15] In Kenya's first and second universal franchise elections in 1961 and 1963, the Kikuyu- and Luo-based KANU under the leadership of Kenyatta—the acknowledged father of Kenyan nationalism but also a Kikuyu ethnic leader—defeated the Kenya African Democratic Union (KADU), which represented smaller and generally less advantaged ethnic groups of the Great Rift Valley and coastal areas. Upon taking power after the 1963 election, Kenyatta began to solidify his broad coalition by picking members from various ethnic groups (as well as from various Kikuyu subgroups) and ideological factions when making ministerial appointments. Most notably, when a republic was declared in 1964 he chose a Luo vice-president—Oginga Odinga—who was, in addition, from the relatively radical faction of KANU. At the same time, KADU was absorbed by KANU through a relatively voluntary merger, encouraged by a conflict within KADU between Luhya and Kalenjin over fertile land in the Great Rift Valley that was resolved by Kenyatta in favor of the Kalenjin as part of the terms of the merger.[16] But KANU was less important as an instrument of rule for Kenyatta than the executive and the bureaucracy, and these institutions came to be staffed disproportionally by Kikuyu. As the Africanization of the former White Highlands took place, the Kikuyu managed to obtain a disproportionate amount of this fertile land at the expense of other groups including the Kalenjin, whose aspirations were conveniently turned westward against the Luhya. Many Kikuyu believed that since they had suffered the most under colonialism, they should benefit the most from independence.

In 1966, another party—the Kenya Peoples Union (KPU)—was formed. The absorption of KADU had strengthened the more conservative faction in KANU, and the more radical faction defected to KPU, primarily because it believed it would have a better chance of changing policies by appealing to the electorate as a separate party. But ethnicity was also involved, because actual electoral support in the 1966 by-elections came almost entirely from KPU leader Odinga's Luo following, partly because Kenyatta used instant land resettlement to undermine the appeal of KPU's Kikuyu leaders. Ethnic violence flared when the most prominent KANU Luo minister, Tom Mboya, was assassinated in 1969, allegedly at the instigation of Kikuyu leaders. The acceleration of Luo-Kikuyu tension caused Kenyatta to rely increasingly on repression, including banning KPU and detaining many of its leaders.

A few months after the departure of Odinga from KANU, Daniel arap Moi, a Kalenjin and a former KADU leader, became vice-president and in 1968 the constitution was amended to make the vice-president interim president in case of the president's death. Since Kenyatta was elderly, there was intense competition over succession, and Moi was initially viewed both by powerful Kikuyu contestants and their by arch-rival Mboya as a nonthreatening official successor. In the mid-1970s, with Mboya no longer a factor, Moi became the most viable non-Kikuyu or, in some eyes, anti-Kikuyu candidate, and a Kikuyu-led group of politicians attempted to change the constitution to deny Moi the advantage of immediate succession. They were unsuccessful in doing so, however, partly because he had two powerful Kikuyu supporters who had been very close to Kenyatta but were not part of the inner circle of leaders from Kiambu District. Moi assumed the presidency on Kenyatta's death in 1978 without incident, and he appointed one of his Kikuyu supporters, Mwai Kibaki, as vice-president and retained the other, Charles Njonjo, as attorney general.

The 1980s saw a continuation of the heated communal contention mixed with conflict over economic policy that had existed under Kenyatta. Without the personal appeal of Kenyatta or the resources made available in the 1960s by Kenya's rapid economic growth and the Africanization of the former White

Highlands, Moi initially attempted to follow Kenyatta's partially implemented policy of ethnically diversifying positions of authority within the Kenyan political structure. This effort achieved only limited success, partly because it involved undoing the disproportionate Kikuyu influence established during the latter years of Kenyatta's reign, and it was seen as an attempt to replace Kikuyu privilege with Kalenjin privilege. At first, Moi managed to attract a limited amount of Kikuyu support—especially among the poor—in districts other than Kiambu, and a greater amount of Luhya support. After the 1979 elections, however, Moi's policy rapidly shifted toward ethnic replacement, leading to disproportional Kalenjin representation in the executive and the administration, substantial economic advances by the Kalenjin, and a substantial narrowing of Moi's support base. Even some Kalenjin subgroups were not fully behind him, and their subgroup identities remain strong.

The one-party state, which had existed de facto since 1969, was mandated legally in 1982 after it was rumored that a socialist party was about to be formed under Odinga's leadership. A few months later, Moi narrowly survived a coup attempt led by the Kenyan air force and allegedly backed by Odinga and other Luo and Kikuyu politicians. As the economy began to stagnate, Asians, who had suffered the consequences of Kenya's policy of Africanization after independence, were allowed a freer economic role, further alienating African support. The two Kikuyu leaders who provided crucial support for Moi's succession, and who held the key posts of attorney general and vice-president, were removed from power in 1983 and 1988, respectively; other Kikuyu entered the cabinet, but in lesser positions.

Conflict in Kenya in the late 1980s and early 1990s has focused on the rise of a real or imagined clandestine left-wing group called Mwakenya and the demand from many quarters for a multiparty system and reduced repression. With a membership that is alleged to be disproportionally Kikuyu and Luo, Mwakenya is perceived by Moi as a direct ideological and ethnic threat. But the regime may be deliberately exaggerating this threat—even to the extent of having invented Mwakenya—to justify its severe repression of all opposition, which has included serious human rights violations. Since 1990 the demand for greater democracy has been too open and too widespread, both geographically and within the class structure, to be blamed on an alleged clandestine organization. In 1991 Odinga and others founded the Forum for the Restoration of Democracy, whose demonstrations were broken up by the police and whose leaders were detained. But by December of that year, Moi and KANU, under pressure from western donors, agreed in principle to allow other parties to form, and two have done so. It is not yet clear how freely they will be allowed to operate, or what manipulations Moi will undertake to keep himself in power, although the recent ban on political meetings—decreed in response to Luo-Kalenjin violence, which opponents accuse Moi of encouraging—may be indicative. It is possible that his actions have already made the Kalenjin a minority at risk, perhaps even at high risk, from a successor government. Meanwhile, the Kikuyu and Luo continue to be at risk because Moi regards the transethnic opposition as led by these two groups.

Largely separate from this pattern of communal contention, but probably contributing to its severity, has been the long history of conflict between the Kenyan state and pastoralist peoples. Around the time of independence this conflict was most severe with the Somali because of their violent separatist campaign to join the neighboring Somali Republic and the Kenya government's violent repression of that campaign. For its own reasons, in 1967 the Somali government ceased to support Kenyan Somali separatism, and since then politicians from this group have consistently declared their loyalty to Kenya. However, the Somali remain at risk because of attacks by Somali *shiftas* (bandits) against other peoples, conflicts between Somali and their culturally different pastoralist neighbors, and the consequent absence of development in the Somali area. Long-term conflict has been most severe with the Masai, because agriculturalists (mainly Kikuyu) have taken so much of their land and left them in a state of great poverty and considerable social disorganization; they are not sufficiently numerous to protect their interests by engaging in communal contention.

Zambia and Kenya both exemplify the politics of communal contention within unstable multiethnic coalitions, but in substantially different ways. In Zambia, smaller differentials, less discrimination, and limited variations in stress (and consequently lower grievances) meant that the institution of a one-party system, combined with economic decline and the formation of a privileged class representing all ethnopolitical groups, could dampen at least the surface manifestations of ethnopolitical conflict. Although there are indications that the process of redemocratization may exacerbate such conflict, it is possible to specify conditions under which this can be avoided (see the conclusion of this chapter). In Kenya, greater differentials, discrimination, stress, and grievances—especially for indigenous pastoralist peoples—combined with more economic growth and an advantaged class that is drawn disproportionally from a few ethnopolitical groups, have meant that a more repressive one-party system has failed to curtail more intense ethnopolitical conflict. These factors may also mean that redemocratization, especially if Moi and KANU attempt to undermine it, will be more likely to exacerbate ethnic strife.

Ethiopia

The pattern of communal contention in unstable multiethnic coalitions emerged in Zambia and Kenya, and elsewhere, out of the partially democratic and relatively peaceful decolonization process in British colonies. Similar patterns were also forged in the slightly less democratic but even more peaceful decolonization process in economically and politically advanced French colonies. A very different pattern of minority versus state conflict, focused on ethnonationalism and including long-term rebellions, emerged in Ethiopia. This pattern developed out of centuries of empire building, interrupted only briefly (for most of the country) by Italian and then British colonial incursions, and almost two decades of social revolution beginning in 1974. The geographical boundaries established during this historical experience are as arbitrary in ethnic terms as those drawn at the Berlin Conference, and the ethnic composition of the populations within those boundaries is as diverse (more than eighty groups are currently recognized), but the process of assimilation that was suspended by colonial administrations elsewhere proceeded apace in Ethiopia.

The origins of contemporary Ethiopia can be traced back to the founding of the Axumite kingdom in about 500 B.C. For many centuries the political and cultural core of the empire was in the northern area inhabited by Tigreans, but it gradually moved southward into what is now the central area, inhabited by the closely related Amhara. These two groups are collectively known as Abyssinian; they share the Coptic Christian religion and many cultural characteristics, but they speak different languages and have a long history of political rivalry within the empire. The Amhara are virtually unique among black African ethnopolitical groups in recognizing the centrality of assimilation rather than common descent in their formation and growth, and in reckoning descent bilaterally so that it is extremely diffuse. As Christopher Clapham states very succinctly:

> Being Amhara is much more a matter of how one behaves than who one's parents were; and without this capacity for assimilating other peoples into a core culture which can be regarded as national, and not the exclusive property of a particular group of people, the Ethiopian state would probably have been unable to sustain itself in the first place. At the same time, it is precisely because Ethiopia has this core identity, associated with one people but also claiming a special national status, that it suffers from much more intense problems of national identity and integration than other African states, in which ethnicity is the result of the almost haphazard process by which different peoples were tossed by colonialism into a common political unit.[17]

Because of this Amhara pan-ethnic nationalism or imperialism, depending on one's point of view, we do not classify the Amhara as a minority. In response, however, the Tigreans and most other groups discussed below have become ethnonationalists.

In the second half of the nineteenth century the empire expanded substantially to the south and southeast, encompassing a number of non-Abyssinian, predominantly Muslim, and frequently pastoralist peoples. By far the largest of these groups—more numerous, in fact, than the Amhara themselves—is the Oromo, an extremely fragmented collection of small agriculturalist or pastoralist, mostly Muslim but sometimes Christian communities spread over southern, western, and even northeastern Ethiopia. Some Oromo—especially in the province of Shoa, which includes the capital city of Addis Ababa—are highly assimilated to Amhara culture, while others are in varying degrees of conflict with it. The Ogaden clan of the Somali inhabits the Ogaden region of southeastern Ethiopia as well as neighboring parts of the country, and they remain totally unassimilated by Ethiopian-Amhara culture. Finally, the negroid peoples of the Ethiopian-Sudanese borderlands comprise eighteen language groups of the Nilo-Saharan family, from which their generic anthropological name is derived. They include the Barta, Anuak, Kunfel, Gumuz, Nuer, Mekan, and Maji. *Shangalla* (or negro) is the Amharic name for this collection of indigenous peoples. There is no sense of collective identity among them.

In 1896, the Ethiopians under Menelik II defeated the Italians, who were seeking to expand their recently established Red Sea coastal colony of Eritrea southward, in the battle of Adwa. As a result the Ethiopians secured the northern frontier of the Ethiopian empire until 1936, when the Italian Fascists briefly occupied Ethiopia itself, but also separated Eritrea from that empire. There are at least nine ethnic groups in Eritrea. The population is about half Muslims and half Tigrinya-speaking Christians. Eritrea was conquered by the British during World War II and was administered by them until 1952, when it was federated with Ethiopia under great pressure from the latter; in 1962 it was annexed outright to the Ethiopian empire. Thus Eritrean nationalism is not, strictly speaking, ethnonationalism; rather, it is anticolonial (Italian, British, and Ethiopian) nationalism similar to that seen elsewhere in black Africa before independence. But because Ethiopian nationalism has a strong Amhara ethnic component, its rejection by Eritrean nationalists has an anti-Amhara ethnic component. There is substantial potential for smaller scale ethnonationalism among Eritrea's Muslim peoples, who have adopted Arabic as their political lingua franca even though it is not the native language of any of them. We have characterized one group—the Afars of the Danikil Plain in southern Eritrea and adjacent areas of Ethiopia proper and the Republic of Djibouti—as a minority at risk in both the Eritrean and broader Ethiopian contexts. The Afars have been especially distant from mainstream Eritrean nationalism, and the Ethiopian government granted them regional autonomy after they rebelled in 1975.

Cultural and physical differences among ethnopolitical groups are even greater in Ethiopia than in Kenya, to say nothing of Zambia. On the other hand, Amhara assimilation of Oromo in Shoa and elsewhere represents an expansion of "primordial" identity on a scale that far exceeds the expansion that has occurred in Zambia, to say nothing of Kenya. The division of the Tigreans by the Ethiopian-Eritrean border has greater political significance than similar divisions of groups in the other countries. In a process also observed in Zambia and Kenya, decentralized primordial groups such as the Somali and the Oromo have substantially strengthened their ethnopolitical identities in response to social change, ethnonationalism, and repression. Economic differentials, discrimination, and grievances as well as variations in demographic and ecological stress are about the same as in Kenya and greater than in Zambia, while political differentials, discrimination, and grievances (regarding both rights and autonomy) are greater—especially in terms of the percentage of the population affected by them—than in either of the other countries. As in Kenya, agriculturalists are more advantaged than pastoralists. In addition, Abyssinians (including assimilated Oromo) are more advantaged than non-Abyssinians, and among the former, the Amhara have been politically and—to a much lesser extent—economically advantaged over Tigrinya speakers. Finally, in contrast to the other two countries, there has been extensive, long-term rebellion in Ethiopia.

Both ethnopolitical mobilization and mass nationalism were rather effectively repressed in imperial Ethiopia until about 1960 and in colonial Eritrea until World War II. Because mobilization occurred first in Eritrea and has been the most intense, it will be discussed first, along with closely related Tigrean mobilization. Somali and Oromo mobilization—also closely, although sometimes negatively, related—will then receive attention. The imperial and revolutionary periods will be treated together because of the essential continuity in the policy of long-time emperor Haile Selassie and Marxist military ruler Mengistu Haile Mariam (both of whom had Oromo ancestors) toward minorities: that policy was to keep minorities in a united Amharic-Ethiopian nation, by manipulation if possible, by force if necessary. The minorities rejected this policy with equivalent continuity. It is important to note at the outset, however, that the widespread radicalism of intellectuals, students, soldiers, and workers after 1960, which brought about the Ethiopian revolution, also deeply affected the mobilization of all minorities except the Somali. The Somali were poorly represented at the University of Addis Ababa, from which radicalism spread, and followed instead the nationalist model of the Somali Republic. Radicalism also stimulated mobilization among the Amhara but, because of their assimilationist outlook, their radicalism took the form of radical Ethiopian nationalism rather than radical ethnonationalism. Most radicals rejected the military regime as fascist, and were in turn rejected by it.

Mobilization in the form of anticolonial nationalism, which soon also became anti-Ethiopian, got a strong boost in Eritrea during the brief period of British rule.[18] Eritrea was ahead of Ethiopia in education, urbanization, and economic development, and the partial openness of British rule combined with the continued presence of Italians in privileged positions created ideal conditions for nationalism. The Ethiopian government immediately began pressing its claim to Eritrea, stressing that it was a victim of both recent Fascist aggression and long-time Italian colonial occupation of what it argued had previously been its territory. Most but not all of the Tigrinya-speaking Christians responded favorably to Ethiopian claims and joined the newly formed Unionist party, while most Muslims opposed any form of union and formed several political movements in support of this position. In 1952, Britain gained UN approval for federation "under the sovereignty of the Ethiopian crown," and conflict temporarily died down. From the beginning, Ethiopia did everything possible to undermine the federation and reduce Eritrea to the status of an ordinary province; Ethiopia gradually attained this goal by manipulating the support of Eritrean Unionists and their Muslim tactical allies. Complete unity was decreed in November 1962.

Mobilization against Ethiopian rule after 1962 continued to be led primarily by Muslims and to be supported by Egypt and Sudan. The Eritrean Liberation Front (ELF), founded in 1960, soon became the dominant movement and retained that position for more than fifteen years. Although perennially rent by ethnic, sectarian, ideological, and personal factionalism, the ELF had a small guerrilla presence in the western lowland areas of Eritrea by 1962. That presence expanded both numerically and geographically in the next decade and a half as large numbers of Eritreans became hostile to the imperial regime because of the severe and diffuse repression to which it subjected them in reprisal for ELF activities. Christians, mainly students who were angry at the imposition of Amharic in the schools and workers who were angry at the Ethiopian crackdown on unions, began joining the movement in the mid-1960s, bringing guerrilla activities to the highlands. Now there were overlapping cleavages in the movement, since the better educated Tigrinya-speaking Christians tended to be more ideologically radical. They led the way in establishing a Labor party within the ELF, which gained considerable influence over the ELF's policies in the early 1970s. A split in the movement resulted, with significant numbers of more conservative Muslims and a small number of more radical Muslims and Christians defecting and joining together temporarily in a loose opposition coalition under radical leadership; considerable fighting between the ELF and this opposition occurred after the split.

After the revolutionary military regime, which initially included Eritreans, seized power in Ethiopia, it made conciliatory gestures toward the Eritrean movements in 1974 and again in 1976; these gestures were ignored, at least in part because of the movements' preoccupation with internal conflicts. The conservative wing of the opposition group split off, and some of its members rejoined the ELF. The now uniformly radical and predominantly Christian opposition adopted the name Eritrean People's Liberation Front (EPLF) in 1976. The high level of disorder that existed in Ethiopia itself as the regime fought various opponents, especially the Somali, gave the Eritrean guerrillas a temporary military advantage in early 1978, which the EPLF used to make itself the strongest movement, both politically and militarily. In the meantime there was much talk about reuniting the two movements, but very little action.

Soon the Ethiopian revolutionary military regime was able to wage a temporarily effective counterattack and regain control of almost all of Eritrea. The ELF never recovered from this setback, and by 1982 it had disintegrated into several small and ineffective organizations. The EPLF was able to hold out and, in close alliance with the Tigrean Peoples Liberation Front (TPLF), to take the offensive again in 1982 and participate in overthrowing the Mengistu regime in 1991. Negotiations between the EPLF and the Ethiopian government continued off and on after 1982 but did not become serious until 1989, by which time the Eritrean-Tigrean coalition was beginning to threaten the Mengistu regime within Ethiopia itself. In the meantime, that regime established a Nationalities Institute with very little power and drew up a new constitution under which severely limited regional autonomy was granted to a number of areas, including Tigray and Eritrea minus the Afar areas of both provinces, which also gained autonomous status as the Assab region. These actions were vigorously rejected by the EPLF and only temporarily assuaged the Afars.

Tigrean mobilization against imperial centralization goes

back to the time of Menelik and reached a high point in the 1940s as the Haile Selassie regime was reimposing central control after the Italians had been driven out. Almost immediately after the revolution Tigrean radicals organized the TPLF in emulation of the EPLF. Its goal has always been autonomy rather than secession, and thus it has maintained an interest in broader Ethiopian politics. The TPLF's focus has been on Tigray Province rather than on all Tigrinya-speaking people, since the latter would include half of the Eritreans and exclude 30 percent of the population of Tigray. This movement had a number of rivals, two of which were all-Ethiopian anti-Mengistu groups, but it was able to defeat them.

The most significant of these rivals, the Ethiopian Peoples Revolutionary party (EPRP), was the main radical group opposing the military regime nationally in the first few years after the revolution, and its members were primarily Amhara and Tigreans. It established a base in Tigray in 1975, and after its membership in Addis Ababa had been decimated by the military regime's "red terror," many of the survivors fled to that base. Although the EPRP was ideologically close to the TPLF and relations between the two movements were initially friendly, the EPRP's assimilationist views were rejected by the TPLF, and violent confrontations between them in 1978 and 1979 ended in complete victory for the TPLF. Believing that defeat of the EPLF would also destroy the TPLF, the Mengistu regime placed low priority on attacking the latter directly until 1983, when it launched the first of a series of attacks. In spite of the attacks, the TPLF retained control of most of Tigray Province and parts of neighboring Welo. By 1989 it began moving southward as the leading element in the newly formed Ethiopian People's Revolutionary Democratic Front (EPRDF), which also contains a number of anti-Mengistu Amhara members from the Ethiopian People's Democratic Movement and military officers from many ethnopolitical groups.

The Somali are the most isolated minority in Ethiopia, as they are in Kenya, because in both cases they have strong ties across the border to the Somali Republic. The Italians and the British stimulated these ties when they occupied all or part of the Somali areas of Ethiopia and attempted to unite all Somali under their tutelage in 1936–41 and 1941–54 respectively. Pan-Somali nationalist mobilization was well underway by the late 1950s.[19] With the independence of the Somali Republic in 1960, assistance in the form of propaganda, weapons, and organizational support began to flow across the border. Separate rebellions, led mainly by traditional leaders, broke out in the Ogaden and in neighboring Bale and Sidamo Provinces in 1963, but they were effectively crushed by the Ethiopian army (by early 1964 in the Ogaden and by late 1969 in Bale-Sidamo), because the Somali government could not supply enough military assistance and, after 1967, desired peace with Ethiopia. A number of guerrillas from both areas fled into the Somali Republic to prepare to fight again at a more propitious time.

The internal disorder and disruption of military ties with the United States caused by the 1974 Ethiopian revolution presented the Somali government and guerrillas with what they considered to be that propitious time. The Western Somali Liberation Front (WSLF) was set up in the Ogaden, and the Somali and Abo Liberation Front (SALF) was established for Bale-Sidamo. (*Abo*, a term of greeting in the regional Oromo dialect, became a convenient political designation for the Oromo of this region.) These movements began guerrilla operations in 1976 and were joined by regular Somali forces in 1977. The Somali government's demand for total control of the operation led to substantial conflict with the guerrillas. Overlapping territorial claims divided the two guerrilla movements. The Ethiopian government, now armed by the Soviets and aided by Cuban troops, was able to drive the Somali and guerrilla forces out of its territory and force the Somali Republic to sue for peace. The guerrillas occasionally carried out raids in the next few years, but they were no longer a threat to the Mengistu regime. The creation of two partially autonomous Somali regions in 1987 was little better received than the autonomous regions in Eritrea-Tigray.

Because of the assimilation of many educated Oromo and a weak sense of common identity among those with less education, Oromo mobilization got a relatively late start, although a group had petitioned for a separate Oromo state at the time of the Fascist occupation. A cultural association with decided political overtones was formed in 1962, but it was banned and its leaders were arrested in 1966. Oromo students at the university took up its ideas in the early 1970s, but the revolution weakened this incipient Oromo nationalism. Oromo were well represented in the military regime and in the radical party (MEISON) with which it initially collaborated in opposition to the EPRP. In addition, Oromo benefited most extensively from the land reform program because so many were peasants on large estates that were expropriated, and the regime's ideology tended to value Oromo identity, equating it with being exploited. But this was not enough for some Oromo radicals, who blamed their exploitation on the colonial situation of the Oromo, and they founded the Oromo Liberation Front (OLF) in the mid-1970s. The OLF demanded a separate state of Oromia, covering a vast stretch of southern Ethiopia that was inhabited by many other peoples, including Somali (and, of course, their Oromo Abo allies), thus putting the OLF in conflict with the Somali nationalists. The movement was able to establish contact with the EPLF through Sudan and receive some training from them, but it has remained small and Christian-led, and an Oromo Islamic Front has split off from it.

Mobilization among the Nilo-Saharans has been virtually nonexistent, despite the fact that they have been pushed off much of their land since the revolution, and especially during the drought years of the 1980s, to facilitate the government's resettlement of Abyssinians. For the most part they have chosen "exit" (to Sudan) rather than "voice."

Conflict in Ethiopia between ethnonationalists and centralists-assimilationists as well as among ethnonationalists is more intense and more difficult to resolve than communal contention for power and economic benefit in Kenya and Zambia. The revolution presented an opportunity for dramatically improving relations between minorities and the state, but this opportunity was missed and relations in fact grew worse. Ethiopian radicals accepted the right of self-determination for minorities in principle, although there was disagreement over whether this right included secession. Had the military regime not distrusted and repressed radical as well as conservative civilian politicians during its first decade in power, it is possible—although by no means certain, as the conflict between the EPRP and MEISON attests—that a strong radical party in control of the government would have been able to unite most or all of the former Ethiopian empire by granting considerable regional autonomy to minorities.

After eighteen additional years of bitter conflict combined with severe famine in many parts of the country, the task of the new government—a loose coalition of the EPRDF and the OLF led by Meles Zenawi of the TPLF—is even more difficult. Since the coalition seized power in May 1991, there have been reports of fighting between the EPRDF and the OLF, as well as a large number of violent localized ethnic conflicts, and several new ethnic parties have formed. The EPRP and MEISON, excluded from the new government, have formed the Coalition of Ethiopian Democratic Forces (COEDF), joined briefly by supporters of the imperial regime, to represent the centralist—if not assimilationist—point of view. On the positive side, the EPLF has agreed to postpone a referendum on Eritrean independence until mid-1993, although it is the de facto government of that territory in the meantime. Given the victory of the coalition of ethnonationalists, all groups in both Eritrea and Ethiopia can be expected to be assertive in the near future; the Oromo in particular can be expected for the first time to demand power proportional to their demographic plurality, and the OLF appears to be concerned that northern liberation movements may not be fully committed to decolonization of the south.[20] The Afar leadership appears to want to be part of Ethiopia rather than Eritrea. Real political parties do not exist, and basic constitutional questions have not been addressed. Finally, it must be remembered that the leaders of all of these groups are radicals, or at least former radicals, and they have already been subjected to western pressure to modify this orientation in order to continue receiving desperately needed aid. The future of Ethiopia remains extremely uncertain.

Conclusion: Prospects for Containment of Conflict

The general analysis and case studies presented in this chapter provide systematic support for the point made by situationalists that politicized communal contention over economic distribution issues is the prevalent form of *politically relevant* ethnicity in Africa. Ethnonationalists are the next most common type of ethnopolitical group, but they are the predominant type only in a few countries such as Ethiopia with atypical histories of intergroup relations. Ethnoclasses are usually confined to relatively small immigrant groups, and the primordial component—while important in influencing the availability of groups for political mobilization and for defining indigenous peoples—enters into conflict less extensively than it does in most other regions. In James McKay's terminology, African ethnic mobilizers tend to be ethnic manipulators.[21] The large number of politically relevant communal groups in Africa, their relatively high geographical concentration, and the relative frequency of conflicts among them not involving the state reflect the superimposition both of colonial divide-and-rule policies and of postcolonial political competition on the primordial ethnic map of precolonial Africa. Most of these groups were coded relatively low on cultural, political, and economic/class differentials; discrimination; all types of grievances; violent and nonviolent protest; and separatism. Consequently, political competition within current state boundaries appears to be a crucial source of group identity and mobilization. Since these groups are defined in large part through participation in political competition, their internal coherence tends to be high.

Although economic differentials and discrimination are low in Africa in comparison to other regions, our analysis shows that these variables are as significant in causing all types of grievances in Africa as they are elsewhere. Political differentials and discrimination also cause some types of grievances. Political action in the 1980s, on the other hand, must be explained primarily in terms of prior mobilization. Both political competition within the context of unstable multiethnic coalitions and ethnonationalist rebellions are initially conflicts over economic and power distribution issues, but these conflicts tend to become self-sustaining regardless of the levels or causes of economic and political differentials or the grievances that result from them.

The general and case study findings presented above can be used to suggest the conditions under which ethnopolitical conflict is most likely to be contained in the context of Africa south of the Sahara. It has been argued in this chapter that the possibilities for containing such conflict are relatively good in at least some black African countries that exemplify the prevailing pattern of unstable multiethnic coalitions. Where the collective disadvantage of significant minorities is not too great or too long-lasting in the population as a whole *and* in the advantaged class, grievances and protest arise in large part from fear of being removed from the ruling coalition or losing power within it. In these situations conflict can be contained by reducing this fear. Reducing the fear of losing power need not involve abandoning either state expansion or democratization, although the specific forms of both processes and the rates of change involved in them will almost certainly affect conflict mitigation. The crucial institutional variables involved in these processes, selected from a wide range of possibilities raised in the literature,[22] are those pertaining to the party system and central-local relations in government and party structures.

Political parties (or at least the ruling party) need stronger organization with greater input from ordinary citizens than has existed in almost all postindependence African parties. Such parties would encompass multiethnic coalitions but would give the coalitions greater stability by introducing effective supra-ethnic party identities and patterns of political interaction. If there is competition among parties, all need to feel that they will continue to have a fair chance to win in the future if they lose the next election. The fear that electoral competition would lead to intense conflict that would threaten the integrity of the state was the justification most frequently given for authoritarian policies, and those policies led to moderate decreases in nonviolent protest and moderate increases in rebellion in the postindependence period. Redemocratization will probably rekindle nonviolent ethnopolitical mobilization and protest to some extent, but strong parties and faith in having a fair chance to win in the future should direct such mobilization into institutionalized channels and keep it from threatening a regime's stability. Delegation of power to local rather than provincial governments and party units needs to be both substantial and institutionalized, so that ordinary people will have an effective voice in the arena that matters most to them and losers in national-level competition will be guaranteed the opportunity to protect their local power bases. Under these conditions, which will probably also strengthen both democracy and state capacity, there will be the sense of political security for both the leadership and the populace that is necessary to keep a broad multiethnic coalition stable and to moderate the self-perpetuating tendency of communal contention.

Such institutional arrangements may work most effectively in situations of economic stagnation or even decline, because economic differentials and discrimination are less salient under these conditions; unfortunately, such conditions are most likely to exist in Africa in the near future. These arrangements will also make economic growth less likely to generate strong grievances, however. If economic decline is too great, of course, all political institutions will be threatened. The formation of a working class that parallels the advantaged class in drawing its membership roughly in proportion from various ethnopolitical groups will help to separate ethnic and class conflict. Finally, the elimination or at least minimization of foreign intervention will also contribute greatly to the containment of ethnopolitical conflict.

The new rulers of Zambia are in a relatively good position to establish the conflict-mitigating conditions discussed above, although it is not clear that they recognize the need for strong parties. In Kenya, the establishment of such conditions will probably require a different set of rulers, and it is not certain who they will be. President Moi has moved in the right direction, however, by creating greater equality among ethnopolitical groups, especially in the privileged class, even if his increasing authoritarianism and his continued reliance on clientelism rather than a participatory party organization have been headed in the wrong direction. In Ethiopia, the task will be to transform ethnonationalism into communal contention, a task that will certainly not be easy given the history of that country. As indicated above, it will probably be more difficult in the 1990s than it would have been shortly after the revolution. But a combination of factors—the heavy costs of conflict in the intervening years, the substantial ethnic equalization that has been achieved within the privileged class, the fragile state of the economy, the ending of the Cold War orientation in foreign aid, and the enlightenment of the current leaders—leads us to believe that there is at least a modicum of hope.

10. Settling Ethnopolitical Conflicts

Some observers have concluded that ethnopolitical conflicts are intractable.[1] The evidence suggests otherwise. All but one of the twenty-four communal minorities in western democracies and Japan have made some gains in response to their political demands, often very significant ones, in the past two decades. The cases reviewed in chapter 6 strongly suggest that western democracies have devised strategies of accommodation that have contributed to a substantial decline in most kinds of ethnic conflict. Among the specific reforms are guarantees of full civil and political rights for ethnoclasses, programs designed to alleviate their poverty, recognition and resources for minority cultures and languages, and greater autonomy and state subsidies for indigenous peoples and regional nationalists. Serious regional conflicts persist in Canada and Northern Ireland, but the Canadian conflict is almost certain to be settled peacefully.

Three authoritarian, multinational states also have relaxed their hold on ethnonationalist peoples in the past several years: the Soviet Union, Yugoslavia, and Ethiopia. The introduction of democratic principles and practices of accommodation played a role in all three. In the USSR, democratization prepared the way for dissolution by facilitating popular nationalist movements in most republics and inhibiting leaders at the center from falling back on discredited Stalinist means to keep the Union intact. Continued commitment to democratic principles by Russia's leaders thus far has restrained loyalists of the old regime from using force to reconstitute the empire (see chapter 7). Yugoslavia went partway down the same path: popular elections brought ethnonationalists to power in Slovenia, Croatia, and Serbia, but Slovenia and Croatia both had to fight for independence because the Serbian leadership tried to maintain

Serbian dominance by force rather than follow the democratic logic of accommodation.[2] The Ethiopian state never made substantive concessions to regional nationalists and after a generation of warfare was defeated by a coalition of its adversaries. The long-range outcome remains in doubt, as shown in chapter 9, but the interim government has made firm commitments to conduct and abide by the results of referendums in mid-1993 that are expected to endorse Eritrean independence and devolution of power to other regions.

Our images of intractable communal conflicts are largely shaped by ethnonationalist wars in the Middle East, Asia, and Africa. Yet for each example of protracted communal conflict in these regions, one can point to neighboring states where similar conflicts have been managed more effectively. In the Middle East the rebellions generated by Kurdish and Palestinian nationalism contrast with the accommodation and incorporation of Berbers by the states of the Maghreb,[3] and the persecution of Baha'is in Iran contrasts with the usually peaceful coexistence of Muslims and Coptic Christians in Egypt (see chapter 8). In Asia the governments of Burma have relied on military means for four decades to suppress the nationalist aspirations of indigenous peoples such as the Karen and Shan, whereas similar insurgencies in Bangladesh (by the Chittagong Hills peoples) and the Philippines (by the Moros) have been defused through a mix of pressure and concessions. In central and west Africa more than a dozen states straddle the cultural and religious divide between the Muslim, Arab-influenced peoples of the savannah and the Christian, European-influenced peoples of the forest and coastal regions. Only in Sudan and Chad have protracted civil wars been fought across this divide (see chapter 9).

It is a mistake to regard ethnopolitical conflicts as intrinsically zero- or negative-sum. As the examples suggest, many strategies have been followed to bring about some form of accommodation between the interests of communal groups and states. In the best of circumstances the result is the institutionalization of peaceful relations between the parties and enduring gains shared by all of them. Ethnic hostilities and inequalities remain a serious issue in the United States despite a generation of public and private effort on civil rights issues, but American society as a whole has benefited politically and materially from the empowerment and incorporation of people of color. Policies of

regional devolution in France, Spain, and Italy demonstrate
that establishing self-managing autonomous regions can be politically and economically less burdensome for central states
than keeping resistant peoples in line by force: autonomy arrangements have transformed destructive conflicts in these societies into positive interregional competition.

The remainder of this chapter examines three general issues
of dispute between communal groups and states—whether aggrieved groups should secede, gain greater autonomy within
the state, or be given equality of status and opportunity—and
evaluates the costs, benefits, and risks of different domestic political means by which these disputes can be accommodated. International forces also affect the dynamics and management of
communal conflicts but are assessed elsewhere.[4] The analysis is
illustrated throughout with examples of compromises and outcomes of ethnopolitical conflicts that are documented in the Minorities at Risk study.

Communal versus State Interests

The interests of communal groups are reflected in their manifest grievances (see chapter 3) and in the objectives of their protest movements and rebellions.[5] The typical interests pursued
by each type of communal group are shown schematically in
figure 10.1. These interests imply that communal groups have
four general orientations to, and demands on, the state that
claims sovereignty over them: exit, autonomy, access, and control.[6] *Exit* implies complete withdrawal and severence of mutual
ties between communal group and state. *Autonomy* and *access*
both imply some degree of accommodation: autonomy means
that a minority has a collective power base, usually a regional
one, in a plural society; access (not mutually exclusive) means
that minorities individually and collectively have the means to
pursue their cultural, political, and material interests with the
same rights and restraints that apply to other groups. *Control* is
the revolutionary aim of a minority or subordinate majority to
establish the group's political and economic hegemony over others. We assume that this objective can be accommodated, if
at all, by some combination of the policies and institutions of
autonomy and power sharing.

Public officials also have interests to protect, the most funda-

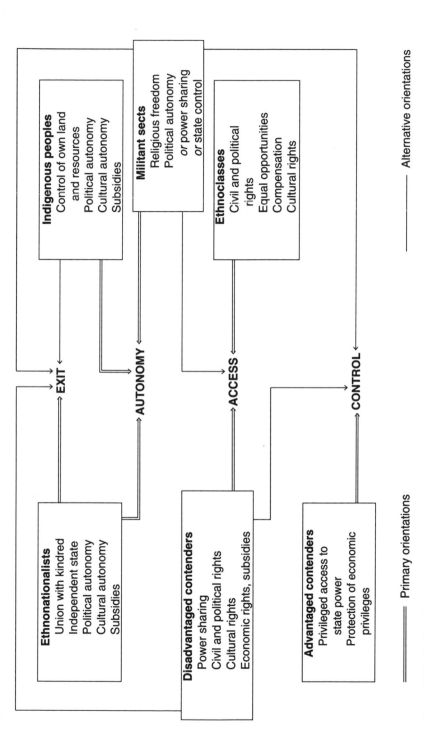

Figure 10.1. Policy Demands and Orientations to the State of Politically Active Communal Groups.

mental of which are (1) maintaining the state's integrity and authority, and (2) securing the support and revenues needed to keep their positions and to pursue their political and programmatic objectives. How officials respond to communal demands is conditioned by these larger interests. It cannot be assumed that officials in multiparty democracies will respond democratically by attempting to accommodate minority demands, if the cost to the continuity and legitimacy of the state is too high. Nor is it surprising that authoritarian leaders sometimes make concessions to minorities: they may calculate that meeting some demands is less costly than investing scarce resources in fighting popular resistance.[7]

Demands for Secession

Communal demands for exit (or secession) are highly threatening, because they challenge the nationalist ideologies held by most dominant groups and imply the breakup of the state. Usually they are resisted by force. Since World War II, thirty of the ethnonationalists in this study have fought protracted wars for national independence or for unification with kindred groups elsewhere. Table 10.1 identifies them and their status as of late 1992.[8] Fourteen groups have made or are on the verge of achieving significant gains, typically in the form of regional autonomy. These peoples are listed in descending order of the extent of gains; the Moros and Baluchis have gotten very limited returns from their political investments in comparison with the independence won by Lithuanians, Ukrainians, and Eritreans.[9] In addition, three of the thirty ethnonationalists are parties to long-term negotiations that may lead to power sharing (for Catholics in Northern Ireland) or autonomy.

On the debit side of the ledger, seven ethnonationalists have suffered what appear to be decisive defeats. The Ibo in Nigeria and the Kurds in Iran have been reincorporated without serious reprisals, the other five are still subject to repression. In six other instances serious conflicts persist or, in the Punjab and in Turkey's Kurdish provinces, are escalating without any prospect of settlement in sight. Rebellion by militant Kurds in Turkey has increased in spite of the Turkish government's acknowledgment, in 1990, of Kurdish identity and aspirations. The acknowledgment was symbolic not substantive, and no concessions were made or promised to the desires of many Kurds for regional autonomy.

Even if independence or autonomy is eventually achieved, grinding and devastating wars are the price paid in most ethnonationalist conflicts that are fought to a conclusion. Serious conflict lasted fourteen years, on average, before autonomy or political recognition was gained by the twelve successful or partly successful ethnonationalists in part 1 of table 10.1 (excluding the two ex-Soviet republics). And in several of these instances, violent conflict continued long after autonomy agreements were implemented. The seven wars that states succeeded in suppressing (see table 10.1, part 3) lasted an average of more than twenty-five years, about as long as the six persisting and escalating conflicts (see part 4).

Faced with the prospect of quarter-century-long wars, state officials may decide that negotiated secession is the most acceptable of a set of unpalatable options. First, the political and material costs of fighting a secessionist civil war may exceed the symbolic and material value of maintaining state boundaries—indeed, may exceed the resources of a poor state.[10] Second, if a state is otherwise homogeneous, the exit of a hostile communal minority may make the remainder more governable. Such assessments presumably were in the mind of an Anglo-Canadian official who recently said that Quebec's secession would be like amputating an arm—painful but the rest of Canada could live without it.[11]

The extent of domestic and international support for secessionist movements plays a critical role in such calculations. Gorbachev and his democratic-minded supporters evidently felt secure enough about the loyalties of the Slavic majority of the Union to countenance autonomy for the peripheral Baltic republics, thinking that the rest of the Union would remain intact. Ethiopia's General Mengistu, governing a more heterogeneous and openly rebellious empire, chose to fight rather than compromise. Events proved both wrong, but the costs of Gorbachev's miscalculation were far less: destructive civil wars were avoided and western material and diplomatic support were maintained.

Until the breakup of the Soviet Union at the end of 1991, only one other postwar ethnopolitical conflict was settled by peaceful participation: Singapore, a previously autonomous member of the Federation of Malaysia, became fully

Table 10.1. Outcomes of Ethnonationalist Wars of Independence, 1944–91.

Group	Countries	Period of Open Conflict[a]	Status in 1992[b]
1. Conflicts Leading to Accommodation			
Lithuanians	USSR	1945–52	Independent 1991
Ukrainians	USSR	1944–mid-1950s	Independent 1992
Eritreans[c]	Ethiopia	1961–91	Members with other groups of a Tigrean-dominated revolutionary coalition, pending autonomy referenda to be held in 1993
Tigreans[c]	Ethiopia	1975–91	
Somali	Ethiopia	1963–91	
Basques[d]	Spain	1959–late 1980s	Regional autonomy 1980
Miskitos[c]	Nicaragua	1981–88	Regional autonomy 1990
Nagas	India	1952–75	Regional autonomy 1972
Tripuras	India	1967–89	Regional autonomy 1972; sporadic conflict
Afars[d]	Ethiopia	1975–85	Regional autonomy 1977
Chittagong Hills peoples[d]	Bangladesh	1975–89	District Councils with limited autonomy 1989
Moros	Philippines	1972–76	Autonomy for part of region 1990
Baluchis[c]	Pakistan	1973–77	Autonomy 1970–73[b]; partially restored 1980
Saharawis	Morocco	1973–90	UN referendum 1992; intermittent conflict
2. Conflicts Leading to Protracted Negotiations			
Catholics	Northern Ireland	1969–present	Intermittent negotiations on power sharing; conflict abating
Kurds	Iraq	1960–present[e]	Negotiations in progress; intermittent conflict
Palestinians[f]	West Bank and Gaza	1968–present	Negotiations in progress; conflict abating
3. Conflict Suppressed without Significant Accommodation			
Ibo	Nigeria	1967–70	Conflict suppressed; reincorporated in state[g]
Kurds	Iran	1945–late 1980s[e]	Conflict suppressed
Palestinians	Lebanon	1965–90	Conflict suppressed by Syrian intervention
Tibetans	China	1959–89[e]	Conflict suppressed

East Timorese	Indonesia	1974–late 1980s	Conflict suppressed
Papuans	Indonesia	1964–86	Conflict suppressed
Karen	Burma	1945–present	Defeat imminent
4. Conflicts Persisting or Escalating			
Kurds	Turkey	1961–present[e]	Political recognition 1990; conflict escalating
Tamils	Sri Lanka	1975–present	Regional autonomy 1987; conflict continues
Sikhs	India	1978–present	Regional autonomy 1966[b], conflict escalating
Southerners	Sudan	1955–72	Autonomy 1973–83[h]; conflict continues
		1983–present	
Kachins	Burma	1961–present	Conflict continues
Shan	Burma	1962–present	Conflict continues

Note: The conflicts listed are sustained or recurrent campaigns of armed force aimed at least in part at securing national independence for a communal group or unification with kindred groups in adjoining states. Conflicts are listed within each group in descending order of the attainment or likelihood of attainment of group objectives.

[a] Beginning and ending dates are approximate because fighting usually begins with sporadic acts of violence that only gradually escalate into campaigns; deescalation usually is even more drawn out.

[b] In the cases of the Baluchis and the Sikhs (in the Punjab), regional autonomy was a response to earlier communal activism but did not prevent later civil wars. Other regional autonomy arrangements and planned referenda reflect efforts to manage secessionist civil wars and terrorist movements. The dates shown for regional autonomy are those in which autonomous regional institutions began operation or held their first elections. Lithuanian and Ukrainian independence are not directly a consequence of their rebellions of the late 1940s.

[c] The aims and situation of the Tigreans are ambiguous. In the early twentieth century they lost their historical dominance of the Ethiopian state to the Amharas. The Tigrean People's Liberation Front in principle sought independence but has emerged as the dominant partner in the revolutionary coalition that now governs Ethiopia. The probable outcomes will be greater regional autonomy for Tigray *and* reestablishment of a leading Tigrean role at the center.

[d] The objective of most rebels and partisans in these conflicts was regional autonomy; independence was talked about or sought by some factions.

[e] Intermittent conflicts, those in which armed combat stopped for substantial periods.

[f] Palestinians in Jordan have supported the cause of independence but, except during "Black September" of 1970, have not warred on the Jordanian state.

[g] The Ibo homeland has been divided into several states that have the same status, powers, and resources as all other constituent states of the Nigerian Federation.

[h] Southern Sudan had regional self-government from 1972 until 1983, when northern efforts to undermine it precipitated the second civil war.

independent in 1965. And in this case Chinese-dominated Singapore did not jump—it was pushed by the Malay-dominated federation, because Singapore's leaders were too successful in building political support among the Chinese minority on the Malay peninsula. One could add to the list Slovenia's secession from Yugoslavia after a brief military confrontation in summer 1991 and the grudging Soviet acceptance of the three Baltic states' independence in 1991, before the failed coup of August that led to the Union's dissolution.

It is likely that the fates of the USSR, Yugoslavia, and Ethiopia are being factored into the calculations of the protagonists in ethnonationalist conflicts elsewhere. The odds of winning independence look better than they have for several decades, which should strengthen the resolve of ethnonationalists. The message for states facing such challenges is more ambivalent: either intensify efforts to crush regional opponents, which is the strategy of the Union of Myanmar (Burmese) government, or opt for negotiations on limited autonomy, as the Israeli and Iraqi governments have done.

Pathways to Regional Autonomy

From the perspective of most public officials, regional autonomy is a less threatening and less costly alternative to civil war and secession. Officials prepared to compromise on this front can find some leaders in virtually all ethnonationalist movements who are open to compromises that guarantee regional autonomy in a federal or confederal framework. Some ethnonationalists pose their demands from the outset in terms of political and cultural autonomy: this is true of most regional movements in western societies, also of some Third World peoples and many indigenous peoples. Seven protracted ethnonationalist wars have led to autonomy agreements and a marked decline in conflict; in seven other instances current negotiations or impending referenda may culminate in autonomy.[12] Specifics of some of these cases are discussed in the following pages.

Communal Interests in Autonomy

One great advantage of regional autonomy over complete independence is that it has many negotiable specifics. Five types of arrangements can be used to accommodate autonomist demands, on the basis of the extent of authority devolved to the communal group: confederalism, federalism, regional autonomism, regional administrative decentralization, and community autonomism.[13] Within any of these frameworks, disputants are better able to work out agreements on more specific issues that surface repeatedly in the programs of communal movements:

- The group's right to teach and use its own language, to practice its religion, and to protect traditional values and lifeways from assimilationist pressures ("cultural autonomy" in figure 10.1).
- Guarantees of group control of its land, water, timber, and mineral resources.
- Powers to ensure that resource and commercial development take place in accordance with group preference.
- Greater funding from the central government for development, education, and medical and welfare assistance ("subsidies" in figure 10.1).
- Communal control of internal security and the administration of justice.
- The right to participate in state decisions affecting the group, and if necessary to veto or modify the implementation of those decisions.
- Protection of the rights of members of the communal group who do not live within regional boundaries.[14]

State Interests in Autonomy

Both state officials and communal representatives may have compelling reasons for resisting accommodation on these issues. For officials, concessions to communal interests may contradict long-standing ideological and political commitments to assimilation of minority peoples and to building a unitary nation-state. This is the prima facie reason for the Turkish state's rejection of expressions of Kurdish or any other nationalism. But as Mikesell and Murphy point out, neither unitarism nor pluralism is an ultimate goal of states: both are "policies pursued in an effort to preserve the territorial integrity of the state and to provide it with at least some degree of legitimacy."[15] The Turkish government's decision late in 1990 to acknowledge the Kurdish language and aspirations seems to reflect a calculation that the state's interests are best served by moving slightly toward pluralism.

Communal demands for control of natural resources have been a flash point in ethnopolitical conflicts from the Australian Outback to the Amazon basin to the Chittagong Hills. Such demands are resisted by state officials because of fear that they will inhibit economic development, which is an essential objective of public policy in both the industrial North and the developing South. The key to bridging this gap is recognition that most communal peoples also want development—provided they can control its pace and enjoy some of its benefits. Two western examples are instructive. In the 1950s, Brittany was France's most impoverished region. Breton aspirations and Parisian policies about investment and promotion of rural development have since combined to make Brittany one of the most productive agricultural regions of the country. In the 1960s Australian Aborigines began land rights protests that eventually led to recognition of Aboriginal autonomy in large tracts of the Northern Territory and South Australia. Protracted litigation and negotiation over mineral exploration and extraction ensued, culminating in agreements that have allowed development with controls on environmental and cultural impact, and have contributed substantial royalties to Aboriginal communities and land councils.[16] The point of both examples is that communal autonomy is consistent with controlled development—and in the Breton case seems to have stimulated it—when it is designed to tap neglected human and natural resources.

Another obstacle to political autonomy for ethnonationalists is state officials' perception that it is a threat to security interests, on either the "camel's nose" theory or the "domino" theory. The camel's nose argument is the one used by some Israelis to reject demands for autonomy for West Bank and Gazaen Palestinians: once the camel's nose is inside the tent, the whole rough beast will soon follow. The domino theory is aptly illustrated by the cascading defection of republics from the USSR and poses a threatening prospect for other heterogeneous states.

Successes and Failures of Autonomy Agreements

Neither in theory nor in practice is there anything inherent in autonomy agreements that leads to future civil war or disintegration of the state. The recent historical record shows that, on balance, autonomy agreements can be an effective means for managing regional conflicts. Eleven instances of autonomy for communal rebels are noted in table 10.1, seven of which led to the deescalation of rebellion and four of which did not. The successful accommodations involved the Basques, Miskitos, Nagas, Tripuras, Afars, Chittagong Hills peoples, and Moros.[17] In four instances rebellions occurred or continued despite grants of autonomy to communal groups. In two of these cases—in Baluchistan and southern Sudan—civil war began or resumed when the central government abrogated autonomy arrangements. These failures were due to defection of the central government from the agreements, not to flaws in the autonomy arrangements per se. In the case of the Tamils, the Sri Lankan government is committed to implementing a 1987 accord that grants extensive regional autonomy; that the accord was negotiated by the Indian and Sri Lankan governments without the participation of Tamil nationalists helps explain why the rebellion continues.

The Sikhs are the only case of eleven that remotely resembles the camel's nose scenario. In 1966, in response to twenty years of separatist pressure, the Indian government reconstituted the Punjab as a majority-Sikh state. The demands of militant Sikhs for complete independence, intensified by the rise of Sikh fundamentalism and Hindu revivalism, led to widespread violence for an independent Khalistan during the 1980s; the violence continues to escalate.[18]

The essential problem for leaders of communal groups considering autonomy is the potential defection of some of their followers if they compromise on the group's demands. Two immediate motives for defection and one longer-term one are evident in the cases we have observed. One immediate motive is the ideological conviction of militants that a key issue—complete independence, or the inclusion of a province such as Navarra or a city such as Kirkuk in the autonomous region, or control of internal security, or subsoil mineral rights—is nonnegotiable. The Irish Republican Army emerged and fought a full-fledged civil war in independent Ireland because Sinn Fein militants rejected the 1921 treaty that created the Irish Free State in the south but left Ulster under British-protected Protestant rule. Nonnegotiable positions are particularly likely to develop in the course of protracted communal conflicts. Leaders who sell out by accepting limited autonomy must then deal with defections by hardliners, attempts to sabotage agreements, and potential assassination.

The second complicating motive is the ambition of alternative or second-tier leaders of an ethnonationalist movement, who seize on compromises as a rationale for claiming that they are the only authentic leaders of the movement. "Authenticity" usually means encouraging defectors from the rank and file and continuing the armed struggle. The interplay of militancy and ambition accounts for the commonly observed fragmentation of ethnonationalist movements during or after attempts to negotiate settlements. In Spain the establishment of regional autonomy for three Basque provinces in 1979–80 precipitated a split in the militant Euzkadi Ta Azkatasuna (ETA) group, both factions of which rejected limits on autonomy (on different grounds) and for the next decade pursued competing strategies of terrorism and discussion with the Spanish government. The Kurdish nationalist movement in Iraq split into two major factions in 1975, when the Patriotic Union of Kurdistan (PUK) emerged to challenge the older Kurdish Democratic party (KDP). Both have alternated between fighting and discussing autonomy with the Baghdad government, but not in synchronization with each other: for example, the PUK negotiated with the government in late 1983, but the KDP did not; whereas in 1991 both negotiated, but the PUK took a harder line.

One political result of factionalism is to strengthen a government's position vis-à-vis ethnonationalists: limited agreements can be reached with a cooperative faction while fighting a more militant faction. The Saddam Hussein regime is one of many that deliberately follows such divide-and-rule tactics toward communal opponents. The Philippine governments of Ferdinand Marcos and Corazon Acquino also benefited from the factional disintegration of regional rebellions by the Moros (1972 to about 1987) and the Cordillera or "Igorot" peoples of northern Luzon (1979 to the end of the 1980s).

The fate of the Moro rebellion illustrates the effectiveness of this approach to the management of secessionist wars. Its main protagonist was the Moro National Liberation Front (MNLF), founded in 1971 by a former university professor and actively supported by Libya, Malaysia, and other member states of the Organization of the Islamic Conference (OIC). After five years of intense conflict in Moro-dominated southern Mindinao and the Sulu archipelago, the OIC was instrumental in brokering a cease-fire and a 1976 agreement between the MNLF and the Marcos government that provided for regional autonomy. In 1979 the government unilaterally implemented its own watered-down version of the autonomy plan over the protests of the OIC and the MNLF. Sporadic insurgency continued until 1987. By this time the Moro movement had split along ethnic-regional lines, and the new Acquino government concluded a new agreement with a weakened MNLF. The government held a 1989 referendum, which the MNLF boycotted with little effect, and in 1990 established the autonomous region of Muslim Mindinao, four provinces separated by areas dominated by Christian settlers. Regional elections confirmed the MNLF's loss of support to traditional local leaders; internationally, the OIC accepted the new arrangements and reduced its financial and diplomatic support for the MNLF.[19] The conflict management strategy followed by both governments worked. concessions short of full regional autonomy attracted substantial Moro support and undercut the militant MNLF's international support.

In the short term, limited autonomy agreements tend to undermine the political cohesion of the communal group and reduce its fighting capacity. The longer-term effects often are positive: some autonomy agreements have enough substance that they gain the active support of most leaders and members of the group. Although many Spanish Basques are dissatisfied with the implementation of the autonomy accords, most Basque politicians work within the regional government rather than support the ETA factions. The most effective autonomy agreements are ones that provide resources and institutions through which groups can make significant progress toward their objectives. Such agreements build long-term support for peaceful solutions and undermine appeals to militant action.

If an autonomy agreement is not fully implemented or observed, then the longer-term motive for defection comes into play. Disillusioned by unkept promises, some ethnonationalists resume militant opposition. The power-sharing agreement of 1972 that ended a seventeen-year civil war in Sudan held for a decade, then collapsed in 1983 when the northern-dominated government violated key elements of the agreement.[20] The second civil war has now lasted nearly a decade, and the failure of the 1972 agreement creates suspicion and cynicism about new efforts at negotiation.

The case of the Baluchis, a predominantly tribal people, provides a more detailed illustration. Baluchistan lost its historical autonomy in 1955 when West Pakistan was consolidated into one province. In 1970 Baluchistan was given its own provincial government and assembly as part of a countrywide shift from martial law to decentralized parliamentary government. Traditional tribal leaders (sardars) held key positions in the regional government. In early 1973, in the aftermath of civil war and secession in East Pakistan, President Bhutto's central government dismissed the Baluchi governor and assembly on grounds that they had encouraged violence and smuggling and had opposed modernization efforts. Political tension between Baluchi leaders and the central government quickly escalated into a civil war that was not suppressed militarily until 1977. A new central government greatly increased development expenditures in the region and in 1980 established a puppet provincial government. Strong support for autonomy and a confederal political system have surfaced repeatedly since then, but in nonviolent form. The outcome was even less favorable than in the Moro rebellion but nonetheless served some Baluchi interests, because key traditional leaders continue to play a role in the regional government.[21]

Most peoples who have gained regional autonomy in the past half-century got it through less destructive political processes than civil war. Finland's Swedish-populated Åland Islands enjoy virtually complete political and cultural autonomy as a consequence of a 1921 international agreement and the more comprehensive 1951 Autonomy Act enacted by the Finnish government.[22] Most of the newer autonomy arrangements in European democracies (see chapter 6) were the outgrowth of peaceful political contention, sometimes punctuated by riots or terrorist bombings.

Some indigenous peoples also have gained communal autonomy by a combination of negotiation, political activism, and alliances with nonindigenous interests. The greatest autonomy has been won by indigenous peoples in western societies. The autonomous status of tribal governments in the United States resulted from the conjunction of indigenous activism and national political developments in the late 1960s. The land rights movement in Australia led a newly elected federal government to empower the first Aboriginal land councils in the early 1970s. In Latin America, however, the autonomy and legal status of native peoples have lagged far behind developments in the advanced industrial democracies. There is limited community autonomy among the Mapuche in Chile and some highland peoples in Colombia (especially the Paez), and there is some recognition of land claims and language rights for indigenous peoples in Argentina, Venezuela, and Costa Rica. Only two native peoples in the region enjoy recognized self-government equivalent to tribal government in the United States, and both of them won those rights through rebellion. They are the 40,000 Kuna Indians who inhabit islands on Panama's Caribbean coast, who fought a successful revolt in 1920, and the 120,000 Miskitos of Nicaragua, who negotiated regional autonomy with the Sandinista government after five years of armed resistance to revolutionary policies.[23]

In conclusion, the outcomes of autonomy agreements as a solution to demand for communal autonomy depend on the political will of leaders on both sides, the resources of the state, and the specifics of the autonomy agreements themselves. Strong and prosperous states such as Spain and the United States have little to fear from granting autonomy to Basques or Navahos. The divided leadership of the economically crippled and institutionally paralyzed USSR had everything to fear from acknowledging the de facto independence of the Baltic states. Similarly, in the aftermath of the Bangladesh civil war and secession, the Pakistani government had compelling reasons for restraining Baluchi nationalists. In general, autonomy agreements in Third World countries are effective means of managing open and impending rebellions *if* they balance the interests of states and ethnonationalists. Balancing means, first, that the majority party among the ethnonationalists gains enough advantages to develop a vested interest in the new regional government, and second, that state officials make a good-faith effort to keep their commitments. Transformation of secessionist conflicts is decisively achieved only when political trust in autonomy arrangements has been established on both sides, and tested in the peaceful resolution of subsequent disputes.

Recognition and Access in a Plural Society

Most ethnonationalist and indigenous political movements are based on the premise that political autonomy is essential for promoting collective interests. In contrast, communal contenders, ethnoclasses, and most militant sects seek recognition and protection of their interests within the political framework of a plural society. Their interests vary depending on their situation. If their culture and beliefs are under pressure, the objective is acceptance: the recognition and protection of their distinctive collective status. If a minority is economically disadvantaged, the objective is access by some combination of public subsidy and enhanced or protected economic opportunities. If the group is politically restricted, or if leaders think access to power is needed to protect other collective interests, the objective is participation. The underlying principle of all three objectives is the same: the communal group seeks equality of status and opportunity with other groups.[24]

Containment: Keeping Minorities Separate and Unequal

The prospects for accommodating communal objectives depend on state interests and patterns of policy. Four broad orientations of public policy toward communal minorities are summarized in table 10.2: containment, assimilation, pluralism, and power sharing.

Containment is the strategy of keeping minorities separate and unequal. Such a strategy may be dictated by a dominant group's racial and religious beliefs, material interests, security concerns, or all three. Islamic doctrine justifies the unequal treatment of heretical Baha'is in Iran and Ahmadis in Pakistan. Similarly, the schism between Sunni and Shi'a Islam reinforces the security interests that dictate restrictive government policies toward Saudi Arabia's Shi'i minority. Doctrines of racial superiority and the material interests of dominant groups are both served by patterns of segregation and discrimination against ethnoclasses and indigenous peoples in western and Latin American societies. The security interests of the state are paramount reasons for policies of containment in multiethnic Third World societies: they help justify restrictions on Kurds and Palestinians in the Middle East, on overseas Chinese in Southeast Asia, and on threatening communal contenders throughout Africa.

"Separate and unequal" policies historically may have met some interests of communal groups. The millets (minority religious communities) of the Ottoman Empire were subject to civil restrictions but were shielded from religious persecution. Indig-

Table 10.2. State Policies toward the Incorporation of Minorities.

General Orientation	Culture	Economy	Politics
Containment	Residential and social segregation Separate and unequal educational facilities Restricted access to higher education Restrictions on religious practice	Forced labor Restrictions on occupations and property ownership Restrictions on place of residence Restrictions on labor organization and action	No or restricted political participation Political organizations banned or curtailed Office holding banned or restricted
Assimilation	Class-based residential and social integration "Remedial" education in dominant language and culture Facilitated access to higher education	Development funds Health and welfare programs Job training Antidiscrimination laws	Civil and political rights guaranteed Selective recruitment into mainstream parties and public office Minority interest groups
Pluralism	Protection of cultural and religious diversity Education and media in multiple languages	Group social and economic entitlements Group representation in public and private employment	Group political parties and interest groups Group representation in legislative assemblies and governing coalitions
Power sharing	Residential and social separation Separate schools, media Separate institutions of higher education or communal quotas	Economic activity organized communally Services allocated communally Group quotas in public and private employment	Group political parties and interest groups Guaranteed participation in decision-making bodies Communal veto power over policies affecting group Territorial or functional autonomy in administration of public services

enous peoples of the Americas and Australia were saved from cultural and physical annihilation by protectionist policies that began to be instituted in the late nineteenth century. The paternalism of public policies during this era is evident in Australia, where surviving Aborigines were resettled on reserves and given the status of wards of the state under the administration of missionaries and officials called protectors of Aborigines. Much of the recent increase in communal protest and rebellion is rooted in reactions to discredited policies of containment: they may still be of value for some native peoples in the Amazon basin, but globally they are a source of bitter grievances and escalating conflict.

Assimilation: Absorbing Minorities into Society

Three alternative strategies to containment are assimilation, pluralism, and power sharing. Each represents a widely practiced approach to reconciling the interests of contending groups, and each has its advocates and opponents. *Assimilation* is an individualistic strategy that gives people incentives and opportunities to subordinate or abandon old communal identities and adopt the language, values, and behaviors of the dominant group. Until the 1960s, assimilation was the preferred strategy for dealing with ethnoclasses and indigenous peoples in most western societies, including immigrant societies such as the United States and Australia, but not Canada. It remains the preferred strategy toward minorities in most of Latin America. The appeal of assimilation to dominant groups in western societies has at least two sources: it is consistent with the values of liberal individualism *and* with ethnocentric nationalism. It also has material and political advantages, because it does not directly threaten the economic and political privileges of dominant groups.

Assimilation also is widely used by Third World states in conjunction with strategies of containment. China's policy toward minorities is based on cooptation of acculturated individuals into the party and state structures, with a mix of communal autonomy and coercive control for others. The Indonesian government has staffed local government and security forces in Irian Jaya with cooperative Papuans at the same time it wars on Papuan nationalists. The Sunni-dominated Iraqi government has actively recruited both Kurds and Shi'i into the Ba'th party, the officer corps, and the bureaucracy. The advantages of such a mixed strategy are obvious: the talents of ambitious members of minorities are diverted to the service of the state—such individuals are more effective than outsiders in controlling their own people, and in the long run the minority will be depleted by a stream of individuals defecting to the dominant society.

Assimilation has met the interests of some kinds of communal groups, especially ethnoclasses and religious minorities. In the guise of integration, it was widely regarded by immigrants and people of color as a means of overcoming discrimination. In practice, integration has worked best for people who are culturally similar to the dominant group, but it has proven difficult or irrelevant for others. Its implementation for people of Third World origin in the United States and Western Europe continues to be impeded by the racial hostility of dominant groups. And it is rejected by those who are not prepared to sacrifice their culture and social autonomy as the price of admission to mainstream society. Historically, assimilation has ended some conflicts by eroding the communal basis for intergroup hostility. But the failures of assimilation have also provided the motivation for new and potentially destructive rounds of intergroup conflict.

Pluralism: Equal Rights, Separate Status

Communal groups in western societies are shifting toward a preference for *pluralism*, an orientation that gives greater weight to the collective rights and interests of minorities. If containment means separate and unequal, then pluralism means equal but separate: equal individual and collective rights, including the right to separate and coexisting identities. Communal advocates of multiculturalism in Canada, the United States, and parts of Europe ask for recognition and promotion of the history, culture, language or dialect, and religion that define their separate identities. Pluralism also has major implications for economic policy and for politics. Economically (see table 10.2) it means a shift from programs designed to enhance individual opportunities toward programs that allocate entitlements and jobs on the basis of ethnicity. Politically, it implies the emergence of institutionalized ethnic politics, with ethnic political parties and guarantees, or expectations, that communal interests will be represented in decision making.[25]

Pluralist policies may be more complex and expensive to implement than policies of assimilation, but pluralism is not fundamentally inimical to state interests in democratic societies. Democratic politics are premised on competition among, and accommodation of, contending interests of parties, classes, and associations; organized communal interests can be dealt with by the same principles and procedures. Pluralism is an approach with great potential for redirecting intergroup conflict into institutionalized and constructive channels.

But pluralism in democratic societies has limits, because it tends to trigger political reactions. Ideologically, it challenges assimilationists' commitment to a homogeneous society and culture. Arthur M. Schlesinger, Jr., recently objected that "militant multiculturalism glorifies ethnic and racial communities at the expense of the common culture."[26] The serious political consequence is countermobilization by members of dominant groups against the material gains and empowerment of minorities. Backlash politics is in the ascendant in virtually every western society that has made concessions to communal pluralism, including the United States, Britain, France, and Germany (see chapter 6). Reaction threatens to derail negotiations between black nationalists and the dominant white minority in South Africa. In India it has spurred political opposition and violence by Hindus who oppose public efforts to improve the status of disadvantaged castes and minorities.

Power Sharing: Organizing Society on Communal Lines

Power sharing is an alternative way of ordering multicommunal societies. It assumes that communal identities and organizations are the basic elements or pillars of society. State power is exercised jointly by the constituent communities, each of which is proportionally represented in government and all of which have mutual veto power. This kind of institutionalized power sharing evolved historically between the Protestant and Catholic communities of the Netherlands, each of which had—and to some extent still has—its own neighborhoods, schools, newspapers, trade unions, associations, and parties. When the socialists became a significant element in Dutch society they too

formed their own "pillar." The same principle has been extended to the new Third World minorities in the Netherlands.
It helps account for their incorporation into Dutch society with
little of the ethnic violence seen in larger European societies.
Power sharing also characterizes the relations of the Flemish
and Walloon peoples in Belgium, with the important qualifications that it has a territorial base and was arrived at only after
extensive conflict and legal tinkering during the 1960s and
1970s. Other versions of power sharing have been urged for
South Africa.[27]

Power sharing has intrinsic appeal to some communal activists because it seems to guarantee that the group has status and
access to power without compromising its cultural integrity. It
has two liabilities, however. The first problem is that such arrangements are not easily constructed, especially not when the
groups begin from an unequal footing. In general, power sharing is most feasible in what Donald Horowitz calls unranked
systems, those in which parallel and more or less autonomous
communal groups coexist. It is much less likely to be established
in societies such as Northern Ireland where there are gross inequalities between hierarchically ordered communal groups.[28]
A basic hindrance to power-sharing arrangements in Belgium
was the historic resentment of the Flemish majority about their
impoverishment and the cultural and political hegemony of the
French-speaking minority. Sustained economic development
since the 1950s has eroded material inequalities; language laws
put both cultures on an equal footing; constitutional reform
provided regional autonomy for the Flemish, the Walloons, and
the smaller German-speaking minority; and all groups are
guaranteed proportional representation in national government.[29]

The second problem is evident in the Third World states,
among them Lebanon, Malaysia, and Nigeria, that have experi-
mented with variants of democratic power sharing. The flaw in
each experiment has been the advantaged position of one communal group—the Maronites in Lebanon, the Malays in Malaysia, and the Muslim Northerners in Nigeria. Each has used the
system to the selective benefit of its own constituency, creating
tensions that contributed to civil war in Lebanon and the collapse of two successive democratic republics in Nigeria. Malaysia
has thus far beaten the odds with a system that restrains but
satisfices the communal interests of Chinese and East Indians in

peninsular Malaysia and accommodates through federalism the regional interests of the peoples of northern Borneo.

Other variants of power sharing are widely distributed in Africa, as illustrated by the case studies of Zambia and Kenya in chapter 9. These and other African states have been governed by informal coalitions that incorporate representatives of most or all major communal groups. They are much less institutionalized than power-sharing arrangements in European societies, which means that there are few means of restraint or redress when a dominant member or coalition decides to exclude one or more groups. Most communal groups in Africa have a territorial base, which means that communal defections and expulsions from ruling coalitions can create the conditions for separatist movements. They also can lead to deadly intercommunal fighting between supporters of the "ins" and "outs" and to civil wars aimed at seizing state power, as happened in Liberia in 1990–91.

Conclusion

Used in creative and appropriate combination, the policies associated with regional autonomy, assimilation, pluralism, and power sharing have the potential for accommodating the essential interests of most disadvantaged and politically active communal groups examined in this study. The previous four chapters document a number of contemporary ethnopolitical conflicts that were resolved or managed by such shifts in public policy. None of these approaches to accommodating communal interests directly threatens the continuity and legitimacy of the state, but each has potential liabilities that are cited above and are worth recapitulating. Regional autonomy arrangments are at risk of defection by governments that fail to implement them fully and by militant factions who prefer to fight rather than accept half a loaf. Assimilation has two problems: some minorities do not want to be assimilated, and some majorities resist pressures to accept people they do not like. Pluralist policies usually mean economic redistribution and greater ethnic access to political power, which generates resentment by other groups that see themselves losing ground, which in turn may push politicians dependent on majority support to retreat from pluralism. Power sharing can be abused by larger and more advantaged communal groups, in which case less advantaged communal groups are tempted to defect. In other words, there are "tipping points" in ethnopolitical conflicts when segments of a group decide that their interests cannot be accommodated within the state and seek exit instead.

All of these unintended consequences are potential sources of new grievances and open conflict. In some worst-case scenarios they have fueled waves of racially motivated murders (in southern France in the 1980s, for example), pograms (e.g., against Ibo living in northern Nigeria in 1965), and civil war (in Nagorno-Karabakh and southern Sudan). The conclusion for states is one of caution: public efforts to manage ethnopolitical conflicts have risks as well as potential gains. If policies of accommodation are to be effective they must be pursued cautiously but persistently over the long term, slowly enough not to stimulate a crippling reaction from other groups, persistently enough so that minorities do not defect or rebel. The conclusion for communal groups is that persistence in the nonviolent pursuit of group interests is a strategic virtue, and so is a willingness to compromise about the specifics of accommodation. A strategy of sustained violence usually alienates groups that would be more helpful as allies and hardens positions so that accommodation and settlements are very difficult to achieve. Violent means in the pursuit of communal interests usually are politically more effective as threats than in actuality.

In conclusion, there are two keys to the constructive management of ethnopolitical conflict. One is to search out politically and socially creative policies that bridge the gaps between the interests of minorities and states. All parties, including outside observers, can contribute to this process. The second is to begin the process of creative conflict management in the early stages of open conflict. It is a well-established principle that protracted conflicts are very resistent to settlement, and some experts contend that effective mediation is likely only when both parties see themselves caught in a hurting stalemate.[30] States and their leaders rarely have the foresight and political will to preempt ethnic conflict before it emerges, but they should be able to respond creatively to political mobilization and protest by communal groups before those groups cross the threshold of sustained violence.

11. Summary and Implications

Since the end of the Cold War, conflicts between communal groups and states have come to be recognized as the major challenge to domestic and international security in most parts of the world. Minority peoples also have become the principal victims of gross human rights violations. At the beginning of 1992 more than twenty million refugees were fleeing from communal conflicts, including nearly 3 percent of the population of Africa south of the Sahara. Communal conflict has devastated Yugoslavia and threatens the stability of most of the successor republics of the Soviet Union. The most protracted conflicts of this century are being fought over ethnonational issues in the Middle East and in Southeast Asia. Communal conflict also is in the ascendant in the West: the most divisive conflicts in the United States in the 1990s arise from ethnic tensions and inequalities. Quebec is edging toward secession from Canada. Virtually every country in Western Europe is beset by growing public antagonism toward immigrant groups of Third World origin.

This volume presents the principal findings of a comparative study of the status, demands, and conflicts of communal groups since the end of World War II, with special attention to the decade of the 1980s. The analysis is based on coded profiles and substantive information on 233 politically active groups in ninety-three countries. Each region's communal groups are analyzed separately, including in-depth discussions of communal tensions in the western democracies, Eastern Europe and the former Soviet Union, the Middle East, and Africa. The status and conflicts of six types of communal groups also are examined: they are ethnonationalists, indigenous peoples, ethnoclasses, militant sects, and advantaged and disadvantaged communal contenders. This concluding chapter does not attempt to recapitulate all the findings and interpretations of the Minorities at Risk study. Instead it draws on the results to suggest answers to some general questions about the nature, causes, and implications of ethnopolitical conflict for the 1990s.

1. *What proportion of the world's population identifies with politically assertive communal groups? Where are they most numerous?* In 1990 more than one-sixth of the global population (17.3 percent, 915 million people) belonged to the 233 groups identified in the Minorities at Risk study. These are groups whose members either have experienced systematic discrimination or have taken political action to assert their collective interests against the states that claim to govern them. Not all people in each group agree about their common identities and interests; most minorities are divided by cross-cutting loyalties to different clans, localities, classes, or political movements. Therefore the aggregate numbers represent the outer bounds of the populations that might be mobilized for collective action on behalf of communal interests. Shared adversity and conflict with dominant groups almost invariably sharpen the sense of common interest and build support for political action.

Africa south of the Sahara has the greatest concentration of minorities at risk, seventy-four groups and more than 42 percent of the regional population. Prior to the breakup of the USSR, the Eastern Europe region had the second largest percentage of minorities at 35 percent. The western democracies and Latin America had the smallest numbers, about 11 percent each. (For specifics and qualifications see chapters 1 and 2, and the Appendix, tables A.1 to A.6.)

2. *Which communal minorities in which world regions are most seriously disadvantaged?* Forty-five ethnoclasses such as Maghrebins in France, people of color in the Americas, and immigrant Chinese communities in Asian countries on average experience greater political and economic inequalities and discrimination than other types of groups. Indigenous peoples face disadvantages nearly as great, and they are threatened by great ecological pressures on their traditional lands and resources as well. Ethnonationalists and communal contenders are less likely to be economically disadvantaged than other types of groups, but they usually face substantial political restrictions, often because their political aspirations are seen as a threat by state elites.

At the beginning of the 1990s, inequalities and discriminatory barriers overall were markedly lower in Eastern Europe and the USSR and in the industrial democracies than in other world regions. Inequalities and discrimination for communal minorities were somewhat greater in Africa and Asia. Indigenous and Afro-American minorities in Latin America, though proportionally small in numbers, experienced the greatest economic differentials and most severe economic discrimination observed in any world region. Communal minorities in the Middle East and North Africa were subject to more severe political restrictions than in any other region. These generalizations, like those that follow, are based on statistical comparisons: a number of groups deviate from these norms. For details and qualifications see chapters 2 and 3.

3. *Are ethnopolitical demands mainly the result of inequalities and discrimination?* The comparative evidence points to two different dynamics that underlie the demands and strategies of activist communal groups. First, contemporary movements for secession or regional autonomy are strongly motivated by a desire to protect and assert group identity. Autonomy demands are concentrated among ethnonationalists and indigenous peoples with a tradition of political independence and sharp cultural differences from dominant groups. The second dynamic is that, in contrast, ethnoclasses, communal contenders, and militant sects usually have more tangible concerns. Their most salient demands are for greater rights within societies, not exit from them. Discrimination motivates demands for greater political and economic rights, while cultural differences prompt demands for protection of the group's social and cultural rights. The evidence for these conclusions is reviewed in chapter 3.

4. *How much has ethnopolitical conflict increased?* Every form of ethnopolitical conflict has increased sharply since the 1950s. The historical profiles we compiled show that nonviolent political action by the 233 communal groups more than doubled in magnitude between 1950 and 1990, and violent protest and rebellion both quadrupled. Trends differ widely among regions and types of groups, however (see chapter 4). In the democracies, communal conflict peaked in the early 1970s and declined through the end of the 1980s. In contrast, ethnic protest and rebellion in Eastern Europe and the USSR were low for most of the postwar period but began to escalate in the early 1980s, before the onset of perestroika and glasnost. Nonviolent protest and rebellion both have steadily increased in Asia and the

Middle East since the 1950s. Communal conflict in Africa was shaped by decolonization and its consequences: protest reached a peak in the decade before 1960, when most African countries gained their independence, but since then a pronounced shift from protest to rebellion has occurred. Latin America has the lowest levels of communal conflict of any region, mainly nonviolent protest by indigenous activists that reached its highest level in 1975–84. Since 1990 there has been a fresh upsurge of activism among Latin American Indians.

Worldwide comparisons of conflict trends for each type of minority show that the indigenous groups in the study had the greatest proportional increase in conflict, a testimony to the influence of the global indigenous rights movement that was established in the 1970s. The long-term global increase in rebellion was mainly attributable to autonomy movements by ethnonationalists, whose magnitudes of rebellion increased five fold between the early 1950s and the 1980s. Communal contenders, a group type found mainly in Africa south of the Sahara, shifted from nonviolent protest toward rebellion. Ethnoclasses, most of whom live in western democracies and Latin America, have used nonviolent protest, which escalated into sporadic episodes of rioting and terrorism from the late 1960s to the early 1980s.

5. *How serious is religiously based communal conflict?* Our comparative evidence and cases suggest that religious cleavages are at best a contributing factor in communal conflict and seldom the root cause. Only eight of the forty-nine militant sects in the study are defined solely or mainly by their religious beliefs. Examples are the politically mobilized Shi'i communities in Iraq and Lebanon, whose goals are political rights and recognition, not propagation of their faith. The other sectarian minorities also have class identifications, such as the Catholics of Northern Ireland and Turkish immigrants in Germany, or nationalist objectives, such as the Palestinians in Israel's Occupied Territories and the Moros in the Philippines. The driving force of the most serious and protracted communal conflicts in the Middle East is not militant Islam but the unsatisfied nationalist aspirations of the Kurds and Palestinians (see chapter 8).

All kinds of political conflict by militant sects were low in magnitude until the 1960s. The doubling of magnitude of sectarian rebellion from then through the end of the 1980s was outpaced by greater increases in rebellion by other kinds of groups, especially ethnonationalists. Overall, groups defined wholly or in part along lines of religious cleavage accounted for one-quarter of the magnitude of rebellions in the 1980s by all groups in the study (see chapter 4).

6. *Is the trend in ethnopolitical activism moving toward protest or rebellion?* It is of the greatest political import whether ethnopolitical conflict takes the form of protest or rebellion. Since 1945, nonviolent political action has been far more common among minorities in western societies, including Latin America, than violent ethnopolitical protest and rebellion (see chapter 4). This was also the case in Eastern Europe and the USSR until 1990. The deadly communal conflicts in Yugoslavia, Moldova, and between Azerbaijan and Armenia distract attention from a significant larger phenomenon: the breakup of the Soviet Union into fifteen independent republics was accomplished without protracted civil wars or rebellions. Ethnic relations in most of the new republics thus far are fractious but seldom deadly (also see chapter 7).

The protagonists in the most persistent communal rebellions of the postwar era have been ethnonationalists such as the Karen and Kachin in Burma, Tibetans, the Nagas and Tripuras in India, the Eritreans and southern Sudanese, the Palestinians and Kurds, and the Basques. Eighty guerrilla and civil wars were fought by these and other communal rebels between 1945 and 1989 (see chapter 4): twenty-six were in Asia, twenty-five in Africa south of the Sahara, twenty-two in the Middle East and North Africa, and only six elsewhere. The numbers have changed as of the end of 1992, but the proportions have not.

7. *Does reform lead toward accommodation or escalation of communal conflict?* Most communal conflicts begin with acts of protest that escalate more or less rapidly into violent conflict. In authoritarian Third World regimes the escalation usually happens very quickly, in part because official responses are more likely to be repressive than reformist. In democracies, though, escalation to violence usually is limited and based on the actions of small, militant factions. All the twenty-four minorities in the western democracies and Japan used nonviolent political tactics at some time between 1945 and 1989, half of them resorted to violent protest, and half had militant factions that used terrorism. Setting aside two movements that used violence from the onset (the Irish Republican Army and Puerto Rican national-

ists), we found that an average of thirteen years elapsed between the establishment of political movements representing communal interests in the western democracies and the first occurrence of violence (see chapter 6). There was ample time for societies to respond to communal grievances while conflict was muted, and the fact that most democratic regimes have attempted reforms helps explain the fact that communal violence in western societies, once it did occur, was usually limited.

8. *Does regional autonomy lead to escalating wars of independence?* Ethnonationalist civil wars are the most protracted and deadly conflicts of the late twentieth century. They are fought with great intensity because communal demands for independence imply the breakup of existing states. Until the dissolution of the USSR in 1990, the only ethnonationalists since 1945 who had won independence from existing states were the Bangladeshis, whose independence was bought at the price of political mass murder and India's intervention. Since then a revolutionary coalition has overthrown the Ethiopian regime and paved the way for Eritrean independence (see chapter 9). Many political leaders on both sides of such struggles have been willing to consider autonomy arrangements. We compared the outcomes of twenty-eight civil wars fought since 1950 in which one of the protagonists sought independence or autonomy (see chapter 10). The ledger is almost evenly balanced between winners and losers. On the positive side, four groups in Ethiopia have won effective autonomy and seven national peoples elsewhere secured autonomy agreements that largely ended open conflict. Outcomes in four cases are under negotiation. On the negative side, seven national movements were suppressed without significant gains, and in six instances serious conflict continues.

Autonomy agreements have helped dampen rebellions by the Basques, the Moros, the Miskitos in Nicaragua, the Nagas and Tripuras in India, the people of Bangladesh's Chittagong Hill Tracts, and the Afars of Ethiopia. They failed to do so in Sudan and Sri Lanka and have been aborted elsewhere. We observed that the success of autonomy arrangements in ending or preempting civil wars lies in the details and the implementation. The details concern the division of powers and responsibilities between the contending parties: successful agreements have required a delicate balancing of communal and state interests, arrived at through protracted negotiations. The challenge for implementation is that both parties must honor the agreements and not defect even in the face of political challenges and the continuation of violence by militant factions.

9. *What approaches work to balance the interests of contending groups within states?* Most politically assertive minorities seek access to political and economic opportunities and protection of their rights in existing societies and states. The question is whether any general lessons can be drawn about how to accommodate their demands and deflect violent conflict. The answers depend on cultural and political context.

Western democracies. Public policy toward minorities in western democracies has evolved during the past half-century from segregation to assimilation to pluralism and, in some countries, power sharing. Pluralism (multiculturalism, as it is known in North America) means arrangements that guarantee communal groups equal individual *and* collective rights, including the right to separate and coexisting identities. A shift toward pluralism, coupled with devolution of power to peripheral regions and indigenous peoples, was mainly responsible for the ebbing of communal conflicts in France, the United States, and other western societies in the 1970s and 1980s. The liability is that pluralism and power sharing, if promoted vigorously, can trigger a backlash from dominant groups. It is particularly problematic whether pluralist approaches to the growing concentrations of Third World immigrants and refugees in western countries can overcome the political and cultural resistance of dominant majorities. For evidence and more detailed discussions see chapters 6 and 10.

Africa south of the Sahara. At the other end of the spectrum of development, most African societies are very heterogeneous, poor, and ruled by weak states led by unstable multiethnic coalitions. With a few exceptions—Nigeria is one—they lack the capacity to either suppress or fully incorporate all their diverse peoples. Two keys to managing communal conflict in these societies are outlined in chapter 9. One is to strengthen and stabilize political parties to ensure that all communal groups have a fair chance at joining governing coalitions—if not now, then in the future. The second is to devolve power to local governments to ensure citizen participation and to protect the local power base of those who lose their place in national coalitions. Both steps are consistent with trends toward democratization that are evident in much of Africa. They also resemble, in a general way, the policies of pluralism and devolution that have dampened communal conflicts in western societies.

Middle East and North Africa. Communal conflicts in the Middle East are more intractable, especially civil wars centered on Palestinian and Kurdish claims for statehood. Inequalities between dominant groups and minorities in the Middle East are greater than in western societies or Africa; sectarian cleavages have deeper historical roots, and ethnoconflict has been more intense and protracted. A few examples of the accommodation of contending communal interests in the region are identified in chapter 8: the governments of the Maghreb have made significant concessions to Berber culture, and the Turkish government has recently and in a limited way acknowledged the existence and aspirations of its Kurdish minority. Elsewhere, however, the role of outside powers is vital for management of communal conflicts in the region. Progress toward settlement of the Palestinian-Israeli conflict hinges on continued U.S. involvement in the peace process as well as internal politics in Israel. The Lebanese civil war abated only after the establishment of Syrian hegemony in central and northern Lebanon and Israeli withdrawal from the south. The outcome of the Gulf War and coalition protection of Iraqi Kurds provided them a rare occasion for negotiating autonomy with the Baghdad government. And the desire of the Iranian regime to rebuild its economy and reestablish its leading role in the region has made it susceptible to international pressures to moderate its repressive policies toward the Baha'is.

Eastern Europe and the Soviet successor states. The collapse of the USSR and of Soviet hegemony in Eastern Europe has transformed communal conflict in the region. Half the Soviet Union's population before the breakup were non-Russians and 40 percent were at risk by the criteria used in this study. Now the sources of communal demands are the new minorities of the successor republics, who constitute as many as 60 percent (in Kazakhstan) of their populations. In the aggregate, the new minorities are 25 percent of the republics' populations, and many are pressing their own claims against new regimes. But thus far most are doing so with the strategies of democratic societies (that is, mass mobilization and civil protest), not the classic forms of armed rebellion (see chapter 7). Most new regimes of Eastern Europe also are responding democratically: the Czechoslovakian government led until recently by Vaclav Havel has negotiated Slovakia's independence, the Bulgarian government aims at pluralistic incorporation of its Muslim Turkish minority. Only the authoritarian Communist regime of Serbia continues to play by Stalinist rules. Its policies of hegemonical nationalism and repression are unlikely to be restrained without international sanctions and military intervention, or reversed except by a democratic revolution from within.

10. *Where are ethnopolitical conflicts most likely to escalate in the 1990s?* The immediate potential for escalating ethnopolitical conflict is greatest in the Soviet successor states. Our optimistic guess is that in the Slavic republics most such conflicts will be settled democratically. The prospects for rebellion, civil war, and deadly intercommunal conflict are considerably greater in the Caucasus and the Central Asian republics. Nonetheless, civil and multicultural societies are likely to prevail in most of the region by the year 2000.

The Western European and North American democracies are in for a resurgence of ethnic conflict. Some will be based on regional claims by people like the Québecois and the Scots, but most will be a consequence of class and communal tensions between dominant groups and minorities of Third World origin. The virtues of democratic politics are that they allow the expression of minority interests and encourage policies of accommodation. The vice is that they also are susceptible to the politics of ethnocentric reaction. Our expectation is that norms of democratic accommodation will prevail and that by 2000 various kinds of pluralist arrangements will be in place in the western societies that do not have them now.

Indigenous activism also is likely to escalate throughout the Americas, especially in the Latin American societies that have been most resistant to the claims of native peoples. Positive responses are most likely in democratic societies in the region, but within limits: indigenous demands for control of land and resources are not likely to be met if they constrain the economic development that Latin American leaders regard as essential to political stability. Eight Central and South American societies also have significant Afro-American minorities, most of whom are seriously disadvantaged and seem likely to remain politically quiescent.

South Asia is likely to suffer the most severe escalation of communal conflicts in the 1990s in the Third World. Long-standing regional conflicts in India are intensifying and

prompting communal demands by other peoples. Religiopolitical tensions are increasing between Muslim and Hindu communities in most countries of the region. Settlers from Bangladesh's densely crowded lowlands continue to push into the
uplands, where they are embroiled in violent communal conflict
with tribal peoples. Pakistani politics are rent by communal
divisions among Pashtuns, Sindhis, Baluchis, and smaller minorities. In the aftermath of Afghanistan's failed Communist
revolution, communal rivalries are intensifying among the
once-dominant Pashtuns and the Tajiks, Hazaris, and others.
The only deescalating communal conflict in the subcontinent
is between Tamils and the Sinhalese-dominated state in Sri
Lanka, and its decline is due more to repression than to
accommodation.

Forecasting the future of communal conflict elsewhere in the
Third World is even more speculative. Most of the Middle East's
conflicts are already manifest, but few are likely to be settled in
the near future. Some ethnopolitical wars in Southeast Asia are
winding down but others may intensify. In Africa the bitter
communal conflicts of Ethiopia and South Africa are being
worked out in the political arena, but others continue in Sudan
and Somalia and may erupt elsewhere. The potential for communal warfare in Nigeria is particularly threatening.

11. *What is the functional place of communal groups in the global
system of states?* The most radical proposal for resolving conflicts
between states and peoples is to reconstruct the state system so
that territorial boundaries correspond more closely to the social
and cultural boundaries among peoples. But such a strategy
would leave unsatisfied the aspirations of many nonterritorial
communal groups. For most others it would create as many
problems as it resolved. The means most likely taken toward
such an objective are destructive civil wars such as those of Yugoslavia, Ethiopia, Moldova, and Georgia. Even if political deconstruction were achieved peacefully, it would create or intensify new communal conflicts. Few ethnonationalist regions are
homogeneous, and the leaders of new states would be caught in
new communal dilemmas.

A more constructive and open-ended answer is to pursue the
positive-sum coexistence of ethnic groups and plural states.
This means both recognizing and strengthening communal
groups within the existing state system. Elise Boulding contends
that greater devolution of authority to communal groups will

help resolve fundamental structural problems of modern states: they are too large in scale and too far removed from many of their citizens to understand or deal with their local concerns.[1] Progress toward the objective of a more pluralist world system requires that the international community of states and peoples accept a common obligation to protect collective rights within such an emergent system. Communal groups should have the protected rights to individual and collective existence and to cultural self-expression without fear of political repression. The counterpart of such rights is the obligation not to impose their own cultural standards or political agenda on other peoples.

Appendix
Basic Data on Minorities at Risk

Background Characteristics of the Groups

The variables displayed in tables A.1 through A.6 are as follows:

GROUP   Three-letter code used for the group in all tables.

NAME   Full name of group. Where two similar groups are combined for purposes of coding, both names are given, separated by a comma. Where a group has a common alternative name, it is given in parentheses. Where two groups have become integrated in a single composite group, their names are separated by a slash (/). See Preface, n. 1, on sources used to standardize group names and spellings.

POP90   Best 1990 estimate of group population.

PROP90   Best 1990 estimate of group size as proportion of country population.

TYPE1   Primary classification of group:
ETHNA = Ethnonationalists
INDIG = Indigenous people
ETHCL = Ethnoclass
SECT   = Militant sect
COMCO = Communal contender

TYPE2   Secondary classification of group (same categories as TYPE1).

ADV80   Advantaged group in the 1980s:
.   = not advantaged
POL   = political advantages only
ECON = economic advantages only
DOM = dominant group, both political and economic advantages

COHERE   Five-category ordinal scale of group coherence, using judgmental categories ranging from value of 1 (category) to 5 (strong identity group).

CONCEN   Six-category ordinal scale of group concentration based on demographic information, ranging from value of 1 (widely dispersed in most urban and rural areas) to 6 (concentrated mainly in one or several adjoining regions).

For all variables, a period (.) means that data are not available or not applicable for the group.

Table A.1. Background Characteristics of the Groups: Western Democracies and Japan.

COUNTRY	GROUP	NAME	POP90	PROP90	TYPE1	TYPE2	ADV80	COHERE	CONCEN
Eurocommunity	ROM	Roma (Gypsies)	1720	.0048	ETHCL	.	.	5	1
France	BAS	Basques	247	.0044	ETHNA	.	.	4	6
France	BRE	Bretons	3816	.0680	ETHNA	.	.	4	6
France	COR	Corsicans	348	.0062	ETHNA	.	.	5	4
France	AAI	Afro-Arabs (Muslims)	1925	.0343	ETHCL	SECT	.	2	2
Greece	MUS	Muslims (Turks)	117	.0116	SECT	.	.	5	6
Italy	GER	South Tyroleans	294	.0051	ETHNA	.	.	5	6
Italy	SAR	Sardinians	1940	.0337	ETHNA	.	.	3	6
Nordic	SAM	Saami	62	.0035	INDIG	.	.	3	3
Spain	BAS	Basques	1780	.0450	ETHNA	.	.	5	6
Spain	CTL	Catalans	3986	.1006	ETHNA	.	.	5	6
Switzerland	JUR	Jurassiens	147	.0222	ETHNA	.	.	3	6
Switzerland	FOR	Foreign workers	959	.1447	ETHCL	.	.	4	1
United Kingdom	BLK	Afro-Caribbeans, Asians	2270	.0397	ETHCL	.	.	3	2
United Kingdom	CAT	Catholics (Northern Ireland)	565	.0099	ETHNA	SECT	.	5	3
West Germany	TUR	Turks	1421	.0233	ETHCL	SECT	.	3	2
Japan	KOR	Koreans	705	.0057	ETHCL	.	.	3	2
Australia	ABO	Aborigines	200	.0120	INDIG	.	.	3	1
New Zealand	MAO	Maoris	340	.1000	INDIG	.	.	4	3
Canada	FCA	French Canadians	6800	.2560	ETHNA	.	.	5	6
Canada	NAT	Native peoples	610	.0230	INDIG	.	.	3	1
USA	BLA	African Americans	30821	.1231	ETHCL	.	.	5	1
USA	HIS	Hispanics	21300	.0840	ETHCL	.	.	2	4
USA	NAT	Native peoples	1650	.0066	INDIG	.	.	3	6
Mean			3501	.0486				3.83	3.75

Table A.2. Background Characteristics of the Groups: Eastern Europe and the USSR.

COUNTRY	GROUP	NAME	POP90	PROP90	TYPE1	TYPE2	ADV80	COHERE	CONCEN
Bulgaria	TUR	Turks	800	.0900	ETHCL	SECT	.	3	4
Czechoslovakia	HUN	Hungarians	643	.0410	ETHNA	.	.	4	6
Czechoslovakia	SLO	Slovaks	4856	.3094	ETHNA	.	.	5	6
Eastern Europe	ROM	Roma	3250	.0231	ETHCL	.	.	5	1
Romania	GER	Germans	372	.0160	ETHNA	.	.	4	3
Romania	HUN	Hungarians	1834	.0788	ETHNA	.	.	3	3
USSR	ARM	Armenians	4713	.0162	ETHNA	.	.	5	5
USSR	AZE	Azerbaijanis	6924	.0238	SECT	INDIG	.	5	5
USSR	CHE	Chechens, Ingushes	844	.0029	SECT	INDIG	.	2	6
USSR	CTA	Tatars	6983	.0240	ETHNA	SECT	.	3	4
USSR	EST	Estonians	1047	.0036	ETHNA	.	.	5	6
USSR	GEO	Georgians	4044	.0139	ETHNA	.	.	5	6
USSR	GER	Germans	2124	.0073	ETHNA	.	.	1	1
USSR	JEW	Jews	2007	.0069	ETHCL	SECT	.	3	2
USSR	KAR	Karachays, Balkars	145	.0005	SECT	INDIG	.	1	5

Country	Code	Group							
USSR	KAZ	Kazakhs	8292	.0285	SECT	INDIG	.	2	6
USSR	KIR	Kyrgyz	2589	.0089	SECT	INDIG	.	5	6
USSR	KUR	Kurds	120	.0004	SECT	INDIG	.	4	3
USSR	LAT	Latvians	1484	.0051	ETHNA	.		5	6
USSR	LIT	Lithuanians	3113	.0107	ETHNA	.		5	6
USSR	ROM	Roma	233	.0008	ETHCL	.		2	1
USSR	TAD	Tajiks	4305	.0148	SECT	INDIG	.	4	5
USSR	TKM	Turkmens (Turkomans)	2764	.0095	SECT	INDIG	.	2	6
USSR	UKR	Ukrainians	44950	.1545	ETHNA	.		5	6
USSR	UZB	Uzbeks	16991	.0584	SECT	INDIG	.	4	6
USSR	RUM	Moldavians	3320	.0114	ETHNA	.		3	6
Yugoslavia	ALB	Albanians	1840	.0771	ETHNA	SECT	.	5	5
Yugoslavia	CRO	Croats	4694	.1967	ETHNA	.		5	5
Yugoslavia	SER	Serbs	8663	.3630	ETHNA	.	POL	5	5
Yugoslavia	SLO	Slovenes	1909	.0800	ETHNA	.	ECON	5	6
China	KAZ	Kazakhs	1005	.0009	SECT	INDIG	.	4	6
China	UIG	Uighurs	6800	.0061	SECT	INDIG	.	2	6
Mean			4802	.0530				3.78	4.78

Table A.3. Background Characteristics of the Groups: Asia.

COUNTRY	GROUP	NAME	POP90	PROP90	TYPE1	TYPE2	ADV80	COHERE	CONCEN
Bangladesh	CHT	Chittagong Hills peoples	570	.0049	INDIG	.	.	3	6
Bangladesh	HIN	Hindus	14120	.1220	SECT	.	.	3	1
Burma	ARA	Arakanese (Muslims)	1530	.0370	SECT	INDIG	.	3	4
Burma	CHN	Zomis (Chins)	990	.0240	ETHNA	INDIG	.	3	6
Burma	KAC	Kachins	455	.0110	ETHNA	INDIG	.	4	6
Burma	KRN	Karens	4210	.1020	ETHNA	INDIG	.	3	6
Burma	MON	Mons	1030	.0250	ETHNA	INDIG	.	4	6
Burma	SHA	Shans	3180	.0770	ETHNA	INDIG	.	3	6
Burma	SMT	Hill tribal peoples	1030	.0250	ETHNA	INDIG	.	2	3
China	HHU	Hui (Muslims)	7800	.0070	SECT	.	.	3	1
China	TIB	Tibetans	4900	.0044	ETHNA	INDIG	.	4	6
India	KAS	Kashmiris	2890	.0034	ETHNA	SECT	.	5	6
India	MUS	Muslims	98600	.1160	SECT	.	.	3	1
India	NAG	Nagas	850	.0010	ETHNA	INDIG	.	5	6
India	SNT	Santals	5610	.0066	ETHNA	INDIG	.	3	3
India	STR	Scheduled tribes	51850	.0610	INDIG	.	.	1	4
India	SIK	Sikhs	15980	.0188	ETHNA	SECT	.	5	5
India	MIZ	Mizos (Lushai)	575	.0007	ETHNA	INDIG	.	.	6
India	TRI	Tripuras	575	.0007	ETHNA	INDIG	.	5	6
Indonesia	CHI	Chinese	5010	.0262	ETHCL	.	ECON	3	2
Indonesia	ETI	East Timorese	765	.0040	ETHNA	.	.	1	6

Country	Code	Group							
Indonesia	PAP	Papuans	1205	.0063	ETHNA	INDIG	.	2	6
Kampuchea	CHA	Cham	175	.0250	SECT	INDIG	.	.	.
Kampuchea	VIE	Vietnamese	315	.0450	ETHNA	.	.	2	1
Laos	HMO	Hmong	440	.1100	INDIG	.	.	3	4
Malaysia	CHI	Chinese	5800	.3400	ETHCL	COMCO	ECON	5	1
Malaysia	DAY	Dayaks	675	.0395	INDIG	.	.	4	6
Malaysia	EIN	East Indians	1415	.0830	ETHCL	COMCO	.	4	3
Malaysia	KAD	Kadazans	665	.0390	INDIG	.	.	5	6
Philippines	CPE	Cordilleras (Igorots)	930	.0140	INDIG	.	.	2	6
Philippines	MOR	Moros (Muslims)	4330	.0650	SECT	INDIG	.	3	5
Singapore	MLY	Malays	395	.1460	ETHCL	SECT	.	4	1
Sri Lanka	ITA	Indian Tamils	940	.0550	ETHCL	.	.	4	2
Sri Lanka	SLT	Sri Lankan Tamils	2150	.1260	ETHNA	.	.	5	6
Taiwan	ATA	Aboriginals	310	.0150	INDIG	.	.	1	4
Taiwan	KMT	Mainland Chinese	2760	.1350	COMCO	.	DOM	5	2
Taiwan	TAI	Taiwanese	17384	.8500	COMCO	.	.	4	1
Thailand	CHI	Chinese	5645	.1000	ETHCL	.	.	1	2
Thailand	MMU	Malay Muslims	1410	.0250	ETHNA	SECT	.	5	6
Thailand	NHT	Northern hill tribes	850	.0150	INDIG	.	.	2	4
Vietnam	CHI	Chinese	1370	.0200	ETHCL	.	.	4	2
Vietnam	MNT	Montagnards	1200	.0175	INDIG	.	.	2	4
Papua New Guinea	BOU	Bougainvilleans	180	.0466	ETHNA	INDIG	.	4	6
Mean			6350	.070				3.34	4.14

Table A.4. Background Characteristics of the Groups: North Africa and the Middle East.

COUNTRY	GROUP	NAME	POP90	PROP90	TYPE1	TYPE2	ADV80	COHERE	CONCEN
Algeria	BER	Berbers	5400	.2100	INDIG	.	.	3	6
Egypt	COP	Copts	4780	.0850	SECT	.	.	2	2
Iran	AZE	Azerbaijanis	14330	.2600	ETHNA	.	.	3	6
Iran	BAH	Baha'is	475	.0086	SECT	.	.	5	2
Iran	BKH	Bakthiaris	900	.0165	ETHNA	INDIG	.	4	6
Iran	BLU	Baluchis	950	.0170	ETHNA	INDIG	.	5	6
Iran	KUR	Kurds	5000	.0905	ETHNA	INDIG	.	3	6
Iran	TKM	Turkomans (Turkmens)	795	.0145	ETHNA	INDIG	.	3	6
Iran	ARB	Arabs	950	.0173	ETHNA	.	.	3	6
Iraq	KUR	Kurds	4150	.2200	ETHNA	INDIG	.	3	4
Iraq	SHI	Shi'is	9800	.5200	ETHCL	SECT	.	2	6
Iraq	SUN	Sunni Arabs	3950	.2100	COMCO	.	DOM	5	2
Israel	ARB	Arabs	800	.1310	ETHCL	SECT	.	4	4
Israel OT*	PAL	Palestinians	1600	.2620	ETHNA	SECT	.	5	6
Jordan	PAL	Palestinians	1070	.3500	ETHNA	.	.	4	1

Country									
Lebanon	DRU	Druze	170	.0445	SECT	COMCO		5	6
Lebanon	MAR	Maronite Christians	1360	.3558	SECT	COMCO	DOM	3	4
Lebanon	PAL	Palestinians	430	.1125	ETHNA	SECT		5	3
Lebanon	SHI	Shi'is	1085	.2839	SECT	COMCO		3	4
Lebanon	SUN	Sunnis	780	.2041	SECT	COMCO	POL	4	1
Morocco	BER	Berbers	9700	.3700	INDIG			3	6
Morocco	SAH	Saharawis	160	.0060	ETHNA	INDIG		5	6
Pakistan	AHM	Ahmadis	3960	.0350	ETHCL	SECT		4	1
Pakistan	BLU	Baluchis	4640	.0410	ETHNA	INDIG		3	5
Pakistan	HIN	Hindus	1800	.0160	SECT		ECON	3	6
Pakistan	PUS	Pashtuns	14710	.1300	INDIG	COMCO		3	6
Pakistan	SIN	Sindhis	11540	.1020	COMCO			5	6
Saudi Arabia	SHI	Shi'is	500	.0300	ETHCL	SECT		2	6
Syria	ALA	Alawis	1620	.1300	SECT	COMCO	POL	4	6
Turkey	KUR	Kurds	10180	.1800	ETHNA	INDIG		2	6
Turkey	ROM	Roma	620	.0110	ETHCL				1
Mean			3813	.1440				3.60	4.58

*Israel's Occupied Territories, the West Bank and Gaza Strip.

Table A.5. Background Characteristics of the Groups: Africa South of the Sahara.

COUNTRY	GROUP	NAME	POP90	PROP90	TYPE1	TYPE2	ADV80	COHERE	CONCEN
Angola	BKO	Bakongo	1230	.1400	ETHNA	COMCO	.	5	6
Angola	OVI	Ovimbundu	2900	.3300	COMCO	.	.	5	6
Botswana	SAN	San	46	.0360	INDIG	.	.	4	6
Burundi	HUT	Hutu	4540	.8300	ETHCL	COMCO	.	4	1
Burundi	TUT	Tutsi	985	.1800	ETHCL	COMCO	DOM	3	1
Cameroon	KRD	Kirdi	2440	.2200	INDIG	.	.	2	6
Cameroon	WES	Westerners	2220	.2000	COMCO	.	.	5	6
Cameroon	BAM	Bamileke	3000	.2700	COMCO	.	DOM	5	6
Chad	NCH	Northerners	2630	.5200	SECT	COMCO	DOM	3	6
Chad	SCH	Southerners	2420	.4800	COMCO	.	POL	4	6
Congo	LAR	Lari (Bakongo)	265	.1150	COMCO	.	.	5	6
Ethiopia	AFA	Afars	2570	.0500	ETHNA	INDIG	.	5	6
Ethiopia	ERI	Eritreans	3850	.0750	ETHNA	SECT	.	3	6
Ethiopia	NSA	Nilo-Saharans	820	.0160	ETHNA	INDIG	.	1	6
Ethiopia	ORO	Oromo	20550	.4000	ETHNA	.	.	3	4
Ethiopia	SOM	Somali	2570	.0500	ETHNA	SECT	.	5	6
Ethiopia	TIG	Tigreans	4620	.0900	ETHNA	.	.	4	6
Ghana	ASH	Ashanti	4265	.2800	COMCO	.	.	5	6
Ghana	EWE	Ewe	1980	.1300	COMCO	.	POL	5	6
Ghana	MDA	Mossi, Dagomba	2440	.1600	COMCO	.	.	4	6
Guinea	FUL	Fulani (Fulbe)	2180	.3000	COMCO	.	.	5	6
Guinea	MAL	Malinke	2180	.3000	COMCO	.	.	5	6
Guinea	SUS	Susu	1160	.1600	COMCO	.	DOM	5	6
Ivory Coast	LEB	Lebanese	160	.0134	ETHCL	.	ECON	5	2

Country	Code	Group								
Kenya	KIK	Kikuyu	5330	.2100	COMCO	COMCO	.	ECON	4	6
Kenya	LUO	Luo	3300	.1300	COMCO	COMCO	.	POL	4	6
Kenya	MAA	Masai	405	.0160	INDIG	INDIG	.	.	4	4
Kenya	SOM	Somali	510	.0200	SECT	SECT	INDIG	.	5	6
Kenya	TRK	Turkana, Pokot	760	.0300	INDIG	INDIG	.	.	2	6
Kenya	REN	Rendille, Borana	250	.0100	INDIG	INDIG	.	.	2	6
Liberia	CRE	Americo-Liberians	75	.0285	ETHCL	ETHCL	COMCO	DOM	5	2
Madagascar	MER	Merina	3070	.2600	COMCO	COMCO	COMCO	DOM	5	4
Mali	TUA	Tuareg	430	.0470	INDIG	INDIG	.	.	5	6
Mali	MND	Mande	3950	.4300	COMCO	COMCO	.	DOM	5	6
Mauritania	KEW	Kewri	410	.2000	COMCO	COMCO	.	ECON	4	6
Namibia	EUR	Europeans	78	.0489	ETHCL	ETHCL	COMCO	DOM	5	2
Namibia	SAN	San	36	.0276	INDIG	INDIG	.	.	4	6
Niger	DSO	Djerema/Songhai	1460	.1900	COMCO	COMCO	.	DOM	5	6
Niger	HAU	Hausa	3540	.4600	ETHNA	ETHNA	COMCO	.	5	5
Niger	TUA	Tuareg	850	.1100	ETHNA	ETHNA	INDIG	.	5	4
Nigeria	HAU	Hausa/Fulani	34470	.2900	SECT	SECT	COMCO	POL	3	6
Nigeria	IBO	Ibo	20210	.1700	ETHNA	ETHNA	COMCO	.	5	4
Rwanda	TUT	Tutsi	840	.1100	ETHCL	ETHCL	COMCO	ECON	4	1
Senegal	DIO	Diola	620	.0800	ETHNA	ETHNA	.	.	4	6
Sierra Leone	CRE	Creoles	80	.0190	ETHCL	ETHCL	COMCO	DOM	5	2
Sierra Leone	LIM	Limba	333	.0800	COMCO	COMCO	.	POL	5	6
Sierra Leone	MEN	Mende	1290	.3100	COMCO	COMCO	.	.	5	6
Somalia	ISS	Issaq	2100	.2500	ETHNA	ETHNA	COMCO	.	4	6
South Africa	ASI	Asians	1030	.0280	ETHCL	ETHCL	COMCO	.	4	2
South Africa	BAF	Black Africans	26935	.7340	ETHCL	ETHCL	COMCO	.	3	1
South Africa	COL	Coloreds	3340	.0910	ETHCL	ETHCL	COMCO	.	3	6
South Africa	EUR	Europeans	5180	.1411	ETHCL	ETHCL	COMCO	DOM	5	1
Sudan	SSU	Southerners	6510	.2600	ETHNA	ETHNA	COMCO	.	5	6

Table A.5. Background Characteristics: Africa South of the Sahara (cont.).

COUNTRY	GROUP	NAME	POP90	PROP90	TYPE1	TYPE2	ADV80	COHERE	CONCEN
Togo	EWE	Ewe	790	.2220	ETHNA	COMCO	DOM	5	6
Togo	KAB	Kabre	500	.1400	COMCO	.	POL	5	4
Uganda	ACH	Acholi	705	.0400	COMCO	.	.	5	6
Uganda	ANK	Ankole	1410	.0800	COMCO	.	.	3	6
Uganda	BAG	Baganda	2810	.1600	ETHNA	COMCO	DOM	5	6
Uganda	KAK	Kakwa	530	.0300	COMCO	.	.	5	6
Uganda	KRA	Karamojong	350	.0200	INDIG	.	.	4	6
Uganda	KON	Konjo, Amba	530	.0300	ETHNA	COMCO	.	5	6
Uganda	LAN	Langi	1060	.0600	COMCO	.	.	3	6
Uganda	LUG	Lugbara, Madi	860	.0490	COMCO	.	.	3	6
Uganda	NYA	Nyarwanda (Rwandans)	1040	.0590	COMCO	.	.	5	6
Zaire	BKO	Bakongo	3640	.1030	ETHNA	COMCO	.	5	6
Zaire	LKA	Luba (Kasai Province)	2155	.0610	ETHNA	COMCO	DOM	5	6
Zaire	LIN	Lingala	7070	.2000	COMCO	.	POL	4	4
Zaire	LYE	Lunda, Yeke	1980	.0560	ETHNA	COMCO	.	5	6
Zaire	KIV	Kivu Region	4600	.1300	ETHNA	.	.	.	6
Zambia	BEM	Bemba	3000	.3700	COMCO	COMCO	.	5	4
Zambia	LOZ	Lozi (Barotse)	570	.0700	ETHNA	.	.	5	6
Zambia	TON	Tonga	1540	.1900	COMCO	COMCO	.	5	6
Zimbabwe	EUR	Europeans	370	.0350	ETHCL	.	.	5	2
Zimbabwe	NDE	Ndebele	2100	.2000	COMCO	.	.	5	6
Mean			3203	.1680				4.33	5.09

Table A.6. Background Characteristics of the Groups: Latin America and the Caribbean.

COUNTRY	GROUP	NAME	POP90	PROP90	TYPE1	TYPE2	ADV80	COHERE	CONCEN
Argentina	JEW	Jews	320	.0100	SECT	.	.	4	2
Argentina	NAT	Native peoples	365	.0113	INDIG	.	.	2	6
Bolivia	NTH	Native highland peoples	4105	.6100	INDIG	.	.	4	6
Bolivia	NTL	Native lowland peoples	135	.0200	INDIG	.	.	3	6
Brazil	BLA	Afro-Brazilians	9475	.0600	ETHCL	.	.	5	6
Brazil	NAT	Native peoples	235	.0015	INDIG	.	.	3	6
Chile	NAT	Native peoples	1070	.0823	INDIG	.	.	5	2
Colombia	BLA	Afro-Americans	2095	.0643	ETHCL	.	.	4	6
Colombia	NTH	Native highland peoples	225	.0069	INDIG	.	.	2	6
Colombia	NTL	Native lowland peoples	110	.0034	INDIG	.	.	2	6
Costa Rica	BLA	Antillean blacks	46	.0150	ETHCL	.	.	4	6
Ecuador	BLA	Afro-Americans	860	.0800	ETHCL	.	.	4	6
Ecuador	NTH	Native highland peoples	2805	.2600	INDIG	.	.	4	6
Ecuador	NTL	Native lowland peoples	108	.0100	INDIG	.	.	3	6
El Salvador	NAT	Native peoples	565	.1000	INDIG	.	.	3	6
Guatemala	NAT	Native peoples (Maya)	3330	.3600	INDIG	.	.	2	4

Table A.6. Background Characteristics: Latin America and the Caribbean (*cont.*).

COUNTRY	GROUP	NAME	POP90	PROP90	TYPE1	TYPE2	ADV80	COHERE	CONCEN
Honduras	BLC	Black Caribs	95	.0180	ETHCL	.	.	4	6
Honduras	NAT	Native peoples	370	.0700	INDIG		.	4	6
Nicaragua	NAT	Native peoples (Miskitos)	126	.0350	ETHNA	INDIG	.	5	6
Panama	BLA	Afro-Caribbeans	121	.0500	ETHCL		.	4	2
Panama	NAT	Native peoples	133	.0550	INDIG			3	6
Paraguay	NAT	Native peoples	115	.0250	INDIG			2	.
Peru	BLA	Afro-Americans	112	.0050	ETHCL			4	6
Peru	NTH	Native highland peoples	8940	.4000	INDIG		.	4	5
Peru	NTL	Native lowland peoples	265	.0120	INDIG		.	3	6
Venezuela	BLA	Afro-Americans	1975	.1000	ETHCL		.	1	.
Venezuela	NAT	Native Peoples	195	.0100	INDIG		.	2	6
Dominican Rep.	BLA	Afro-Americans	650	.0870	ETHCL		.	4	.
Mexico	NAT	Native peoples	10425	.1200	INDIG		.	2	4
Mean			1702	.0920				3.31	5.35

Indices of Intergroup Differentials and Discrimination

The variables displayed in tables A.7 through A.12 are as follows. See chapter 2 for scale categories, traits, and dimensions.

CULDIF   Five-category scale (values from 0 to 4) of cultural differentials derived from codings of six cultural traits.

ECODIF   Seven-category scale (values from −2 to +4) of intergroup differentials in economic status and positions derived from codings of six dimensions.

POLDIF   Seven-category scale of intergroup differentials in political status and positions (same scale values as ECODIF, and parallel categories) derived from codings of six dimensions.

DEMSTRESS   Sum of three ordinal scales (each with values from 1 to 3) of three demographic traits signifying group poverty.

ECOSTRESS   Sum of three ordinal scales (each with values from 1 to 3) of three kinds of pressures on group land and resources.

ECODIS   Five-category ordinal scale (values from 0 to 4) of severity of economic discrimination affecting group members.

POLDIS   Five-category ordinal scale (values from 0 to 4) of severity of political discrimination affecting group members.

AUTLOST   Indicator (values from 0 [no historical autonomy] to 6) of loss of historical autonomy derived from codings of magnitude of loss and group status prior to loss, weighted by length of time since loss.

For all variables, a period (.) means that data are not available or not applicable for the group.

Table A.7. Codings of Intergroup Differentials and Discrimination: Western Democracies and Japan.

COUNTRY	GROUP	CULDIF	ECODIF	POLDIF	DEMSTRESS	ECOSTRESS	ECODIS	POLDIS	AUTLOST
Eurocommunity	ROM	3	4	4	9	0	3	3	.0
France	BAS	2	1	0	0	0	1	0	1.0
France	BRE	2	1	0	0	0	1	0	1.3
France	COR	3	3	0	0	0	1	0	1.3
France	AAI	4	4	3	1	0	3	4	.0
Greece	MUS	3	1	1	2	2	3	1	.0
Italy	GER	2	0	1	0	0	0	0	.7
Italy	SAR	2	1	0	0	0	1	0	.5
Nordic	SAM	3	2	0	2	0	1	0	.8
Spain	BAS	2	0	1	0	0	0	0	1.3
Spain	CTL	2	0	1	0	0	0	1	1.5
Switzerland	JUR	1	0	0	0	0	0	0	1.0
Switzerland	FOR	3	4	3	3	0	2	4	.0
United Kingdom	BLK	3	3	1	4	0	3	1	.0
United Kingdom	CAT	3	2	2	2	0	3	1	.7
West Germany	TUR	4	4	3	6	0	1	4	.0
Japan	KOR	2	4	4	.	.	3	4	.0
Australia	ABO	4	4	1	5	0	1	1	.0
New Zealand	MAO	4	4	1	5	0	2	1	1.3
Canada	FCA	2	0	0	0	0	0	0	1.0
Canada	NAT	4	3	2	3	0	3	1	.7
USA	BLA	2	2	0	6	0	1	1	.0
USA	HIS	3	3	1	5	0	2	1	.5
USA	NAT	3	3	0	7	0	1	1	.7
Mean		2.75	2.21	1.21	2.50	0.08	1.50	1.21	0.60

Table A.8. Codings of Intergroup Differentials and Discrimination: Eastern Europe and the USSR.

COUNTRY	GROUP	CULDIF	ECODIF	POLDIF	DEMSTRESS	ECOSTRESS	ECODIS	POLDIS	AUTLOST
Bulgaria	TUR	4	3	4	3	1	4	4	.0
Czechoslovakia	HUN	3	3	2	0	0	2	2	.7
Czechoslovakia	SLO	1	0	0	1	0	0	0	1.0
Eastern Europe	ROM	3	3	2	9	2	1	1	.0
Romania	GER	2	0	1	0	0	0	0	.0
Romania	HUN	3	2	1	0	0	0	0	4.0
USSR	ARM	2	0	0	1	0	0	0	1.7
USSR	AZE	4	0	0	3	0	0	0	.0
USSR	CHE	4	2	2	3	0	1	1	.0
USSR	CTA	2	0	1	0	0	0	2	.0
USSR	EST	3	−1	0	0	0	0	2	3.0
USSR	GEO	2	−1	0	0	0	0	0	1.7
USSR	GER	1	0	3	0	0	0	2	2.0
USSR	JEW	1	0	2	0	0	0	3	.0
USSR	KAR	4	0	0	1	0	0	0	.0

		2.91	0.83	1.07	1.47	0.16	0.77	1.28	1.05
USSR	KAZ	4	2	2	.2	0	1	1	.0
USSR	KIR	4	2	2	3	0	1	1	1.3
USSR	KUR	3	0	1	0	0	0	0	.0
USSR	LAT	3	-1	0	0	0	0	2	3.0
USSR	LIT	3	-1	0	0	0	0	2	3.0
USSR	ROM	3	2	2	2	0	2	2	.0
USSR	TAD	4	2	1	3	0	1	1	.0
USSR	TKM	4	2	2	3	0	1	1	.0
USSR	UKR	1	0	0	0	0	0	0	1.7
USSR	UZB	4	2	1	3	0	1	1	1.3
USSR	RUM	3	3	1	4	0	3	3	1.0
Yugoslavia	ALB	4	2	1	6	0	1	4	1.0
Yugoslavia	CRO	1	0	0	0	0	0	0	.0
Yugoslavia	SER	2	1	-2	0	2	0	1	2.0
Yugoslavia	SLO	3	-2	2	0	0	4	3	.7
China	KAZ	4	·	·	·	·	·	1	2.0
China	UIG	4	·	2	·	·	·	1	2.5
Mean		2.91	0.83	1.07	1.47	0.16	0.77	1.28	1.05

Table A.9. Codings of Intergroup Differentials and Discrimination: Asia.

COUNTRY	GROUP	CULDIF	ECODIF	POLDIF	DEMSTRESS	ECOSTRESS	ECODIS	POLDIS	AUTLOST
Bangladesh	CHT	4	3	1	3	8	4	4	3.0
Bangladesh	HIN	1	4	0	0	3	3	3	1.0
Burma	ARA	1	0	4	0	0	.	3	1.5
Burma	CHN	4	4	2	0	0	2	2	1.5
Burma	KAC	4	.	.	0	0	2	3	1.5
Burma	KRN	2	0	2	0	0	0	0	2.5
Burma	MON	1	0	0	0	0	0	0	.8
Burma	SHA	2	.	3	0	0	0	0	2.0
Burma	SMT	4	4	4	0	0	2	2	1.5
China	HHU	1	.	.	0	0	.	.	.0
China	TIB	4	4	3	3	0	1	3	2.5
India	KAS	4	1	2	0	0	1	1	2.5
India	MUS	2	3	4	1	0	3	3	1.0
India	NAG	4	3	1	0	4	3	4	2.5
India	SNT	4	4	4	3	3	3	3	.8
India	STR	4	4	4	3	5	3	3	.5
India	SIK	4	1	1	0	2	2	2	1.3
India	MIZ	4	2	2	0	3	1	1	2.5
India	TRI	4	4	3	3	6	1	1	1.5
Indonesia	CHI	3	-1	3	0	0	4	4	.0
Indonesia	ETI	4	4	1	3	3	3	2	2.0

Country	Code								
Indonesia	PAP	4	3	3	2	5	3	4	2.0
Kampuchea	CHA	3	.	.	.	.	1	0	.0
Kampuchea	VIE	1	.	.	0	0	.	4	.0
Laos	HMO	4	4	3	3	3	1	3	3.0
Malaysia	CHI	4	−2	1	0	0	4	0	.0
Malaysia	DAY	4	4	2	3	3	3	2	2.0
Malaysia	EIN	3	3	3	0	2	2	3	.0
Malaysia	KAD	4	.	2	.	.	1	2	1.0
Philippines	CPE	2	.	2	0	3	2	1	.8
Philippines	MOR	2	2	1	0	4	3	1	1.5
Singapore	MLY	4	4	2	0	0	2	3	.0
Sri Lanka	ITA	3	3	3	2	0	2	2	.0
Sri Lanka	SLT	3	0	2	0	2	0	1	1.3
Taiwan	ATA	3	4	3	0	0	3	3	.0
Taiwan	KMT	2	0	−2	0	0	0	0	.0
Taiwan	TAI	1	0	1	0	0	0	4	1.0
Thailand	CHI	2	−2	2	0	0	0	.	.0
Thailand	MMU	3	2	2	0	1	1	1	1.3
Thailand	NHT	4	4	4	3	6	3	2	.0
Vietnam	CHI	2	−1	4	0	2	2	4	.0
Vietnam	MNT	4	.	.	0	7	1	1	1.0
Papua New Guinea	BOU	1	.	0	0	0	0	0	.5
Mean		2.98	2.12	2.16	0.74	1.83	1.80	2.08	1.11

Table A.10. Codings of Intergroup Differentials and Discrimination: North Africa and the Middle East.

COUNTRY	GROUP	CULDIF	ECODIF	POLDIF	DEMSTRESS	ECOSTRESS	ECODIS	POLDIS	AUTLOST
Algeria	BER	3	1	1	8	0	1	3	.0
Egypt	COP	1	0	1	0	0	0	3	.0
Iran	AZE	2	0	0	.	.	0	0	2.5
Iran	BAH	1	3	4	.	.	4	4	.0
Iran	BKH	3	3	3	.	.	2	2	.0
Iran	BLU	4	4	3	2	0	3	2	1.3
Iran	KUR	4	4	3	2	1	3	4	2.5
Iran	TKM	4	4	4	0	2	3	4	1.0
Iran	ARB	4	4	4	.	.	4	4	.0
Iraq	KUR	3	4	4	3	5	3	4	.7
Iraq	SHI	1	3	2	2	2	2	1	.0
Iraq	SUN	1	-2	-2	0	0	0	0	.0
Israel	ARB	4	4	4	8	6	3	4	2.5
Israel	PAL	4	4	4	8	6	4	4	2.5

Jordan	PAL	1	0	3	4	0	0	4	.0
Lebanon	DRU	2	0	0	0	0	0	0	1.3
Lebanon	PAL	1	4	4	3	0	2	4	2.5
Lebanon	MAR	1	-1	-2	0	0	0	0	1.7
Lebanon	SHI	1	4	3	9	2	3	2	.7
Lebanon	SUN	1	-1	-1	1	0	0	0	.0
Morocco	BER	4	3	2	8	3	2	3	.0
Morocco	SAH	3	.	.	3	0	2	2	2.0
Pakistan	AHM	1	0	3	0	0	4	4	.0
Pakistan	BLU	4	3	2	0	0	3	3	.0
Pakistan	HIN	2	1	1	0	0	4	4	.0
Pakistan	PUS	3	0	0	0	0	0	0	.8
Pakistan	SIN	3	4	2	0	0	3	3	1.0
Saudi Arabia	SHI	1	.	4	3	0	0	3	.0
Syria	ALA	2	2	1	0	0	1	0	.0
Turkey	KUR	3	3	3	3	5	3	4	.7
Turkey	ROM	3	4	.	6	0	3	3	.0
Mean		2.42	2.10	2.07	2.35	1.19	2.00	2.52	0.77

Table A.11. Codings of Intergroup Differentials and Discrimination: Africa South of the Sahara.

COUNTRY	GROUP	CULDIF	ECODIF	POLDIF	DEMSTRESS	ECOSTRESS	ECODIS	POLDIS	AUTLOST
Angola	BKO	1	·	2	0	0	·	3	1.3
Angola	OVI	1	·	2	0	0	3	·	.0
Botswana	SAN	3	3	1	2	3	3	2	.0
Burundi	HUT	2	3	3	0	3	4	4	.0
Burundi	TUT	1	-2	-2	0	0	0	0	.0
Cameroon	KRD	3	4	1	2	0	1	3	.0
Cameroon	WES	1	2	1	0	0	3	3	1.0
Cameroon	BAM	2	-2	-2	0	0	0	0	.0
Chad	NCH	3	0	2	0	0	0	0	.0
Chad	SCH	3	0	3	0	0	0	3	.0
Congo	LAR	1	0	2	0	0	0	3	.0
Ethiopia	AFA	4	3	1	·	·	3	1	1.5
Ethiopia	ERI	1	0	4	2	0	0	0	4.0
Ethiopia	NSA	4	4	4	2	3	3	4	.5
Ethiopia	ORO	2	1	1	·	·	3	3	1.3
Ethiopia	SOM	4	4	4	2	1	3	4	1.0
Ethiopia	TIG	1	0	1	3	3	2	2	.0
Ghana	ASH	1	1	1	0	0	0	3	1.5
Ghana	EWE	1	1	1	0	0	0	0	1.5
Ghana	MDA	2	2	2	0	0	2	2	.0
Guinea	FUL	2	·	2	0	0	·	3	1.3
Guinea	MAL	1	·	2	0	0	·	4	.0
Guinea	SUS	1	-2	-1	0	0	0	0	.0
Ivory Coast	LEB	4	2	3	0	0	4	·	.0
Kenya	KIK	2	1	1	0	3	0	4	.0

Kenya	LUO	1	2	1	0	0	0	.0
Kenya	MAA	3	3	1	0	2	2	.0
Kenya	SOM	3	3	2	2	0	2	1.0
Kenya	TRK	3	2	2	2	2	4	.0
Kenya	REN	3	3	2	2	1	3	.0
Liberia	CRE	3	2	2	0	0	0	.0
Madagascar	MER	2	1	2	0	0	0	1.3
Mali	TUA	3	3	·	0	0	4	1.3
Mali	MND	2	-2	-2	0	0	0	.0
Mauritania	KEW	3	2	1	0	0	0	1.0
Namibia	EUR	4	-2	-2	0	0	0	.7
Namibia	SAN	4	4	3	2	3	3	.0
Niger	DSO	1	-1	-2	0	0	0	.0
Niger	HAU	1	1	2	0	0	0	1.3
Niger	TUA	3	3	2	2	1	2	1.3
Nigeria	HAU	2	2	-1	2	0	1	.0
Nigeria	IBO	2	·	1	0	0	·	5.0
Rwanda	TUT	1	2	1	0	0	4	.0
Senegal	DIO	2	2	1	2	0	2	.7
Sierra Leone	CRE	3	2	1	0	0	0	.0
Sierra Leone	LIM	2	0	-2	0	0	0	.0
Sierra Leone	MEN	1	0	2	0	0	0	.0
Somalia	ISS	1	0	2	0	0	0	3.0
South Africa	ASI	3	2	2	0	0	4	.0
South Africa	BAF	3	4	4	7	3	4	.0
South Africa	COL	1	3	3	2	0	4	.0
South Africa	EUR	4	-2	-2	0	0	0	.0
Sudan	SSU	4	4	3	3	4	4	1.5
Togo	EWE	1	1	1	0	0	3	.7
Togo	KAB	1	1	1	0	0	0	.0

Table A.11. Differentials and Discrimination: Africa South of the Sahara (*cont.*).

COUNTRY	GROUP	CULDIF	ECODIF	POLDIF	DEMSTRESS	ECOSTRESS	ECODIS	POLDIS	AUTLOST
Uganda	ACH	2	2	2	0	0	1	1	.0
Uganda	ANK	1	−1	−1	0	2	0	0	2.0
Uganda	BAG	2	−1	−1	0	0	0	0	2.0
Uganda	KAK	3	2	2	0	0	1	1	.0
Uganda	KRA	3	3	2	2	1	1	1	1.0
Uganda	KON	2	2	2	0	2	1	1	1.0
Uganda	LAN	2	2	2	0	0	1	1	1.0
Uganda	LUG	2	2	1	0	0	1	1	.0
Uganda	NYA	3	3	4	0	5	4	4	.0
Zaire	BKO	1	2	1	0	0	0	3	1.0
Zaire	LKA	1	1	1	0	0	0	0	1.0
Zaire	LIN	1	.	2	0	0	0	0	.0
Zaire	LYE	1	.	2	0	0	0	4	4.0
Zaire	KIV	1	2	1	0	0	.	4	4.0
Zambia	BEM	1	0	0	0	0	0	0	.0
Zambia	LOZ	2	1	0	0	0	1	0	.0
Zambia	TON	2	0	0	0	0	0	0	.0
Zimbabwe	EUR	3	−2	0	0	0	0	0	.0
Zimbabwe	NDE	1	0	1	1	0	0	2	.0
Mean		2.09	1.31	1.25	0.57	0.57	1.28	1.92	0.69

COUNTRY	GROUP	CULDIF	ECODIF	POLDIF	DEMSTRESS	ECOSTRESS	ECODIS	POLDIS	AUTLOST
Argentina	JEW	1	0	0	0	0	0	0	.0
Argentina	NAT	4	4	3	2	5	3	3	.0
Bolivia	NTH	4	4	2	2	0	3	2	.0
Bolivia	NTL	4	4	2	3	3	3	3	.0
Brazil	BLA	2	4	3	0	0	2	2	.0
Brazil	NAT	4	4	2	3	8	4	2	1.0
Chile	NAT	4	4	3	3	3	3	4	3.0
Colombia	BLA	1	4	2	0	0	3	2	.0
Colombia	NTH	2	4	3	0	3	3	2	.0
Colombia	NTL	4	4	3	0	3	3	3	.7
Costa Rica	BLA	2	2	1	0	0	2	2	.0
Ecuador	BLA	1	2	1	0	0	3	3	.0
Ecuador	NTH	4	4	1	1	3	3	3	.0
Ecuador	NTL	4	4	2	1	3	3	3	.0
El Salvador	NAT	3	0	0	0	3	0	0	.0
Guatemala	NAT	4	4	3	3	5	4	4	.7
Honduras	BLC	2	4	1	4	1	2	2	.0
Honduras	NAT	4	4	3	0	3	2	2	.7
Nicaragua	NAT	4	2	3	0	9	2	3	.7
Panama	BLA	3	1	1	0	0	2	0	.0
Panama	NAT	3	1	1	0	5	2	1	.7
Paraguay	NAT	4	4	4	2	3	4	4	.0
Peru	BLA	1	2	0	0	0	2	2	.0
Peru	NTH	2	4	2	0	0	1	1	1.0
Peru	NTL	4	4	2	2	3	3	3	.0
Venezuela	BLA	1	4	1	0	0	2	2	.0
Venezuela	NAT	4	4	3	2	3	3	3	.0
Dominican Rep.	BLA	2	4	4	5	3	4	4	.0
Mexico	NAT	3	4	2	0	2	3	3	.0
Mean		2.93	3.24	2.00	1.14	2.45	2.55	2.34	0.29

Indices of Group Grievances and Conflict in the 1980s

The variables displayed in tables A.13 through A.18 are as follows.
See chapter 3 for scales and weights. Guttman coding scales for
PROT, RIOT, and REBEL are given in table 4.1.

ECOGR   Demands for greater economic rights: sum of codings
            on six ordinal scales.
SOCGR   Demands for greater social and cultural rights: sum of
            codings on four ordinal scales.
POLRI   Demands for greater political rights other than auton-
            omy: sum of codings on five ordinal scales.
AUTGR   Demands for greater political autonomy: sum of codings
            on four ordinal scales.
COMCON   Conflict with communal groups not associated with the
            state: sum of Guttman scale scores for each decade
            1940s to 1980s.
PROT   Extent of nonviolent group protest in the 1980s: sum of
            Guttman scale scores for nonviolent protest 1980–84
            and 1985–89.
RIOT   Extent of violent group protest in the 1980s: sum of
            Guttman scale scores for violent protest 1980–84 and
            1985–89.
REBEL   Extent of group rebellion in the 1980s: sum of Guttman
            scale scores for rebellion 1980–84 and 1985–89.

For all variables, a period (.) means that data are not available or not
applicable for the group.

Table A.13. Codings of Group Grievances and Conflict in the 1980s: Western Democracies and Japan.

COUNTRY	GROUP	ECOGR	SOCGR	POLRI	AUTGR	COMCON	PROT	RIOT	REBEL
Eurocommunity	ROM	4	2	4	0	1	3	2	0
France	BAS	0	1	0	1	0	2	0	3
France	BRE	3	2	1	1	0	2	0	0
France	COR	4	2	2	1	1	2	0	4
France	AAI	4	4	2	0	3	0	0	0
Greece	MUS	3	2	2	0	0	1	0	0
Italy	GER	0	2	0	1	2	0	0	2
Italy	SAR	3	1	1	1	0	0	0	1
Nordic	SAM	1	1	2	1	0	3	0	0
Spain	BAS	1	2	2	4	0	4	0	4
Spain	CTL	0	2	2	3	0	4	0	2
Switzerland	JUR	0	1	0	1	1	2	0	0
Switzerland	FOR	2	1	3	0	0	4	0	0
United Kingdom	BLK	4	2	5	0	3	6	7	0
United Kingdom	CAT	2	6	6	2	5	4	5	4
West Germany	TUR	3	1	1	0	3	2	0	0
Japan	KOR	0	0	0	0	0	0	4	0
Australia	ABO	4	2	2	0	0	7	0	0
New Zealand	MAO	3	2	0	1	0	6	0	0
Canada	FCA	0	2	2	3	0	4	0	0
Canada	NAT	4	2	2	2	0	5	0	0
USA	BLA	4	2	3	0	1	6	5	0
USA	HIS	4	2	3	1	0	4	0	2
USA	NAT	6	2	1	1	0	5	1	0
Mean		2.46	1.92	1.92	1.00	0.83	3.33	0.83	0.92

Table A.14. Codings of Group Grievances and Conflict in the 1980s: Eastern Europe and the USSR.

COUNTRY	GROUP	ECOGR	SOCGR	POLRI	AUTGR	COMCON	PROT	RIOT	REBEL
Bulgaria	TUR	2	6	4	0	0	6	4	0
Czechoslovakia	HUN	0	0	0	0	0	0	0	0
Czechoslovakia	SLO	0	0	0	2	0	4	0	0
Eastern Europe	ROM	3	2	3	0	1	4	0	0
Romania	GER	0	3	0	0	0	0	0	0
Romania	HUN	2	4	2	2	0	4	0	0
USSR	ARM	0	2	1	2	5	5	5	1
USSR	AZE	0	6	2	0	5	4	5	1
USSR	CHE	0	0	0	0	0	2	0	0
USSR	CTA	0	0	2	0	0	5	0	0
USSR	EST	3	2	3	2	0	7	0	0
USSR	GEO	2	2	2	2	5	8	5	1
USSR	GER	0	0	2	1	0	2	0	0
USSR	JEW	0	2	4	2	0	4	0	1
USSR	KAR	0	0	0	0	0	0	0	0
USSR	KAZ	0	0	0	0	0	3	4	0

USSR	KIR	0	4	2	2	0	1	7	0
USSR	KUR	0	0	0	0	0	0	0	0
USSR	LAT	2	2	2	2	0	8	2	0
USSR	LIT	0	4	2	2	0	8	2	0
USSR	ROM	0	0	0	0	0	0	0	0
USSR	TAD	0	4	0	0	0	3	4	0
USSR	TKM	0	3	0	2	0	0	2	0
USSR	UKR	0	4	0	2	0	7	2	2
USSR	UZB	0	4	2	1	5	4	5	0
USSR	RUM	0	2	0	3	0	4	3	0
Yugoslavia	ALB	4	2	2	0	4	8	9	3
Yugoslavia	CRO	0	0	0	1	0	3	1	1
Yugoslavia	SER	3	1	2	2	8	7	0	0
Yugoslavia	SLO	3	3	2	3	2	4	0	0
China	KAZ	1	2	2	1	.	0	0	0
China	UIG	2	0	1	1	0	7	8	1
Mean		0.84	1.88	1.25	1.06	1.09	3.81	2.13	0.34

Table A.15. Codings of Group Grievances and Conflict in the 1980s: Asia.

COUNTRY	GROUP	ECOGR	SOCGR	POLRI	AUTGR	COMCON	PROT	RIOT	REBEL
Bangladesh	CHT	4	6	6	3	5	4	0	9
Bangladesh	HIN	0	6	0	1	.	4	0	0
Burma	ARA	2	4	2	1	5	4	0	6
Burma	CHN	0	4	2	2	0	2	0	0
Burma	KAC	0	4	6	2	0	4	0	10
Burma	KRN	2	2	2	2	0	4	0	10
Burma	MON	0	0	4	2	0	4	0	3
Burma	SHA	0	2	0	2	0	4	0	8
Burma	SMT	2	0	2	2	0	4	0	10
China	HHU	0	0	0	0	.	0	0	0
China	TIB	5	4	8	2	0	4	4	1
India	KAS	0	4	5	3	0	6	2	2
India	MUS	5	6	2	1	5	4	0	0
India	NAG	2	2	2	3	0	7	0	2
India	SNT	8	2	4	2	0	4	0	2
India	STR	2	1	2	1	.	.	.	.
India	SIK	6	6	2	3	8	6	4	4
India	MIZ	0	0	2	2	3	4	0	3
India	TRI	4	4	6	2	6	8	4	8
Indonesia	CHI	2	4	4	0	.	0	0	0
Indonesia	ETI	2	0	3	2	0	0	0	6

Country	Code								
Indonesia	PAP	2	2	2	3	1	0	2	6
Kampuchea	CHA	0	0	0	0	0	0	0	0
Kampuchea	VIE	2	2	2	0	0	0	0	7
Laos	HMO	0	0	1	1	0	4	0	0
Malaysia	CHI	1	3	4	0	0	5	0	0
Malaysia	DAY	4	2	2	1	0	2	0	0
Malaysia	EIN	4	2	1	0	0	2	0	0
Malaysia	KAD	6	2	4	2	0	6	0	6
Philippines	CPE	2	2	5	2	.	4	0	4
Philippines	MOR	2	4	5	2	0	4	5	0
Singapore	MLY	1	0	1	0	5	4	0	0
Sri Lanka	ITA	3	4	2	2	9	3	0	0
Sri Lanka	SLT	4	6	8	3	0	4	0	10
Taiwan	ATA	1	1	1	0	0	0	0	0
Taiwan	KMT	0	0	2	2	0	6	2	0
Taiwan	TAI	0	0	6	1	0	0	0	0
Thailand	CHI	0	0	0	0	0	0	0	0
Thailand	MMU	1	4	1	3	0	1	0	3
Thailand	NHT	0	0	0	0	0	0	0	0
Vietnam	CHI	0	0	0	0	.	0	0	0
Vietnam	MNT	2	0	2	2	0	2	0	1
Papua New Guinea	BOU	4	0	4	1	0	2	0	3
Mean		1.98	2.21	2.72	1.47	1.27	2.95	0.55	2.95

Table A.16. Codings of Group Grievances and Conflict in the 1980s: North Africa and the Middle East.

COUNTRY	GROUP	ECOGR	SOCGR	POLRI	AUTGR	COMCON	PROT	RIOT	REBEL
Algeria	BER	4	2	4	0	0	7	5	0
Egypt	COP	4	3	2	0	3	2	0	0
Iran	AZE	0	2	4	2	.	2	0	0
Iran	BAH	2	6	4	0	0	4	0	0
Iran	BKH	0	0	0	0	.	0	0	0
Iran	BLU	4	4	4	2	3	0	0	3
Iran	KUR	4	4	4	2	.	0	0	4
Iran	TKM	4	6	4	2	0	0	0	3
Iran	ARB	4	2	8	2	0	0	0	2
Iraq	KUR	4	2	7	4	0	6	0	8
Iraq	SUN	0	0	0	0	0	0	0	0
Iraq	SHI	2	2	2	0	0	4	0	8
Israel	ARB	7	4	7	3	4	9	4	2
Israel	PAL	4	2	6	4	4	10	7	4

Jordan	PAL	0	0	0	0	0	3	2	1
Lebanon	DRU	0	4	3	2	6	4	0	10
Lebanon	PAL	2	2	3	2	12	4	0	10
Lebanon	MAR	2	4	4	1	12	6	0	10
Lebanon	SHI	8	4	4	2	6	4	0	10
Lebanon	SUN	0	2	2	0	0	4	0	10
Morocco	BER	4	2	4	3	0	0	0	0
Morocco	SAH	0	0	2	0	0	3	0	10
Pakistan	AHM	0	4	2	0	3	0	0	0
Pakistan	BLU	2	0	2	0	0	1	1	1
Pakistan	HIN	1	0	2	2	0	2	0	0
Pakistan	PUS	2	2	0	2	5	0	0	8
Pakistan	SIN	4	2	2	2	5	8	10	6
Saudi Arabia	SHI	5	1	4	0	0	0	2	0
Syria	ALA	0	0	0	0	3	0	0	0
Turkey	KUR	5	3	7	3	0	4	0	6
Turkey	ROM	1	1	1	0	0	0	0	0
Mean		2.55	2.26	3.16	1.23	2.36	2.81	1.00	3.74

Table A.17. Codings of Group Grievances and Conflict in the 1980s: Africa South of the Sahara.

COUNTRY	GROUP	ECOGR	SOCGR	POLRI	AUTGR	COMCON	PROT	RIOT	REBEL
Angola	BKO	0	0	3	2	0	0	0	0
Angola	OVI	1	0	3	0	5	0	0	10
Botswana	SAN	5	2	1	0	0	0	0	0
Burundi	HUT	4	4	6	0	5	0	3	0
Burundi	TUT	1	2	0	0	5	0	0	1
Cameroon	KRD	1	1	1	0	0	0	0	0
Cameroon	WES	4	2	2	1	0	3	2	0
Cameroon	BAM	3	2	1	0	.	0	0	0
Chad	NCH	0	0	0	0	0	0	0	0
Chad	SCH	0	2	2	0	0	0	3	7
Congo	LAR	0	0	2	0	0	2	0	0
Ethiopia	AFA	2	2	1	1	0	0	0	3
Ethiopia	ERI	2	0	5	2	0	0	0	10
Ethiopia	NSA	2	4	3	1	0	0	5	0
Ethiopia	ORO	2	2	5	1	0	0	0	4
Ethiopia	SOM	2	2	2	3	0	0	0	4
Ethiopia	TIG	2	0	3	2	0	0	0	10
Ghana	ASH	1	0	2	1	0	4	0	1
Ghana	EWE	0	0	0	1	0	2	0	1
Ghana	MDA	1	0	2	0	0	4	0	0
Guinea	FUL	0	0	2	1	0	0	0	0
Guinea	MAL	0	0	2	0	0	0	3	1
Guinea	SUS	0	0	0	0	.	1	0	0
Ivory Coast	LEB	1	0	1	0	.	0	0	0

Kenya	KIK	0	0	2	0	4	0	0	0
Kenya	LUO	0	0	1	0	2	0	0	0
Kenya	MAA	2	1	1	4	0	0	0	0
Kenya	SOM	3	2	4	0	6	0	0	2
Kenya	TRK	3	4	3	0	3	0	0	0
Kenya	REN	1	2	3	0	0	0	0	0
Liberia	CRE	0	0	2	0	·	2	0	0
Madagascar	MER	0	0	1	1	0	2	0	0
Mali	TUA	0	0	0	0	0	0	0	0
Mali	MND	0	0	0	1	0	0	0	0
Mauritania	KEW	2	2	1	1	0	0	0	0
Namibia	EUR	2	1	2	2	0	0	0	0
Namibia	SAN	3	2	1	0	0	0	0	0
Niger	DSO	0	0	0	1	0	0	0	0
Niger	HAU	1	0	3	1	0	2	0	1
Niger	TUA	4	0	3	2	3	2	0	0
Nigeria	HAU	2	1	1	0	3	5	0	0
Nigeria	IBO	1	4	2	1	·	0	0	0
Rwanda	TUT	2	2	6	1	0	1	0	0
Senegal	DIO	2	0	1	1	0	0	2	0
Sierra Leone	CRE	0	0	0	0	0	3	0	0
Sierra Leone	LIM	2	0	0	1	·	3	3	0
Sierra Leone	MEN	0	0	2	0	0	0	0	0
Somalia	ISS	0	2	3	1	0	5	0	8
South Africa	ASI	2	1	7	0	0	5	0	0
South Africa	BAF	6	2	7	0	0	9	8	5
South Africa	COL	·	2	7	0	0	4	0	0
South Africa	EUR	0	2	0	0	0	3	0	0

Table A.17. Grievances and Conflict: Africa South of the Sahara (*cont.*).

COUNTRY	GROUP	ECOGR	SOCGR	POLRI	AUTGR	COMCON	PROT	RIOT	REBEL
Sudan	SSU	4	4	6	2	6	0	0	10
Togo	EWE	0	0	2	1	0	0	0	1
Togo	KAB	0	0	0	0	0	0	0	0
Uganda	ACH	2	3	4	0	0	3	5	5
Uganda	ANK	0	0	0	0	0	2	0	5
Uganda	BAG	4	2	5	2	0	3	0	5
Uganda	KAK	2	1	2	0	0	0	6	7
Uganda	KRA	1	2	1	1	6	2	3	2
Uganda	KON	2	4	4	2	0	2	0	0
Uganda	LAN	2	3	2	1	3	1	5	5
Uganda	LUG	2	0	2	0	0	0	0	4
Uganda	NYA	5	2	4	0	3	1	0	0
Zaire	BKO	0	0	0	0	0	0	0	0
Zaire	LKA	0	0	0	0	0	0	0	0
Zaire	LIN	0	0	0	0	0	0	0	0
Zaire	LYE	0	0	1	1	0	0	0	6
Zaire	KIV	3	2	2	2	0	4	0	0
Zambia	BEM	2	0	1	0	0	4	3	0
Zambia	LOZ	3	0	1	0	0	0	0	0
Zambia	TON	2	0	1	0	0	0	0	0
Zimbabwe	EUR	2	1	1	0	1	4	0	0
Zimbabwe	NDE	1	2	2	0	.	8	4	6
Mean		1.47	1.06	2.06	0.59	0.82	1.19	0.74	1.68

COUNTRY	GROUP	ECOGR	SOCGR	POLRI	AUTGR	COMCON	PROT	RIOT	REBEL
Argentina	JEW	0	3	0	0	0	0	0	0
Argentina	NAT	6	3	2	0	0	0	0	0
Bolivia	NTH	4	2	3	0	0	4	0	0
Bolivia	NTL	7	2	5	0	0	4	0	0
Brazil	BLA	5	2	4	0	0	2	0	0
Brazil	NAT	6	2	4	2	0	0	10	0
Chile	NAT	6	4	3	2	0	6	0	0
Colombia	BLA	1	1	1	0	0	0	0	0
Colombia	NTH	6	2	5	0	0	3	0	1
Colombia	NTL	2	3	1	2	0	2	0	0
Costa Rica	BLA	3	2	2	0	0	0	0	0
Ecuador	BLA	3	0	1	0	0	0	0	0
Ecuador	NTH	5	2	2	0	0	4	0	0
Ecuador	NTL	2	3	3	0	0	4	0	0
El Salvador	NAT	0	0	0	0	0	0	0	0
Guatemala	NAT	4	3	5	2	0	6	0	7
Honduras	BLC	2	2	2	0	0	0	0	0
Honduras	NAT	3	4	1	1	0	2	0	0
Nicaragua	NAT	2	3	2	2	0	0	0	8
Panama	BLA	2	2	2	0	0	1	0	0
Panama	NAT	2	0	2	4	0	.	.	.
Paraguay	NAT	5	4	3	0	0	0	0	0
Peru	BLA	1	1	0	0	0	0	0	0
Peru	NTH	5	2	5	1	0	6	0	0
Peru	NTL	3	4	6	1	0	4	0	0
Venezuela	BLA	1	1	0	0	0	0	0	0
Venezuela	NAT	3	2	0	0	0	4	0	0
Dominican Rep.	BLA	2	0	2	0	0	3	0	0
Mexico	NAT	4	3	2	0	0	4	0	0
Mean		3.28	2.14	2.43	0.59	0.00	2.11	0.36	0.57

Notes

Preface

1. There are alternate names and spellings for many of the communal groups included in this study. In general we use the names preferred at present by groups' political representatives and advocates: Blacks rather than Bantu (or tribal names like Zulu and Xhosa) in South Africa, Roma rather than Gypsies, native peoples or Native Americans rather than American Indians, Arab citizens of Israel or Arabs in Israel rather than Arab-Israelis, Hmong rather than Meo. For the peoples of the former USSR we rely on the Soviet ethnographic and census studies cited in chapter 7, note 8. For groups with multiple names and alternative spellings we adopt the form most commonly used by regional experts: for example, we refer to the adherents of Shi'ism as Shi'is rather than Shi'ites or Shi'as because Shi'i is the term preferred by most Islamic scholars writing in English. The most definitive general guide to group names, and our source of last resort, is the Minority Rights Group, *World Directory of Minorities* (Chicago and London: St. James Press, n.d. [1990]).

2. Three recent books offer important generalizations based on analysis of a wider range of case studies and observations: Donald L. Horowitz, *Ethnic Groups in Conflict* (Berkeley, CA: University of California Press, 1985); Joseph V. Montville (ed.), *Conflict and Peacemaking in Multiethnic Societies* (Lexington, MA: Lexington Books, 1990); and Hurst Hannum, *Autonomy, Sovereignty, and Self-Determination: The Accommodation of Conflicting Rights* (Philadelphia: University of Pennsylvania Press, 1990).

3. All indicators of group traits analyzed in this book were developed for the Minorities at Risk project, under the direction of the author. Scales and coding categories were devised in a lengthy experimental period during which the author and Monty G. Marshall

independently coded information on a half-dozen groups, then compared codings and either discarded or refined the scales. New coders
were trained by using sample case materials. All coders either had substantial prior knowledge of the regions on which they were working,
or worked under the close supervision of project members who had
such knowledge. Questions about the interpretation of particular
groups and events were regularly discussed among coders and the project director, and amendments were made to coding guidelines where
necessary. All codings were reviewed by the author and additional
source materials often were sought to resolve specific ambiguities.
Some area experts were consulted about which groups met our general criteria and about problematic codings and interpretations. The
scales that could not be coded for specific groups because information
was not available, ambiguous, or not applicable are indicated by a period (.) in the data cell in the Appendix tables. The project director
and his assistants continue to compile materials on the groups
in the study and have made some retrospective adjustments in the
codings and interpretations reported in this book. Limited resources
kept us from following two more technical procedures: testing
the reliability of the coded data by statistically comparing independent codings of the same groups by different coders; and assessing the validity of the codings by having them reviewed by panels of
experts.

4. As reported by T. R. Gurr and Erika B. K. Gurr, "Group Discrimination and Potential Separatism in 1960 and 1975," in Charles
Lewis Taylor and David Jodice (eds.), *World Handbook of Political and
Social Indicators*, 3d ed., vol. 1 (New Haven: Yale University Press,
1983), 50–57, 66–75.

5. T. R. Gurr and James R. Scarritt, "Minorities Rights at Risk: A
Global Survey," *Human Rights Quarterly* 11, no. 4 (1989):375–405; T. R.
Gurr, "Ethnic Warfare and the Changing Priorities of Global Security,"
Mediterranean Quarterly 1, no. 1 (1990):82–98; and T. R. Gurr, "Third
World Minorities at Risk Since 1945," in Sheryl J. Brown and Kimber
M. Schraub (eds.), *Resolving Third World Conflict: Challenges for a New
Era* (Washington, DC: United States Institute of Peace Press, 1992),
51–88.

6. Barbara Harff and T. R. Gurr, "Victims of the State: Genocide,
Politicide and Group Repression Since 1945," *International Review of
Victimology* 1, no. 1 (1989):23–41; T. R. Gurr, "The Internationalization of Protracted Communal Conflicts Since 1945: Which Groups,
Where, and How," in Manus I. Midlarsky (ed.), *The Internationalization
of Communal Strife* (London: Routledge, 1992), 3–25; and T. R. Gurr,
"Why Minorities Rebel: A Global Analysis of Communal Mobilization and Conflict since 1945," *International Political Science Review*
14, no. 2 (April 1993):161–201.

I. Identifying Communal Groups

1. Walker Conner makes the same point in his prescient 1972 analysis of the enduring significance of ethnonationalism: "The essence of the nation is not tangible. It is psychological, a matter of attitude rather than of fact"; "Nation-Building or Nation-Destroying?" *World Politics* 26(April 1972):337.

2. The conventional meanings of *minority, ethnic group, ethnie* (a term widely used by French scholars), and *national people* are subsumed by our definition of *communal group*. A collaborative social science effort to standardize terminology in this research area is summarized in Fred W. Riggs, "Ethnicity, Nationalism, Race, Minority: A Semantic/Onomantic Exercise" (Honolulu: Department of Political Science, University of Hawaii, 1991), who concludes that ethnicity is the most general of these concepts. Our field of vision is broader than Riggs's, because we include forty-nine politically active religious groups, such as the Catholics of Northern Ireland, most of whom are not ethnically distinct from dominant groups. A collaborative effort by Dutch scholars to clarify the concept of minorities for comparative and international legal purposes leads to the following definition, which approximates our conception of communal groups except that it seems to exclude subordinate groups such as black South Africans who are numerical majorities: "A minority is composed of a group of persons differing from the rest of a population with markedly distinct ethnic, religious, linguistic characteristics, cultural bonds or ties, numerically in an inferior and non-dominant position, showing a will, if only implicitly to preserve and develop their patterns of life and behavior." From Oldrich Andrysek, *Report on the Definition of Minorities* (Utrecht: Netherlands Institute of Human Rights, SIM Special Report No. 8, 1989), 60.

3. The plasticity of ethnic group identity has been recognized and analyzed by many scholars, most influentially by Frederik Barth in his introduction to *Ethnic Groups and Boundaries: The Social Organization of Culture Difference* (London: Allen and Unwin, 1969), 9–38; Donald L. Horowitz in *Ethnic Groups in Conflict* (Berkeley, CA: University of California Press, 1985), 41–54; and Anthony D. Smith in *The Ethnic Origins of Nations* (Oxford and New York: Basil Blackwell, 1986). Recent studies focus on "ethnogenesis," the ways in which migration, conflict, and other processes of increased contact among groups enhance or even generate communal identities; see especially the case studies in Nancie L. Gonzalez and Carolyn S. McCommon (eds.), *Conflict, Migration, and the Expression of Ethnicity* (Boulder, CO: Westview Press, 1989); and Eugeen E. Roosens, *Creating Ethnicity: The Process of Ethnogenesis* (Newbury Park, CA: Sage Publications, 1989), who has studied the process among the Hurons and others.

4. These views are expressed, with qualifications, by Clifford

Geertz, "The Integrative Revolution: Primordial Sentiments and Civil Politics in the New States," in Geertz (ed.), *Old Societies and New States* (New York: Free Press, 1963), 105–157; by some contributors to John F. Stack, Jr. (ed.), *The Primordial Challenge: Ethnicity in the Contemporary World* (New York: Greenwood Press, 1986); and by Pierre L. van den Berghe, "Race and Ethnicity: A Sociobiological Perspective," *Ethnic and Racial Studies* 1(October 1978):401–411.

5. An analysis of ethnogenesis among immigrants to the United States is Jonathan D. Sarna, "From Immigrants to Ethnics: Toward a New Theory of 'Ethnicization'," *Ethnicity* 5(1978):370–378.

6. One of the most influential statements of the situationalist perspective is Michael Hechter, *Internal Colonialism: The Celtic Fringe in British National Development, 1536–1966* (London: Routledge and Kegan Paul, 1975). Two useful reviews and critiques of this approach are William A. Douglass, "A Critique of Recent Trends in the Analysis of Ethnonationalism," *Ethnic and Racial Studies* 11(April 1988):192–206, and Oystein Gaasholt, "Traditional Culture as a Motive Force in Ethnic Autonomy Movements: The Case of Aboriginal Peoples" (Paper presented to the European Consortium for Political Research, Paris, April 1989). Both argue that the strength and persistence of communal movements cannot be understood without recognizing the importance of people's nonrational "affect" or "passions" for threatened cultural forms and lifeways.

7. Interpretations consistent with ours include those of James McKay, "An Exploratory Synthesis of Primordial and Mobilizationist Approaches to Ethnic Phenomena," *Ethnic and Racial Studies* 5(October 1982):395–420, and George M. Scott, Jr., "A Resynthesis of the Primordial and Circumstantial Approaches to Ethnic Group Solidarity: Towards an Explanatory Model," *Ethnic and Racial Studies* 13(April 1990):147–171. In this chapter and in chapter 3 we discuss the existence of multiple interests, factions, and leaders in most politicized communal groups.

8. Bernard Nietschmann, "The Third World War," *Cultural Survival Quarterly* 11, no. 3 (1987):1–16.

9. Gunnar Nielsson and Ralph Jones, "From Ethnic Category to Nation: Patterns of Political Modernization" (Paper presented to the International Studies Association, St. Louis, March 1988). An earlier phase of the study is reported in Gunnar P. Nielsson, "States and Nation-Groups: A Global Taxonomy," in Edward A. Tiryakian and Ronald Rogowski (eds.), *New Nationalisms of the Developed West: Toward Explanation* (Boston: Allen and Unwin, 1985). The 575 ethnic groups include 45 nations such as Iceland and the Koreas that (a) have their own states in which (b) minorities are less than 10 percent of the population.

10. Prepared and edited by the staff of the Minority Rights Group (Chicago and London: St. James Press, n.d. [1990]). The directory is compiled mainly from the Minority Rights Group's series of reports on specific groups and countries and does not claim to be comprehensive. It excludes some of the ethnoclasses and many of the communal contenders covered in the Minorities at Risk study, for example. Eighty-five of the 170 groups in the directory are included in the present study; the others either fall below our size threshold (one hundred thousand people or at least 1 percent of country population) or are not at risk. There also are differences in the ways groups are aggregated in the two studies: for example, the directory treats Amerindians of Latin America as one group whereas the Minorities at Risk study analyzes thirteen separate groups; and the directory distinguishes among Canada's Indians, Metis, and Inuits, whereas our data set treats them as a single group.

11. Alan Gewirth says that the most basic human rights are the rights to "the essential preconditions of action, such as life, physical integrity, and mental equilibrium"; *Human Rights: Essays on Justifications and Applications* (Chicago: University of Chicago Press, 1982), 55–56. Barbara Harff narrows the list of basic rights to the preservation of life itself: "The right to live . . . is an economic right and, by implication, a political one. In its absence, no other right is significant"; *Genocide and Human Rights: International Legal and Political Issues.* Monograph Series in World Affairs, vol. 20, book 3 (Denver, CO: University of Denver, 1984), 77. The question whether communal groups have *collective* rights—for example to cultural self-expression and autonomy—is more controversial. A wide-ranging assessment is Hurst Hannum, *Autonomy, Sovereignty, and Self-Determination: The Accommodation of Conflicting Rights* (Philadelphia: University of Pennsylania Press, 1990).

12. A preliminary list is reported in T. R. Gurr and James R. Scarritt, "Minorities Rights at Risk: A Global Survey," *Human Rights Quarterly* 11(1989):375–405.

13. Iran, Iraq, Turkey, and the USSR. The Kurdish minority in Syria falls below the one hundred thousand or 1 percent size threshold, according to our principal sources; other sources say it numbers as many as half a million. See Stephen C. Pelletiere, *The Kurds and Their Agas: An Assessment of the Situation in Northern Iraq* (Carlisle, PA: Strategic Studies Institute, U.S. Army War College, 1991), n. 24.

14. The scale could not be coded for five groups. The scores of each group are listed in Appendix tables A.1 to A.6 with the variable label COHERE.

15. Martin Heisler has made a persuasive case for treating both of these groups as politicized minorities (personal communication).

16. The results of the 1973 census were repudiated by the Nigerian federal government in 1975; the 1963 census has since been the only politically acceptable one. A new 1991 census was supposed to provide the basis for electoral districting that is essential to complete the transition to the democratic Third Republic.

17. See L. R. Smith, *The Aboriginal Population of Australia* (Canberra: Australian National University Press, 1980), 6–66. Aborigines were socially stigmatized until the 1950s, politically controversial in the 1960s, beneficiaries of major public assistance programs in the 1970s, and romanticized in the 1980s. It is not surprising that people of part-Aboriginal descent should acknowledge it as a primary identity at one time and deny it at another.

18. For Corsicans we calculate this datum from census reports and expert estimates. For most other regionally concentrated peoples we use estimates of the regional population.

19. Robert Clark, *The Basque Insurgents: ETA, 1952–80* (Madison: University of Wisconsin Press, 1984), 147.

20. For most African groups we use population estimates derived according to this procedure, which also is employed by Donald George Morrison et al., *Black Africa: A Comparative Handbook, Second Edition* (New York: Irvington Publishers and Paragon House, 1989).

21. A working definition of indigenous peoples is provided by Julian Burger, *Report from the Frontier: The State of the World's Indigenous Peoples* (London: Zed Press, 1987), 9. Indigenous people are those who meet several of these criteria: (a) they are descendants of original inhabitants of a territory that has been overcome by conquest; (b) they are nomadic and seminomadic peoples and practice a labor-intensive form of agriculture; (c) they do not have centralized political institutions but instead organize at the level of the community; (d) they share a common language, religion, culture, and a relationship to a particular territory, but they are subjugated by a dominant culture or society; and (e) they have a custodial and nonmaterialistic attitude toward the land and natural resources and want to pursue separate development. Scott McDonald identified indigenous peoples for this study by applying Burger's criteria to information in the Minorities at Risk files and data set.

22. The Maghrebins are first-generation immigrants from Islamic North Africa, the Beurs (the French word for Arab pronounced backward) are the citizen-descendants of Muslim immigrants; see chapter 6.

23. Contenders, sects, and ethnoclasses whose only advantages are economic (see Appendix tables A.1 to A.6, variable ADV80), almost invariably are subject to political restrictions by politically advantaged groups.

24. That Somalia is one of the few culturally and linguistically homogeneous countries in Africa has not spared it from deadly intergroup conflict. Rivalries among regionally concentrated clans and subclans have shaped Somali politics since independence in 1960; see Said S. Samatar, *Somalia: A Nation in Turmoil* (London: Minority Rights Group, 1991). We regard the clans as communal contenders. The secession of northern Somalia, though unrecognized internationally, has largely sheltered it from the anarchic violence that devastated the remainder of the country in 1991–92.

25. The reference to Indians in Sri Lanka is to the Indian Tamils whose ancestors were recruited as plantation workers in the late nineteenth and early twentieth centuries. They live in the central highlands and have played little part in the separatist civil war of the northern Tamils, whose ancestors have lived on the island for more than a millenium.

2. The Status of Minorities

1. The comparisons reported in tables 2.1, 2.3, and 2.4 show that indigenous peoples and ethnoclasses are about equally disadvantaged with respect to economic differentials and economic discrimination; indigenous peoples experience more ecological stress than any other type of group.

2. The Minorities at Risk study does not treat migrant workers or refugees as minorities unless they and their descendants are settled more or less permanently, and in substantial numbers, in the receiving country. Migrants in most Middle Eastern and African countries are subject to expulsion on political and economic grounds, as happened to Yemeni workers in Saudi Arabia in 1990 and most Palestinians in Kuwait in 1991.

3. Contemporary leaders can and do recreate and manipulate group traditions to mobilize political movements, but they cannot invent a credible belief in historical victimization out of whole cloth.

4. Politically advantaged minorities are excluded from most of the analyses reported in this chapter.

5. For discussion of procedures used for coding groups see chapter 1, especially n. 2.

6. The assignment of ratings from 1 to 4 on the summary scale does not necessarily correspond precisely to the numbers of dimensions on which differentials were observed. Coders were instructed that the category counts were guides to judgment, not firm rules. Coders of the African groups were particularly likely to judge that the differentials they identified were significant mainly for group leaders, not ordinary people, and therefore rated the group one or two categories lower than was indicated by the number of dimensions checked. The Minorities at Risk data set includes the codings on each specific dimension checked. They are not reported or analyzed here.

7. The cultural and religious rights of the Turkish minority were restored in 1990 by the first freely elected Bulgarian government. They gained politically in the October 1991 elections, prompting a backlash of resurgent anti-Turkish nationalism by other parties, but no renewal of old restrictions.

8. For historical overviews see Doug McAdam, *Political Process and the Development of Black Insurgency, 1930–1970* (Chicago: University of Chicago Press, 1982), and Hugh Davis Graham, *The Civil Rights Era* (New York: Oxford University Press, 1990).

9. Most population estimates for the Roma are conjectural. Efforts to settle and incorporate them were somewhat more effective in the Socialist states than in Western Europe, but their social deficit is pronounced throughout the continent as well as in Turkey and the USSR. See Grattan Puxon, *Roma: Europe's Gypsies*, revised ed. (London: Minority Rights Group, 1987).

10. The problems of population displacement associated with communal conflicts are far too severe and complex to be analyzed by using the Minorities at Risk data set. For global data see the *World Refugee Survey* issued annually by the U.S. Committee for Refugees (Washington, DC); for comparative analyses see Aristide Zolberg, Astri Suhrke, and Sergio Aguayo, *Escape from Violence: The Refugee Crisis in the Developing World* (New York: Oxford University Press, 1989), and Goeran Rystad (ed.), *The Uprooted: Forced Migration as an International Problem in the Post-War Era* (Lund: Lund University Press, 1990).

11. A perfect correlation is 1.000; the proportion of variance of one variable "explained" by another is the square of the coefficient, for example $.634^2 = .402$. By the standards of aggregate analysis this is a relatively strong relationship; correlations over .80 ($r^2 = .64$) are very strong. The statistical significance of correlation coefficients is indicated by asterisks, as explained in the note to table 2.5.

12. This may seem a heavy weight of interpretation to place on the results of analysis using one summary indicator of cultural difference. We also constructed an alternative indicator of minorities' ethnocultural traits (ETHDIF, not shown in the Appendix) that made finer distinctions based on differences in language, physical appearance, and religion. For all groups ETHDIF correlates .774 with CULDIF, and its global, regional, and group type correlations with differentials and discrimination show very similar patterns. The ETHDIF results provide supporting evidence for the interpretations.

3. "Give Us the Means"

1. The phrase "give us the means to the future" was used by Aboriginal poet and author Kath Walker in a July 1969 paper presented to the Federal Council for the Advancement of Aborigines and Torres Straits Islanders and is quoted by C. Jennett in "Ethnic Politics: Aboriginal Black Power and Land Rights Movement of the 1970s" (Paper presented to the 22nd Annual Conference of the Australasian Political Studies Association, Canberra, August 1980).

2. For evidence on inequalities among groups in the USSR see John M. Echols (ed.), "Racial and Ethnic Inequality: The Comparative Impact of Socialism," special issue of *Comparative Political Studies* 13, no. 4 (1980), and Ralph S. Clem, "The Ethnic Dimension of the Soviet Union," in Jerry G. Pankhurst and Michael Paul Sacks (eds.), *Contemporary Soviet Society: Sociological Perspectives* (New York: Praeger, 1980), 11–62.

3. Thirty-one of the Asian communal groups are classified as indigenous, ethnonationalist, or both (see Appendix table A.3).

4. Peoples such as the Tibetans and some of the Hmong who resisted cultural accommodation and political assimilation to Asian Communist regimes have been forcibly suppressed. In the early 1990s Laos and Cambodia repudiated doctrinaire communism; the implications for minority policies are not yet clear.

5. Copts have been subject to occasional episodes of harassment and violence by Egyptian Muslims, most recently in 1991–92, but state policy aims at evenhanded control of communal conflict.

6. The foregoing discussion follows from a reading of the evidence on a number of communal political movements and from theoretical analyses of the mobilization and actions of groups in conflict. Especially relevant are Lewis A. Coser's classic *The Functions of Social Conflict* (New York: Free Press, 1956); James DeNardo, *Power in Numbers* (Princeton: Princeton University Press, 1985); Mark Irving Lichbach, "Deterrence or Escalation in Repression and Dissent," *Journal of Conflict Resolution* 31(1987):266–297; T. David Mason, "Nonelite Response to State-Sanctioned Terror," *Western Political Quarterly* 42(1986):467–492; and Charles Tilly, *From Mobilization to Revolution* (Reading, MA: Addison-Wesley, 1978), chaps. 3 and 4.

7. U.S. Commission on Security and Cooperation in Europe, *Document of the Copenhagen Meeting of the Conference on the Human Dimension of the CSCE* (Washington, DC: U.S. Government Printing Office, 1990), 16–17.

8. The Kemalist revolutionaries of the 1920s established a strong assimilationist policy in response to foreign intervention that exploited minority and nationality tensions. Historically the politicized minorities of Anatolia have included Greeks (virtually all of whom fled in the 1920s), Armenians (still present in small numbers despite genocide and emigration), Azeris of eastern Kars Province (formerly under Russian rule), Circassians, and Tatars as well as Kurds. For an anthropological analysis see Peter Alford Andrews (ed.), *Ethnic Groups in the Republic of Turkey* (Wiesbaden: Dr. Ludwig Reichert Verlag, 1989), esp. 17–42.

9. These marginalized groups presumably had some grievances, but so far as we know from limited source materials, they did not have any associations pursuing communal interests or engage in protest or rebellion that expressed collective demands.

10. Five of the 120 groups expressing autonomist demands do not have a modern history of independence or political transfer. They include the Soviet Jews, whose ancient history helped justify contemporary demands for freedom to emigrate to Israel; the Tigreans of Ethiopia and the Tutsi of Rwanda, for whom "autonomy" is a surrogate for reassertion of their lost political influence; and the Arabs of Iran and Indian Tamils of Sri Lanka, whose demands were stimulated by external political conflicts.

11. Politically advantaged communal contenders are eliminated from all the following analyses. Their grievances are few, as shown in table 3.1, and cannot be attributed to collective disadvantages.

12. The construction of the indicator is described in T. R. Gurr, "Why Minorities Rebel: A Global Analysis of Communal Mobilization and Conflict Since 1945," *International Political Science Review* 14, no. 2 (April 1993):161–201, Appendix table 3.

13. A more nuanced analysis of the economic basis of ethnonationalism is provided by Walker Connor, "Eco- or Ethno-Nationalism?" *Ethnic and Racial Studies* 7(July 1984):342–359. Other useful analyses are Martin Heisler and B. Guy Peters, "Scarcity and the Management of Political Conflict in Multicultural Polities," *International Political Science Review* 4, no. 3 (1983):327–344; and Milton J. Esman, "Ethnic Politics and Economic Power," *Comparative Politics* 19(July 1987): 395–418.

14. Political and economic differentials have very similar correlates with demands for political rights (not shown in table 3.3). Cultural differentials, on the other hand, have little or no impact on demands for political rights, as shown in part 3 of the table.

15. The correlation between the severity of economic discrimination (ECODIS) and the intensity of economic grievances (ECOGR) among ethnoclasses is nil, but inspection of the data shows that this is a statistical artifact of constrained variation on both variables: ethnoclasses tend to have high scores on both ECODIS and ECOGR, and a

direct causal linkage between them is evident in the claims made by their representatives.

16. Albert O. Hirschman, *Exit, Voice and Loyalty: Responses to Decline in Firms, Organizations, and States* (Cambridge, MA: Harvard University Press, 1970).

4. When Minorities Rebel

1. Our estimate is based on information summarized by Herbert K. Tillema, "Foreign Overt Military Intervention in the Nuclear Age," *Journal of Peace Research* 26(1989):179–195.

2. For a more detailed analysis of the international dimensions of communal conflicts see T. R. Gurr, "The Internationalization of Protracted Communal Conflicts since 1945: Which Groups, Where, and How," in Manus I. Midlarsky (ed.), *The Internationalization of Communal Strife* (London: Routledge, 1992), 3–25.

3. From Barbara Harff and T. R. Gurr, "Toward Empirical Theory of Genocides and Politicides: Identification and Measurement of Cases since 1945," *International Studies Quarterly* 32(September 1988): 359–371.

4. Our tabulation from data in *World Refugee Survey 1992* (Washington, DC: U.S. Committee for Refugees, 1992), 32–34. Estimates of internally displaced people are fragmentary.

5. Group conflict scores for the 1980s, but not for the entire 1945–89 period, are given in the Appendix, tables A.13 to A.18. A similar procedure was used to score violent conflicts with other communal groups (COMCON in the Appendix). Intercommunal conflict is not analyzed here.

6. We also included situations in which a communal group took part in a civil or international war initiated by others, when it is clear that the group did so to advance its own interests. In the early 1980s the indigenous Miskitos and several related peoples joined in the Contra insurgency against Nicaragua's Sandinista government because they sought to reestablish their rights and regional autonomy, not because they wanted to overthrow the Managua regime.

7. We think that virtually all major protest campaigns and rebellions by communal groups have been identified and taken into account in the coding. Localized nonviolent protest by communal groups in the Third World, especially in the 1940s and 1950s, is more likely to have gone unreported in our sources. We made substantial use of code 9 (= no basis for judging) for groups and periods for which there was little information, but we converted these missing data to 0 for purposes of constructing the indicators used for regional and trend analyses.

8. Table 4.3 is organized on the logic of the Guttman scale: groups are counted according to their highest level of rebellion at any time between 1945 and 1989. For example, a group responsible for both a short-term terrorist campaign and a short-lived guerrilla war is counted under guerrilla war only. A group that supported both terrorism and a guerrilla war in three successive coding periods is counted under protracted war only.

9. The guerrilla and civil wars in this region occurred at the end of World War II in the Baltics and Ukraine. The only protracted terrorist campaign was waged by Croats, mainly from exile.

10. If recent conflicts are more likely to be reported than historical ones, then the upward trends are inflated. Our sources and coders suggest otherwise: while less detail is reported about some historical conflicts, even brief references usually are enough for coding the scales. Moreover our coders usually were satisfied that they had enough historical and journalistic information for reliable coding: data codes are no more often missing for earlier periods than for recent ones. In fact, missing data codes are somewhat more common for the 1985–89 period than for earlier ones, because at the time the coding was completed, we lacked current (1989) information for some groups. So the upward trend for the 1980s is, if anything, understated.

11. These are overlapping sets: eighteen escalated from previous protest only, three escalated from lower to higher rebellion only, and twenty-five did both. Another thirty-three episodes showed neither pattern.

12. Statistical evidence of contagion effects in the 1970s and 1980s is reported in T. R. Gurr, "Why Minorities Rebel: A Global Analysis of Communal Mobilization and Conflict since 1945," *International Political Science Review* 14, no. 2 (April 1993):161–201.

13. The dataset includes all indigenous Latin Americans in the fifteen countries where they are present in significant numbers. In four countries (Bolivia, Ecuador, Peru, Colombia) we distinguished and coded separately highland and lowland peoples, hence the data set profiles nineteen indigenous groups.

14. "Ecuador Indians March for Rights," *Christian Science Monitor*, April 24, 1992, 6.

15. In the mid-1970s the Maya of Guatemala began to be heavily recruited by revolutionary guerrilla organizations. The Miskitos were encouraged by the Contras to armed resistance against Sandinista efforts to impose revolutionary policies on their region. It has been suggested that the native peoples of Peru also qualify, since they provide part of the support base for the revolutionary war being waged by Sendero Luminoso. We disagree because (a) Sendero doctrine emphasizes revolutionary class struggle, it does not appeal to *indiginista* interests, and (b) the movement's tactics toward the indigenous peoples in its areas of operation are mainly coercive and terroristic.

16. In Brazil, Colombia, Costa Rica, Ecuador, Honduras (black Caribs), Nicaragua, Panama, Peru, and Venezuela. The only numerically significant minority at risk in Latin America that is not indigenous or of African origin is the Jewish community of Argentina.

5. Why Minorities Rebel

1. In T. R. Gurr, "Why Minorities Rebel: A Global Analysis of Communal Mobilization and Conflict Since 1945," *International Political Science Review* 14, no. 2 (April 1993):161–201.

2. The relative deprivation perspective is developed most fully in T. R. Gurr, *Why Men Rebel* (Princeton, NJ: Princeton University Press, 1970). It is similar to the "emergent human needs" theory used by Edward E. Azar and John W. Burton to account for protracted communal conflicts, in *International Conflict Resolution: Theory and Practice* (Sussex: Wheatsheaf Books, and Boulder, CO: Lynne Reinner, 1986). A comprehensive statement of the mobilization perspective is Charles Tilly, *From Mobilization to Revolution* (Reading, MA: Addison-Wesley, 1978). The approaches are compared and contrasted by James B. Rule, *Theories of Civil Violence* (Berkeley, CA: University of California Press, 1988), chaps. 6 and 7.

3. This debate is reviewed briefly in the opening pages of chapter 1. The quotation is from William A. Douglass, "A Critique of Recent Trends in the Analysis of Ethnonationalism," *Ethnic and Racial Studies* 11, no. 2 (1988):192.

4. Coalition formation can be as important for successful ethnopolitical movements as it is for revolutionary movements; see the comparative analysis in Jack A. Goldstone, T. R. Gurr, and Farrokh Moshiri (eds.), *Revolutions of the Late Twentieth Century* (Boulder, CO: Westview Press, 1991), chap. 14.

5. Salience of group identity and extent of group cohesion are equivalent, respectively, to Charles Tilly's concepts of CATNESS (the extent to which members of a group form a distinctive, self-conscious social category) and NETNESS (the extent to which they are linked into networks). See Tilly, *From Mobilization to Revolution*, 62–68 (see n. 2). The definition of mobilization used here is consistent with Tilly's analysis of the process of mobilization, in the same source, 69–91.

6. President Kennedy played a key role in prompting the Dutch withdrawal from Western New Guinea, now Irian Jaya, in 1962, which paved the way for the Indonesian takeover in 1963 that provoked a series of harshly repressed rebellions. In neither this instance nor the Indonesian invasion of East Timor in 1975, which also led to a protracted communal rebellion, did the United States openly oppose Indonesian policies of assimilation at gunpoint. Rather, developmental and military assistance continued, including provision of military equipment used against communal rebels.

7. The Angolan civil war of 1975–91 was a left-right struggle superimposed on an underlying communal conflict. The southern Ovimbundu people, represented by UNITA, relied on U.S. and South African assistance in a protracted conflict with the Soviet- and Cuban-supported government in Luanda, which was controlled by the Mbundu, eventually in coalition with the Bakongo. The Indian government initially intervened in the war betwen Sri Lanka and Tamil rebels as a peacekeeping force, with the reluctant agreement of the Sri Lankan government. Failing in their effort to disarm the Tamil rebels, the Indian troops became combatants but were no more successful at suppressing the insurgency than the Sri Lankan government, and they withdrew at that government's request.

8. The concept of political opportunity is commonly used in analyses of the origins and dynamics of social movements, for example, by William Gamson, *The Strategy of Social Protest* (Homewood, IL: Dorsey Press, 1975); Anthony Oberschall, *Social Conflict and Social Movements* (Englewood Cliffs, NJ: Prentice-Hall, 1973); and especially Tilly, *From Mobilization to Revolution* (see n. 2). It is less often used in the analysis of ethnopolitical conflict, an important exception being Doug McAdam, *Political Process and the Development of Black Insurgency, 1930–1970* (Chicago: University of Chicago Press, 1982). The concept needs more elaboration than we can give it in this macroanalysis.

9. This summary account is from T. R. Gurr, "Outcomes of Public Protest Among Australia's Aborigines," *American Behavioral Scientist* 26, no. 3 (1983):360. For more detail see M. A. Franklin, *Black and White Australians* (Melbourne: Heinemann Educational, 1976), 209–212.

10. The terms *diffusion* and *contagion* sometimes are used interchangeably. A conceptual analysis of these and other international effects on internal conflicts is William Foltz, "External Causes," in Barry M. Schutz and Robert O. Slater (eds.), *Revolution and Political Change in the Third World* (Boulder, CO: Lynn Reinner, 1990). A recent empirical study of contagion effects is Stuart Hill and Donald Rothchild, "The Contagion of Political Conflict in Africa and the World," *Journal of Conflict Resolution* 30(December 1986):716–735.

11. From Franke Wilmer, *From Time Immemorial: The Indigenous Voice in World Politics* (Newbury Park, CA: Sage Publications, in press).

12. A number of contemporary states besides the USSR and Yugoslavia are candidates for political deconstruction. By the time this book is published Czechoslovakia will have fissioned peacefully into two independent republics. Others, in descending order of immediacy, are Ethiopia, Canada, Sudan, Iraq, Sri Lanka, South Africa, India, Burma, and Pakistan. In Canada, and possibly Ethiopia and South Africa, the next steps in the process are likely to be peaceful; all the others are or have been wracked by protracted communal wars.

13. As reported in Gurr, "Why Minorities Rebel" (see n. 1), based on data for 227 groups. The scope of state power is measured as of 1986; the rate of change in state power is measured across the period 1960–86. Protest and rebellion are measured using 1980s codings.

14. Israel and South Africa are not included among the democracies in our analyses, or in these generalizations, because large communal groups under each country's control have been denied political and economic rights. The two states are best characterized as quasi-democracies.

15. The prevalence of protest over rebellion is a characteristic of all kinds of conflict in democracies; for evidence and interpretation see T. R. Gurr, "Protest and Rebellion in the 1960s: The United States in World Perspective," in Gurr (ed.), *Violence in America*, vol. 2: *Protest, Rebellion, Reform* (Newbury Park, CA: Sage Publications, 1989), 111–115. On the problematic consequences of the recent wave of democratization see Samuel P. Huntington, "Democracy's Third Wave," *Journal of Democracy* 2(Spring 1991):12–34.

16. The breakup of the USSR has transformed some communal conflicts, such as the one between Armenia and Azerbaijan, into interstate conflicts; and has intensifed hostilities between newly dominant groups and Russian and other non-national minorities in each of the new states. For a thorough analysis see chapter 7.

6. Western Democracies and Japan

1. On this and other distinctive traits of ethnicity in western societies see Martin O. Heisler, "Ethnicity and Ethnic Relations in the Modern West," in Joseph V. Montville (ed.), *Conflict and Peacemaking in Multiethnic Societies* (Lexington, MA: Lexington Books, 1990), 21–52; and Barbara S. Heisler and Martin O. Heisler, "Citizenship—Old, New and Changing: Inclusion, Exclusion and Limbo for Ethnic

Groups and Migrants in the Modern Democratic State," in Juergen Fijalkowski et al. (eds.), *Dominant National Cultures and Ethnic Identities* (Berlin: Free University of Berlin, 1991), 91–128.

2. For evidence on public backlash against communal and ethnic terrorism see Jeffrey Ian Ross and T. R. Gurr, "Why Terrorism Subsides: A Comparative Study of Terrorism in Canada and the United States," *Comparative Politics* 21(July 1989):405–426.

3. Jurg Steiner, "Power-Sharing: Another Swiss 'Export Product'?" in Montville (ed.), *Conflict and Peacemaking*, 107–114 (see n. 1).

4. Some small groups that meet the general criteria, such as the Ainu, fall below our 1 percent or one hundred thousand size threshold. Others (e.g., the Inuit) are incorporated in aggregate groupings: native peoples in Canada are treated as a single group, as they are in the United States. The Scandinavian Saami are counted as a single group; so are the Roma, who are dispersed widely throughout Western Europe.

5. Belgium has a history of divisive communal conflict between French and Flemish speakers, which was settled but not entirely resolved by federalization in the 1970s. See Martin O. Heisler, "Managing Ethnic Conflict in Beligum," *Annals* 433(September 1977):32–46; and Liesbet Hooghe, *A Leap in the Dark: Nationalist Conflict and Federal Reform in Belgium* (Ithaca, NY: Cornell University Press, 1991). Heisler contends that the civil and political rights of 1.2 million French speakers who do not live in Wallonia have been curtailed (personal communication).

6. A few groups are cross-classified, for example, the Catholics of Northern Ireland, who in addition to being ethnonationalists are a religious minority and have some ethnoclass traits. Hispanics in the United States and its territories include Puerto Rican nationalists, but the vast majority of Hispanics live in the continental United States and have the status and aspirations of ethnoclasses. For purposes of this chapter each such group is classified with the minorities with which it has most in common.

7. The data for these and most of the following comparisons are given in the Appendix.

8. This comparison is based on the analysis of the Minorities at Risk project's indicator of ethnocultural differences, which is not shown in the Appendix. See chapter 2, n. 12.

9. The five are the Roma; immigrant workers in France, Switzerland, and Germany; and Koreans in Japan.

10. Economic discrimination is coded high (3 or 4) for blacks and Northern Irish Catholics in the United Kingdom; the Roma; Afro-Arabs in France; Muslims in Greece; Koreans in Japan; and native peoples in Canada.

11. The two lowest categories on the rebellion scale are sporadic terrorism (= 1) and campaigns of terrorism (= 2). None of the democratic minorities had higher scores on this indicator in any postwar period.

12. The average is calculated from conflict profiles coded for successive five-year periods; lags are thus rounded to the nearest five years. In two of the fifteen cases the first evidence of nonviolent and violent political action is coded for the same five-year period; narrative information shows that in both cases (the Jurassiens and the French Canadians), nonviolent political action was under way for several years before the first bombs exploded.

13. Most Roma in Western Europe make several moves each year, usually for economic reasons, and rarely are encouraged to settle permanently. The socialist regimes of Eastern Europe used offers of jobs and housing, and coercion, to settle significant numbers. See Grattan Puxon, *Roma: Europe's Gypsies* (London: Minority Rights Group Report No. 14, revised 1987 ed.).

14. Summarized in Joel Kotkin, "Europe Won't Work," *Washington Post*, September 15, 1991, C4.

15. For references on ethnogenesis see chapter 1, n. 3 and n. 5. A country study of ethnogenesis in Europe is Rinus Penninx, "Ethnic Groups in the Netherlands: Emancipation or Minority Group-Formation?" *Ethnic and Racial Studies* 12(January 1989):47–62. The process is not confined to Western Europe; it is well under way among the hundreds of thousands of Caribbeans and Africans who have migrated to Canadian cities since the liberalization of immigration policies in the late 1960s; see "Quebec's New Minority Issue: Blacks Charge Bias," *New York Times*, August 16, 1991.

16. Ethnocentrism and antiforeign prejudice are present in all European societies, including the Netherlands; see survey studies by Peter Scheepers, Albert Felling, and Jan Peters, "Ethnocentrism in The Netherlands: A Typological Analysis," *Ethnic and Racial Studies* 12(July 1989):290–308; and by Louk Hagendoorn and Joseph Hraba, "Foreign, Different, Deviant, Seclusive and Working Class: Anchors to an Ethnic Hierarchy in The Netherlands," *Ethnic and Racial Studies* 12(October 1989):441–467. But violence and open discrimination against foreigners are much less pronounced in the Lowlands and Scandinavia than elsewhere.

17. This section incorporates materials from Michael Banton, *Promoting Racial Harmony* (Cambridge, UK: Cambridge University Press, 1985); John Benyon and John Solomos (eds.), *The Roots of Urban Unrest* (Oxford: Pergamon Press, 1987); Louis Clairborne and others, *Race and Law in Britain and the United States*, Minority Rights Group Report 22, 3d ed. (London: Minority Rights Group, 1983); Brian D. Jacobs,

Black Politics and Urban Crisis in Britain (Cambridge, UK: Cambridge University Press, 1986); Tony Kushner and Kenneth Lunn (eds.), *The Politics of Marginality: Race, The Radical Right and Minorities in Twentieth Century Britain* (London: Frank Cass, 1991); Vaughan Robinson, *Transients, Settlers, and Refugees: Asians in Britain* (Oxford: Clarendon Press, 1986); John Solomos, *Black Youth, Racism and the State: The Politics of Ideology and Policy* (Cambridge, UK: Cambridge University Press, 1988); and a number of scholarly articles and news items.

18. Alison M. Bowes, Jacqui McCluskey, and Duncan F. Sim, "Racism and Harassment of Asians in Glasgow," *Ethnic and Racial Studies* 13(January 1990):71–91.

19. In January 1992, Muslim militants convened a "parliament" in London that rejected government policies of racial integration and urged a campaign of civil disobedience. "Muslim Parliament Divides Britons," *Christian Science Monitor*, January 8, 1992, 3.

20. *Afro-Arab* is our word. In French discourse, people of Muslim North African birth are called Maghrebins, French citizens of North African descent are Beurs (the French word for Arab pronounced backwards) or Franco-Maghrebins. Substantial numbers of black Africans from the Senegal basin also live and work in France. All these peoples are sometimes characterized by the catchall word Muslims.

21. Important comparative studies of the status of immigrant workers in Europe include Stephen Castles and Godula Kosack, *Immigrant Workers and Class Structure in Western Europe*, 2d ed. (New York: Oxford University Press, 1985), and Zig Layton-Henry, *The Political Rights of Migrant Workers in Western Europe* (London: Sage Publications, 1990). Sources on the current status of the Maghrebins include Miriam Feldblum, "Who's Wearing the Veil? 'Franco-Maghrebins' and Ethnic Politics in France" (Paper presented at the Annual Meeting of the American Political Science Association, San Francisco, August-September 1990); a series of papers by William Safran, including "The French State and Ethnic Minority Cultures: Policy Dimensions and Problems," in J. R. Rudolph, Jr., and R. J. Thompson (eds.), *Ethnoterritorial Politics, Policy, and the Western World* (Boulder, CO: Lynne Rienner, 1989); and correspondence and other materials from William Safran, Martin O. Heisler, and Sarah V. Wayland.

22. North African citizens living legally in France number about 1.5 million, plus 125,000 black Africans, to which we have added an estimated 200,000 to 300,000 illegal Maghrebin immigrants. See Ronald Koven, "Muslim Immigrants and French Nationalists, *Society* 29(May-June 1992):25–33, and Kotkin, "Europe Won't Work," C4 (see n. 14).

23. Catherine Withol de Wenden, "Du culturel au politique," *Cahiers du CIEMI*, no. 1 (January 1988):43–63.

24. Estimates of France's Muslim citizens range from 1 million (Feldblum, "Who's Wearing the Veil," 10) to 1.5 million (Koven, "Muslim Immigrants," 26). Martin O. Heisler suggests (personal communication) that the Beurs and other French citizens of Third World origin also meet our criteria for minorities at risk.

25. This interpretation is drawn from a book manuscript in preparation by Marc Howard Ross, Department of Political Science, Bryn Mawr College, "Managing Conflicts Constructively," chapter 1. Another analytic account is Feldblum, "Who's Wearing the Veil," 11–24.

26. Important comparative analyses of European ethnonationalism and responses to it include Edward A. Tiryakian and Ronald Rogowski (eds.), *New Nationalisms of the Developed West* (Boston: Allen and Unwin, 1985); Mark O. Rousseau and Raphael Zariski, *Regionalism and Regional Devolution in Comparative Perspective* (Westport, CT: Praeger, 1987); Rudolph and Thompson (eds.), *Ethnoterritorial Politics* (see n. 21); and Claire Palley and others, *Minorities and Autonomy in Western Europe* (London: Minority Rights Group, 1991).

27. Tiryakian and Rogowski (eds.), *New Nationalisms of the Developed West*, 376–377 (see n. 26).

28. On the Basque autonomy movement and the governmental response to it, see the writings of Robert P. Clark, including *The Basque Insurgents: ETA, 1952–1980* (Madison: University of Wisconsin Press, 1984); and "Spanish Democracy and Regional Autonomy: The Autonomous Community System and Self-Government for the Ethnic Homelands," in Rudolph and Thompson, *Ethnoterritorial Politics* (see n. 21). A useful empirical study is Goldie Shabad and Francisco Jose Llera Ramo, "The Effects of Political Violence in a Democratic State: Basque Terrorism in Spain" (Paper presented at the Annual Meeting of the American Political Science Association, Atlanta, 1989). The status of ETA in spring 1992 is analyzed by William Drozdiak, "Avowed 'Decapitation' of Basque Group in Doubt as Olympics Near," *Washington Post*, May 4, 1992.

29. Detailed studies of Breton nationalism include Jack E. Reece, *The Bretons Against France* (Chapel Hill: University of North Carolina Press, 1977); and M. J. C. O'Callaghan, *Separatism in Brittany* (Trewolsta, UK: Dyllansow Truran, 1983). This section also makes use of Michael Keating, "The Rise and Decline of Micronationalism in Mainland France," *Political Studies* 33(1985):1–18; recent news articles; and observations by William Safran (personal communication).

30. The Socialist government's major shift in national policy toward all ethnic and communal minorities is analyzed in William Safran, "The Mitterand Regime and Its Policies of Ethnocultural Accommodation," *Comparative Politics* 18, no. 1 (October 1985):41–35; and, by the same author, "Minorities, Ethnics, and Aliens: Pluralist Politics in the Fifth Republic," in Paul Godt (ed.), *Policy-Making in France: From de Gaulle to Mitterand* (London and New York: Pinter Publishers, 1989), 186–190.

31. The bombings rarely do serious damage or injury and commonly have been targeted at symbols of the large numbers of non-Corsicans who have emigrated to the island, many of them resettled *pieds noirs* from Algeria. See Peter Savigear, "Corsica: Regional Autonomy or Violence?" *Conflict*, no. 149 (1983):2–16; and the listings for Corsica in Henry W. Degenhardt (ed.), *Revolutionary and Dissident Movements: An International Guide*, 2d ed. (Harlow, UK: Longman House, 1988).

32. Historical background is provided by Peter J. Katzenstein, "Ethnic Political Conflict in South Tyrol," in Milton J. Esman (ed.), *Ethnic Conflict in the Western World* (Ithaca, NY: Cornell University Press, 1977). More current information comes from news accounts and political chronologies such as Degenhardt, *Revolutionary and Dissident Movements* (see n. 31).

33. On the emergence of modern Québec see Kenneth McRoberts and Dale Postgate, *Quebec: Social Change and Political Crisis*, rev. ed. (Toronto: McClelland and Stewart, 1984); on separatism, William D. Coleman, *The Independence Movement in Quebec 1945–1980* (Toronto: University of Toronto Press, 1984); on the Front de Liberation de Québec, Louis Fournier, *FLQ: The Anatomy of an Underground Movement* (Toronto: NC Press, 1984); on the decline of terrorism, Ross and Gurr, "Why Terrorism Subsides" (see n. 2); on recent political and constitutional developments, Eloise Forgette Malone, "Canada: The Independence Movement and Internal Security" (Paper presented at the Annual Meeting of the American Political Science Association, Washington, DC, 1991).

34. In the slogan "Je me souviens" (I remember), which supposedly echoed across the Plains of Abraham after the French lost the decisive battle for Quebec there on September 13, 1759.

35. The five groupings analyzed in this study comprise many distinct clans and tribes that are identity groups in their own right. There are more than four hundred recognized tribes in the United States alone.

36. On the politics of Aboriginal protest and policy see T. R. Gurr, "Outcomes of Public Protest Among Australia's Aborigines," *American Behavioral Scientist* 26, no. 3 (1983):353–373.

37. The numbers of people identifying their race to census takers as Native American between 1970 and 1990 far outpaced natural increase. In effect it has become more acceptable to self-identify as a

Native American. Identification is not the same as descent: surveys in 1979 and 1980 found that seven million to ten million Americans claimed some indigenous heritage. See "More Americans Declaring Indian Identity," *Washington Post*, February 11, 1991, 1, 4. The 180,000 native Hawaiians are not included in this or most analyses of native peoples because of their different culture (Polynesian), distinct political history (more or less voluntary annexation to the United States in 1898), and status (though somewhat disadvantaged economically, they do not qualify as a minority at risk).

38. Douglas Emory did background research for this section. A general history and analysis of white-Indian relations in the United States is Stephen Cornell, *The Return of the Native: American Indian Political Resurgence* (New York: Oxford University Press, 1988). On the history of federal policy toward Native Americans see American Indian Policy Review Commission, *Final Report* (Washington, DC: U.S. Government Printing Office, 1977). On the American Indian Movement see Robert Burnette and John Koster, *The Road to Wounded Knee* (New York: Bantam, 1974). Recent analyses of the political and economic status of native peoples in Canada are J. Anthony Long and Menno Boldt (eds.), *Governments in Conflict: Provinces and Indian Nations in Canada* (Toronto: University of Toronto Press, 1988); and Bruce Alden Cox (ed.), *Native People, Native Lands: Canadian Indians, Inuit and Metis* (Toronto: Oxford University Press, 1988).

39. This summary is based mainly on news accounts, the most important of them "Canada's Native Uprising," *Christian Science Monitor*, October 18, 1990, 10–11; "Ontario Recognizes Indian Self-Government," *New York Times International*, August 7, 1991; and "Accord to Give the Eskimos Control of a Fifth of Canada," *New York Times*, December 17, 1991, 1, 7. In May 1992 a plebiscite in the Northwest Territories approved the separation of the Nunavut region.

40. For an overview see Mervyn Jones, *The Sami of Lapland* (London: Minority Rights Group, Report No. 55, 1982). Oystein Gaasholt of the University of Aarhus, Denmark, provided supplementary information for this case.

41. See the section on "Ethnoclasses," earlier in this chapter, and the opinion surveys cited in Charles F. Andrain and Michael P. Byron, "Political Attitudes toward Ethnic Tolerance in the European Community" (Paper presented to the International Society for Political Psychology, San Francisco, July 1992).

42. Jean Marie Domenach, cited by Joel Kotkin, "Europe Won't Work," 1991, n. 13. For a more thorough analysis see William Safran, "Islamization in Western Europe: Political Consequences and Historical Parallels," *Annals of the American Academy of Political and Social Science* 485(1986): 98–112.

7. Eastern Europe

The author thanks William Reisinger, Vicki Hesli, Kristen Hill Maher, Robert Grey, Donald Smith, and Ted Robert Gurr for their reactions to earlier versions of the manuscript of this chapter.

1. Functional linkages between and among individuals are, in the aggregate, a complex network of personal connections that binds human beings and their functional organizations into civil societies and polities. It is perhaps ironic that Stalin's strategy of social change focused on severing interpersonal linkages and substituting state-controlled organizational linkages to impose political controls. The present situation involves the weakening or severing of organizational linkages and the strengthening of personal linkages. It is the individual's personal linkages that are essentially political and potentially mobilizable.

2. The distinction between client and agent regimes differentiates between the principal benefactors of those regime types. The client regime is defined as "one dependent on the patronage or protection of another," implying that the exogenous patron's interests take precedence in regime decisions. The agent regime is defined as "one that acts for or as a representative of another," implying that the regime is primarily responsive to its (endogenous) citizens' interests. Definitions are from *The American Heritage Dictionary*, 2d ed.

3. The old, centralized Soviet Union has been reformed as the new, decentralized Commonwealth of Independent States. Yugoslavia is now the official name of what is little more than a truncated Greater Serbia.

4. For a theoretical treatment of this issue, see Robert O. Keohane, *After Hegemony: Cooperation and Discord in the World Political Economy* (Princeton: Princeton University Press, 1984). While Keohane's work was not originally intended to be applied in analysis of the breakdown of Socialist regimes, its arguments are very helpful in understanding the alternatives of regime transformation and in anticipating what might follow the loss of Soviet hegemony in this region.

5. The Kazakhs and Uighurs of the People's Republic of China are not considered in the analyses of this chapter.

6. Actual policies toward ethnic and religious minorities, however, have periodically deviated from the professed official line, and usually for political or strategic purposes. The Stalin regime especially showed great interest in accelerating the "natural" assimilation of members of ethnic subcultures into the Soviet (Russian) superculture, often forcefully.

7. Although only four groups in this region are coded as ethnoclasses, recent changes are likely to promote the politicization of many more such minority groups in the near future; see pp. 204–206.

8. Uzbekistan is the least homogeneous (71 percent), followed by Turkmenistan (72 percent), Belarus (78 percent), Lithuania (80 percent), Russia (82 percent), Azerbaijan (83 percent), Romania (89 percent), Slovenia (90 percent), Bulgaria (91 percent), Armenia (93 percent), Albania (97 percent), Poland (98 percent), and Hungary (99 percent). The data on the countries of Eastern Europe are compiled from IU. V. Bromlei (ed.), *Narody Mira: Historico-etnograficheskii spravochnik* (Moscow: *Sovetskaya Entsyklopediya*, 1988); the data on the former republics of the USSR are from the 1989 All-Union census (see annex 1); the data on Yugoslavia are from the 1981 All-Union census (see annex 2).

9. The percentages of the primary ethnic groups in Kazakhstan are—Kazakhs 40 percent, Russians 38 percent.

10. The ethnic group percentages for the trinational state of Bosnia and Hercegovina are Bosnian Muslims (40 percent), Serbs (32 percent), and Croats (18 percent).

11. In mid-1992, Yugoslavia comprised the Serbian, Macedonian, and Montenegrin autonomous republics and the Vojvodina (Hungarian) and Kosovo (Albanian) autonomous regions within Serbia (although the autonomy of Kosovo was suspended in July 1990). The Macedonian Republic claimed independence in 1992 but was refused recognition by the European Community until it met certain criteria, including changing its name; Greece claimed title infringement over the use of the term "Macedonia." A referendum on independence was held in Kosovo in May 1992, leading to an immediate Serbian military buildup in that province; the Albanians, unlike the Croats and Bosnian Muslims, are an unarmed minority.

12. The majority percentage and those of the primary ethnic contenders in the Commonwealth of Independent States are as follows: Russians 52 percent, Ukrainians 16 percent, and Turkic and Mongol peoples 16 percent.

13. The term *korenizatsiya* or indigenization refers to the twin policies of educating and socializing the populace through their own native language and customs, and training loyal cadres of indigenous elites to assume regional administrative responsibilities.

14. Members of the dominant (Russian) ethnic group were not required and rarely made the effort to acquire a second language, thus remaining monolingual even when living outside the Russian republic. Despite official education policies designed to promote Russian language usage most members of the non-Russian minorities living in their national homelands rejected bilingualism in favor of retaining their native language. See M. N. Guboglo, "The General and Particular in the Development of the Linguistic Life of Soviet Society" and

"Factors and Tendencies of the Development of Bilingualism among the Russian Population Living in the Union Republics," in Martha B. Olcott (ed.), *The Soviet Multi-National State* (Armonk, NY: M. E. Sharpe, 1990).

15. As an integral part of the *perestroika* reforms, most of the ethnic republics passed laws in 1989 establishing the official language (or languages) of each of the republics to be that of the main ethnic group (or groups); Russian was designated by the central government on April 24, 1990, to be the official language of internationality or inter-republic communication.

16. Serbia controls two autonomous provinces, Vojvodina in the north and Kosovo in the south.

17. The General League of Jewish Workingmen in Lithuania, Poland, and Russia, commonly known as the Bund, was very active in the Marxist opposition to the Russian autocracy at the turn of the century. The Bund was affiliated with the Russian Social Democratic Labor party but disagreed with the Bolshevik faction's policy on the Jewish question. Ethnic Jews were also very active and prominent among the revolutionary Bolshevik leadership: in August 1917, six of the twenty-one members of the Bolshevik Central Committee were ethnic Jews, including Trotsky, Kamenev, and Zinoviev. Stalin was able to effectively eliminate the Jewish influence in the party in the early years of his reign. See Zvi Y. Gitelman, *Jewish Nationality and Soviet Politics: The Jewish Sections of the CPSU, 1917–1930* (Princeton: Princeton University Press, 1972); and Louis Rappoport, *Stalin's War Against the Jews* (New York: Free Press, 1990).

18. On July 17, 1992, Czechoslovakia succumbed to the wave of nationalism unleashed by the Gorbachev reforms. On that day, a declaration of sovereignty by the Slovak Republic made the demise of the Czech and Slovak union official, effective January 1, 1993.

19. Six transmigrant groups are coded at risk: Turks in Bulgaria, Hungarians in Czechoslovakia, Hungarians and Germans in Romania, and Germans and Tatars in the former Soviet Union.

20. Lenin himself characterized the Russian state in this way. He abhorred the oppression of the subject peoples of the Empire as much as he abhorred the oppression of the Russian working classes.

21. The Albanians in Yugoslavia and the Turks in Bulgaria are historical transmigrant ethnic groups that are also Muslim.

22. The most noted arguments in the debates among the European Marxists were voiced by Karl Kautsky (Germany), Karl Renner and Otto Bauer (Austria), Rosa Luxemburg (Germany and Poland), and V. I. Lenin.

23. See V. I. Lenin, "Imperialism, the Highest Stage of Capitalism," in *Collected Works*, vol. 22 (Moscow: Foreign Languages Publishing

House, 1962). Lenin's general argument is that the resource demands of the capitalist industrial mode of production made necessary ever larger economic bases for the state. The nationality-based political identity of the nation-state rationalized the exclusion of other-nationality outgroups, causing the internal economic dynamic toward expansion of the material base to be expressed in imperialist—that is, dominant-versus-submissive—relations between social groups over the control of material resources. Because these relations were based in inequity, oppression of the less powerful groups was necessary for the implementation of the industrial mode. Existent ethnic groupings were simply too small to provide the necessary material foundation for the transition to an industrial mode. Imperialism was a short-term solution to this problem in that its system of oppression stimulated intergroup hostility rather than fostering the social cohesion necessary for systemic maintenance.

24. I have written extensively about this early twentieth-century debate in an unpublished manuscript, "Soviet Nationalities Policy: A Theoretical Account of Lenin's Final Victory," May 1990. See n. 22 for a list of major voices in the debate.

25. Lenin's principle of national self-determination first came under heavy attack at the Eighth Congress of the Russian Communist Party (Bolshevik) in 1919. Bukharin took up Stalin's argument of limiting the principle of self-determination to the national proletariat, leading to a lengthy debate. Lenin's argument was that only the national proletariat itself could objectively and reliably distinguish between the two faces of national self-determination: bourgeois nationalism and proletarian internationalism. Lenin's argument eventually prevailed, however tenuously, only by the strength of his powers of persuasion. Lenin's defense of this principle was again called on during the events of 1922, the so-called Georgian affair and the drafting of the Union Treaty.

26. V. I. Lenin (1922), "On the Establishment of the USSR", in *Collected Works*, vol. 42 (Moscow: Progress Publishers, 1969).

27. Dictated to a personal secretary by a stricken Lenin in 1922. Translation provided in an afterword titled "Lenin's Article on the National Question (In Three Parts)," in Bertram D. Wolfe, *Khrushchev and Stalin's Ghost* (New York: Frederick A. Praeger, 1957), 271–272.

28. Cultural autonomy, or cultural-national autonomy, differs fundamentally from national self-determination over the relationship of a people with the territory they inhabit. In Stalin's own words (January 1913), under a policy of cultural autonomy ". . . [the state] would represent not a union of autonomous regions, but a union of autonomous nationalities, constituted irrespective of territory." He goes on to explain, "It means . . . that the national institutions which are created . . . are to have jurisdiction only over 'cultural,' not 'political' questions."

See J. V. Stalin, "Marxism and the National Question," in *Works*, vol. 2 (Moscow: Foreign Languages Publishing House, 1953), 332. In this work, commissioned by Lenin, Stalin condemns the incompatibility of this policy with the stated policy of the party (i.e., national self-determination). The civil war experience and the use of the border-lands as staging areas for campaigns by the counterrevolutionary White forces supported in part by foreign powers appear to have changed Stalin's position in this matter. As Gerhard Simon has explained, "Although Stalin agreed with Lenin that, as in any other nation, Russia's fringe regions had the inalienable right to secede from Russia, he also explicitly declared that *after* the socialist revolution and in the interests of the masses, he would consider the demand for secession of the fringe regions an altogether counterrevolutionary demand." Gerhard Simon, *Nationalism and Policy Toward the Nationalities in the Soviet Union* (Boulder, CO: Westview Press, 1991), 21. Stalin's original (1920) statement can be found in J. V. Stalin, "The Policy of the Soviet Government on the National Question in Russia," in *Works*, vol. 4 (Moscow: Foreign Languages Publishing House, 1953), 366.

29. Many disagree with the claim that Lenin favored federalist policies, because Lenin continually insisted that the vanguard party must remain a unitary organization, resisting all attempts to nationalize it. However, he also insisted that the policy of self-determination dictated a federal structure in political administration (i.e., the state). The claim of Lenin's commitment to democratic process is perhaps even more controversial, but this claim is not essential to the present argument and therefore will not be defended here.

30. A comparison between the censuses of the USSR and Yugoslavia illustrates this point: the USSR census does not include an option for the identification "Soviet" in its ethnic classification; the Yugoslavian census allows respondents to choose either the identification "Yugoslav" or none at all, in addition to ethnic classifications.

31. See, for example, Michael Kirkwood (ed.), *Language Planning in the Soviet Union* (London: Macmillan, 1989).

32. Of the deported ethnic groups, all were politically rehabilitated and returned to their ancestral lands as part of Khrushchev's de-Stalinization campaign, except the Crimean Tatars, the Germans, and the Meskhetians. These groups have been petitioning the central government for reinstatement of their former status and the right to return to their former lands.

33. Gorbachev, like Lenin, was never an advocate of national independence as the preferred expression of self-determination, as many western analysts have pointed out. His preferred strategy was to change the relations of groups within the Union so that the severing of political ties between groups was not deemed necessary or efficacious. He did oversee All-Union legislation that provided legal provisions for secession from the Union, something for which no other modern state makes similar provisions. He demanded, however, that any separation take place according to the law and insisted that the law and the Union Treaty be upheld, by force if necessary.

The old Russian system was not prepared for the transition to socialism in 1917, as Lenin was well aware. Both Lenin and Trotsky were agreed on the impossibility of the fledgling Soviet state attaining socialism without outside assistance from the revolutionary states in the more advanced capitalist states of Western Europe. Russia was the least likely candidate for a successful socialist revolution. When it became clear that the revolution would not be joined by the proletariat in the capitalist states, Lenin instituted the New Economic Policy, by which he intended to promote a state-controlled and regulated capitalist economy. Stalin advocated a continuation of the policies of war communism as the most efficient path to socialist development. Lenin strictly opposed the forced transformation of civil society; Trotsky continued to oppose Stalin's policies from his exile in Mexico.

34. This strategy is reminiscent of that symbolized by Lenin's famous exhortation, "All power to the Soviets!" If the old system resists necessary reform or is incapable of such reform, there must be an alternative system that both challenges the prevailing order and stands able to assume authority if the old system fails.

35. Of course, a conservative reaction was triggered, resulting in the unsuccessful August 1991 coup. The failure of that attempt points to the relative success of the attempt to legitimize the reform process within the Soviet system. The current post-Communist, democratic reforms in the former republics of the USSR are being led by the former opposition *within* the party (i.e., reform Communists), not by the political opposition *to* the party.

36. A paradox is evident in the relative development of these indigenous groups. In comparison with other groups in their political systems, these groups are relatively disadvantaged, but they are relatively advantaged in comparison with other referent indigenous groups outside the borders of their political systems. This development paradox accentuates the impact of environmental context and resource endowments on the developmental capabilities of groups as one of the determinants of group differences.

37. Kisangani N. Emizet and Vicki L. Templin, "The Disposition to Secede: An Analysis of the Soviet Case" (Paper presented at the Annual Meeting of the Midwest Political Science Association, Chicago, April 18–21, 1991); Donald L. Horowitz, *Ethnic Groups in Conflict* (Berkeley: University of California Press, 1985).

38. This situation could change dramatically as a result of the resurgence of the political role of Islam among the minorities we coded as indigenous peoples and militant sects. The establishment of Islamic states would likely make the republics of Central Asia more separatist vis-à-vis the Slavic core.

39. These eleven groups are the Slovaks in Czechoslovakia; the Estonians, Latvians, and Lithuanians of the Baltics; the Armenians, Georgians, Ukrainians, and Moldavians in the USSR; and the Croats, Serbs, and Slovenes of Yugoslavia.

40. These nine groups are the Azerbaijanis, Chechens-Ingushes, Karachays-Balkars, Kazakhs, Kyrgyz, Tajiks, Turkmens, and Uzbeks of the USSR and the Albanians of Yugoslavia.

41. A seminal work from this perspective is Immanuel Wallerstein, *The Modern World System* (New York: Academic Press, 1974).

42. See, for example, Valerie Bunce, "The Empire Strikes Back: The Evolution of the Eastern Bloc from a Soviet Asset to a Soviet Liability," *International Organization* 39, no.1 (Winter 1985):1–46.

43. All the ethnic republics of the USSR became independent with the official dissolution of the Soviet Union in December 1991 (except the three Baltic republics whose independence was recognized by the Soviet government in September 1991). Their relationships with the successor Commonwealth of Independent States remain uncertain as of early 1993.

44. The Lechinskaya *raion* is inhabited primarily by Kurds and was once known as Red Kurdistan. The Kurds have become involved in the regional conflict primarily as a matter of self-protection; Armenia is courting the Kurds in hopes of securing a friendly link to the beseiged Nagorno-Karabakh enclave.

45. The Soviet regime set up a short-lived, independent Azerbaijani state in Iranian territory at the end of World War II.

46. The concept of the protracted social conflict is associated with the work of Edward E. Azar; see, especially, Azar, Paul Jureidini, and Ronald McLaurin, "Protracted Social Conflict; Theory and Practice in the Middle East," *Journal of Palestine Studies* 8, no. 1 (1978):41–60. In a recent study I proposed several hypothesized relationships and tested some of the effects of protracted social conflicts on regional security factors: "Conceptualizing Regional Insecurity: The 'Protracted Conflict Region'" (unpublished manuscript, June 1989). The hypothesized "concentric rings" effect of regional insecurity was well supported. Unfortunately, the limitations of the available data prevented testing any of the stochastic effects in the *processes* of the dispersion of insecurity and the diffusion of violence.

47. Georgia was a nominally independent state from 1918 to 1921 when security and other political exigencies caused the Menshevik leadership to seek unification with the Soviet state, thus setting the stage for the infamous "Georgian affair" noted earlier in this chapter.

48. These former ethnic republics are now known as the independent states of Kazakhstan, Kyrgyzstan, Tajikistan, Turkmenistan, and Uzbekistan (see n. 43).

49. A notable exception is the rioting that took place in Alma-Ata in 1986 after the ouster of the popular, yet purportedly corrupt, Kazakh leader of the Kazakh union republic during the anticorruption campaign that signaled the beginning of the Gorbachev restructuring period.

50. See Martha B. Olcott, "The Basmachi or Freemen's Revolt in Turkestan 1918–24," *Soviet Studies* 23, no. 3 (July 1981):352–369; and Marie Broxup, "The Basmachi," *Central Asian Survey* 2, no. 1 (July 1983):57–81.

51. Joint Publications Research Service, "Emigration Figures by Republics Detailed," *Soviet Union: Political Affairs*, JPRS-UPA-90-066 (December 4, 1990), 23–24. The U.S. Committee for Refugees estimated that there were 750,000 internally displaced persons in the Soviet Union at the end of 1990; *World Refugee Survey 1991* (Washington, DC: U.S. Committee for Refugees, 1991), 34, 76–77.

52. Gregory Gleason, "Leninist Nationality Policy: Its Source and Style," in H. R. Huttenbach (ed.), *Soviet Nationality Policies* (London: Mansell, 1990), 9; emphasis was added by Gleason.

53. The concepts of *sblizhenia* and *sliiania* represent the main social processes of the theoretic formula for social group integration proposed by Lenin. Social psychological studies by Muzafer Sherif and his colleagues (i.e., the "Robbers' Cave" experiments) on the conditions that lead to social group integration show that cooperative solutions to common problems and mutually beneficial participation in the implementation of those solutions (i.e., the pursuit of superordinate goals) lead to social integration. Compare Muzafer Sherif, *In Common Predicament: Social Psychology of Intergroup Conflict and Cooperation* (Boston: Houghton Mifflin, 1966).

54. Alexander Motyl, *Will the Non-Russians Rebel? State, Ethnicity, and Stability in the USSR* (Ithaca and London: Cornell University Press, 1987).

55. Since the breakup of the multinational states, calls for assistance in mediating disputes have often been directed to and involved international organizations such as the United Nations, the European Community, and the Council on Security and Cooperation in Europe.

56. All three quotes are found in Giovanni Sartori, *The Theory of Democracy Revisited* (Chatham: Chatham House Publishers, 1987), 32.

57. "Greed," 1924, directed by Erich von Stroheim and based on the novel *McTeague*, by Frank Norris.

8. North Africa and the Middle East

1. See chapter 4, table 4.3. The average scores for violent protest by groups in this region from 1945 to 1989 exceed those for all other regions; nonviolent protest ranks second to groups in the western democracies and Japan; and rebellion ranks second to Asian groups.

2. This chapter examines representative minorities in the Arab world and North Africa. Groups in Pakistan are not included in the case studies, because communal politics in Pakistan are sharply distinct from those elsewhere in the region. Groups in Afghanistan were not included in the Minorities at Risk study, because no clear patterns of dominance and subordination were evident among them in the 1980s. A pattern of communal contention began to emerge after the fall of the Soviet-backed Najibullah government in 1992 in which the principal players are the Pashtuns (most of whom fled to Pakistan during the civil war), the Tajiks (most of whom remained and at first dominated the new government), the Hazaras, the Uzbeks, and the Turkmens. See Nassim Jawad, *Afghanistan: A Nation of Minorities* (London: Minority Rights Group, February 1992).

3. Turkey, Iraq, and Iran. Syrian Kurds were not included because the Minorities at Risk project relied on sources that put them below the population threshold used; but see n. 7.

4. General sources on the Palestininans include Roy R. Andersen, Robert F. Seibert, and Jon G. Wagner, *Politics and Change in the Middle East*, 3d ed. (Englewood Cliffs, NJ: Prentice Hall, 1990); Massoud Ahmad Egbarieh, "Arab Citizens in Israel: The Ongoing Conflict with the State" (Ph.D. dissertation, Department of Government and Politics, University of Maryland, 1991); Deborah J. Gerner, *One Land, Two Peoples: The Conflict over Palestine* (Boulder, CO: Westview Press, 1991); Don Peretz, *Intifada: The Palestinian Uprising* (Boulder, CO: Westview Press, 1990); Charles D. Smith, *Palestine and the Arab-Israeli Conflict* (New York: St. Martin's Press, 1988); Ehud Sprinzak, *The Ascendance of Israel's Radical Right* (New York and Oxford: Oxford University Press, 1991); and Joshua Teitelbaum and Joseph Kostiner, "The West Bank and Gaza: The PLO and the Intifada," in Jack A. Goldstone, T. R. Gurr, and Farrokh Moshiri (eds.), *Revolutions of the Late Twentieth Century* (Boulder, CO: Westview Press, 1991).

5. For detailed data see *B'TSELEM: Violations of Human Rights in the Occupied Territories 1990/1991* (Jerusalem: The Israeli Information Center for Human Rights in the Occupied Territories, n.d. [1992]).

6. David Menashri, "Khomeini's Policy toward Ethnic and Religious Minorities," in Milton J. Esman and Itamar Rabinovich (eds.), *Ethnicity, Pluralism, and the State in the Middle East* (Ithaca, NY: Cornell University Press, 1988), 217.

7. General sources on the Kurds include Esman and Rabinovich, *Ethnicity, Pluralism and the State* (see n. 6), especially chaps. 13 and 14; Edmund Ghareeb, *The Kurdish Question in Iraq* (Syracuse, NY: Syracuse University Press, 1981); David McDowall, *The Kurds*, Minority Rights Group Report 23, rev. ed. (London: Minority Rights Group, 1985); Stephen C. Pelletiere, *The Kurds: An Unstable Element in the Gulf* (Boulder, CO: Westview Press, 1984); and Stephen C. Pelletiere, *The Kurds and Their Agas: An Assessment of the Situation in Northern Iraq* (Strategic Studies Institute, U.S. Army War College, September 16, 1991). On Kurds in the USSR see Nadir Nadirov, "A Scattered People Seeks Its Nationhood," *Cultural Survival Quarterly* 16(Winter 1992):38–40. Population figures on the Kurds are unreliable. For a review of alternate estimates see Charles G. MacDonald, "The Kurdish Question in the 1980s," in Esman and Rabinovich, *Ethnicity, Pluralism, and the State* (see n. 6), 236. Pelletiere, *The Kurds and Their Agas*, believes that there are about four million in Iran and one-half million in Syria.

8. On the status of the Kurds in Iraq see Mustafa Al Karadaghi, "A Report on the Kurdish Situation Following Allied Withdrawal From Kurdistan on July 15, 1991" (Fairfax, VA: Kurdish Human Rights Watch, November 17, 1991); Scott B. McDonald, "The Kurds in the 1990s," *Middle East Insight* (January-February 1990):29–35; Munir H. Nasser, "Iraq, Ethnic Minorities and Their Impact on Politics," *Journal of South Asian and Middle Eastern Studies* 8, no. 3 (1985):22–37; Siyamend Othman, "Kurdish Nationalism: Instigators and Historical Influences," *Armenian Review* 42(Spring 1989):39–59; Pelletiere, *The Kurds and Their Agas* (see n. 7); and Richard Sim, "Kurdish National Movement in Iraq," *Conflict* 124 (1980).

9. Sources include news items; Marianne Laanatza, "Ethnic Conflicts in Islamic Societies: Politization of Berbers in North Africa and Kurds in Iraq," in Sven Taegil (ed.), *Regions in Upheaval: Ethnic Conflict and Political Mobilization* (Stockholm: Scandinavien University Books/ Esselte Studium, 1984); and Robert Montagne, *The Berbers: Their Social and Political Organisation*, translated with an introduction by David Seddon (London: Frank Cass, 1973).

10. In addition to the sources in n. 4 see Asher Arian, *Politics in Israel: The Second Generation*, rev. ed. (Chatham, NY: Chatham House, 1989); Gregory S. Mahler, *Israel: Government and Politics in a Maturing State* (Orlando, FL: Harcourt Brace Jovanovich, 1990), especially chap. 10; William B. Quandt (ed.), *The Middle East: Ten Years after Camp David* (Washington, DC: The Brookings Institution, 1988); and Sammy Smooha, "Jewish and Arab Ethnocentrism in Israel," *Ethnic and Racial Studies* 10, no. 1 (1987). Data on Arab attitudes are from surveys reported by Egbarieh, "Arab Citizens in Israel," 41 and 111, and Peretz, *Intifada*, 144 (see n. 4).

11. See Ibrahim Abu-Lughod and Eqbal Ahmad (eds.), "The Invasion of Lebanon," *Race and Class: A Journal for Black and Third World Liberation* 24, no. 4 (1983):327–428; Michael C. Hudson, *Arab Politics: The Search for Legitimacy* (New Haven: Yale University Press, 1977); and Sean McBride et al., *Israel in Lebanon: Report of the International Commission to Enquire into Reported Violations of International Law by Israel During Its Invasion of Lebanon* (London: Ithaca Press, 1983).

12. See Juan R. I. Cole and Nikki R. Keddie (eds.), *Shi'ism and Social Protest* (New Haven: Yale University Press, 1986); Stuart E. Colie, "A Perspective on the Shiites and the Lebanese Tragedy," *Middle East Review* 9(Fall 1976):16–24; Hudson, *Arab Politics* (see n. 11); Augustus Richard Norton, "Political Violence and Shi'a Factionalism in Lebanon," *Middle East Insight* (August-October 1983):9–16; Norton, "Shi'ism and Social Protest in Lebanon," in Cole and Keddie; and Elizabeth Picard, "Political Identities and Communal Identities: Shifting Mobilization Among the Lebanese Shi'a Through Ten Years of War: 1975–1985," in Dennis L. Thompson and Dov Ronen (eds.), *Ethnicity, Politics, and Development* (Boulder, CO: Lynne Rienner, 1986).

13. See Shaul Bakhash, *The Reign of the Ayatollahs* (New York: Basic Books, 1984); Katherine R. Bigelow, "A Campaign to Deter Genocide: The Baha'i Experience," in Helen Fein (ed.), *Genocide Watch* (New Haven: Yale University Press, 1991); and Roger Cooper, *Baha'is in Iran*, Minority Rights Group Report 51 (London: Minority Rights Group, 1982), quotation from p. 4.

14. See Rafiq Zakaria, *The Struggle within Islam: The Conflict between Religion and Politics* (New York: Penguin Books, 1988).

15. See John L. Esposito, *Islam and Politics* (Syracuse: Syracuse University Press, 1984), 217.

9. Africa South of the Sahara

1. For more detailed discussions of this type of conflict, see Ted Robert Gurr and James R. Scarritt, "Minorities Rights at Risk: A Global Survey," *Human Rights Quarterly* 11(1989):387–388; and Donald L. Horowitz, *Ethnic Groups in Conflict* (Berkeley: University of California Press, 1985), 427–437.

2. Robert H. Bates, "Modernization, Ethnic Competition, and the Rationality of Politics in Contemporary Africa," in Donald Rothchild and Victor A. Olorunsola (eds.), *State Versus Ethnic Claims: African Policy Dilemmas* (Boulder, CO: Westview Press, 1983), 152–171.

3. The primordialist position is put forth in a somewhat milder form in Clifford Geertz, "The Integrative Revolution: Primordial Sentiments and Civil Politics in the New States," in Clifford Geertz (ed.), *Old Societies and New States* (New York: Free Press, 1963), 105–157. The situationalist position is explicated, again in somewhat milder form, in Jonathan Y. Okamura, "Situational Ethnicity," *Ethnic and Racial Studies* 4(October 1981):452–465.

4. See, for example, Paul Brass, "Ethnic Groups and the State," in Brass (ed.), *Ethnic Groups and the State* (Totowa, NJ: Barnes and Noble, 1985), 24–49; Naomi Chazan et al., *Politics and Society in Contemporary Africa* (Boulder, CO: Lynne Rienner, 1988), 102–105; Horowitz, *Ethnic Groups in Conflict*, 3–92 (see n. 1); Nelson Kasfir, "Explaining Ethnic Political Participation," *World Politics* 31(April 1979):365–388; James McKay, "An Exploratory Synthesis of Primordial and Mobilizationist Approaches to Ethnic Phenomena," *Ethnic and Racial Studies* 5(October 1982):395–420; Donald G. Morrison and Hugh M. Stevenson, "Integration and Instability: Patterns of African Political Development," *American Political Science Review* 66(September 1972):902–927; Jeffrey A. Ross, "The Mobilization of Collective Identity: An Analytical Overview," in Jeffrey A. Ross and Ann Baker Cottrell (eds.), *The Mobilization of Collective Identity: Comparative Perspectives* (Lanham, MD: University Press of America, 1980); John S. Saul, "The Dialectic of Class and Tribe," in Saul, *The State and Revolution in Eastern Africa* (New York: Monthly Review Press, 1979), 391–423; and George M. Scott, Jr., "A Resynthesis of the Primordial and Circumstantial Approaches to Ethnic Group Solidarity: Towards an Explanatory Model," *Ethnic and Racial Studies* 13(April 1990):147–171.

5. A recent analysis that presents a very similar picture of African ethnopolitics is Martin Doornbos, "Linking the Future to the Past: Ethnicity and Pluralism," *Review of African Political Economy* 52(November 1991):58–59.

6. We code the average number of transnational segments in black Africa as one per group, slightly below the global mean. Because the colonial powers drew the political boundaries of black Africa without any concern for ethnic boundaries, many primordial groups straddle international boundaries. Because of our interest in ethnopolitics, we code the existence of transnational segments only for those cases in which at least a minimal sense of common identity has survived these political divisions.

7. Robert Molteno, "Cleavage and Conflict in Zambian Politics: A Study in Sectionalism," in William Tordoff (ed.), *Politics in Zambia* (Berkeley: University of California Press, 1974), 62–63.

8. James R. Scarritt, "From Tribalism to Sectionalism?: Political Cleavages in Zambia and Uganda," *Umoja* 2, no. 2 (1975):1–12.

9. For detailed treatments see Thomas Rasmussen, "Political Competition and One-party Dominance in Zambia," *Journal of Modern*

African Studies 7, no. 3 (1969):407–424; and Tordoff, *Politics in Zambia*, 62–196 (see n. 7).

10. Bornwell Chikulo, "Electoral Politics in Zambia's Second Republic" (Discussion paper, Department of Political and Administrative Studies, University of Zambia, 1986), 76.

11. Cherry Gertzel (ed.), Carolyn Baylies, and Morris Szeftel, *The Dynamics of the One-Party State in Zambia* (Manchester: Manchester University Press, 1984), 17–20.

12. A more complete treatment of the changes discussed in this paragraph is found in Gerzel et al., *Dynamics*, 29–106 (see n. 11).

13. For a more detailed analysis of MMD support, see James R. Scarritt, "Dilemmas of Democratization in Zambia," *Association of Concerned Africa Scholars Bulletin* 32(Winter 1991):5–8.

14. The most comprehensive and balanced work on the complex topics covered in this paragraph is Carl G. Rosberg, Jr., and John Nottingham, *The Myth of Mau Mau* (New York: Praeger, 1966).

15. The discussion in the next three paragraphs about mobilization during the Kenyatta era relies on Cherry Gertzel, *The Politics of Independent Kenya 1963–8* (Evanston, IL: Northwestern University Press, 1970); and Henry Bienen, *Kenya: The Politics of Participation and Control* (Princeton, NJ: Princeton University Press, 1974), 66–153.

16. David W. Throup, "The Construction and Destruction of the Kenyatta State," in Michael G. Schatzberg (ed.), *The Political Economy of Kenya* (New York: Praeger, 1987), 46. The following analysis of Moi's role in Kenyan ethnopolitics relies extensively on this source.

17. Christopher Clapham, *Transformation and Continuity in Revolutionary Ethiopia* (Cambridge: Cambridge University Press, 1988), 24.

18. The following discussion of Eritrea and Tigray relies most heavily on John Markakis, *National and Class Conflict in the Horn of Africa* (Cambridge: Cambridge University Press, 1987), 57–69, 91–94, 104–145, 245–258. Clapham, *Transformation and Continuity in Revolutionary Ethiopia*, 204–214; and Edmond J. Keller, *Revolutionary Ethiopia: From Empire to People's Republic* (Bloomington: Indiana University Press, 1988), 150–155, 208–212, were also helpful. An interesting treatment from a pro-Ethiopian but anti-Selassie and anti-Mengistu perspective is found in Dawit Wolde Giorgis, *Red Tears: War, Famine and Revolution in Ethiopia* (Trenton, NJ: Red Sea Press, 1989), 69–117.

19. The following discussion of Somali and Oromo mobilization relies on Markakis, *National and Class Conflict*, 169–181, 191, 201, 222–234, 258–264 (see n. 18); Clapham, *Transformation and Continuity in Revolutionary Ethiopia*, 214–219 (see n. 17); and Keller, *Revolutionary Ethiopia*, 156–163, 202–207 (see n. 18).

20. John W. Harbeson, *The Ethiopian Transformation: The Quest for the Post-Imperial State* (Boulder, CO: Westview Press, 1988), 163.

21. McKay, "An Exploratory Synthesis," 404–407 (see n. 4).

22. The literature on the resolution of ethnic conflict is quite extensive, but see especially Horowitz, *Ethnic Groups in Conflict*, 563–684 (see n. 1); and Joseph V. Montville (ed.), *Conflict and Peacemaking in Multiethnic Societies* (Lexington, MA: Lexington Books, 1990), 451–541. For an explanation of why these institutional variables were selected over others that are frequently advocated, such as consociationalism, federalism, and multiparty pluralism, and a discussion of their relation to democracy and state capacity, see James R. Scarritt and Shaheen Mozaffar, "Toward Sustainable Democracy in Africa: Can U.S. Policy Make a Difference?" in William Crotty (ed.), *Post-Cold War Policy: Foreign and Military* (Boston: Nelson-Hall Publishers, forthcoming).

10. Settling Ethnopolitical Conflicts

1. This is the implication of such titles as Nietschmann, "The Third World War" (chap. 1, n. 8); Richard N. Haass, *Conflicts Unending: The United States and Regional Disputes* (New Haven: Yale University Press, 1990); and the contributors to Louis Kriesberg et al. (eds.), *Intractable Conflicts and Their Transformation* (Syracuse, NY: Syracuse University Press, 1989).

2. Croatia's intensely nationalist leaders contributed to the conflict by refusing to acknowledge or accommodate the political and cultural interests of its Serbian minority, who make up 12 to 20 percent of Croatia's population. Had such commitments been made, Serbians would have had less reason to go to war. See Misha Glenny, "The Massacre of Yugoslavia," *The New York Review*, January 30, 1992, 30–35. In the tragic case of Bosnia, Muslim leaders offered such assurances but they were not enough to satisfy Bosnian Serbs, whose leaders started a preemptive war to avoid the losses suffered by Serbs in Croatia.

3. It might be argued that the groups are not comparable, because the Palestinians and Kurds seek their own states whereas the Berbers do not. Yet the Berbers fiercely resisted French and Spanish colonial rule in defense of their traditional autonomy, and Kablye Berbers rebelled against the newly independent Algerian government in 1963–65 and 1967–68 on behalf of regional interests. The point is that the responses of the Algerian and Moroccan governments to Berber regional and cultural interests have been sufficient to keep conflict from escalating into ethnonationalist civil wars.

4. In T. R. Gurr, "The Internationalization of Protracted Communal Conflicts Since 1945: Which Groups, Where, and How," in Manus I. Midlarsky (ed.), *The Internationalization of Communal Strife* (London: Routledge, 1993); and in T. R. Gurr and Barbara Harff,

Ethnic Conflict in World Politics (Boulder, CO: Westview Press, in preparation).

5. We assume that many, but not necessarily all, members of communal groups want some kind of redress of the grievances articulated by their leaders. Collectivities may have other "objective" or "latent" interests, but what counts in the political world of action and response are their expressed demands.

6. This is a refinement of distinctions drawn in chapter 3, "Sources of Group Demands," derived from Albert O. Hirschman, *Exit, Voice and Loyalty: Responses to Decline in Firms, Organizations, and States* (Cambridge, MA: Harvard University Press, 1970).

7. Maintaining the state's authority and revenues is fundamental to the achievement of any and all other partisan and policy objectives. "Democracy" and "autocracy" refer to different sets of principles, procedures, and institutions by which officials secure the state's general interests and define and pursue specific objectives. This view is derived from an extended analysis of state interests in T. R. Gurr and Desmond S. King, *The State and the City* (Chicago: University of Chicago Press, 1987), 7–28. For a discussion of how general state interests mesh with minority objectives see Marvin W. Mikesell and Alexander B. Murphy, "A Framework for Comparative Study of Minority-Group Aspirations," *Annals of the Association of American Geographers* 81, no. 4 (1991):588–590.

8. The roster includes groups that have relied on terrorist as well as guerrilla strategies, with campaigns lasting for five years or more. In most of these armed conflicts, independence was one of several alternative political objectives, not the only one. The list excludes rebellions and civil wars that were concerned mainly or exclusively with redress of grievances, intercommunal rivalries, and cultural autonomy.

9. The recent independence of Lithuania and Ukraine is a reflection but not a direct consequence of the nationalism that motivated anti-Soviet guerrilla wars in those regions in the late 1940s. Similar nationalist rebellions were fought by Estonians and Latvians but were of lesser magnitude and more quickly suppressed than conflicts in Lithuania and Ukraine. Adding them to the list would not alter any of the conclusions drawn from it.

10. Careful analyses of the economic costs of civil war are very rare. An exception is John M. Richardson, Jr., and S. W. R. de A. Samarasinghe, "Measuring the Economic Dimensions of Sri Lanka's Ethnic Conflict," in Samarasinghe and Reid Coughlin (eds.), *Economic Dimensions of Ethnic Conflict* (London: Frances Pinter, 1991). The primary, secondary, and tertiary costs of ethnic and political conflict in that country between 1983 and 1988 are estimated at US$4.2 billion, equal to 68 percent of Sri Lanka's 1988 gross domestic product.

11. Such views are sharply at odds with the official policy of Prime Minister Brian Mulroney's government, which is that Canada's unity must be preserved, but they are reflective of an emerging political realism. See, for example, David J. Bercuson and Barry Cooper, *Deconfederation: Canada Without Quebec* (Toronto: Key Porter Books, 1991).

12. The seven relatively successful autonomy agreements are listed in part 1 of table 10.1, beginning with the Basques and concluding with the Moros. The conflicts that may culminate in autonomy involve the Eritreans, Tigreans, Somali, Saharawis, Catholics in Northern Ireland, Iraqi Kurds, and Palestinians in Israel's Occupied Territories.

13. From Mikesell and Murphy, "Framework for Comparative Study," 587–588 (see n. 7). Their analysis of alternative policies for meeting communal demands, developed independent of this study, parallels ours in a number of respects. A more general analysis of regional devolution is Mark O. Rousseau and Raphael Zariski, *Regionalism and Regional Devolution in Comparative Perspective* (New York: Praeger, 1987).

14. Hurst Hannum, *Autonomy, Sovereignty, and Self-Determination: The Accommodation of Conflicting Rights* (Philadelphia: University of Pennsylvania Press, 1990) provides detailed case studies of nine regional autonomy arrangements (pp. 123–327) and a listing of the basic issues underlying autonomy disputes (pp. 458–68).

15. Mikesell and Murphy, "Framework for Comparative Study," 588 (see n. 7).

16. This conflict is analyzed in T. R. Gurr, "The Politics of Aboriginal Land Rights and Their Effects on Australian Resource Development," *Australian Journal of Politics and History* 31, no. 3 (1985):474–489. The arrangements meet one of the tests of successful accommodation: aside from lawyers, none of the interested parties are entirely satisfied—not Aborigines, because they have been pressured by government to accept some unwanted mineral development projects; not mineral corporations, because projects are delayed and more costly; not environmentalists, because mining inevitably has *some* environmental impact. State governments in Queensland and Western Australia have been more resistant to Aboriginal demands and more responsive to developers' interests.

17. "Success" is used in the narrow sense of reduction of intense conflict. In none of these instances did communal nationalists get all or even most of what they sought. These are instances of conflict management, not conflict resolution.

18. The Sikhs are only a slight majority in the Punjab. The origins and escalation of Sikh ethnonationalism are more complex than this sketch suggests; for recent analyses of the Punjab crisis see Paul R. Brass, *Ethnicity and Nationalism: Theory and Comparison* (New Delhi:

Sage Publications, 1991), chaps. 5 and 6; and Hannum, *Autonomy, Sovereignty, and Self-Determination*, chap. 8 (see n. 14).

19. This sketch of the Moro insurgency is based on background research and chronologies prepared by Monty G. Marshall and Scott McDonald.

20. Three shifts in government policies coincided to precipitate the second civil war: the proposed partition of the south into three regions, the imposition of Islamic laws on the entire country (the south is partly Christian), and the transfer of southern troops (former rebels who had been integrated into the army) to the north. See Francis Mading Deng, "The Identity Factor in the Sudanese Conflict," chap. 20, in Joseph V. Montville (ed.), *Conflict and Peacemaking in Multiethnic Societies* (Lexington, MA: Lexington Books, 1990).

21. This sketch is based on background research and a chronology prepared by Shin-wha Lee.

22. The Aland Autonomy Act, with 1991 extensions, is widely regarded as a model for regional autonomy elsewhere. Its history and provisions are summarized by Antony Alcock, "Finland—The Swedish-Speaking Community," in *Minorities and Autonomy in Western Europe* (London: Minority Rights Group Report, October 1991), 12–15.

23. This passage is derived from a comprehensive review by Michael Hartman of the status of native peoples in Latin America. The victories of the Kuna and Miskitos are unusual outcomes. The Maya in Guatemala who have supported leftist revolutionaries have suffered grievously from government repression and forced relocation; their interests have not been accommodated in any way. An even more devastating fate befell the Ashaninka people of Peru's Amazon basin, who joined the Tupac Amaru insurgency in 1965–66; see Michael F. Brown and Eduardo Fernandez, *War of Shadows: The Struggle for Utopia in the Peruvian Amazon* (Berkeley: University of California Press, 1991).

24. This threefold distinction among minority objectives is used by Mikesell and Murphy in "Framework for Comparative Study," 588–589 (see n. 7).

25. For a general analysis of cultural pluralism in Europe see Antony E. Alcock, Brian K. Taylor, and John M. Welton (eds.), *The Future of Cultural Minorities* (London: Macmillan, 1979). "Multiculturalism" in American political discourse is usually a euphemism for the claims of people of color to a distinct history and status. The policies and objectives of pluralism (which includes multiculturalism) are much more widely applicable. Recent analyses of multicultural arrangements include Fathali M. Moghaddam and Elizabeth A. Solliday, "'Balanced Multiculturalism' and the Challenge of Peaceful Coexistence in Pluralistic Societies," *Psychology and Developing Societies* (forthcoming); and

Thomas Hylland Eriksen, "Ethnicity versus Nationalism," *Journal of Peace Research* 28(August 1991):263–278, a study that draws on examples from northern Norway, Trinidad, and Mauritius.

26. Arthur M. Schlesinger, Jr., "Writing, and Rewriting, History," *The New Leader*, December 30, 1991, 14. He spells out the details of his critique of radical multiculturalism in *The Disuniting of America: Reflections on a Multicultural Society* (New York: Norton, 1991).

27. This model of power sharing in democratic societies, or consociational democracy, is most closely associated with the work of Arend Lijphart, especially *Democracy in Plural Societies* (New Haven: Yale University Press, 1977). He proposes an application to South Africa in *Power-Sharing in South Africa*, Policy Paper in International Affairs No. 24 (Berkeley: University of California, Institute of International Studies, 1985).

28. Donald L. Horowitz, *Ethnic Groups in Conflict* (Berkeley: University of California Press, 1985), 21–36, 601–652.

29. See R. E. M. Irving, *The Flemings and Walloons of Belgium* (London: Minority Rights Group, Report 46, 1980); and Alexander B. Murphy, *The Regional Dynamics of Language Differentiation in Cultural-Political Geography* (Chicago: University of Chicago Geography Research Series No. 227, 1988).

30. The concept of hurting stalemate is associated with I. William Zartman, who is directing a comparative study of Negotiating Internal Conflicts at the Johns Hopkins University's Paul Nitze School of International Studies. See his *Ripe for Resolution: Conflict and Intervention in Africa* (New Haven: Yale University Press, 1989), chap. 6. There is a substantial literature on the settlement of civil wars, most of which is beyond the scope of this study. Important comparative studies are reported in Roy Licklider (ed.), *Stopping the Killing: How Civil Wars End* (New York: New York University Press, 1992); Hugh Miall, "Peaceful Settlement of Post-1945 Conflicts: A Comparative Study," (Paper presented at the United States Institute of Peace Conference on Conflict Resolution in the Post-Cold War Third World, Washington, October 1990); and Ralph M. Goldman, *From Warfare to Party Politics: The Critical Transition to Civilian Control* (Syracuse, NY: Syracuse University Press, 1990). Comparative studies of the settlement of communal conflicts include Montville, *Conflict and Peacemaking* (see n. 20); and John M. Richardson, Jr., and Jianxin Wang, "Peace Accords: Resolving Conflicts in Deeply Divided Societies," in Kingsley M. de Silva and S. W. R. de A. Samarasinghe (eds.), *Ethnic Peace Accords* (London: Frances Pinter, forthcoming). Case studies that draw general conclusions about when and how civil wars might be settled include Hizkias Assefa, *Mediation of Civil Wars: Approaches and Strategies—The Sudan Conflict* (Boulder, CO: Westview Press, 1987); and Will H. Moore, "Why Internal

Wars End: The Decision to Fight, Negotiate or Surrender" (Ph.D. diss., Department of Political Science, University of Colorado at Boulder, 1991).

11. Summary and Implications

1. Elise Boulding, "Ethnicity and New Constitutive Orders: An Approach to Peace in the Twenty-First Century" (Paper prepared for a Festschrift for Kinhide Mushakoji, n.d. [1990]).

Index

Page numbers in italic refer to illustrations. The designation *t* following a page number indicates that the reference is to a table. The reader is also directed to the Appendix tables that begin on page 326 for additional data on specific groups and specific countries. (Names of authors and other subjects in the notes are not included.)

United States Institute of Peace

The United States Institute of Peace is an independent, nonpartisan federal institution created and funded by Congress to strengthen the nation's capacity to promote the peaceful resolution of international conflict. Established in 1984, the Institute meets its congressional mandate through an array of programs, including grants, fellowships, conferences and study groups, library services, publications, and other educational activities. The Institute's Board of Directors is appointed by the President of the United States and confirmed by the Senate.

Jennings Randolph Program for International Peace

As part of the statute establishing the United States Institute of Peace, Congress envisioned a fellowship program that would appoint "scholars and leaders of peace from the United States and abroad to pursue scholarly inquiry and other appropriate forms of communication on international peace and conflict resolution." The program was named after Senator Jennings Randolph of West Virginia, whose efforts over four decades helped to establish the Institute.

Since it began in 1987, the Jennings Randolph Program has played a key role in the Institute's effort to build a national center of research, dialogue, and education on critical problems of conflict and peace. Through a rigorous annual competition, outstanding men and women from diverse nations and fields are selected to carry out projects designed to expand and disseminate knowledge on violent international conflict and the wide range of ways it can be peacefully managed or resolved.

The Institute's Distinguished Fellows and Peace Fellows are individuals from a wide variety of academic and other professional backgrounds who work at the Institute on research and education projects they have proposed and participate in the Institute's collegial and public outreach activities. The Institute's Peace Scholars are doctoral candidates at American universities who are working on their dissertations.

Institute fellows and scholars have worked on such varied subjects as international negotiation, regional security arrangements, conflict resolution techniques, international legal systems, ethnic and religious conflict, arms control, and the protection of human rights, and these issues have been examined in settings throughout the world.

As part of its effort to disseminate original and useful analyses of peace and conflict to policymakers and the public, the Institute publishes book manuscripts and other written products that result from the fellowship work and meet the Institute's high standards of quality.

Michael S. Lund
Director